PIMLICO

102

# KEEPERS OF THE FLAME

Biographer, critic and poet, Ian Hamilton has worked as the Editor of *The Review* and *The New Review*, Poetry and Fiction Editor of *The Times Literary Supplement* and presenter of BBC TV's 'Bookmark'. He has published collections of his own poems and editions of the work of Alun Lewis and Robert Frost. His books include *Robert Lowell*, *In Search of J. D. Salinger* and *Writers in Hollywood*.

# KEEPERS OF THE FLAME

## Literary Estates and the Rise of Biography

### IAN HAMILTON

PIMLICO

PIMLICO
An imprint of Random House
20 Vauxhall Bridge Road, London SW1V 2SA

Random House Australia (Pty) Ltd
20 Alfred Street, Milsons Point Sydney
New South Wales 2061, Australia

Random House New Zealand Ltd
18 Poland Road, Glenfield
Auckland 10, New Zealand

Random House South Africa (Pty) Ltd
PO Box 337, Bergvlei, South Africa

Random House UK Ltd Reg. No. 954009

First published in Great Britain by Hutchinson 1992
Pimlico edition 1993

1 3 5 7 9 10 8 6 4 2

Printed and bound in Great Britain by
Mackays of Chatham PLC, Chatham, Kent

ISBN 0-7126-5970-6

# CONTENTS

Foreword     vii

1   John Donne the Younger     7

2   Surviving Shakespeare     16

3   Be Kind to My Remains: Marvell, Milton, Dryden     30

4   Pope's Bullies     46

5   Boswell's Colossal Hoard     63

6   The Frailties of Robert Burns     85

7   Byron and the Best of Friends     109

8   At the Shelley Shrine     128

9   John Forster, of Dickens Fame     144

10   Froude's Carlyle, Carlyle's Froude     158

11   Keeping House: Tennyson and Swinburne     177

12   Legends and Mysteries: Robert Louis Stevenson and Henry James     197

13   Remembering Rupert Brooke     222

14   Authorised Lives: Hardy and Kipling     241

15   James Joyce's Patron Saint     267

16   Provisional Posterities: Sylvia Plath and Philip Larkin     291

Notes     311

Index     332

## Acknowledgements

I am grateful to the following for their advice and practical assistance during the preparation and writing of this book: Gillon Aitken, Nicolas Barker, Humphrey Carpenter, Richard Cohen, Matthew Hamilton, Sir Rupert Hart-Davis, Eric Homberger, Olwyn Hughes, Elizabeth Inglis (University of Sussex Library), Hermione Lee, Robert Bernard Martin, Karl Miller, Andrew Motion, Norman Page, R. N. R. Peers (Dorset County Museum), Charis Ryder, Martin Seymour-Smith, Chris Sheppard (Brotherton Collection, University of Leeds), Robyn Sisman, Ahdaf Soueif, Jon Stallworthy, Ann Thwaite, Anthony Thwaite, Juliet Townsend, and Patricia Wheatley. My thanks also to Mrs T. S. Eliot for permission to quote from Eliot's report on Lord Birkenhead's biography of Kipling; to the National Trust for permission to quote from Elsie Bambridge's notes on Birkenhead; to the Estate of Charles Carrington for permission to quote from Carrington's excerpts from Carrie Kipling's diaries.

# FOREWORD

A book about literary estates has to be about many other things as well: about changing notions of posterity, about copyright law, publishing, the rise of English Studies, the onset of literary celebritism. Principally, or so I discovered as I wrote, it has to be about biography, the history and ethics of. How much should a biographer tell? How much should an executor suppress? And what would the biographee have wanted – do we know?

These questions are still under debate, and they continue to generate much heat and high-mindedness. Rarely does a month pass without some new biographical 'controversy' making the headlines. Two widows have been at each other's throats; a family is divided; an authorised biographer has been expelled. Or maybe a cache of old letters has been found, revealing our hero to be less than perfect – is it right that they should now be embargoed for a hundred years? He burned her diary; she scissored his erotic juvenilia. And so it goes.

Sometimes, arguing about biography is like arguing about abortion or capital punishment: minds tend to be made up before you start. There are revealers and there are concealers. The agents of reticence have no truck with the agents of disclosure. Privacy is sacred, the public has a right to know. Thus, depending on your point of view, or on the nature of your personal involvement, the biographer is either a sleaze-hound or 'an artist on oath', the executor either a secretive parasite or a protector of imperilled decencies.

In this atmosphere, it seems to me, there is some call for a review of continuities and precedents. When did these quarrels start and how did they proceed? If we look hard enough, can we trace patterns: Boswellism versus Romanticism, Victorianism versus Stracheyism? Did such patterns actually impinge on the specific human dramas of the past? Are they still in place today? Or was it – is it – all to do with human nature, a matter of competing vanities and envies, deadlocked special interests, cash? What is a keeper of the flame and what manner of flame is it that he (or she) tries to keep? And who or what is it kept for?

I have tried to explore a dozen or so case-histories, each of them marking some development or alteration in the function of literary executors, or custodians, in how they were seen and how they saw themselves, and what they did. In this book, flames have a double presence: there is the gem-like flame of art and there is the private bonfire, 'the trustful guardian of secret matters'. I have tried also to chart the several and curious ways in which authors themselves have taken a hand in the shaping of their own posterities.

With two exceptions (both of which I happen to feel close to), I have stuck to 'dead', or out-of-copyright, estates. I learned enough from my study of these to shy away from too much probing of the present-day – and not just for legal reasons. My overall conclusion about the biography debate would run more or less as follows: writers, indeed any potential or probable biographees, should follow Henry James and try to serve as their own keepers of the flame. If they don't, or if they fail to cover all the angles (as James did), then it seems to me that fifty years is not too long for us to wait for the 'whole truth' about a private life. In the meantime, no one should burn anything, however certain he or she might feel about what the lost loved one 'really would have wished'. All this may sound fishy, coming as it does from the biographer of Robert Lowell (d. 1977) and the near, would-be or failed biographer of J. D. Salinger (1919–   ), but there it is. We live and learn.

Ian Hamilton

# CHAPTER ONE

# JOHN DONNE THE YOUNGER

In the summer of 1634, John Donne the Younger, son of the recently deceased Dean of St Paul's, was out riding in the streets of Oxford with a friend, another Christ Church man. An eight-year-old boy named Humphry Dunt accidentally startled one of the horses. Donne dismounted and set on the boy, whipping him four or five times about the head. For several days afterwards, little Humphry complained of headaches and was put to bed. Two weeks later, he died. John Donne the Younger was tried for unlawful killing and would no doubt have been put away for a long stretch if he had been found guilty. He was acquitted: two surgeons and a physician testified that 'they could not assign the cause' of little Humphry's death, 'since there was no appearance of hurt'. And to this day, there are those who would also testify that if Donne had hit the kid a few more times, had left some marks, we might never have been told that 'No man is an island' nor 'for whom the bell tolls'. We would certainly not have known, or cared, much about John Donne the Younger.

The history of literary estates is filled with such what-might-have-beens: what might have been destroyed, what might have been preserved, what might have been distorted or inked over. John Donne the Younger may not be the first noteworthy keeper of the flame (the family of Sir Philip Sidney had forty years earlier gone to the courts to prevent piracies of *Astrophel and Stella*) but he probably is the first to have been given an individual entry in the *Dictionary of National Biography* and to have had his character and motives scrutinised in the scholarly periodicals. And one can easily see why this is so. Donne Senior's writings were largely unpublished at his death and he himself was deeply equivocal on the matter of how their posterity should be administered. Donne was also the first important English writer to leave a substantial collection of letters and the first to be taken as the subject of a literary biography (again, if we except Sidney, whose none-too-literary Life was written by Fulke Greville but not published until 1652). John Donne the Younger was in at the birth of nearly all the elements and 'issues' that will come to dominate our narrative.

And this was in an age when literary property was not greatly prized nor very energetically protected, when notions of Fame were very different from our own ('A man should seek great glorie and not broad'), and when connections between the Writing and the Life – or the Repute – were not perceived as controversial. When Izaak Walton set to work on his 'best plain picture' of the Life of Donne there was in English no such title as 'biographer'. Anecdotalists, encyclopedists, antiquarians: each of these was to some extent in the business of life-writing, or fame-fixing, but they would generally be lumped together as 'historians'. Plutarch had been translated into English sixty years before; he was read and admired but nobody took much notice of his claim that the *Lives* he wrote were something other than straight-forward histories – something perhaps lowlier, and by being lowlier, more accurate, maybe. For all his homely and incisive touches, the Greek was scrutinised as ancient history, and as a source-book for up-and-coming playwrights. Plutarch came under 'history' just as surely as the concocters of Saints' Lives came under 'God'.

But then in those days, everything – including history – came under 'God'. In an epoch of special pleading, an epoch in which pleading sometimes had to be very special indeed if the pleader prized his neck, there was of course something weird and suspect in the idea of one writer electing to recount another writer's Life: the more so if the subject was of recent memory. Walton in 1639 would surely have had in mind Sir Walter Ralegh's cautionary text: 'Whosoever in writing a modern history shall follow truth too near the heels, it may haply strike out his teeth.' This was an age of martyrs and near-martyrs, favourites and ex-favourites. Only two years earlier, Charles I had tightened the screws on writers and printers so that all of them lived in terror of 'fines impossible to be paid and penal pains almost too horrible to endure'. Life-writing was either exemplary or admonitory (and very soon the Royalist Walton would note that it was either pro- or anti-Parliament). What is this Life meant to teach us; what are we supposed to be talked into here, or out of? These would have been the questions that Walton might have expected to face from his 'reviewers'.

Walton is now praised as the first Life-writer to have approached his task with conscious literary skill, and there is merit in this claim. The skill, however, was necessarily tempered by the requirements of avoidance and suppression. For a Dean of St Paul's Donne had a somewhat dodgy past. Although Walton knew him only in his later, holy years, he would have known about the danger-spots. Donne had been brought up as a Catholic: this was common knowledge. But how adhesive were those early Jesuit connections? And then there was the rakish youth, the runaway marriage, the sponging, prospectless, near-suicidal years in Mitcham. These would have to be referred to, of course, but without revealing any of Donne's tendency to opportunism, both spiritual and professional (not to mention spiritual-professional): an opportunism perpetually at odds with an obscured and yet deep-running vein of anger and impulsiveness.

There was plenty to play down and if Walton is now thoroughly forgiven for the errors and adjustments of his Life of Donne, this is because the playing down is done so charmingly, with such 'ambling unpretence'. It seems certain that Walton believed himself to be doing the Life in more or less the way Donne would have wished. The chief complaint against the Life – that it says next to nothing about the poetry – would not have been Donne's own. And in any case, Walton's original title was 'The Life and Death of Dr Donne'. This was a memorial, meant to be set alongside all the other exequies and elegies and hymns of praise that had been got up in honour of this holy man.

John Donne died in 1631 and his death-bed performance has rightly been praised for its histrionic flair, its consummate stage-management. Although Donne the poet seems not to have cared much about the disposition of his literary remains, Donne the man of God approached the task of dying with an artist's rigour and fixity of purpose. The death-bed extravaganza is well-known but has not been better described than by Walton, one of its near-witnesses. First of all, as a prelude, there was the business of Donne's final sermon, called *Death's Duell*. The Dean was on his sick-bed, wasted by consumption, and everyone was telling him he would be mad to travel up to London from his Essex home, in the dead of winter, for what would surely turn out to be his last public appearance. Donne was not to be dissuaded. 'It hath been my desire,' he said, 'and God may be pleased to grant it, that I might die in the pulpit; that is, die the sooner by occasion of those labours.' And so he made the trip, amazing his beholders as much by the spectacle of his 'decayed body' and his 'dying face' as by anything he had to say. His text was 'To God the

Lord belong the issues from death'. Many of those who 'saw his tears and heard his faint and hollow voice' considered the text 'prophetic-ally chosen and that Dr Donne had preached his own Funeral Sermon'.

Returned to his sick-bed, Donne was easily persuaded that a monument should now be made to him. After all, as Walton drily observed, a wish for self-perpetuation – on earth as it may be in heaven – is surely 'rooted in the very nature of man'. Donne may have succeeded in tugging out from his interior garden the worst weeds of self-flattery but even he had not altogether been able to kill off those that disguise themselves as 'a desire of glory or commendation'. Such as these, says Walton, are innate, ungraspable: 'like our radical heat'.

> A monument being resolved upon, Dr Donne sent for a carver to make for him in wood the figure of an urn, giving him directions for the compass and height of it; and to bring with it a board, of the just height of his body. 'These being got [Walton here quotes from an eyewitness report], then without delay a choice painter was got to be in readiness to draw his picture, which was taken as followeth. – Several charcoal fires being first made in his large study, he brought with him into that place his winding sheet in his hand, and having put off all his clothes, had this sheet put on him, and so tied with knots at his head and feet, and his hands so placed as dead bodies are usually fitted, to be shrouded and put into their coffin, or grave. Upon this urn he thus stood, with his eyes shut, and with so much of the sheet turned aside as might shew his lean, pale and death-like face, which was purposely turned towards the East, from whence he expected the second coming of his and our Saviour Jesus.' In this posture he was drawn at his just height; and when the picture was fully finished, he caused it to be set by his bedside, where it continued and became his hourly object till his death, and was then given to his dearest friend and executor, Dr Henry King, then Chief Residentiary of St Paul's, who caused him to be thus carved in one entire piece of white marble, as it now stands in that church.

And so it stands today, the one St Paul's monument to have survived more or less intact the Great Fire of 1666: 'One toe is broken off, and the conflagration has just swept across the surface of the urn.'

'The estate which I should leave behind me,' write Donne, '. . . is my poor fame, in the memory of my friends, and therefore I would be curious of it, and provide that they repent not to have loved me.' Donne's will – made three months before he died – was evidently pondered with 'mature deliberation' and it is certainly not short on detail. It lists all manner of trifling bequests: specific paintings for specific friends, mementoes that would have personal significance for the chosen legatee, carefully judged charitable donations, and so on. It makes no mention, though, of any of Donne's writings.

Shortly before he died, Donne put various manuscripts into the hands of Henry King and, as Walton says, he did name King as one of his executors (the other was John Mountford, another colleague at St Paul's). King was a secret poet himself, and a good one, but his relationship with Donne was not that of a fellow writer. Like Walton, King dealt only with the later Donne and he seems not to have thought that his duties as executor went much beyond overseeing the funeral and the making of the monument and ensuring that the will was properly enacted. It had been at King's urging that Donne had prepared some of his sermons for possible future publication but the executor printed only one of them, the last. The mass of material left in his care – sermons, poems, letters, disquisitions, literary jottings – was put into a cabinet and might well have stayed there but for the intervention of John Donne the Younger.

There is disagreement about the nature of this intervention: the evidence can be made to serve more than one version of the case. What seems certain, though, is that after his Oxford acquittal young Donne thought it wise to absent himself from the scene of his disgrace. He spent the next two years in Italy, pondering what now appeared a gloomy set of prospects. Before the Humphry Dunt episode, he had been angling for a job at Christ Church. Son of a renowned divine, he had church contacts galore, and although he dithered before seeking ordination, the signs were that he would climb steadily once he had made up his mind. (The date of his ordination is unknown but is thought to be post-Italy.) Like his father, he was an ingenious and zestful sycophant and would before long have landed some middling to lofty ecclesiastical position. Now, thanks to a moment's rush of blood, even the Christ Church job was out of reach. The best Donne Jr could hope for was one or two low-level rural rectorships or livings. He might even have to live *in* one of his livings.

This was clearly a fate to be avoided at all costs. In Italy, it seems to have dawned on Donne Jr that, scandal or no scandal, he was still his father's son. After all, had not his father, at about his own age – John Jr was thirty in 1634 – also been disgraced, indeed imprisoned? Admittedly, father's crime was to have secretly married John Jr's mother, but even so: was it not rumoured that Donne Sr's young manhood had been deeply stormy and profane, that at one time he had been 'a great visiter of ladies, a great frequenter of playes, a great writer of conceited verses'? And yet, despite these early lapses, the wily rogue had managed to become Dean of St Paul's. Had he lived, he would soon have been made up to Bishop. By associating himself more closely with his father's fame, John Jr might gain access to a whole new set of openings.

Quite apart from his father's near-saintly reputation as a cleric, there was the interesting matter of those 'conceited verses' to be studied. Before the Oxford scandal, John Jr would have seen two posthumous volumes of Donne's work in print. There had been *Juvenilia* (1632), a collection of youthful Problems and Paradoxes, and *Poems* (1633). *Poems* included the 'Songs and Sonnets' that most people now think of as Donne's finest work.

So far as we can tell, both publications were unauthorised: but then 'authorised' did not mean much in the 1630s. In theory, books could be published only by members of the Stationers' Company, incorporated in 1556 'to control the printing and dissemination of printed matter in the interests of Church and State'. The drill was that a member who wished to claim a copyright had to enter the title of his intended publication on the Company's register and seek approval from its Wardens – ie from the Church and State. By 1634, this system – never watertight – was beginning to collapse. Archbishop Laud's war against the books was into its stride and the pirates were at their most intrepid and resourceful. In 1634 – the year of John Donne Jr's trial in Oxford – authors and publishers were being regularly pilloried in London. In February, the Puritan William Prynne 'was sentenced to a fine of £5000, to be degraded from the Bar, to stand in the pillory at Westminster and Cheapside, were he was to have one of his ears cropped at each place, and to be imprisoned for life. An eyewitness to his punishment in the pillory at Cheapside says that while he stood there "they burnt his huge volumes under his nose, which had almost suffocated him." ' Three years later Prynne was at it again: 'a second fine of £5000, together with the renewed degradation of the pillory, the loss of what remained of the stumps of his ears, and, most infamous of all, the mutilation of both cheeks with the letters "S.L." '. 'S.L.' stood for 'seditious libeller' but Prynne whimsically translated it as 'Stigmata Laudis'.

In a generally maddened climate, the living author could just about control the publication of his works. The dead author was fair game, unless there was someone to pursue his cause with vigour. Although not officially his father's executor, John Jr decided to appoint himself custodian of the literary side of the estate. After all, no one else seemed to be in charge, least of all Henry King.

John Donne not only made no mention of his poems in his will; during his lifetime, he spoke of them but rarely and then with – in the main – superb offhandedness. Poetry, he would say, was the mistress of his youth; divinity was the wife of his maturity. His tenebrous early verses were referred to as 'evaporations', 'vanities'. The pieces he would put his name to tended to be those which, from time to time, he submitted to highborn dedicatees, in the hope of some preferment. On the one occasion that he did rush into print, he regretted it. His regret, it seems, had much to do with the feeling that he had committed a social faux pas: he speaks of having 'descended' to the act of publication. Before the accession of James I, the smart versifier's ideal was a Sidneyesque aloofness from the printer's shop. The courtier-poet wrote for a courtly coterie, for other connoisseurs: what was the point of publication when only about half a dozen people could get what you were getting at? Sidney, it was said admiringly, would have been most indignant if any upstart publisher had suggested putting his works up for sale. When the publisher of the anthology *England's Helicon* 'innocently affixed the names of some writers to their pieces' there was alarm among his contributors, and 'he was driven to the clumsy expedient of pasting slips of paper over their names.'

Sidney, of course, was of patron stock and felt himself to be a natural enemy of the democratising print-machines. For Donne, the rules were different. Even so, as a frequent client of the patronage system, he had no good reason to challenge the illusion on which that system thrived: that poems were addressed, not to the world, but to a single, revered addressee. 'I will have no such readers as I can teach,' he said. His single verse-publication, the first of his *Anniversaries*, was in fact a product of the system and its distribution earned him 'many censures'. (The poem was in super-extravagant mourning for the death of his patron's daughter. As Ben Jonson famously pointed out, the stricken Donne had never met the girl.)

When James I started publishing his own works, the familiar, snooty attitudes were somewhat called in question. Chiefly, though, the feeling was that James had rather let the side down. There were furtive murmurs that 'since writing of books had grown into a trade, it was as discreditable for a king to become an author as it would be for him to be a practitioner in a profession.' When James came to assemble his collected works he thought it prudent to instruct one of his bishops to pen an explanatory preface. The bishop rather exceeded his brief: with stunning topicality he set to arguing for nothing less than a divine right of royal authorship:

> The majesty of kings . . . is not unsuited to a writer of books . . . The first royal author is the King of Kings – God himself, who doth so many things for our imitation. It pleased his divine wisdom to be the first in this rank, that we read of, that did ever write.

As Izaak D'Israeli comments: 'How James and the bishop looked on one another at their first meeting, after this preface was fairly read, one would like to learn; but here we have the age!'

For Donne such royal sanction came too late. He had already decided that publication would not be in keeping with his solemn office: it was not smartness he now aimed for, but seemliness. There were even those around him who believed that the very making of verses did not fit well with his 'yeares and place'. As to the writings of his youth, he remained nervous about these to the end: after all, they exhibited aspects of his nature which he had long ago suppressed. He had always worried that his manuscripts would get into the wrong hands. He had circulated them – in sets – to a small group of friends and at least once he implored a member of that circle not to make any copies, saying that he felt 'fear' and 'perhaps shame' at the idea of any wider distribution. Often, it seems, he did not himself keep copies of the verses he sent out. According to Jonson, 'Donne repented highly and sought to destroy all his poems.'

The 1633 edition of Donne's poems was printed by one Thomas Marriot, who explained that he had produced the book in haste so as to forestall any foreign piracy: a thin tale, when one considers how difficult it would have been even for an English publisher to gather in works which, says Walton, 'were loosely, God knows too loosely scattered in his youth'. Marriot also claimed that he was acting 'on the best warrant that can be, public authority and private friends', and sure enough the book was well-stocked with encomia from several of Donne's literary chums, though not all of these tributes suggested first-hand acquaintance with the work. The book also carried a dozen of Donne's letters. Plans for the publication would have had to be set in motion during 1631 or 1632: years in which, as Edmund Gosse has put it, Donne's verses must have 'hung on the verge of extinction'.

Gosse was perhaps exaggerating, but not by much. In ten years' time, there would be Civil War. During the Commonwealth, private libraries were ransacked, studies broken into: many papers were destroyed and altogether there was a more efficient censorship. If Donne's work had not been collected in a hurry, it seems probable that at least some of it would have disappeared. Although there was a Donne vogue in the decade after his death, it was already tailing off in the mid-1640s and might never have happened at all if Marriot had not acted as he did (although the private circulation of manuscripts would no doubt have been stepped up).

If Donne's writings had disappeared from view, it is unlikely that future – that's to say near-future – scholars would have exerted themselves on his behalf. Donne and his imitators enjoyed no critical favour in the eighteenth century: after 1719, his 'Heap of Riddles' found no new editor for 130 years. 1631–41 was the key decade for ensuring Donne's survival into the safe-keeping of his nineteenth-century admirers who in turn paved the way for Herbert Grierson, T. S. Eliot and the GCE. The job of preservation was well done, but we are still not certain who ought to be thanked.

And here we return to the enigma of John Donne the Younger. No one has been able to reconstruct a precise and plausible chronology of John Jr's involvement in his father's literary estate; a certain amount of conjecture has been unavoidable. The most popular narrative would have him returning from Italy in 1636, anxious to live down the Oxford scandal, and wakening up to the possibility of cashing in on his father's now burgeoning reputation as a poet. Such a presentation has to assume that in 1631–2 he took no part in preparing his father's poems for the press, even though in those years he was safely riding the streets of Oxford and was available for consultation. The argument here is that Donne Sr probably would not have shown any of his poems to his son, for whom he entertained clerical ambitions. The middle-aged friends who helped to organise the 1633 publication perhaps felt similarly furtive. And when the book appeared, John Jr may simply have elected to keep his distance: a quick reading would have told him that there had indeed, as rumoured, been two John Donnes, that dad had led a double life. Double lives were dangerous.

Once the book was out in the open, though, and had been praised by some important people, John Jr may have felt that it was safe to make a move. By the mid-1630s, his father's work was being hailed as 'incomparable' and was therefore being widely borrowed from: the vogue was under way. What we do know for certain is that in 1637, shortly after his return to England, John Jr began to petition for control of his father's literary estate. He denounced the existing editions as 'erroneous' and requested that their sale be stopped. In a letter to the Archbishop of Canterbury, he claims that he has often warned the publishers of their 'abuses' and told them 'that if they desisted not they should be proceeded against before your Grace, that they seem so much to slight, that they professe soddainly to publish new impressions, verie much to the grief of your petitioner, – and the discredite of ye memorie of his Father'. Marriot indeed took no notice of all this but perhaps agreed to give John Jr a share of any profits. And this, some have surmised, could have been the petition's principal objective. It took John Jr another thirteen years to gain full control of the estate and when he produced his own version of his father's *oeuvre*, he included all the 'erroneous' poems from the Marriot edition.

John Jr's link with the poems, then, is shadowy – not to say a trifle shady. On the matter of the prose, we seem to be on surer ground. Here most chroniclers concede that it was John Jr who saved the day. We last saw Donne's prose manuscripts being stored away in the cabinet of Henry King. When next heard of, they are somehow in the possession of John Jr and are being prepared for a stage-by-stage publishing programme that ran well into the 1660s. How this transfer was effected no one knows, although the word 'filched' has more than once been used. What seems certain is that at some time during the 1630s – and possibly within months of his father's death – John Jr 'borrowed' the papers from King, using Izaak Walton as an intermediary. The borrowing was permanent. As late as 1664, King is writing ruefully to Walton:

> How these [manuscripts] were got out of my hands, you, who were the Messenger for them, and how lost both to me and your self, is not now seasonable to complain: but, since they did miscarry, I am glad that the general Demonstration of his Worth was so fairly preserved and represented to the World by your pen in the History of his Life.

Twenty years earlier, in 1643, King had been Bishop of Chichester and his palace had been overrun by Parliamentary soldiers. According to a contemporary report, the Cromwellians did a thorough job of pillaging the Bishop's library: they 'rent the books in pieces, and scattered the torn leaves all over the Church, even to the covering and the Pavement.' Had John Jr not 'borrowed' his father's papers when he did, they would perhaps have been similarly rent and scattered. Or so the story goes. In fact, John Jr himself suffered some mild persecution during the Civil War. Writing a year after the assault on Chichester Cathedral, he says: 'Since the beginning of the war my study was often searched, and all my books and almost my brains by their continual alarms sequestered for the use of the committee.'

Nonetheless, it seems fair to give him credit for the survival of the prose. Perhaps he stole the manuscripts from King; certainly he told lies in his petition. And he has also been accused of bungling the various publications he eventually engineered. The 1651 edition of the *Letters to Severall Persons of Honour* is widely regarded as a joke, with its wrong attributions, its invented addressees: 'no such important work was ever thrown upon the world in a more slovenly way'. There is also the controversial question of *Biathanatos*, Donne's treatise declaring that 'Self-Homicide is not so naturally Sin, that it may never be otherwise', published by John Jr in 1644. Donne himself called this 'a book written by Jack Donne and not by Dr Donne' and was always nervous about it; he instructed a friend: 'Publish it not, yet burn it not; and between those do what you will with it.' John Jr has been denounced for 'disregarding his father's wishes' and for the 'characteristic brutality' with which he 'made merchandise of the Mss'. In his 1644 Preface the son notes that his father has forbidden 'both the Presse and the Fire' but goes on to argue that 'I could find no certain way to defend it from the one but by committing it to the other'. In the current climate, 'two dangers appeared more eminently to hover over this, being then a manuscript, a danger of being utterly lost, and a danger of being utterly found.'

To write like this in 1644 involved a certain risk, but the preface is rather wittily composed and makes good sense. And the same might be said of John Jr's Preface to his 1661 edition of his father's *XXVI Sermons*, in which he apologises for having sought Commonwealth protection before bringing out an earlier collection. His belief was, he says, that if he had acted differently the sermons would have been burned by the public executioner. By publishing, he had helped to safeguard 'the banks of the Church against that torrent of Heretiques that did then invade her . . . for now began to swarme and muster the Ebionites, Sabellians, Jovinians, Euticheans, Corpocratians, Sethians,

11

Cerinthians, Theodotians, Nicolaitans, Samocetanians, Apolena-
rians, Montaneans, all against the second Person of the Trinity.'

In this mildly 'fantastical' flight we can discern a possible key reason
for John Jr's unpopularity over the years with his father's more po-
faced adherents. In all his writings there is a compulsive wish to come
across as an irresistibly jocular sort of fellow, full of erudite and artful
levity. This kind of ambition can grate on the nerves. Those who wish
to berate John Jr have seized with glee on Anthony Wood's near-
contemporary character-sketch:

> He had all the advantages tendered to him to tread in the steps of his
> virtuous father, but his nature being vile, he proved no better all his
> lifetime than an atheistical buffoon, a banterer, and a person of over-free
> thoughts.

Wood was, of course, a notorious curmudgeon and rarely spoke
kindly about anyone. (It was for him that Aubrey collected his *Brief
Lives*, thus earning from Wood a title – 'magotie-headed' – that, not
surprisingly, has stuck.) Even Wood, though, had to concede that, in
spite of everything, John Jr was also a man possessed of 'humour' and
of 'sense'. These modifying judgements have not often been passed on
to us by later commentators.

For the twentieth century the most damaging account of John Jr
comes in Augustus Jessop's short article in the *Dictionary of National
Biography*. Canon Jessop laboured for fifty years on Donne's theological writings and almost collaborated with Edmund Gosse on his 1899
biography; the collaboration did not work because Jessop 'had never
been able to feel much enthusiasm for Donne as a poet'. To him the
Donne who mattered was the author of the *Sermons* and the *Essays in
Divinity*. One might have thought, therefore, that he would feel
gratitude to the original custodian of the materials which had provided
his life's work. But no: Jessop's piece is savage in its hostility; he
recounts the Humphry Dunt episode, he quotes the nastiest bits from
Anthony Wood, he lets us know that John Jr was neglectful of his
duties as a parish priest (as, so it seems, he was), and he deplores his
'dissipated habits'. About John Jr's executorship, he says nothing
except that the son 'managed to get possession of all the books and
papers which had been bequeathed to Dr John [*sic*] King, and to retain
them in his own hands during his life'.

The clinching paragraph comes near the end, when we are told that

John Jr, a few months before he died, published some of his own writings: 'a very gross volume in small 8vo, entitled *Donnes Satyr; containing a short map of Mundane Vanity, a cabinet of Merry Conceits, certain pleasant propositions and questions, with their merry solutions and answers*. . . . They are full of the most shocking indecencies.' We cannot be sure that Jessop actually perused the book in question. His verdict was taken on trust, however, so that thirty years later we can find a responsible historian making casual reference to John Donne the Younger as 'despicable', 'hateful', 'notorious for his profligate habits', and as one who 'left manuscripts of his own which, from all accounts, were unspeakably obscene and succeeded in publishing a volume of his indecencies only six months before his death.'

John Jr's *Satyr* is in fact not in the least indecent, obscene, shocking or any of those things. It is an innocuous bit of play-acting that was perhaps self-consciously composed in the huge shadow of his father's fame. The title *Donnes Satyr* surely invites us to look at it this way. The book seems almost to be saying: I'm nowhere near as good as *he* was, but I'm not entirely without merits of my own. There are attempts at learned wit; abstruse, ebullient conceitedness; there are worldly-wise aphorisms and outlandish speculations. In other words, the period bag of tricks – but delivered with a near-simpering unpretentiousness. Here is Jolly Jack Jr at play; you can ignore him if you wish but surely you can't help but like him just a little. To give something of the flavour, here is one of a series of jests manufactured according to the signs of the Zodiac:

### Of the Sun Tavern

> One staggering out of the Sun Tavern came
> And being far in drink, and out of frame,
> A friend him meets and greets, but not a word
> This stupefied Sot could him afford;
> And if he did (a wager might be laid)
> He would not stand to anything he said;
> His face being foully fleckt, and both his eyes
> With drink main red, his friend to him thus cries,
> I know where you were late I'll hold a gun,
> For your face shows that you were in the Sun.

John Jr's habit is to play the fool: to exhibit something of his father's comic resourcefulness, but pointlessly. There is even a suggestion in one of his pieces that Donne Sr's elaborate funeral arrangements are being offered as good for a laugh:

13

Earth is the Womb from whence all living came,
So is't the tomb, all go unto the same;
And as at first all naked thence were born,
So as naked thither all at last return;
Unless they carry thence a Winding sheet,
To hide their weak frail nakedness, most meet.

John Jr's little book was probably put together in 1661, a year after
Charles II's return to England. It was meant to catch the mood of
cavalier rejoicing: 'after melancholy, mirth is the more musical,
sweet, acceptable, delightful and pleasant'. We know very little about
John Jr's circumstances under the Commonwealth; our guess is that,
in spite of some harassment, he managed merrily to muddle through.
A certain amount of compromise and opportunism was no doubt
required, and making best use of his father's celebrated legacy was just
one more way of turning a guinea during seriously adverse times. In
the preface to his *Satyr*, John Jr quotes Machiavelli: 'who cannot
dissemble cannot live' – a 'Heathenish' insight, he admits, but one that
'was never put more in practice than in these Phanatick times':

> for he that cannot metamorphose his shape like Proteus, vary his hiew like
> the Polypus, change his colour like the Camelion, bear two faces under a
> hood like Janus, comply with every Planet like Mercury, vary and change
> like the Moon constantly, turn with the weathercock, adulate with
> Aristippus, equivocate with Synon, dissemble with Gnatho, hunt with the
> Hound, and hold with the Hare, carry fire in the one hand, and water in the
> other; and in a word, who cannot temporise at all times, with all persons,
> and in all places, that man knows not how to look or live in this
> hypocritical, perverse and crooked Generation.

Behind the garrulity there is more than a hint of bitterness and self-
reproach. Even so, the overall effect is of a too-effortful facetiousness.
As satire, it would have been dismissed as puny stuff by John Donne
Sr. And this is what makes it rather sad and likeable. We get much the
same feeling when we read John Jr's Last Will and Testament – the
legacy of one who is known to history only as a legatee. Anthony
Wood, in his character-sketch, makes a point of scoffing at John Jr's
'fantastical and conceited will' and sure enough the thing *is* played for
laughs. It is as if the family fund of death-bed sonority had been
entirely used up by the Dean, with his burning braziers, his urn, his
effigy. John Jr's Act V, Scene 5 is marked by its jocund rejection of

14

theatricality, its determined prankishness of tone. 'I have not lived by juggling', he says, 'therefore I desire to dye and be buried without any'. He also warns his executor against any well-meaning improvisation: 'I desire my executor to interpret my meaning in this request by my word, and not by his own discretion; who, peradventure, for fashion sake, and apprehending we shall never meet, may think to order things better for my credit' (which surely is a clause that ought to be built into all literary wills). On the matter of the actual bequests, John Jr again finds it hard to keep his face straight. Some of them he lists as follows:

> To my honourable friend, Sir Allen Broderick, I give my cedar table, to add a fragour to his excellent writing. To my kind friend, Mr. Tho. Killigrew, I give all my doves, that something may descend upon a courtier that is an emblem of kindness and truth. To my servant Mary Web, if she be with me at the time of my death, I give all my linen that belongs to my personal use, and forty shillings above her wages, if it does not appear that she hath occasioned my death; which I have often lived in fear of, but being alone could never help, although I have often complained of my sad condition to my nearest relations, 'twas not fit to trouble others.

John Donne the Younger died in 1662, and was outlived by both Izaak Walton and Henry King, Donne's other keepers. They too are remembered in the will:

> To the Reverend Bishop of Chichester, I return that cabinet that was my father's, now in my dining room, and all those papers which are of authors analysed by my father; many of which he hath already received with his Common Place Book, which I desire may pass to Mr Walton's son, as being more likely to have use for such a help, when his age shall require it.

# CHAPTER TWO

# SURVIVING SHAKESPEARE

Although John Donne the Younger took a modest pride in his versifying gifts, we know little of any of his other writings. There is one piece, though, which he is fairly confidently believed to have co-authored. It is entitled 'Certain Verses written by several of the Author's friends, to be reprinted in the Second Edition of *Gondibert*'. The title was heavily sarcastic; the piece is actually an item of 'Wit-Combat' directed at Sir William Davenant, who at the time was known to be working on a vast new epic poem. 'Certain Verses' was anthologised in 1653 but probably issued as a pamphlet a couple of years earlier.

William Davenant was two years younger than John Donne the Younger and one of the leading literary figures of the day. A successful theatre manager, he had taken over from Ben Jonson as unofficial Poet Laureate in 1638. On the strength of *Gondibert*, his epic-in-progress, he was beginning to be mentioned in the same breath as Chaucer, Spenser, Donne. Maybe this is what irritated John Donne Jr. He and Davenant were almost exact contemporaries; their fathers had known each other slightly. In the year that Davenant became Poet Laureate, John Jr was still struggling to live down his Oxford scandal. As John Jr manoeuvred for promotion in the church, Davenant was cutting a brilliant figure in the London theatre. Even before the Oxford scandal, Davenant was way ahead: he had scored a stage triumph with *The Witts* and was in demand for the presentation of Court masques. And now, in 1650, here was news of *Gondibert*.

*Gondibert* was indeed a grandiose project, an elaborate attempt at a genuinely English epic, in quatrains, and its appearance was being preceded by much portentous theorising on the part of the author and his allies. Davenant was not afraid to place himself in a direct line from Homer and Virgil, nor to announce candidly that he was in pursuit of a Fame similar to theirs. By 'Fame' he meant 'reputation' for the living and 'a musical Glory' for the dead: 'I will gravely tell thee he who writes an Heroick poem leaves an estate entailed; and he gives a greater gift to Posterity, than to the Present Age.' To Davenant's foes, such lofty talk was deliciously provoking: they crowed back that *Gondibert* would be at best a poem with which a wit might 'wipe the Taile'. As things turned out, Davenant got bored by his great undertaking around the middle of Book III. In 1650, though, when John Jr and his friends conceived their satire, *Gondibert* seems to have been the coming event in literary circles. And when the first two books appeared, in 1651, 'the courtiers with the Prince of Wales would never be quiet about the piece'. These courtiers were presumably doing their chattering in Paris. John Jr and his associates were, of course, trying to get by in London.

A further stimulus to ridicule was provided by Davenant's personal appearance: 'there was a feature in his face, or rather no feature at all, that served as a perpetual provocative'. As a consequence of some early 'mishaps among the women', his nose had become eroded by disease. (In the *Dictionary of National Biography* we are told that 'an illness resulted in the loss of his nose'; the more primitive Aubrey records that 'He gott a terrible clap of a black handsome wench that lay in Axe-yard . . . which cost him his nose'). Even an admirer like Suckling had to concede that 'In all their records, in verse or prose/ There was none of a Laureat who wanted a nose'. It was also perceived that Davenant was touchy on the subject of his humble origins, his 'untaught childhood': he was the son of a vintner, landlord of the Crown Inn, Oxford. When he inserted a Gallic, or 'aristocratic', apostrophe into the spelling of his name – calling himself D'Avenant – the wits made a great business of trying to locate on the map of France a place called Avenant, observing the while that Davenant had 'made a Notch in's name, like that in's face'.

Davenant's performance in the Civil War was also sneered at by his literary enemies, although in fact he seems to have carried out some hazardous assignments. At various times, he acted as ordnance officer, gun-runner, dynamite-plotter, secret agent, courier and general factotum to the exiled Queen. It was he who in 1646 was chosen by the Queen to take a message from Paris to the cornered Charles I in Newcastle. The drift of the message was that the King should 'part with the church for his peace and security' – in other words, cave in. Charles got the impression that Davenant's own attitude to the church was insufficiently respectful and, according to Clarendon's great history, was 'transported with indignation' and 'gave [Davenant] a sharper reprehension than was usual for him to give to any other man, and forbade him to presume to come again into his presence. Whereupon the poor man, who had in truth very good affections, was exceedingly dejected and afflicted.' Davenant returned to Paris, where he had lodgings in the Louvre, and began laying down the scheme of *Gondibert*.

By the time the Preface to *Gondibert* appeared, Davenant must have seemed a safe target for the London satirists. From his long exile in Paris, he had set sail for America (in the spring of 1650). His ship was intercepted by Parliamentary soldiers and Davenant was transported to the Tower, where he remained for two years: 'pretty certain that I shall be hanged next week'. (It is said that Milton saved Davenant from execution and that ten years later Davenant was able to return the favour.) He was released on bail in 1652 but was re-arrested because of debts that had piled up 'in his absence'. His final release did not come until August 1654. It was during this long, low period that John Donne the Younger and his intrepid co-satirists had been making merry with Davenant's literary reputation.

For our purposes, it is piquant that John Donne the Younger should have chosen to go gunning for Davenant. In his different, rather nobler way, Davenant was also the keeper of a flame. Throughout much of the Commonwealth and well into the Restoration period, he was generally regarded as the chief guardian of Shakespeare's somewhat precarious repute. There was even a current rumour, believed by many and not discouraged by Davenant himself, that he was Shakespeare's son: William Shakespeare the Younger, so to speak. The Bard, it seems, used to lodge at the Crown when he was in Oxford and according to Anthony Wood – who else? – the landlord's wife was 'a very beautiful woman, of a good wit and conversation, in which she was imitated by none of her children but by this William'. We also know that, two years after Shakespeare's death, the twelve-year-old Davenant wrote an Ode in his 'Remembrance'. The truth appears to be that Davenant was Shakespeare's godson but that, when he was in his cups, 'it seemed to him that he writ with the very same spirit that Shakespeare did, and was contented enough to be thought his son.' Later on, Pope would tell a story about Davenant that, as a small boy, he used to run from school to meet Shakespeare, when the playwright was in town, and that once 'being asked where he was running, by an old townsman, replied "to see my Godfather,

Shakespeare", "There's a good boy," said the old gentleman, "but have a care that you don't take God's name in vain".' Keeping abreast of modern thinking on the matter, we should perhaps also cite Frank Kermode on 'Shakespeare's Learning': 'Whether or not Davenant is speaking the truth in his scurrilous account of how Shakespeare amused himself when passing through Oxford, it seems unlikely that he went into Bodley to read.'

There was, to be sure, something recognisably filial in Davenant's approach to Shakespeare's memory, as we shall see, but the hero-worship ran deep and was unshakeable. From this point of view, the timing of events could hardly have been better. Shakespeare's First Folio – the first attempt at a collected edition of his plays – appeared in 1623, shortly after the young Davenant had moved from Oxford to London and was beginning to make his mark in literary and theatrical circles. Arguably the most important event in publishing history, this edition would have had huge significance for the ambitious godson of its author. It was not usual for plays to be put into print and a Collected Plays was almost without precedent. Of Shakespeare's contemporaries only Ben Jonson had been able to secure homage of this order, Ben having 'told them plainly he deserv'd the Bayes/For his were called Works, where others were but Plaies.' Jonson, who was much criticised for his presumption, took a hand in the elevation of Shakespeare to his own high rank.

In itself, the First Folio was an awe-inspiring act of devotion, and of literary conservation. The editors were two of Shakespeare's fellow actors, John Heming and Henry Condell, each of whom had been remembered in the playwright's will – he left them 28s 6d to buy a mourning ring. In their Dedication they spoke convincingly of their wish to 'keepe the memory of so worthy a friend and fellow worker alive as was our Shakespeare'. Their claim – and they were well-placed to make it – was that all the plays were here 'set forth according to their first originals': not just the unpublished pieces but also – 'now cur'd and perfect in their limbs' – the plays that had been printed during Shakespeare's lifetime, even those 'diverse stolne and surreptitious copies maimed and deformed by the frauds and stealths of injurious imposters'. Thanks to the First Folio, eighteen of Shakespeare's plays were rescued from oblivion – these include *Lear*, *The Tempest* and *Macbeth* – and several others from being handed down in texts that would soon have become irretrievably corrupt. Davenant, proud of his personal connection, already a fervent admirer of the work, and now contemplating a role in the theatre for himself, could scarcely not have been intrigued by this talk of making Shakespeare safe.

It would be some years, though, before he was able to announce himself as the successor to Heming and Condell. Before the Civil War, Davenant was the manager of a small theatre in Drury Lane, the Phoenix, but he had not been permitted to mount Shakespeare productions there. The plays were the property of Shakespeare's old company, The King's Men, who were still in business at the Globe. In 1642 the theatres were shut down and by the time Davenant came out of jail all the old acting companies had been broken up and dispersed. For a theatre impresario anxious to resurrect his old career, the situation clearly demanded some masterstroke of cunning. Davenant rose splendidly to the demand. He began staging so-called 'musical productions'. The government, he had noted, was prepared to tolerate musical entertainments provided that they seemed to be good for the soul. Given in private houses to a ticket-buying audience, these Davenant presentations, or 'declamations', ingeniously contrived to skirt the law. They also introduced a number of new theatrical gimmicks that would be effectively developed later on: scene-changes, women actors, stage-machines. One of Davenant's own compositions, *The Siege of Rhodes*, is now thought of as the first 'opera' in English. These musical evenings, begun in 1656, were viewed with suspicion by the Parliamentary authorities – there were 'questions in the House' – but were never actually closed down. The diarist John Evelyn attended one of them and marvelled 'that in a time of such public consternation such a vanity shd. be kept up or permitted'. Davenant, it should be said, was canny enough during these years to issue the odd strategic piece of verse: notably, there was an *Epithalamion* for the marriage of Cromwell's daughter. After all, he was – he supposed – still Poet Laureate.

Somehow Davenant kept his 'theatre' going and after a time even managed to stage some of his productions at the Phoenix. With the Restoration he was well placed to take a leading role in the reopening of the London theatres – a process which, luckily for him, was managed gradually. In August 1660, Charles II issued warrants to two theatre companies: the King's, to be run by Thomas Killigrew (he to whom John Donne the Younger would soon bequeath his doves) and the Duke's, or Duke of York's, which would be run by Davenant. The King's would operate from Drury Lane and Davenant would have his playhouse (which became known as 'The Opera') in Lincoln's

Inn Fields. Killigrew's company was seen as the more conservative of the two, with older actors and a programme built around the works of Jonson. Davenant's manifesto was rather more progressive: his youthful troupe would handle Shakespeare.

To this end, Davenant secured from the King an exclusive right to 'perform and reform' certain Shakespeare plays: four comedies, four tragedies and one 'spectacle' (this was *Henry VIII*). His moment had arrived: 'he had waited eighteen years for his opportunity, he was now fifty-four, and there was no time to be lost.'

During his 'musical' years, Davenant had developed a taste for the spectacular; he had become fond of wires and trapdoors. Soon he would have *Macbeth*'s witches whizzing through the air. He had also acquired, or so he thought, a shrewd sense of audience requirements. The younger playgoers of the day not only had never seen Shakespeare; more likely than not, they had never seen a play. Davenant's entrepreneurial nose (one might have said) persuaded him that, wonderful as Shakespeare was, some revamping must be done. For one thing, the language in places required clarification and polish. Lines like 'Screw your courage to the sticking place' should surely read 'Bring but your courage to the fatal place' and 'Sleep that knits up the ravelled sleeve of care' might well trip more fluently if altered to 'locks up the senses from their care'. Also, some of the plays badly needed restructuring: for example, *Much Ado*'s Beatrice and Benedick slot neatly into *Measure for Measure* which, in any case, had to be retitled: *The Law Against Lovers* had a more contemporary feel. In general the plots would benefit from being purged of low-life drollery.

In 1667, the year before he died, Davenant teamed up with the young John Dryden and swiftly converted him to the cause of Shakespeare, perhaps seeing in him an appropriately gifted heir apparent. Together, the pair of them produced what seems to have been a memorably ghastly Restoration version of *The Tempest*. It was later well-described by Dr Johnson: 'The effect produced by the conjunction of these two powerful minds was that to Shakespeare's monster Caliban is added a sister-monster Sycorax; and a woman who in the original play had never seen a man is in this brought acquainted with a man that had never seen a woman.' There was also a 24-piece orchestra and a genuinely flying Ariel, plus *corps de ballet*.

Involving Dryden in the perpetuation of Shakespeare's glory might seem to us to have rendered dubious rewards. Dryden, of course, thought Shakespeare was 'divine' but, like Davenant, he could see that there were barbarities – 'bombast, obscurity, incoherence' – to be attributed to Shakespeare's faulty education in the classics. These old plays had none of that instinctive care for symmetry which made it possible for the author of *Heroic Stanzas on the Late Lord Protector* to publish, one year later, 'A poem on the happy Restoration and Return of his Sacred Majesty King Charles the Second'. Ten years later, Dryden was established as Shakespeare's principal 'refiner', setting a fashion for other, lesser, rewrite-men like Shadwell, Cibber, Rymer, and so on. In his preface to his version of *Troilus and Cressida*, Dryden has the air of a man who is stating the obvious: 'It must be allowed to the present age, that the tongue in general is so much refined since Shakespeare's time, that many of his words, and more of his phrases, are scarce intelligible. And of those which we understand, some are ungrammatical, others coarse; and his whole style is so pestered with figurative expressions, that it is as affected as it is obscure.'

We can chuckle now at these complacencies but we also know that this is how literary history works: each generation 'corrects' the errors of its ancestors, 'each generation, like each individual, brings to the contemplation of art its own categories of appreciation, makes its own demands upon art, and has its own uses for art.' There is indeed a troublesome cocksureness about Restoration and eighteenth-century attitudes to Shakespeare: we tend to think that in this one extra-ordinary instance, 'correction' could have been, well, just a bit less 'incorrect'. At the same time, though, we have to concede that, in the 1660s, Shakespeare might have done worse than claim the imperfect attentions of two of the most gifted poets of the day – two poets, moreover, who happened to span two generations. Had Shakespeare not been 'refined', he might well have been ignored and this would, in some obvious and no doubt several hidden ways, have altered the literature that followed, the literature we now possess – the stock, in other words, that is now available for our 'correction'.

When the theatres re-opened in 1660, Shakespeare was not well-known. If he was talked of at all, it was rather as Dryden talked of him, although without Dryden's sense of his essential genius: for the average literatus, he was just another of those rude Elizabethans. By 1668, however, he was generally revered as one of England's greatest poets. Even Samuel Pepys, who enjoyed relatively few of his numerous nights at the theatre, had one or two admiring words for Davenant's *Hamlet* 'done with scenes' (although, it must be said, he thought *A Midsummer Night's Dream* 'silly and ridiculous' and *Romeo and Juliet* the worst play he had ever seen). Simply in terms of maintaining the continuity of Shakespeare's fame, it was the happiest of accidents that Davenant, its keeper, was where he was in 1660. At that date, it would have occurred to no one else to invest so heavily in Shakespeare.

Davenant died intestate (odd, this, for one who so often pondered the enticements of posterity) and his funeral at Westminster Abbey was a low-key affair, notable chiefly for the number of children who attended it – Davenant was thrice-married – and for the absence of 'any lawrel upon his coffin, which [Aubrey presumed] was forgotten'. Although the inscription on his marble – 'O rare Sir Will' – echoed Ben Jonson's, in most of the numerous eulogies that followed his death, his name was linked to Shakespeare's. Opponents like Richard Flecknoe imagined Davenant arriving in Elysium to a frosty welcome from the various bards assembled there; 'Nay, even Shakespeare, whom he thought to have found his greatest friend, was so much offended with him as any of the rest, for so spoiling and mangling his plays' (Flecknoe, whose own posterity Dryden would soon be taking care of, believed – with some justice – that it was his *Ariadne* that had first brought Italian opera into English). For Davenant's admirers, though, the championing of Shakespeare was thought to be one of his chief triumphs. 'Their quick inventions were the same,' said one, without a trace of irony.

Davenant passed the Shakespeare flame to Dryden but in his theatre company there was another protégé who would turn out to have a significant supporting part to play. The actor Thomas Betterton, himself a writer of plays and operas, was a Davenant-trained Shakespeare devotee. The Olivier of his age, Betterton was adored even by Pepys: indeed, it was often to see Betterton that Pepys went to Shakespeare plays. At Davenant's urging, the actor had made it his business to take on all the great Shakespearean roles and for these – it has been claimed – he had the advantage of being coached by an old actor called John Taylor who at one time worked with Shakespeare. The story is that Taylor coached Betterton for his celebrated Hamlet, thus providing the actor with a direct line to the exact requirements of the Bard. 'Betterton,' it was later said, 'performed the part as if it had been written on purpose for him, as if the author had conceived it as he plays it.' Pepys was so struck by Betterton's Hamlet that he did a musical setting of the 'To be or not to be . . .' speech, and in this tried to capture 'some echo of the intonations of the great actor'. Pepys' setting has survived and one respectable commentator has mused on it as follows:

> it is no extravagance to suggest that a note here and there enshrines the modulation of the voice of Shakespeare himself. For there is the likelihood that the dramatist was Betterton's instructor at no more than two removes. Only the lips of Davenant, Shakespeare's godson, and of Taylor, Shakespeare's acting colleague, intervened between the dramatist and the Hamlet of Pepys' diary.

There is always a slight air of desperation about these Shakespeare stories, an almost spiritualist need to 'make contact', any contact. There is also an air of exasperation. How could so little have been written down by those who lived and worked with this now-vaunted figure? Shakespeare had been dead for nearly fifty years before any 'biographical notices' started to appear: by this time, most sources of information had dried up. In reference works of the late seventeenth century, one or two facts were noted but in general the encyclopedists were reduced to listing Shakespeare's works and leaving it at that.

Even a relatively early work like Thomas Fuller's *Worthies* (1662) had only half a page on Shakespeare, and this mostly speculation. Fuller was an unusually diligent researcher; he travelled round the country in search of 'delightful stories' with which to 'flesh out' the 'skeleton of Time' but, for his Shakespeare entry, he seems not to have greatly stirred himself. If Fuller had gone to Stratford, he could have interviewed some of Shakespeare's family – a brother and a sister still survived – and he could also have checked the gravestone for the dates of Shakespeare's birth and death, both of which he has some trouble with. When Fuller was doing his research, though, Shakespeare was not high on the list of England's worthies.

'Hard has been the fate of many a great genius that while they have conferr'd immortality on others, they have wanted themselves some friend, to embalm their names for posterity.' Rather aptly, these words appear in a preface to Nicholas Rowe's translation of the Roman poet Lucan. Rowe's other claim to fame (apart from the Lucan and a brief spell as Poet Laureate) is that in 1709 he became the first 'critical editor' of Shakespeare and, with his forty-page 'Some Account of the Life', published as a preface to his six-volume edition of the *Works*, he laid claim to be thought of as the first biographer.

Rowe's edition was badly needed at the time. It corrected printers' errors, supplied modern spelling and punctuation, and in general smartened up the presentation. Rowe even added a few illustrations. His editorial work provided a starting point for the great textual battles of the eighteenth century and so was shortly to be superseded. His 'Life', though, was not substantially added to for another hundred years.

If Shakespeare had indeed had a friend, a contemporary, who had wished to 'embalm' his name for posterity, Rowe's task would have been a bit less hopeless. There were legends and anecdotes – Greene's insult, Jonson's jealousy, Davenant's parentage, and so on – but almost nothing in the way of documentation. Some of Rowe's legends and anecdotes are to this day under strenuous discussion in the Shakespeare Institutes and will probably never become more (or less) believable than they were when he first heard them. The problem was – and is – that Shakespeare seems not to have had the kind of friends who wrote things down. Also his fame as a writer was in suspense during the years in which one might have expected the chroniclers to go about their business. And then there was the Civil War. Aubrey had interviewed Davenant for his *Brief Lives* and had done some of the necessary legwork (possibly as early as the 1640s) but his unpublished manuscript was locked up in the Ashmolean Museum in 1693 and would not be properly published until 1898. All that the world knew of Aubrey's jottings was in the material Anthony Wood used for his dictionary of Oxford worthies, or was in reports of Aubrey's conversation.

Unlike Aubrey, Nicholas Rowe was not the energetic type. As an editor, he peculiarly failed to track down a copy of the First Folio but used subsequent, even more error-strewn printings as his working texts. As a biographer, he exhibited a similar passivity. And this is where Betterton came in. In his old age – probably in 1708, when he was seventy-three – the actor decided that he would make a journey to Stratford 'on purpose to gather up what Remains he could of a name for which he had so great a place'. It was Betterton to whom Rowe would own 'a particular obligation' for the 'most considerable part' of his biography. In effect, the distinguished actor served as Rowe's principal researcher.

Betterton, it seems, checked parish registers and school records. He may even have importuned a few grizzled Stratford residents. He made errors and Rowe did not double-check, but the information Betterton picked up, coupled with all the Davenant yarns he was able to remember, made him as close to a 'living witness' as Rowe could hope to get. There are grounds for suspecting that by this time in his life Betterton had worked up a nice line in Shakespeare-Davenant stories, but Rowe was presumably eager to accept whatever he was given. When the 'Life' was being written, Rowe was thirty-five, a popular new playwright; Betterton was in impoverished semi-retirement. In 1709, Rowe composed a prologue for a benefit evening for Betterton that raised £500 – not bad, when one thinks that Betterton at his peak earned £4 a week. From the accounts of his contemporaries, Rowe was of personable manners and appearance, witty and convivial, but somewhat deficient in imagination: more of a scholar than a poet, some would say. 'He seldom pierces the heart' but he 'often improves the understanding' was Dr Johnson's summing-up. Betterton, by this time, had become something of a relic, honoured for his reputation but criticised for his tendency to cling on to the past – playing young-man roles long after he was physically out of shape. Not the ideal team, perhaps, but remembered now as the fathers of Shakespearean biography.

After Rowe and Betterton, it would not be long before biography began to get entangled with Bardolatry. Soon enough, Thomas Sharpe would be selling toothpicks cut from the authentic mulberry tree that used to stand in the garden at New Place. Soon enough, there would be David Garrick's ludicrous Stratford Jubilee, with processions, pageants, unveilings, declamations and, of course, much toast-quaffing from Sharpe's seemingly endless supply of mulberry goblets. Garrick's essential message was: 'A demi-god is born.' To this 'Avonian Willy', the famous actor addressed many verses and songs specially composed for the occasion. We can only surmise, and hope, that as he delivered them, he drank deeply from the magic cup:

> Behold this fair goblet, 'twas carved from the tree,
> Which, O my sweet Shakespeare, was planted by thee;
> As a relic I kiss it, and bow at the shrine.
> What comes from thy hand must be ever divine.

By the mid-eighteenth century the Shakespeare industry was launched, unstoppably, and Stratford had indeed become a shrine. Sixty years after Betterton's pioneering visit to the town, this puff for Garrick's Jubilee was printed in the *Gentleman's Magazine*, accompanied by the world's first-ever picture of the Birthplace:

The Gothic glories of the ancient Church, the modern elegance of the Civic Hall, cease to be regarded, when it is remembered that the humble shed, in which the immortal bard first drew that breath which gladdened all the isle, is still existing; and all who have a heart to feel, and a mind to admire the truth of nature and splendour of genius, will rush thither to behold it, as a pilgrim would to the shrine of some loved saint; will deem it holy ground, and dwell with sweet though pensive rapture, on the natal habitation of the poet.

There is a Henry James story called 'The Birthplace, 1903' in which these cadences are mimicked and in which James, while deploring the industry, cannot disguise his admiration for the Bard's gifts of self-promotion: the way for a writer to promote himself, James perceives, is by *not having a self* to promote. The point about relics is that there must be very few of them, and even these should be of questionable authenticity.

In the story, Morris Sledge is appointed custodian of the birthplace of a great dead poet – 'the supreme poet, the Mecca of the English-speaking race'. As a genuine admirer of the poet's work, Sledge feels much honoured, saying to his wife: 'The more we *know* him, the more we shall love him. We don't as yet, you see, know him so very thoroughly.' Sledge has no difficulty in discriminating between his own 'wish to know' and that of the unlettered tourists who flock to inspect the birthplace: what can they *know* of 'the enshrined Presence', 'the great spirit'?

Gradually, though, Sledge's mystical approach falls victim to some nagging doubts. What if the birthplace is a fake? 'Well, we don't know. There's very little *to* know. He covered his tracks as no other human being has ever done.' Sledge fears that if he gives voice to his doubts, he will surely get the sack, so he keeps quiet. It all comes to a head, though, when a pair of stylish Jamesian Americans turn up, a husband and wife, bearing with them 'a nature, a culture, a facility of some sort'. She is 'vaguely, delicately, irregularly but mercilessly pretty' and he, of course, is rich, cultivated, thoughtful and relaxed. Overheard by Sledge, they speak as follows:

HE: I'm interested in what, I think, is *the* interesting thing – or at all events the eternally tormenting thing. The fact of the abysmally little that, in proportion, we know.

SHE: In proportion to what?

HE: Well, to what there might have been – to what in fact there *is* – to

27

> wonder about. That's the interest; it's immense. He escapes us like a thief at night, carrying off – well, carrying off everything. And people pretend to catch Him like a flown canary, over whom you can close your hand and put Him back; he won't *come* back. He's not . . . such a fool: it makes Him the happiest of all great men.

Sledge is mightily impressed and weighs in with a speech about the poet's work being invulnerable to the intrusion of all this low biographical curiosity. 'It's all I want,' he says, 'to let the author alone. Practically there *is* no author; that is, for us to deal with. There are all the immortal people – *in* the work; but there's nobody else.' To this the husband adds his, and James's final word: 'Yes, that's what it comes to. There should really, to clear the matter up, be no such person.'

As for Sledge: his epiphany complete, and knowing himself to be a fraud, he decides to hang on to his job. Indeed, he now evolves a curator's performance of such excessive gravity and sub-poetic power that he himself becomes something of a celebrity: around the world, tourists speak with awe of his unforgettable birthplace address. Instead of being fired for his loss of faith, he gets a raise. And the demi-god, he's pretty sure, would not have grudged him this.

Henry James's suggestion is that bardolatry is fuelled by the absence of biography, that if we knew more we would worship less. James, though, was writing in an age of journalism, an age in which the superior spirit believes itself to be pursued as prey, to be tied down, examined, reduced – though never, of course, comprehended. He admires and envies Shakespeare for having given no interviews, for having left no clues, for having escaped us, as a thief at night. There is now 'no such person'; hence, the Bacon theory, the Marlowe theory, theories born of an exasperated curiosity, a thwarted love.

And yet, even as we talk of Shakespeare's disappearance, we also pay tribute to his omnipresence. Just a few years before his friend David Garrick pranced through the streets of Stratford with his mulberry wand and goblet, Samuel Johnson offered, in the preface of his *Shakespeare*, a noble delineation of the playwright's continuing aliveness as a literary classic:

> The poet, of whose works I have undertaken the revision, may now begin to assume the dignity of an ancient, and claim the privilege of established fame and prescriptive veneration. He has long outlived his century, the test commonly fixed as a test of literary merit. Whatever advantages he

might once derive from personal allusions, local customs, or temporary opinions, have for many years been lost; and every topick of merriment or motive of sorrow, which the modes of artificial life afforded him, now only obscure the scenes which they once illuminated. The effects of favour and competition are at an end; the tradition of his friendships and his enmities has perished; his works support no opinions with arguments, nor supply any faction with invectives: they can neither indulge vanity nor gratify malignity, but are read without any other reason than the desire of pleasure, and are therefore praised only as pleasure is obtained; yet, thus unassisted by interest or passion, they have passed through variations of taste and changes of manners, and, as they devolved from one generation to another, have received new honours at every transmission.

T. S. Eliot said that any poet would forgo his corner in Westminster Abbey in exchange for words like these: 'no poet can ask more of posterity than to be greatly honoured by the great'. Johnson's homage to Shakespeare is, of course, free of bardolatry – he avoided Garrick's Jubilee, causing Boswell to comment: 'When almost every man of eminence in the literary world was happy to take part in this festival of genius, the absence of Johnson could not but be wondered at and regretted' – and it is also unclouded by any temptation to evoke 'the man'. There is no guesswork, no companionable reconstruction. Johnson, the inveterate biographer, measures the greatness of this poet by what has been outlived.

# CHAPTER THREE

# BE KIND TO MY REMAINS:
# MARVELL, MILTON, DRYDEN

These are to certifie every ingenious Reader, that all these poems, as also the other things in this Book contained, are Printed according to the exact copies of my late dear Husband, under his own Hand-writing, being found since his Death, among his other Papers, Witness my Hand this 15th day of October, 1680.

*Mary Marvell*

So reads the notice 'To the Reader' at the front of Andrew Marvell's *Miscellaneous Poems, 1681.* During his famously 'manysided' lifetime, Marvell published only one or two of his poems: as with Donne, the songs we now most like him for were kept well out of sight. After his death, his widow came upon a 'few Books and Papers at a small value'. Among the papers were Marvell's lyric poems: 'To His Coy Mistress', 'The Garden', and so on. Hence the publication three years after his death: seemingly a tender and pious act of widowhood.

Marvell's friends, though, were taken by surprise when they read his *Miscellaneous Poems.* It was not just that they did not know about the poems; they also knew nothing of the widow. So far as they had known, Marvell was unmarried. She who called herself 'Mary Marvell' was actually one 'Mary Palmer', the poet's landlady. And so she was. Mary Palmer, so the story goes, assumed the widowhood as part of a complicated plot to get hold of some funds that were owed to the poet's estate. Publication of the poems was a ploy: a means of declaring her entitlement. 'Mary Marvell' was a legal fiction.

The full story of Mary's supposed intrigue was not told until 1938, in a *PMLA* article by Fred S. Tupper, but even Marvell's earliest biographers were sceptical. In 1726, Thomas Cooke wrote of the poems:

[These] were published with no other but a mercenary view, and indeed not all to the honour of the deceased, by a woman with whom he lodged, who hoped by this stratagem to share in what he left behind him. He was never married.

And in 1776, Edward Thompson entered his agreement:

After the death of Mr Marvell, a work was published, said to contain the compositions already published, and other posthumous writings of the late ingenious Mr Marvell, by a woman who assumed his name, and pretended to be his wife: but as it was well known that he had never married, this cheat was detected, and the woman proved to be the keeper of the lodging he last possessed, and she had taken this disingenuous means of raising money at the expense of his fame. He had no wife, and his gallantries are unknown.

The two commentators echo the deposition of one of Mary Palmer's legal opponents at the time: 'Is it probable that the said Andrew Marvell who was a member of the House of Commons for many a year together and a very learned man would undervalue himself to intermarry with so mean a person as shee?'

Tupper's clinching evidence against Mary's claim was that she had the name 'Palmer' put on her gravestone. And he offered other impressive-seeming evidence: the 'plot' involved fugitive bankrupts, false testimonies and a mountain of depositions and counter-depositions (all to do with money that the bankrupts had lodged with their friend Marvell in order to keep it out of the hands of creditors). His article concluded: 'Andrew Marvell never married.' And this verdict has been generally accepted. And yet several doubts still nag. William Empson has imaginatively challenged Tupper's reading of several of the original documents, but even an amateur perusal of Tupper's essay leaves an impression that the argument is being pushed too hard. For example, Mary in one of her depositions went so far as to name the date of her wedding with Marvell and the church where it took place. Tupper discovered that the relevant church records had (by 1938) gone missing and in his essay ventured the explanation that Mary, some two hundred and fifty years earlier, might have *made* them disappear: 'it is not a completely fantastic possibility that Mrs Palmer herself, fearing eventualities, saw to it that that particular volume of registers disappeared. The missing volume . . . covers the period through 1683.' In its 'scholarly' context, this surely has an over-eager ring. But then, as Empson points out, everyone seems over-eager to dissociate Marvell from 'so mean a person as shee'. At the same time, no one can pretend to know enough about him even to guess what sort of woman it would have been 'in character' for him to marry. He remains one of the most unknowable of poets: an 'elusive, unrecorded character'. Until the marriage register of the Church of the Holy Trinity in the Little Minories actually turns up, we cannot be certain that Marvell's poems were *not* saved by Mrs Mary Marvell. In any event, she has a strong claim to be thought of as our first literary widow.

The real poignancy of the Marvell story, though, is that it seems to fit so well with what we know of Marvell's personality: there is in it a nice balance between expedient motive and elevated outcome that the poet might indeed have smiled on. Marvell died suddenly, of a 'tertian ague' (possibly malaria, although 'Whether Fate or Art untwined his thread/Remains in doubt'; there were rumours that the Jesuits had poisoned him because of his recent pamphlet protests against creeping 'popery'). So far as we know, he made no arrangements for preserving or handing on his poetry: he left no will. And yet his manuscripts show that he was a serious craftsman: he wanted to build poems that would last.

Known now as the laureate of Cromwell, Marvell was also the laureate of early retirement – a post for which, it must be said, there are numerous contenders. A good book could be written – perhaps has been written – on the cult of retirement in seventeenth- and eighteenth-century verse. No doubt Marvell believed that he would get around to organising things just as soon as he was finally 'settled in some secret nest' out in the country. His habits of secrecy and paradox were so ingrained as to have become almost instinctual and yet there is a yearning for the disentangled at the heart of his best work. And as to the matter of his poetic fame, it is hard to believe that his close association with Milton was not without its moments of modestly emulative awe.

Indeed Marvell – had he reached retirement – might have made an ideal literary executor for the 'mighty poet' he had worked for, protected and – in the year of Milton's death, it is believed – so subtly praised:

> Pardon me, mighty Poet, nor despise
> My causeless, yet not impious, surmise.

But I am now convinc'd, and none will dare
Within thy Labours to pretend a Share.
Thou hast not miss'd one thought that could be fit,
And all that was improper dost omit:
So that no room is here for Writers left,
But to detect their Ignorance or Theft.

In the seventeenth century, of course, the title 'literary executor' was not in use. Authors dreamed and wrote of fame, and most of them (however coy or sheepish in their public manner) took it for granted that literary repute was worth pursuing, but nobody did much about trying to set his posterity in order. In part, this was because there was no such thing as a 'literary profession' in the sense that we conceive of it today. Also the idea of a 'posterity' was mostly nebulous, and deeply interfused with the idea of heaven, with Temples of Fame, celestial roll-calls, good talk in the Elysian Fields.

In 'Lycidas', Milton seeks to console his dead young poet friend with evocations of perpetual fame but makes it clear that 'Fame is no plant that grows on mortal soil . . . In Heav'n expect thy meed.' Some authors of later epochs would see this as scant comfort, and we suspect that Milton also saw it thus: after all, the poet he mourned had not lived long enough to secure much earthly recognition. Milton himself was customarily contemptuous of his literary contemporaries – 'libidinous and ignorant Poetasters' – and seemingly unsusceptible to their influence and commendation. But he would not have been content to settle – in perpetuity – for other-worldly fame. A poet by vocation, for a time he is lured by duty into prose, but he leaves us in no doubt that the sacrifice should be thought of as momentous.

For Milton, the idea of 'belonging to the immortals' did indeed suggest rewards in heaven: it meant pleasing the 'great taskmaster' and praying 'to that eternall spirit who can enrich with all utterance and knowledge, and sends out his seraphim with the hallowed fire of his Altar to touch and purify the lips of whom he pleases', but it also meant exactly what it said. It meant defeating death, on earth, by force of language. It meant an acknowledgement, by the world, that he had joined the company of Homer, Virgil, Ariosto, Tasso; it meant inheritance and procreation. It also meant, for Milton, Englishness: the adorning of his native tongue, the interpreting and expounding 'of the best and sagest things among mine own citizens throughout this island in the mother dialect'. The idea of an English epic, or the idea that by no other means could English be sufficiently 'adorned' as to begin ranking with the languages of the immortals, can be traced back to Spenser – via Davenant, if we so please – but in Milton the idea is promoted with a new and urgent gravitas that would have to be reckoned with by his descendants.

John Dryden, nearing the end of his life and preparing to offer to the world his versions of 'our old English poet Chaucer', had a clear enough image of an English literary family tree:

> For Spenser and Fairfax both flourished in the reign of Queen Elizabeth: Great Masters in our Language; and who saw much further into the Beauties of our Numbers, than those who immediately followed them. Milton was the poetical son of Spenser, and Mr Waller of Fairfax; for we have our Lineal Descents and Clans, as well as other Families: Spenser more than once insinuates that the Soul of Chaucer was transfus'd into his Body; and that he was begotten by him Two hundred years after his decease.

In a century obsessed with questions of 'lineal descent', it was natural enough for Dryden to defend the native literary tradition as if it were a threatened dynasty: he is the first great writer to promote the idea of a specifically English tradition. When critics of the day compared the moderns unfavourably with the Great Masters of antiquity, Dryden arraigned them as literary traitors, as 'auxiliary troops turned our enemyes' or as 'insects' who 'manifestly aim at the destruction of our Poetical Church and State'.

Dryden felt that he was Shakespeare's heir, with filial rights of emendation: when Shakespeare was disparaged by outsiders (that is to say, by critics other than himself), it was evident to Dryden that the attacks were really aimed at him. Indeed, with this writer, we can often take 'modern' to mean 'me'. His vanity aside, though, the importance of Dryden's several ruminations on tradition is that he understood, as no one else did, that literary inheritance is more to do with overlaps than with handovers. He saw that the question never could be either/or. It was understandable enough, and perhaps healthy, for modern writers to think of the past as a burden, and understandable too that the present should now and then demean itself with talk of 'the giant Race before the flood'. There was a difference, however, between a studious, correctly – even correctively – filial veneration of the old and the sort of polemical opportunism which

Dryden believed to be at the base of his opponents' assaults upon the new.

In one of his best, and best-known, poems, 'To My Dear Friend Mr Congreve', Dryden addressed the 23-year-old William Congreve as his heir:

> Oh that your Brows my Lawrel had sustain'd,
> Well had I been Depos'd, if you had reign'd!
> The Father had descended for the Son;
> For only you are lineal to the Throne.
>       . . . Thou shalt be seen,
> (Tho' with some short Parenthesis between:)
> High on the Throne of Wit; and seated there,
> Not mine (that's little) but thy Lawrel wear.

This concept of literary inheritance was nothing to do with money or manuscripts or wills, but it was not a fanciful abstraction. For Dryden, in spite of all the self-centredness, it had a genuinely vital meaning. Although he left no will, nor any directions for his funeral (so that wildly improbable accounts of that event circulated for many a year afterwards – see Johnson's *Life* for the funniest and cruellest version), Dryden made sure that everybody knew what he would like to happen next. The poem to Congreve was written as a Prologue to that playwright's newest work, *The Double Dealer*, and it marked Dryden's own retirement from the theatre. When the old poet hands his laurel to the new, he is, to be sure, thumbing his nose at other possible contenders, and showing that high appointments are in *his* gift too. But Dryden did genuinely like and admire Congreve (who, a year earlier, had said of Dryden's Persius translations: 'Old Stoick Virtue, clad in rugged lines/Polish'd by you, in Modern Brilliant shines') and there is no hint of cunning or affectation in his plea: 'Be kind to my remains'. Just as he, Dryden, has been prepared to do battle for his great predecessors, so he would hope now to deserve some protection from his youthful legatee:

> Already I am worn with Cares and Age;
> And just abandoning th'Ungrateful Stage:
> Unprofitably kept at Heav'ns expence,
> I live a Rent-charge on his Providence:
> But You, whom ev'ry Muse and Grace adorn,
> Whom I foresee to better Fortune born,

Be kind to my Remains; and oh defend,
Against Your Judgement Your departed Friend!
Let not the Insulting Foe my Fame pursue;
But shade those Lawrels which descend to You:
And take for Tribute what these Lines express:
You merit more; nor cou'd my Love do less.

When Dryden wrote this, he was sixty and had seven more years
to live. Congreve was twenty-three, and newly famous. It was a
generous tribute and it 'sank deep into the heart of Congreve'. In 1718,
Congreve introduced Dryden's *Works* in six volumes and in his
Dedication wrote as follows: 'In some very Elegant, tho' very partial
Verses which he did me the Honour to write to me, he recommended
it to me to *be kind to his Remains*. I was then, and have been ever since
most sensibly touched with that Expression: and the more so, because
I could not find in my self the means of satisfying the Passion which I
felt in me, to do something answerable to an Injunction laid upon me
in so Pathetick and so Amicable a manner.' The collected edition was
his answer.

As Congreve presumably well knew, Dryden had recommended
other duties to his care and these were not so easy to fulfil. Two years
before Dryden died, Congreve was attacked by Jeremy Collier in a
*View of the Immorality and Profaneness of the English Stage*. Dryden, who
was included in the attack, kept silent; indeed later on he seemed
almost to concede that the eloquently censorious Collier might have
had a point. Congreve took the field alone, and was trounced. He was
not in Collier's league as a polemicist and in any case adopted a
foolishly near-apologetic line of self-defence, pleading in effect that
Collier had read into the plays indecencies that were not there.
Collier's victory was conceded on all sides; Congreve was humiliated;
it was later said that he was 'too much hurt' to defend himself
effectively. It may also have been, as Congreve admitted, that Collier
'had a fair appearance of Right on his side'. Two years later, in the year
of Dryden's death, Congreve announced *his* retirement from the
stage, at the age of thirty, and shortly after the first performance of his
best play, *The Way of the World*. So much for Lineal Descent.

Congreve's retirement has been much grumbled at, by Johnson,
Macaulay, Voltaire, and others: as if, in Johnson's wording, he was
guilty of 'ingratitude' to the Muses. These great and energetic writers
have seemed baffled by the spectacle of lapsed ambition. Unluckily

there are some comic aspects to the playwright's long years of literary leisure (although he was not *that* leisured and the poetry he wrote post-1700 has been unfairly scorned), and when he died he managed further to offend Johnson and the others by leaving all his money – some £10,000 – to his 'close friend', the Duchess of Marlborough, 'in whose immense wealth such a legacy was as a drop in the bucket'. So said Johnson. And Macaulay gave us the following report on poor Congreve's 'keeper of the flame':

> The great lady buried her friend with a pomp seldom seen at the funerals of poets . . . Her Grace laid out her friend's bequest in a superb diamond necklace, which she wore in honour of him, and, if report is to be believed, showed her regard for him in ways much more extraordinary. It is said that a statue of him in ivory, which moved by clockwork, was placed daily at her table, that she had a wax doll made in imitation of him, and that the feet of the doll were regularly blistered and anointed by doctors, as poor Congreve's feet had been when he suffered from the gout.

Another account has the statue life-sized, dressed in Congreve's clothes, and so contrived by the Duchess 'as to nod mechanically when she spoke to it'. A far cry, it might seem, from the effigy of Donne, as described for us by Izaak Walton.

There remains, though, a puzzle attaching to Congreve's refusal of Dryden's great bequest. We can find the puzzle exasperating, if we are so inclined; or we can read into it a poignancy and say that the coincidence of dates (*The Way of the World* opened in March 1700; Dryden died in May) has in itself a troubling sort of power, one that might even led us to conjecture: 'What if Dryden had lived on?' Would Congreve have had the nerve to set aside the laurel if his master had been watching?

The probability is that Congreve was never, temperamentally, disposed to the succession and indeed was intimidated by it. By all accounts, he was an equable, unhurried figure, not often in good health. Later commentators have been irritated by his sloth, but at the time Congreve enjoyed huge respect from his contemporaries and from the up-and-coming men. What to Johnson and Macaulay was annoying, to them seemed strangely admirable: here was an eminent who stood above the battle. Even Pope, the most tirelessly manipulative literary figure of the day, was impressed by Congreve's rich aloofness, his detachment from the all-engrossing fray.

Maybe if Johnson and Macaulay had not been so eager to write off the last thirty years of Congreve's life as wasted time, they might have read with more sympathy the last poem Congreve wrote, not long before he died. As a legacy, it does not perhaps eclipse the £10,000 (which in any case has now been explained: the money, it seems, was meant for Congreve's daughter by the Duchess), but it does rather affectingly reveal why Dryden's crown proved too weighty for his chosen heir. It was addressed to Lord Cobham (formerly Sir Richard Temple), Congreve's closest friend:

> When Leisure from affairs will give thee Leave,
> Come, see thy Friend, retir'd without Regret,
> Forgetting Care, or striving to forget;
> In easy Contemplation soothing Time,
> With Morals much, and now and then with Rhime,
> Not so robust in Body, as in Mind,
> And always undejected, tho' declin'd;
> Not wondering at the World's new wicked Ways,
> Compar'd with those of our Fore-fathers' Days,
> For Virtue now is neither more or less,
> And Vice is only varied in the Dress;
> Believe it, Men have ever been the same,
> And all the Golden Age is but a dream.

A weird footnote can be added to the story of the Dryden–Congreve transaction: a sort of enactment of it in reverse. During the early years of Congreve's retirement, one of the more amusing sights around literary London was that of his contemporary William Wycherley, now something of a relic, and certainly long out of fashion, being followed everywhere – 'like a little dog' – by the eager, teen-age Alexander Pope. Pope was a country-boy prodigy and was at first entranced by the idea of Wycherley, who had once been praised by Dryden and could still turn a few good Restoration anecdotes. Wycherley in his turn saw Pope as a useful factotum in his bid to make a comeback, this time as a bawdy poet. He permitted Pope to tidy up his verses, affecting a certain disdain for the young man's command of 'method', and the pair of them exchanged some heavily literary letters. Later on, Pope would tidy these up too, but not until things had turned a little sour between the pair of them. Pope began to tire of the old man's dreadful doggerel, and of the pontificating that went with it, and Wycherley found it hard to adjust to the stripling's growing condescension – or plain-dealing, as Pope preferred to call it.

When Pope began saying things like: 'To *methodise* in your case is full as necessary as to *strike out*', it was evident that the balance of the relationship had altered. Pope continued to rise, and Wycherley to decline, but separately. Ironically, the editor called in to 'methodise' Wycherley's chaotic papers at his death in 1715 was none other than Lewis Theobald, he who ten years later would seek to tidy up Pope's *Shakespeare*, thus securing for himself the throne of Dullness in *The Dunciad*.

In his prologue to his last play, *Love's Triumphant*, Dryden formally announced his retirement from the theatre, and distributed some further, more trifling bequests. He did it in the form of a mock Last Will and Testament. The 'you' addressed here is, of course, the audience:

> He leaves you, first, all plays of his inditing;
> The whole estate which he has got by writing.
> The beaux may think this nothing but vain praise;
> They'll find it something, the testator says;
> For half their love is made from scraps of plays.
> To his worst foes he leaves his honesty,
> That they may thrive upon't as much as he.
> He leaves his manners to the roaring boys,
> Who come in drunk, and fill the house with noise.
> He leaves to the dire critics of his wit,
> His silence and contempt of all they writ.

This is the kind of will that most writers, certainly most playwrights, would like to leave, but don't. Beneath the rather awkward pugnacity, however, there is the recognisably paternal fear that, unprotected, the sons of his imagination may prove vulnerable to insult or unfair neglect and that posterity, like some other great powers he has known, might turn out to be susceptible to bad advice.

Milton's view of posterity was more spacious and grandiose, less literary–political. Like Dryden, he spent much of his life squabbling and pamphleteering in the immediate public arena, but he did it out of deep conviction rather than under the pressure of strategic necessity. Milton's first publication was a verse in praise of Shakespeare, and he never relinquished his youthful conviction that with hard work his 'strong propensity of nature' might one day yield 'something so written to after-times as they should not willingly let die'.

These are stirring words, and strongly felt, but when Milton came to dictate his will he was far more interested in chiding the 'unkind children' of his first marriage than in directing the future of his literary offspring. Like most other writers of the time, he was hoping for the best. So far as there was any model of conduct in these matters of literary estates, it would probably have been Walton's *Lives*. In each of his five short biographies, Walton provides a death-scene, to which the making of a will is central, but not one of his subjects is shown to have provided for the management of his literary effects. Of Donne we learn that his manuscripts were passed to King, and of George Herbert (Walton's other 'literary' subject) that his writings went to his widow who 'preserved many . . . which she intended to make public, but they and Highnam House were burnt together, by the late rebels, and so lost to posterity'. In Walton's terms, the loss to posterity was of yet more evidence of the spiritual excellence of one who 'lived . . . like a saint, unspotted of the world, full of alms-deeds, and all the examples of a virtuous life; which I cannot conclude better than with this borrowed observation:

> . . . all must to their cold graves;
> But the religious actions of the just
> Smell sweet in death, and blossom in the dust.

Mr George Herbert's have done so to this, and will doubtless do so to succeeding generations.' (In passing we might note that the poet James Shirley could have done with a literary executor: in my books, his final couplet reads: 'Onely the actions of the just/Smell sweet, and blossom in their dust.' Shirley was writing about Ajax and Ulysses.)

Individual writers did now and then spell out their posthumous literary requirements. Ben Jonson, before his death in 1637, passed 'several of his writings and works' to Kenelm Digby, 'to dispose of at his will and pleasure. To whose care and trust the said Benjamin left the publishing and printing of them and delivered him true and perfect copies for his better and more effectual doing thereof.' And thirty years later, Abraham Cowley hoped in his will that his 'dear friend' Thomas Sprat would:

> trouble himself with the collection and revision of all such writings of mine (whether printed before or not) as he shall think fit to be published, beseeching him not to let any passe which hee shall judge unworthy of the name of his friend and most especially nothing (if any of yt kind have

escaped the pen) which may give the least offence in point of religion and good manners.

Behind these instructions, there was a reasonable fear of the 'unauthorised', of mangled texts and of several possible varieties of plagiarism. There seems not to have been any particular nervousness about biography. Jonson would not have suspected that his loose-mouthed chats with William Drummond of Hawthornden would in time be printed 'for the use and benefit of the common reader'. Indeed, he had probably forgotten all about those long, slurred Scottish evenings, the dirty jokes, the idle savaging of literary rivals. In Drummond's late-night shorthand, Jonson comes over as an intellectual bully, a sort of Renaissance Mr Big, and of course we hear nothing of Drummond's prompts or repartee. Even so, no account of Jonson's personality would now be attempted without copious quotation from the Drummond sessions.

In the case of Cowley, the poet had no idea, when he entreated his 'dear friend' to protect his name, that he would be condemning Sprat to a small, inglorious slot in literary history. Sprat's *Life of Cowley* is now remembered chiefly for having been mocked by Dr Johnson ('the mist of panegyric') and for the pioneering timidity of its preface, in which Sprat apologises for writing the life of a mere author, and argues the first-ever case against the use of private letters:

> The familiar way of verse puts me in mind of one kind of prose wherein Mr Cowley was excellent; and that is in his letters to his private friends . . . But I know you agree with me that nothing of this nature should be published . . . The very same passages which make writings of this nature delightful among friends, will lose all manner of taste, when they come to be read by those that are indifferent. In such letters the souls of men should appear undressed; and in that negligent habit, they may be fit to be seen by one or two in a chamber, but not to go abroad in the streets.

If Drummond's jottings had been pirated in, say, 1650 (Drummond died in 1649) or if a rival biographer had got his hands on Cowley's letters, there was nothing much that either Digby or Sprat could have done to prevent publication. They could have protested and petitioned but the accepted method of asserting publication rights – ie by putting out their own 'authorised' version of the text – would, self-evidently, not have served their cause.

Under the prevailing legislation, the author had no defined rights.

41

The concept of non-corporeal property had not yet even come up for discussion. There was merely a common-law assumption that the writer was the original owner of his works and could therefore sell them to an individual publisher (or 'bookseller'). The publisher in turn assumed, when he acquired such works, that they belonged to him in perpetuity.

For a seventeenth-century author to have challenged the publisher's assumption would have been, to say the least, undignified. Authors in those days, as we have noted, were keen to be thought of as amateurs: if they needed money, the only acceptable way of getting it was to operate within the patronage system, to hope that by shrewd dedications (in themselves not always worth much in straight money terms) they would win preferment in His Lordship's entourage. Very little could be made from the sale of printed books – about £6 from the outright sale of an entitlement – and only small amounts could be picked up from subsidiary literary tasks, like proof-reading or the penning of pamphlets (about £2 a time for these).

The necessary bridge between patronage and the market-place was in fact already under construction, but the process was gradual. Spenser, as long ago as 1589, had signalled the way forward by dedicating the *Faerie Queene* to the 'court in general' rather than to any individual patron, and by appending to his text not one but sixteen dedications addressed to a range of influential figures in that court. The wheeze caught on and there are accounts of Elizabethan works being pledged to as many as fifty-six individual patrons (Thomas Dekker talks of 'one booke' that had 'seven score patrons').

It was this enterprising promiscuity that led eventually to the system of subscription selling, a method of which Dryden was an early beneficiary. Under this method, an author would announce his plan of work and then solicit subscriptions from the friendly and the great, half to be paid in advance, and the other half on publication. Another approach was to get the publisher to supply a large number of free copies which the author could then offer for subscription. The appeal of subscription selling was that it kept the patronage system ticking over (a subscriber could, after all, donate as much as he liked over the basic selling price), whilst at the same time it opened up a direct route to a paying readership. And it was often very profitable. It did not, however, challenge the publisher's right to the proceeds of any subsequent printings of the work. So far as the author was concerned, the first edition was the one that mattered.

In 1667, Milton helped to call this assumption very faintly into question by agreeing a contract for *Paradise Lost* which required the publisher to pay him, in effect, a royalty: £5 on signature, £5 for a first printing of 1300 copies, and a further £5 each for second and third impressions, if these turned out to be required. After the third impression, the rights would revert to the publisher. Milton collected his payment for the first edition but at his death in 1674, the second edition was still in print and his widow sold 'all her claims' for one last payment, of £8.

This does not sound much of a deal and, on the face of it, seems designed more to protect the publisher than to profit the author. 1667 was a particularly shaky year for the publishing trade. The Great Fire had devastated a number of their offices and print-shops, not to mention the odd epic poem: apparently, the manuscript and entire stock of John Ogilby's *The Carolies* were consumed in the blaze. Milton's publisher, one Samuel Simmons, had been spared, and no doubt wished to take advantage of a market vacuum; in other circumstances, Milton's political record would have given him pause. As to Milton himself, he was probably pleased enough that there was a publishing house still standing that was prepared to take a risk with his great work. In *Areopagitica*, he had fumed extravagantly against the licensing system and, to judge from that somewhat over-puissant text, might have been expected to give any publisher a hardish time. But circumstances had changed a lot since 1644 and in any case (if Aubrey is right about the date of its completion) *Paradise Lost* might have gone the same way as *The Carolies*. All the same, his contract did imply that an author could, by arrangement, enjoy a renewable stake in the fortunes of his work. It also implied that his widow's 'claims' might carry legal weight. Indeed, it has been pointed out that if Mrs Milton had not relinquished her interest, the poet's last descendants would not have died – as they eventually did – in poverty. But she would have needed unusual gifts of foresight (and of sympathy) to see it in this way.

The point, though, about the tale of Milton's contract is that it signifies a slight weakening of the publisher's power of outright purchase. Discussion of late-seventeenth-century publishing practice tends now to centre on the Miltons and the Drydens but publishing, for most of its practitioners, had little to do with highbrow literary works. It was increasingly a matter of pamphlets, broadsides, newsbooks: in short, the media – in embryo. The readership could no longer be thought of, except wistfully, as a 'fit audience . . . though few'. A new appetite had to be satisfied, an appetite for the 'barbarous dissonance' of controversy, rumour, current goings-on. And a new type of publisher was on the rise, a type disinclined to seek permission from the Stationers' Company before setting out his wares.

The story of publishing in the last two or three decades of the seventeenth century is a story of deepening nervousness on the part of the regular publishers as they saw the controls that had protected them, however changeably, since 1557, begin to fall apart. Because publishing had become so heavily politicised, it was even more difficult than usual to draw a distinction between 'regulation' (the wish to protect a literary property) and 'censorship' (the wish to exterminate the opposition). Charles II set things on the road to final chaos by putting the Royalist bully Roger L'Estrange in charge of implementing a tough new Licensing Act. L'Estrange did his best to terrorise the industry, with midnight raids, spies, bribes, and an extravagant use of the blue pencil, and the effect in the end was to stimulate the clandestine sector and to bring the legitimate into contempt. L'Estrange was removed by the Revolution of 1688. By then his office and the law it was supposed to implement were floundering and for the next ten years or so the drift – compounded by the ineptitudes of the new controller, Edmund Bohun – was towards a general free-for-all.

Between 1701 and 1708 fewer than four publications a year were entered on the Stationers' Company Register. Not even those who supported the rules thought it worth bothering to obey them. It was during these years that the rule-supporters began lobbying for legislation that would make obedience worthwhile. At first, these publishers expressed fears for the safety of the 'body politic' but soon settled into a more plausible statement of their aims. In 1707, they straightforwardly petitioned for the protection of their 'literary property'. As the trade historian John Feather comments: 'The faint cultural overtones of the word "literary" could not disguise the fact that what they were actually asking for was legal protection for their copies.'

In April 1710 there was passed an Act for the Encouragement of Learning (now known as the first Copyright Act). It had the following preamble:

Whereas Printers, Booksellers and other Persons have of late frequently taken the Liberty of Printing, Reprinting and Publishing, or causing to be Printed, Reprinted and Published Books, and other Writings, without the consent of the Authors or Proprietors of such Books and Writings, to their very great Detriment, and too often to the Ruin of them and their Families . . . For Preventing therefore such Practices for the future, and for the Encouragement of Learned Men to Compose and Write useful Books; May it please your Majesty . . .

The Act gave the publishers what they wanted, or so it seemed: it required registration of titles in the Stationers' Register, as before, and it gave 'copy-owners' the right to take proceedings against piracy. It also imposed specific penalties for infringement. All in all, it reaffirmed the publisher's right to repel any trespass on his commercial territory.

From the publishers' point of view, the Act simply re-empowered what they regarded as the legal status quo. There were other clauses in it, though. A time limit was set for the ownership of literary property. Anything the publishers now owned, they could keep for a further twenty-one years. Any new titles they signed up would be theirs for fourteen years. From the authors' angle, it was the Act's final clause that was significant: 'after the expiration of the said term of fourteen years, the sole right of printing or disposing of copies shall return to the authors thereof, if they are living, for another term of fourteen years.'

And then? Nobody seemed to know. The question of who owned the 'perpetual copyright' was not dealt with by the Act, although the imposition of time limits did seem to challenge the old common-law assumptions. In the short term, however, what mattered was that the word 'authors' had somehow been smuggled into a piece of legislation that was intended to secure for the publishers a more 'durable' protection of their rights. Many would now say that this final clause in the Act of 1710 announced the birth of the literary profession.

# CHAPTER FOUR

# POPE'S BULLIES

Literary 'professionalism' had in fact already been blue-printed by John Dryden. In 1679, when he stopped writing for the theatre, Dryden needed to make a living from his poetry and prose and, with this in view, he teamed up with the publisher Jacob Tonson. It was an unprecedentedly deliberate liaison. 'We get the feeling,' says one historian, 'that both were exploring uncharted regions, on the lookout for surprises and misadventures at every step. This was the beginning of the relationship between publisher and author.'

As it turned out, Dryden found in Tonson an ingeniously innovative partner and over the next ten years several lucrative and worthy schemes were hatched: Dryden's *Life of Plutarch*, a series of *Miscellanies* (forerunners of the literary magazine), the subscription selling of Dryden's translation of the *Iliad*. Tonson, even at this early point, knew how to make the most of the copyrights he owned and was cautiously alert to the possibilities of an expanding readership. Dryden was happy to be paid line by line and on the nail for couplets which he could almost manufacture in his sleep.

Although they quarrelled over money ('I find all your trade are sharpers,' Dryden said) and although they were of opposite political persuasions, their partnership was brilliantly effective. Tonson had sufficient taste, but he also had a touch of the vulgarian: he was not above advertising his publications in the newssheets nor above lightening his miscellanies with a bit of fashionable bawdy. For Dryden – 'the old Tory, Roman Catholic and Jacobite who was abhorred at court' – it was luck indeed to have found himself a well-placed Whiggist sharper who happened also to entertain a proper reverence for his great genius.

Tonson tends to be harshly caricatured in the histories, and his authors have not always in this respect been useful to him. Even Dryden portrayed him as 'leering', 'bull-faced', with 'frowzy pores that taint the ambient air'. But this sort of thing might be taken merely as one further symptom of the author's nascent professionalism. When Tonson died, it was popularly rumoured that, with his last breath, he expressed 'the wish to live his life over again and at the end to leave one hundred thousand pounds instead of eighty thousand'. The rumour, we can be pretty certain, was started by one of his authors.

Tonson himself would have wished to be thought of by the wits as a conscientious guardian of what he called 'the esteem of ye author'. He would no doubt have said that he kept Milton's reputation alive during a period around the turn of the century when it was somewhat in the balance, and that he performed similar services for Shakespeare and for Dryden. And it is true enough that Tonson's 1695 edition of *Paradise Lost* (with heavy annotation and commentary by Patrick Hume) was the first 'scholarly' edition of an English poet. His publication of Rowe's *Shakespeare* in 1709 served purposes we have already noted. And when Tonson perceived that Dryden's pre-eminence was being posthumously undermined by Addison and his coffee-house 'senate', he kept up a steady run of editions, both folio and popular. It was Tonson who commissioned Congreve's preface to the *Plays*.

Tonsons would be needed in the years to come, but he was the first of his kind: the first publisher to be thought of as having an active influence on literary taste, and the first to be accorded prestige by the writing community. To be on Tonson's list was to be of the elect. In 1706 (thanks, incidentally, to a tip from Congreve), Tonson wrote to the young Alexander Pope:

> Sir: I have lately seen a Pastoral of yours in Mr Walsh's and Mr Congreve's hands, which is extremely fine, and is generally approved of by the best judges in poetry. I remember I have formerly seen you at my shop, and am sorry I did not improve my acquaintance with you. If you design your poem for the press, no person shall be more careful in the printing of it, nor no one can give greater encouragement to it than, sir, your, &c/ Jacob Tonson.

Pope did not need Wycherley to tell him that this was his first step on the path to fame: 'You will make Jacob's ladder raise you to immortality.'

In the end, though, Tonson was a literary businessman and the Act of 1710 had inadvertently decreed that, for the next hundred years or so, and in spite of any good intentions, publishers and authors would stand face to face, as foes. Tonson, for all his merits, would soon be training his heirs to fight for their imperilled copyrights and – as the incentive to acquire new authors sharpened – he himself would be learning to fight dirty. And it would not be long before Pope was learning to outsmart him: 'Jacob creates poets as kings do knights, not for their honour but their money.'

Of course, the literary milieu in which both Pope and Tonson functioned was saturated with suspicion: any publisher or author worth his salt had to be a connoisseur of the mendacious and the underhand. Pope's own labyrinthine plots and vendettas (he could not 'take tea without a stratagem') were at first modelled on Dryden's great battles with the Shadwells and the Settles, and were similarly based in the culture of the coffee-house, with its so-called dictators of taste and their variously motivated hangers-on. But by the time Pope was launched, these centres of intrigue had become over-crowded and ill-tempered. The literary world, now distanced from the court, had begun to take on the aspect of a self-contained republic, with its nostalgic, disdainful aristocracy, its inky new Grub Street proletariat, its shifty and pretentious middle-class. Books, it had long been known, could be formidable weapons but in this new 'Augustan' literary realm, the warrior-pen was not often employed to any elevated or even conscientious purpose: books mainly battled against other books.

In Pope, the age miraculously found a poet who could thrive in this unhealthy atmosphere, could take it as his subject and his inspiration. It also found a professional whose temperament insisted that he should control every aspect of his own career. This poet's other-worldliness found its expression in a mastery of the techniques of worldliness: the alienated sensibility put him a venomous yard or two ahead of his competitors. Indeed, the agonies and satisfactions of Pope's writing life often seem so vehemently present-tense that it is hard now to get a clear picture of how he felt about matters of posterity and after-fame. It is not that such matters did not interest him; they did, and deeply. But there was almost always something else, something more immediate, to be attended to: a publisher to be worked over, a rival scribbler to be punished, a law-suit to be master-minded, and so on. And in any case, was fame itself not compromised, contaminated? In 'The Temple of Fame' (written when Pope was in his early twenties) the poet's rapt contemplation of the wondrously jewelled throne of fame is soon interrupted by dark thoughts of all the 'vast numbers' of bogus pretenders who are 'prest around the shrine'. He ends up praying that heaven will:

> Drive from my breast that wretched lust of praise,
> Unblemish'd let me live, or die unknown;
> Oh grant an honest fame, or grant me none!

Pope was the first literary celebrity of the type we are nowadays familiar with. No earlier writer had needed to complain, as he did, about 'invasion of privacy':

> Shut, shut the door, good John! fatigu'd I said,
> Tye up the knocker, say I'm sick, I'm dead.
> The Dog-star rages! nay 'tis past a doubt,
> All Bedlam, or Parnassus, is let out:
> Fire in each eye, and papers in each hand,
> They rave, recite and madden round the land.
>   What walls can guard me, or what shades can hide?
> They pierce my thickets, thro' my Grot they glide,
> By land, by water, they renew the charge,
> They stop the chariot, and they board the barge.
> No place is sacred, not the Church is free,
> Ev'n Sunday shines no Sabbath-day to me:
> Then from the Mint walks forth a man of rhyme,
> Happy! to catch me, just at Dinner time.

The complaint, of course, is actually a boast. Pope loved this kind of thing: that is to say, he would, after a time, have found it hard to live without it. A spoiled child, his appetite for flattery was boundless. Like most celebrities, however, he was never famous enough, or never famous in quite the way he wanted to be famous. He was forever tinkering with the detail of his public image. Johnson said of him: 'Pope had been flattered till he thought himself one of the moving powers of life' and there is indeed something close to demonic in his attempts to organise the way he was adored. 'Pope may be said to write always with his reputation in his head.'

Of course, he started out with a string of natural disadvantages: a tiny, deformed body, a desultory education; he was a Roman Catholic, his private means were meagre. And all this must be kept in mind when we try to account for his appetite for self-promotion.

There was a sort of frenzy in it. Usually, this frenzy worked to his advantage; now and then it betrayed him into an excess of ingenuity. There is, for example, the saga of his Letters and of his mighty duel of wits with Edmund Curll.

Curll was a key figure of the day. He was the rogue-publisher, Grub Street's answer to the likes of Jacob Tonson. The story was that he invariably had three hack writers sleeping in his rotting garret, on 24-hour call for the swift composition of seditious and pornographic pamphlets, or for an urgent translation job, or for a preface to a pirated edition. Curll's role 'in the first half of the eighteenth century resembles nothing more than that of some foul bird acting as a scavenger for a literary battle-field'. In the histories, Curll is always 'unspeakable', 'notorious', or 'vile'. He had been sued and pilloried and had had his ears removed but nothing could shake him from his top spot as the prince of pirates. He was also a trail-blazer, in his way, and now has his niche as the first-ever pedlar of scandalous biographies:

> It occurred to him that, in a world governed by the law of mortality, men might be handsomely entertained on one another's remains. He lost no time in putting his theory into action. During the years of his activity he published some forty or fifty separate Lives, intimate, anecdotal, scurrilous sometimes, of famous and notorious persons who had the ill-fortune to die during his life-time. He had learned the wisdom of the grave-digger in *Hamlet*, and knew that there are many rotten corpses nowadays, that will scarce hold the laying in. So he seized on them before they were cold, and commemorated them in batches . . . His books commanded a large sale, and modern biography was established.

Dr Arbuthnot said that Curll had added 'a new terror to death' and Swift in his lines 'On the Death of Dr Swift' was accurate in his forecast that:

> He'll treat me as he does my Betters.
> Publish my Will, my Life, my Letters,
> Revive the Libels born to dye;
> Which Pope must bear, as well as I . . .

The explanatory footnote reads: 'Curl hath been the most infamous Bookseller of any Age or Country: His Character may be found in Mr Pope's *Dunciad*. He published three Volumes all charged to the Dean

[Swift], who never writ three Pages of them. He hath used many of the Dean's friends in almost as vile a manner.'

By 1735, the year of their climactic battle, Pope and Curll had been engaged in open warfare for almost two decades. Not only had Curll published unauthorised editions of Pope's work, he had also – as with Swift – put out collections of other people's writings under Pope's name. He had from time to time sponsored attacks on Pope in which insults like 'Hunchback'd Papist' and 'Ludicrous Animal' were offered as routine. Pope had retaliated with pamphlets giving an 'Account of the Most Deplorable Condition of Mr Curll' and, of course, saw to it that the publisher made a sizeable showing in *The Dunciad*, to which Curll responded with, among other items, the *Popiad*, a sort of 'best of' anthology of earlier attacks on Pope.

The enmity between the two went back to the time of Curll's first 'borrowing' of Pope's name. To this offence Pope had responded by slipping an emetic into Curll's drink, causing his foe to believe that he had been fatally poisoned. Within hours of the deed, Pope was arranging for the publication of 'A Full and True Account of a Horrid and Barbarous Revenge by Poison on the Body of Mr Edmund Curll'. After this little exchange, there would be no holds barred. Any Popeana, authentic or fake, that Curll could lay his hands on, he turned to his hostile advantage.

In 1726 Curll issued an unauthorised printing of some of Pope's private letters to his friend Richard Cromwell. An ex-mistress of Cromwell's had sold them to Curll. This was a novel sort of outrage: the market for literary correspondence was untested. Pope manifested fury but he also noted with some interest that the book was a success. So much of a success, indeed, that Curll was soon advertising in the papers – for *more* letters by Alexander Pope. Pope was alarmed by this: the idea of Curll putting out forged, doctored or nastily footnoted material was deeply repugnant, and the effusiveness of some of his letters to Cromwell had made him squirm. At the same time, he was intrigued by the possibilities. In 1729, he found an excuse to publish his 'edited' correspondence with Wycherley (publication had been forced on him, he said, by the appearance a year earlier of an unworthy memoir). This time he was unequivocally pleased by the reception. The letter, he began to see, offered a means of showing to the world a humbler, kinder, much more human Pope than it may have grown used to from a reading of his verses and his controversial pamphlets. His first *Dunciad* had recently appeared and caused an outcry. (On

51

publication day 'a Crowd of Authors besieg'd the Shop; Entreaties, Advices, Threats of Law, and Battery, nay cries of Treason, were all employ'd to hinder the coming out of the *Dunciad*'.)

Pretending to be chiefly concerned about the outcome of the Curll advertisements, Pope began asking friends to return to him any letters of his which, perchance, they might have kept. Having amassed a decent-sized collection, Pope then began polishing the letters to his taste: altering dates so as to encourage esteem for his precocity, running two or three letters into one, here and there refashioning the prose. The next step was to arrange for their redistribution.

In other words, he badly wanted to get the letters into print. Naturally, he could not himself be seen to have been a party to such vanity. The solution he hit on was wonderfully double-edged: he would *arrange* for Curll to steal them. Thus a mysterious Mr P.T. one day approached the publisher with the offer of a cache of Pope's private correspondence. Curll was suspicious but hugely tempted. He did some checking, but P.T.'s tracks were covered and in the end Curll took the plunge. Pope, on learning of this latest 'piracy', took legal action – but on a technicality which he knew would not succeed. And then, with Curll's improper edition on the market, he began collecting subscriptions for the 'Authentic Edition' of Pope's Letters. As he explained in his preface, the villainous Curll had left him no alternative:

> A Bookseller advertises his intention to publish your Letters. He openly promises encouragement, or even pecuniary rewards to those who help him to any; and ingages to insert whatever they shall send: Any scandal is sure of a reception, and any enemy who sends it skreen'd from discovery. Any domestick or servant, who can snatch a letter from your pocket or cabinet, is encouraged to that vile practice. If the quantity falls short of a volume, any thing else shall be join'd with it . . . which the collector can think for his interest, all recommended under your Name: You have not only Theft to fear, but Forgery.

A step-by-step account of the intrigue, of which there have been several, reveals the astonishing intricacy of Pope's planning: the creation and the passing off of the still-unidentified P.T. ('a man in a clergyman's gown, but with a lawyer's band' acted as his agent), the audacious lawsuit, and so on. As it transpired, the ruse was not totally successful. Several people expressed suspicion and when Johnson came to write his *Life of Pope*, in 1780, the main facts were available

(Johnson probably got clues from Richard Savage: he was seeing a lot of Savage at the time of the intrigue, and Savage was then in receipt of occasional 'donations' from Pope). But overall, as Johnson says, the object was achieved: 'Pope's private correspondence, thus promulgated, filled the nation with praises of his candour, his tenderness and benevolence, and the fidelity of his friendship.'

In this affair, Pope seems not to have minded much that he would almost certainly be rumbled by posterity. Indeed, the author of *The Dunciad* perhaps envisaged with amusement future bibliographers and textual scrutineers puzzling out his fiendish machinations. His underlying conviction may have been that his talents so dwarfed those of all his dunce-opponents that in the end he would either be vindicated or forgiven. If he did so reckon, he was right. The disposition nowadays is to chuckle over the amount of effort expended on the plot and to suggest that for Pope there was more than mere vanity at stake: with Curll to contend with, his scheme was legitimately self-protective.

Pope died in 1744, at the age of fifty-six. It could hardly be expected that the handling of his immediate after-fame would be tranquil and judicious, but even he might have been dismayed by the titanic struggle that took place over his remains.

Like most heroes, Pope had a need for heroes of his own. Dryden, then for a moment Wycherley, then Swift: these were the heroes of his youth. After Swift came Henry St John, 1st Viscount Bolingbroke, once mighty in the land as Secretary of War, twice Secretary of State, and chief architect of the Treaty of Utrecht (in 1713, at which date he was thirty-five). Ousted after the death of Queen Anne, and then impeached, he fled to join the Pretender's government-in-exile and – after the 1715 débâcle – was ousted from this too. He then made unsuccessful overtures to George I.

Pope had always admired the famous Jacobite. Indeed, in '15, he had rather bravely dedicated the first book of his *Iliad* to this disgraced 'Genius . . . not more distinguished in the great Scene of Business than in all the useful and entertaining parts of Learning'. And the admiration never really faltered. In Bolingbroke he discovered 'something superior to anything I have seen in human nature'. Students of Bolingbroke's political record find it hard to fathom the intensity of the poet's admiration (and of Swift's also: the Dean spoke of Bolingbroke as 'the greatest young man I ever saw'). Such tributes cannot altogether be accounted for by the known tendency of poets to go weak at the knees when they encounter well-read politicians. In truth, Bolingbroke was not just well-read; he was dazzlingly learned in areas that Pope had barely dabbled in. He was versed in Huygens, Hooke and Halley, mathematicians, physicists, cosmologists, and spent his hours not quarrelling with Curll but mastering the Universe.

In 1725, Bolingbroke was allowed to return to England, but on condition that he took no further part in politics. Needless to say, he continued to intrigue, but in an abstract way, giving voice to his thoughts on concepts of good government. To the world, though, his posture was that of giant-in-retirement. He bought a manor house near Uxbridge and sat among the haycocks, deep in thought. Pope, always inclined to sentimentality about the country settings of his childhood, was re-entranced. Under the great man's influence, or at his 'instigation', he began work on *An Essay on Man*, a long poem that considers 'Man in the Abstract, his Nature and his State', with respect to the Universe, to Himself, as an Individual, to Society, and – finally – to Happiness. It was a 'noble' scheme and – post-*Dunciad* – just the sort of project that Pope's admirers had been urging on him: 'Employ not your precious Moments and great Talents on little men and little things, but choose a Subject every way worthy of you'. The poem begins and ends with fulsome tributes to Lord Bolingbroke, 'my Friend, my Genius, Oh master of the poet, and the song!'

> Oh! while along the stream of Time thy name
> Expanded flies, and gathers all its fame,
> Say, shall my little bark attendant sail,
> Pursue the triumph, and partake the gale?
> When statesmen, heroes, kings, in dust repose,
> Whose sons shall blush their fathers were thy foes,
> Shall then this verse to future age pretend
> Thou wert my guide, philosopher and friend?

*An Essay on Man* enjoyed wide distribution and was much pondered on the Continent. This was Pope's bid for international status as a poet capable of handling the largest themes. Unluckily, the text fell into the hands of a Swiss theologian, Jean Pierre de Crousaz, who in 1737 published a long critique of the poem in which he accused Pope of having disseminated a 'fatalistic' philosophy which was potentially 'destructive of all religion and morality'. Pope's vision of cosmic harmony was at odds with Christian doctrines of divine revelation.

Curll saw to it that the Crousaz critique was translated into English and Pope became seriously troubled. He was not a trained philosopher: what if de Crousaz turned out to be right? Freethinkers could end up in jail. Bolingbroke was out of the country and this time Pope was not able to deliver the sort of contemptuous riposte of which he was a proven master: Crousaz wrote in prose.

It was a tricky situation but miraculously, as it seemed, help was at hand. William Warburton, a priest who had trained as a lawyer, was building a great reputation in the field of theological disputation. He was skilled in paradox and, lawyer-like, could argue pugnaciously from seemingly opposed positions. Indeed, it was his chief delight to do so. And Warburton was also famously brutal with anyone who presumed to take him on. He boasted that he had hung one batch of his opponents 'as they do vermin in a warren, and left them to posterity to stink and blacken in the wind'. At other times, he talked of being obliged to hunt down like wolves the 'pestilent herd of libertine scribblers with which the island is over-run'. His energy, his erudition and his rough debater's manners seem, in concert, to have left most readers unsure about his actual beliefs, but there was no questioning of his essential orthodoxy. The impression is that no one would have dared so to interrogate him.

Warburton's affinities with Pope are perhaps clearer to us now than they were in 1738. It so happens that the theologian had more than once spoken harshly about Pope: 'Dryden borrowed for want of leisure and Pope for want of genius' was one of his recorded *mots*, and he had privately sided with the loathed Theobald in that scholar's assault on Pope's Shakespeare edition. He had even, at small gatherings, denounced *An Essay on Man* for its 'atheism, spinozaism, deism, hobbism, fatalism, materialism, and whatnot'.

Although he was happily ignorant of these particular slanders, Pope's sleepless antennae would almost certainly have directed him to think of Warburton as a likely foe. He was therefore as surprised as everybody else seems to have been when this rigorous disputant decided to take up arms against de Crousaz. In a series of articles, Warburton demonstrated to the general satisfaction that the Swiss had lamentably misread Pope's *Essay*, and that the poem was in fact 'a justification of Providence against the impious objections of Atheistical Man'. Pope's 'cosmic harmony', as any fool should see, *implied* a divine presence, a Supreme Harmoniser, so to speak.

Crousaz was trounced, and Pope could barely contain his gratitude.

Not least, he was delighted to learn that *this* was what his poem meant. He wrote off eagerly to Warburton: 'You have made my system as clear as I ought to have done, and could not'; 'I know I meant just what you explain, but I did not explain my own meaning as well as you. You understand me as well as I do myself, and you express me better than I could myself.'

From this day until the end of Pope's life – and, in many ways, thereafter – Warburton would serve as the poet's adviser, defender, commentator and editor. When the two met, Pope did not have very long to live and Warburton, it was said, saved his belief. Pope in return opened important doors which led the priest to a rich wife and thence (via her *very* rich and influential uncle) to a bishopric and a palatial estate. It was, shall we say, a harmonious arrangement, with Warburton laying down the law and Pope happy to cast himself in the role of a grateful dependant. He hoped that he and his commentator would 'go down together to posterity', 'I mean, to as much of posterity as poor moderns can reach to, where the commentator, as usual, will lend a crutch to the weak poet to help him limp a little further than he could on his own feet.'

With Bolingbroke it had been he, Pope, who had dreamed of hitching a ride on the statesman's ship of fame, and altogether there seems to have been less of the worshipful in his attitude to Warburton. One of Warburton's chief attractions was his willingness to worship Pope, to tell him 'in strains of rapturous commendation . . . that he is the only poet who hath found out the art of uniting wit to sublimity': once more able to 'express' the poet better than he could express himself. Pope called Warburton the best 'general critic' he had ever come across.

As Warburton established himself in what Johnson calls 'the closest intimacy' with Pope – advising on new editions, laboriously annotating the poet's texts – Bolingbroke was necessarily rather shouldered to one side. Pope tried to bring his two heroes together and to this end he helpfully despatched to Bolingbroke some of Warburton's impromptu annotations to one of the philosopher's important texts. Bolingbroke did not believe himself in need of annotation. As Izaak D'Israeli has reported it: 'The style of the great dogmatist, thrown out in heat, must no doubt have contained many fiery particles, all of which fell into the most inflammable of minds. Pope soon discovered his officiousness was received with indignation.' From now on, the two heroes were in opposition. 'The two most arrogant geniuses who ever lived, in vain exacted submission from each other: they could allow no divided empire, and they were born to hate each other.'

It was between these two competing emperors that Pope divided his literary estate. In his will, he left all his unpublished manuscripts to Bolingbroke, giving him the power to destroy or preserve them as he saw fit, and to Warburton all his copyrights: 'the property of all such of my works already printed, as he hath written or shall write commentaries or notes upon, and which I have not otherwise disposed of or alienated; and all the profits which shall arise after my death from such editions as he shall publish without future alterations.'

The trouble began almost immediately. When Bolingbroke (who had cried 'for a quarter of an hour like a child' beside the poet's death-bed) took delivery of Pope's unpublished papers, he discovered that a work of his own, *The Idea of a Patriot King*, had been secretly printed by Pope in an edition of 1500 copies. It seems that he had given Pope the manuscript in 1738, with the suggestion that he might like to print up a few copies to be passed around to mutual friends, adding that 'they should never go into any hands except those of five or six persons who were then named by him.' This secretly stored cache of printed copies smacked of treachery. And worse still, almost, Pope had presumed to 'tidy up' Bolingbroke's text. Bolingbroke was furious: in an instant the dead Pope became his enemy.

Pope's 'treachery', in fact, was but a further mark of his veneration of Bolingbroke: he had believed that he would outlive his friend and would serve him as his 'Porte feuille'. He knew that Bolingbroke 'designed to suppress' *The Patriot King* and, believing the work 'too valuable to the world to be so used', had taken steps to save it. His was a pre-emptive, and some might think excessive, act of literary guardianship. But Bolingbroke, already simmering with resentment because Warburton had been given the more prestigious slice of Pope's estate, refused to see it in this way. He buried the 1500 copies in his garden and when later on, in response to a pirate serialisation, he issued his own authorised text, he prefaced it with a nasty attack on 'the turpitude of a man with whom I lived in the intimacy of friendship'. Bolingbroke never forgave Pope; indeed, henceforward 'his thirst of vengeance excited him to blast the memory of the man over whom he had wept in his last struggles.'

It is generally agreed that this thirst of vengeance directed Bolingbroke's strange conduct in the much-discussed case of the 'Atossa' verses. These verses were originally intended by Pope as an attack on Sarah Churchill, Duchess of Marlborough, but later on (after the poet had made friends with her) they were re-targeted to damage a quite different Duchess: really they were an attack on a certain type of high-born shrew, or termagant, and Bolingbroke surely had sense enough to see this. What he actually did, though, was to publish the piece surreptitiously as 'Verses upon the Late D—ess of M— by Mr P—' and to add a note to them:

> These verses are Part of a Poem, entitled *Characters of Women*. It is generally said, the D—ess gave Mr P £1000 to suppress them. He took the Money, yet the World sees the Verses, but this is not the first instance where Mr P's practical Virtue has fallen very short of those pompous Professions that he makes in his Writings.

Bolingbroke's posthumous mud-slinging seemed out of character: by now he was seriously ill and some say that he was being egged on by his literary assistant (and executor-designate), the egregious David Mallett – né Malloch. Whatever the explanation, the sorry business made it possible for Warburton to step forward as the true keeper of the flame, a man of reason and responsibility. On the matter of the *Patriot King* furore, he was able to enquire:

> Are the laws of friendship then so slight, that *one* imprudent action committed against the humour of a friend (in a mistaken fondness for his glory which came near to Adoration), that *one* shall obliterate the whole merit of a life of service, though flowing from the warmest heart that the Profession of Friendship ever took possession of?

To this Bolingbroke mustered the following retort:

> You [Warburton] have signalised yourself to be the Bully of Mr Pope's memory, into whose acquaintance, at the latter end of the poor Man's Life, you was introduced by your nauseous flattery.

And in the same year, 1749, there appeared a pamphlet addressed to Bolingbroke and reputedly written 'under the eye of Warburton' in which Pope's tribute to his 'guide, philosopher and friend' is most cruelly re-designed:

> I venture to foretell that the name of Mr Pope, in spite of your unmanly endeavours, shall survive and blossom in the dust, from his own merits,

and presume to remind you, that *yours*, had it not been for *his* genius, *his* friendship, his idolatrous veneration for *you*, might, in a short course of years, have died and been forgotten.

And here we do feel a pang of sympathy for Bolingbroke. The pamphleteer largely got it right: Bolingbroke has his place in the history books but no one writes of him as Pope did.

When Bolingbroke died in 1751, 'a soured and disappointed man', he had a small bombshell of his own to leave behind: papers that would reveal him to have all along been 'secretly hostile to all forms of revealed religion'. Publicly the philosopher had always been careful to champion the Established Church; in his ministerial days he had helped to frame the Schism Acts, which were directed against religious dissenters. But strangely enough, this exposure of his inner thoughts, which caused a great stir at the time, depends for its continuing notoriety on a memorial built by another distinguished literary man. In Boswell's *Life of Johnson*, we read of the day in 1754 when Bolingbroke's *Works* appeared under the editorship of David Mallett:

> The wild and pernicious ravings, under the name of *Philosophy*, which were thus ushered into the world, gave great offence to all well-principled men. Johnson, hearing of their tendency, which nobody disputed, was roused with a just indignation, and pronounced this memorable sentence upon the noble authour and his editor: 'Sir, he was a scoundrel and a coward. a scoundrel, for charging a blunderbuss against religion and morality; a coward, because he had not resolution to fire it off himself, but left half a crown to a beggarly Scotchman, to draw the trigger after his death!'

One cannot help reflecting that what Bolingbroke might have needed, after all, was some paradoxical annotation by Warburton.

Warburton's annotations are now – and were then – the object of a certain ribald awe: prolix, condescending, argumentative and full of 'what must, I fear, be called ratiocinative virtuosity' (the 'I' here is George Sherburn). A poem by Pope, after Warburton has toiled over it, is a most peculiar sight: sometimes we get a thin two-line strip of verse along the top of a page black with Warburtonian analysis; in the more 'difficult' poems the verse-allocation, per page, is rarely more than half a dozen lines. To come across a stretch of verse without annotation is at first to feel headily set free and then to marvel that

Pope, so glitteringly epigrammatic a poet, should have solicited explication from so leaden an exponent of the obvious: 'This definition is very exact', 'We must here remark the poet's skill', 'Our author, having thus far, by way of Introduction, explained the nature, use and abuse of Criticism, in a figurative description of the qualities and characters of Critics, proceeds now to deliver the precepts of the art. The first of which, from Ver. 47 to 68, is . . .'.

Although Warburton can be amusing when he is in a temper, he often seems ridiculously out of key with Pope's, well, sense of the ridiculous. For example, when Pope writes:

> Words are like leaves, and where they most abound
> Much fruit of sense beneath is rarely found:
> False eloquence, like the prismatic glass,
> Its gaudy colours spread at every place

we might hope that Warburton would experience some faint tremor of self-consciousness, or even elect to pass over these disconcerting lines in silence. Not at all; the annotation reads as follows:

VER 311. *False eloquence, like the prismatic glass, etc.* This simile is beautiful. For the false colouring given to object by the prismatic glass, is owing to its untwisting, by its *obliquities*, those threads of light, which Nature had put together in order to spread over its works an ingenuous and simple *candor*, that should not hide, but only heighten the native complexion of the objects. And *False Eloquence* is nothing else but the straining and *divaricating* the parts of *true Expression*; and then daubing them over with what the Rhetoricians very properly term COLOURS; in lieu of that candid light now lost, which was reflected from them in their natural state, while sincere and entire.

There is a story that the Bolingbrokean Lord Marchmont said to Pope: 'You are one of the vainest men living.' 'How so?' asked Pope. 'Because, you little rogue, it is manifest from your close connexion with your new commentator you want to show posterity what an exquisite poet you are, and what a quantity of dullness you can carry down on your back without sinking under the load.' It is an attractive theory but just for once we have to wonder if Pope's ingenuity has not been exaggerated. On the other hand, posterity *has* responded much as Marchmont said it would.

Warburton brought out his edition of Pope's *Works* in 1751, seven years after the poet's death. Although he and Pope had together prepared several poems for the press (with slabs of Warburton's response to de Crousaz now attached to the text of *An Essay on Man*) there was still much on which his comments seemed to him to be required: and Pope's will, after all, had given him permission to indulge himself.

Examining the first of the nine volumes, we are at once struck by the frontispiece, on which winged nymphs and cherubs sport and symbolically recline around a centrally placed bust of Warburton; one of the smaller cherubs is pointing upwards to a smaller depiction of the head of Pope. The artist who did the engraving has testified that Warburton insisted on being made 'the principal figure, and Pope only secondary in the picture, and that in consequence, the light, contrary to the rules of art, goes upwards from Warburton to Pope'. And so it does.

Next comes Warburton's introduction, or Advertisement. It is characteristically bellicose and self-important, boasting of Warburton's close liaison with the poet during his last years and of the solemn trust that has been placed in him. He quotes at length from a letter of Pope's in which he, Warburton, is hailed as a 'sensitive and reflecting judge' and pays tribute to his own editorial labours on *The Dunciad*, or *The New Dunciad*, as it became under his guidance. He tells how he saved Pope from frivolity, directed his gifts to the 'ends of virtue and religion' and all in all ensured that the work be purged of 'anything that might be suspected to have the least glance towards *Fate* and *Naturalism*' (originally, Warburton had wanted Pope to write a new *Essay on Man*, this time with Warburton in charge, not Bolingbroke). *The New Dunciad* is Warburton's pride and joy. He had urged Pope to rewrite *The Dunciad* and to round it off with a more 'metaphysical' fourth book; he had been at the poet's elbow as he wrote. His notes unstintingly celebrate his supreme act of editorial appropriation – amounting almost to co-authorship, he might have murmured.

Warburton loved to see himself as Pope's saviour, but he also enjoyed stepping forward as his bodyguard, his muscle. It was a role that gave Warburton the opportunity to work off some of his own deep-running grievances – his nature being just as retributive as Pope's. The bodyguard impulse was, if anything, intensified after the poet's death:

Together with his Works, he hath bequeathed me his DUNCES. So that as the property is transferred, I could wish they would now let his memory alone. The veil which Death draws over the Good is so sacred, that to tear it, and with sacrilegious hands, to throw dirt upon the Shrine, scandalises even Barbarians. And tho' Rome permitted her slaves to calumniate her best Citizens on the day of Triumph, yet the same petulancy at their Funeral would have been rewarded with execration and a Gibbet.

The message to all 'miserable scribblers' is clear: you have been warned.

Warburton outlived Pope by thirty-five years, becoming richer and grander by the year. For a time, though, it seems as if he *became* Pope, even handing out books from the poet's library inscribed 'From Alexander Pope'. And the identification lingered to the very end. Maynard Mack tells that 'in his last years, though by then well gone in senility, [Warburton] is reported to have come suddenly alert, during a conversation when Pope was being censured, with the exclamation, "Who talks against Pope? He was the best of friends, and the best of men." '

# CHAPTER FIVE

# BOSWELL'S COLOSSAL HOARD

> As they returned in the same carriage together from Twickenham, soon after the death of Mr Pope, and joined in lamenting his death, and celebrating his praises, Dr Warburton said he intended to write his life; on which Mr Spence, with his usual modesty and condescension, said that he also had the same intention; and had from time to time collected from Mr Pope's own mouth, various particulars of his life, pursuits and studies; but would readily give up to Dr Warburton all his collections on the subject, and accordingly communicated them to him immediately.

Recorded here, some have said, is one of the great lost opportunities of English literary history: one commentator has even gone so far as to describe the happening as a catastrophe. The idea is that if Dr Warburton had been less proprietorial and Mr Spence less compliant, we might not have had to wait nearly fifty years for Boswell to write the first 'major' literary Life. Spence would have got there first. To call this catastrophic is perhaps to exaggerate but the very least that can be said is that Spence had all the right credentials; he knew more than anybody else about Pope's life and, if Warburton had given him permission to proceed, he would have found out more – more than we actually now know.

The Reverend Joseph Spence met Pope in 1726 and immediately declared: 'I'm in love with Mr Pope: he has the most generous spirit in the world' – generous enough, certainly, for Pope to help the young Oxford critic get elected as Professor of Poetry in 1728. Around this time, Spence first began to think that he might write a life of Pope, if only to show the world that the maligned author of The Dunciad was not the vindictive monster that he seemed. With this in mind, he began jotting down Pope's 'conversation', and collecting remarks and anecdotes about him. The established French vogue for ana (as in Popeana) had not yet made its way to England, but in the coffee-houses the art of conversation, or table talk, was greatly prized.

Spence, who confessed himself 'always a mighty man for getting acquainted with authours', was a conscientious, not to say ingenuous, good listener – not just to Pope but to any literary celebrities or notables who crossed his path. No doubt there were many other admiringly cocked ears. The difference with Spence was that he thought to write down what he heard.

By the time Pope died (with Spence also in attendance at the crowded bedside) a substantial collection of Popeana had been assembled: enough, certainly, on which to base a fairly detailed Life. If Spence had been allowed to persevere, he had the energy and the patience to approach the task methodically: he would have been delighted to interview a range of living witnesses. He was well-liked in the cut-throat literary world: 'meek' and 'sweet-tempered' are the words most often used of him (as they were of Izaak Walton). Pope's acquaintances, both pro and con, would probably have trusted him and – with tongues untied by Pope's demise and with memories relatively fresh – would surely have supplied a mass of new material.

It was Spence's sweet temper, though, that allowed him to be bullied by Warburton into handing over his precious sheaf of notes and abandoning his plans for a biography – plans that Pope himself had known of and approved. And it was not as if Warburton really *needed* the notes, since his own plans turned out to be mostly theoretical. He made use of Spence's material in his edition of the *Works* and, in his Introduction to that publication, declared that a biography would shortly follow – 'The Author's Life deserves a just volume, and the editor intends to give it' – but he felt no real enthusiasm for the project. His idea of a biographer was derived from his observation of Curll's hacks and in any case his suspicious and defensive temperament set him against what he called the 'impertinent' curiosity of the life-writer. His interest in Pope was always a bit disembodied.

As Warburton procrastinated, a few hack Lives of Pope did make an appearance: the author of one of them complaining that he had become weary of waiting for the 'so-long-promised' biography by 'the Colossus-bully of literature'. Warburton took no notice of these, nor was he stung into swift action by Joseph Warton's 1756 *Essay on the Genius and Writings of Pope*, a work that uses facts supplied by Spence. It was not until 1767 – twenty-three years after he had been handed Spence's notes – that Warburton commissioned an official Life. He gave the job to a 'dull, plodding' lawyer named Owen

Ruffhead and then sat over him as he composed, or transcribed, a biography largely based on Spence or on already published letters. Ruffhead was not encouraged to undertake much energetic research; in any case, by this time, much of the material was not there to be researched. It has been thought suspicious that Ruffhead's biography came out a year after the death of Spence: Warburton's habit was to 'speak contemptuously' of the humble chronicler and he perhaps feared that Spence might somehow lay claim to bits of Ruffhead's *Life*.

It seems unlikely that Spence would have done so. He enjoyed collecting his anecdotes but was never sure what he wanted to do with them: 'anecdote', in those days, meant 'something yet unpublished, secret history'. At Spence's death, his collection was in the hands of a publisher but his executors were equipped with discretionary powers. They in turn decided that the material was too recent or too trivial for publication and the manuscript passed into the hands of the Duke of Newcastle (from whom Johnson borrowed it when he was working on *his* Life of Pope), and it remained in the Duke's keeping until its eventual publication in the early nineteenth century. Spence's *Anecdotes* is now established as a key source book for background on the world of Pope; Ruffhead is more or less forgotten – although now and then someone points out that Johnson owed Ruffhead more than was summarised in the verdict: 'he knew nothing of Pope and nothing of poetry.'

Johnson himself, of course, was not the most conscientious of biographers. 'If it rained knowledge I'd hold out my hands,' he said, when working on his Pope, 'but I would not give myself the trouble to go in search of it.' His *Lives of the Poets* was commissioned by a consortium of London publishers in yet another of their attempts to consolidate their copyrights. He wrote the essays very quickly for a ludicrously small fee. At the time of his 'treaty with the booksellers', Johnson was sixty-five, a great name in the land, and would not readily have demeaned himself by going about in search of background information. Such work was 'tedious and troublesome', he said. 'I wrote them in the usual way, dilatorily and hastily, unwilling to work, and working with vigour and haste.' Even Johnson's much earlier *Life of Savage* (1744), for all the famed largeness of its sympathies, was sketchily researched: the 'mother' railed against by both Savage and his biographer was still alive when Johnson wrote but he chose not to approach her. Nobody cares much about such lapses now. Savage lives on as a Grub Street rascal-victim, vain, self-pitying, deluded, yet – in Johnson's tale – possessing a 'complicated virtue'. He is for us the character Johnson wanted him to be and is now filed under Johnson Studies.

Although Savage owes his immortality, such as it is, to the ministrations of the sage, it is hard to think of Johnson as the keeper of anybody's flame. His intelligence was naturally lordly and his narrative habit was to inspect his subjects from above. In this sense, he was a biographer well ahead of his time. In the short term, though, he was inimitable. Although Johnson let it be known that the biographer need not be an acolyte, that he could assume at least an equality with his subject, he might not have approved such condescension if it had sprung from pens other than his own.

And yet Johnson did considerably open up the field for humbler practitioners. With *Savage* he offered not an exemplum but an object of compassion; he required of his readers not that they admire but that they understand, that they ask themselves: had they been in Savage's condition, would they have lived and written better than Savage? This was a new sort of question, requiring a 'complicated virtue' in response. Merely by asking it, Johnson supplied his genre with new aspirations; biography could indeed turn out to be a 'more philosophical and a higher thing than history'.

Johnson would have been happy for biography to usurp, at the outset, territory which we now know was reserved for fiction. When he wrote his *Life of Savage* there were to hand a multitude of what might be called 'novel-biographies', half fiction and half fact: not just Curll's fake memoirs of celebrities but *Robinson Crusoe* and *Moll Flanders*, and Mrs Manley's 'Secret Memoirs and manners of several persons of quality, of both sexes, from the New Atlantis, an island in the Mediterranean'. Soon there would be the 'blockhead' Henry Fielding. In 1744, neither the novel nor the biography had 'attained artistic certainty'. The 300-page bibliographical supplement to Donald A. Stauffer's *The Art of Biography in Eighteenth Century England* is bulging with items which, to judge from their subtitling, could easily go either way: 'Strange Adventures', 'True Histories', 'Compleat Accounts' abound. As Stauffer says:

> Sometimes writers of romances will center their 'memoirs' upon some notorious foreign name, in the hope that popular curiosity about genuine characters will sell their weak inventions. This procedure, however, is reversed in a more popular type, in which the lives of real people are told

under romantic pseudonyms. Disguises of this sort, in cases of current scandal or of political acrimony, may have been necessary. Secret histories soon became a habit; keys were issued to identify the baffling initials, the Mirabels or the Hilarias; and the public, delighted by mysteries, almost assumed that the more 'secret' the history, the more certain its truth. The most bewildering variant of all is the pseudo-biography which introduces both historical and imaginary personages, who laugh and frown at each other, and converse. Few of these mongrel productions possess literary value.

This may be so, but there they were, with potentially retarding consequences for the serious literary life-writer. The fear of being tainted by association with such vulgar stuff might easily have induced a more resolute stuffiness, a reinvigorated piety. Also, the exotic flavour of these popular bio-fics could have made the 'strange adventures' of the literary man seem dull enough either to be ignored or to be irresponsibly spiced up. Nobody could call the *Life of Savage* dull or pious – it had adulteries, murders, debts, imprisonments – and yet it was self-evidently a work of troubling seriousness. Johnson had a high standing in 'aristocratic' literary circles, the world of Pope and Warburton, but because of his own early struggles, he also had a passion for the dramas of the low-level scribbling career. He was perhaps better placed than anyone to confer prestige on an emerging genre. In a 1760 *Idler* he wrote memorably as follows:

> It is commonly supposed that the uniformity of a studious life affords no matter for a narrative: but the truth is, that of the most studious life a great part passes without study. An author partakes of the common condition of humanity; he is born and married like another man; he has hopes and fears, expectations and disappointments, griefs and joys, and friends and enemies, like a courtier or a statesman; nor can I conceive why his affairs should not excite curiosity as much as the whispers of a drawing room or the factions of a camp.
>
> Nothing detains the reader's attention more powerfully than deep involutions of distress, or sudden vicissitudes of fortune, and these might be abundantly afforded by memoirs of the sons of literature. They are entangled by contracts which they know not how to fulfil, and obliged to write on subjects which they do not understand. Every publication is a new period of time, from which some increase or declension of fame is to be reckoned. The gradations of a hero's life are from battle to battle, and of an author's from book to book.
>
> All this, modified and varied by accident and custom, would form very

amusing scenes of biography, and might recreate many a mind which is very little delighted with conspiracies of battles, intrigues of a court, or debates of a parliament.

When Johnson wrote this, he had not yet met James Boswell, but in many respects the most interesting 'gradations' and 'declensions' of his own career had taken place. He was fifty-one, his wife was dead, his *Dictionary* was done. Five days before writing the *Idler* piece he had privately made reference to 'the change of outward things which I am now to make' and had prayed 'that the course which I am now beginning may proceed according to thy laws, and end in the enjoyment of thy favour'. Although later in the same year Johnson made a list of several resolutions ('to rise early', 'to drink less strong liquor', 'to keep a journal', and so on), we have no idea what great alterations of his life he had in prospect. Boswell notes: 'he did not, in fact, make any external or visible change'. But we read the *Idler* words a little differently when we have been made aware that they were written at a crisis point in Johnson's own biography. Johnson knew enough about himself to know that his life-story would not, if told truthfully, be at all short of 'deep involutions of distress or sudden vicissitudes of fortune'. He also knew, or thought he knew, that 'those relations are commonly of most value in which the writer tells his own story. He that recounts the life of another . . . lessens the familiarity of his tale to increase its dignity . . . and endeavours to hide the man that he may produce a hero.'

In 1775, William Mason's 'biography' of Thomas Gray made its appearance, and although Johnson (who was never keen on Gray) did not take much notice of it, the book's unusual method made its mark on Boswell, who by that date was securely installed as Johnson's principal disciple. Mason had held a similar position in Gray's life:

> a faithful and affectionate henchman, full of undisguised admiration of Gray and fear of his sarcasm, not unlike Boswell in his persistence, and in his patience in enduring the reproofs of the great man. Gray constantly crushed Mason, but the latter was never offended, and after a few tears, returned manfully to the charge.

When Gray died, it was directed in his will that Mason should take charge of 'all his books, manuscripts . . . old papers of all kinds to preserve or destroy at his own discretion'. Mason prepared an edition of the poems and then had the original idea of constructing a biography out of Gray's letters, to which he would merely add a linking commentary, so that in effect 'Mr Gray will become his own biographer': 'I am well aware that I am here going to do the thing which the courteous and courtly Dr Sprat (were he now alive) would highly censure.' (Sprat, it will be remembered, took a stand against the use of letters in his *Life of Cowley*.) Mason's plea was that, by his method, the biographer would be yielding the task of final judgement to the reader. The conventional procedure was for the biographer to narrate the facts of his subject's life and then go on to offer a 'character' summation:

> The method in which I have arranged the foregoing pages has, I trust, one degree of merit – that it makes the reader so well acquainted with the man himself as to render it totally unnecessary to conclude the whole with his character . . . I might have written his life in the common form, perhaps with more reputation to myself, but surely not with equal information to the reader.

It so happened that Mason was here being vastly disingenuous: he had actually manipulated the evidence far more extensively than would have been possible had he employed the 'common form'. The letters on display were heavily doctored: passages silently omitted, phrasings altered, colloquialisms ironed out, and so on. Quite often, a single letter was in fact a patchwork of several different letters, some of these written at intervals of many years. The overall motive was to present Gray as a virtuous 'Scholar and Poet'; Mason was simply 'brushing his clothes and washing his hands for him before allowing the world to see him'. But there was a certain brutality in the procedure. Many of the original letters were destroyed and Mason did what he could to ensure that his monument would be the first and last. It was not until the middle of the nineteenth century that the range and detail of his tampering was finally revealed, in the painstaking editions of John Mitford. (Mitford's labours, incidentally, gave rise to one of textual scholarship's great horror stories: Edmund Gosse in 1884 took it upon himself to 'correct' some of Mitford's wrong transcriptions and announced with great solemnity that he had arranged for Gray's letters to be 'scrupulously printed, as though they had never been published before, direct from the originals'. It turned out that Gosse neglected to do the copying himself but employed a copyist who, 'wearying of the script, and finding that the letters had been published

69

by Mitford, soon began to copy from the printed word in preference to the MSS . . . Gosse's amanuensis had let him down.')

Boswell, of course, was unaware of Mason's doctorings, although he may well have heard rumours, and in his *Life of Johnson* he makes a point of acknowledging a debt:

> Instead of melting down my materials into one mass, and constantly speaking in my own person, by which I might have appeared to have more merit in the execution of the work, I have resolved to adopt and enlarge upon the excellent plan of Mr Mason, in his Memoirs of Gray.

Boswell's mode of biography – in his view 'the most perfect that can be conceived' – combines the methods of Mason (the extensive use of letters) with the habits of Spence (the recording of the subject's 'conversation'). The extra ingredient is Boswell. Unlike his exemplars, this biographer is a character in his own book – the main character, some have complained.

With Boswell, the processes of biography are dramatised: how the facts were collected, how rival biographers were dealt with, how the biographer first met his subject, how their relationship developed, and so on. Now and then he employs the language of hagiography but he undermines it from within, with impious winks and nods. There is no reverential distancing: not even, all the time, much tact. For Boswell, admiration is a busy, intimate affair: we never feel him to be the mere recorder he pretends to be, nor would he wish us to. An enormously vain man, he is yet a stranger to embarrassment, and this unusual mix can often seem to be his greatest strength. The worshipper bears in on the worshipped; he wants to get out of him more of the good stuff that he knows is there. If this means rude rebuffs, too bad: the job has to be done. But at the same time Boswell wants more than mere biography: he wants to imprint his own personality on the life he plans to write, even as that life is being lived. And Johnson was 'well apprised of the circumstances'. Whether fond or irritated – and with Boswell he could easily be both – he too needed to be on his toes. He would not have wished to disappoint one so transparently susceptible to disappointment; and he had seen enough of Boswell's journals to know the kind of *Life* that he would write.

Boswell had the 'highest reverence . . . a sort of mysterious veneration' for Johnson. He spent three years fishing for an introduction and when they finally met he was gratified to be treated with a proper brusqueness: after all, Johnson's brusqueness was well-known. When they began to see each other by arrangement Boswell 'felt no little elation at having now so happily established an acquaintance of which I had been so long ambitious', and when it began to seem that Johnson liked him he experienced 'a pleasing elevation of mind beyond what I had ever before experienced'. This is the stock language of the seasoned hero-hunter. Boswell was addicted to the famous; Rousseau and Voltaire were two of his prize scalps, and he was forever writing letters to celebrities in order to connect their names with his. 'The fear that his wavering flame would be overcome by the darkness of contemporary unconcern or of future forgetfulness was with him an obsession.' Like many another hero-worshipper, Boswell believed that his own gifts and temperament were nearer to the heroic than to those of the mediocre mass: he *deserved* to be close to Johnson – more than an incompetent sycophant like Goldsmith did, for instance. By keeping Johnson's flame he would also be attending to his own. And from this point of view, he has been thoroughly triumphant. The Dr Johnson of the popular imagination is indeed Johnson as first imagined by James Boswell: Ursa Major, the Great Cham, the auld dominie, and all the rest of it, have been drawn directly from the *Life*. The verb 'to Boswellise' now has a meaning in the language.

Every so often, efforts are made to liberate Johnson from the ardent custody of his disciple, to insist that Johnson – never 'Dr Johnson', if you please – was a *writer* not a chop-house aphorist, that he had an inner life which Boswell had no access to and would not have understood, that the testimony of other authoritative memoirists (like Mrs Thrale) has been unfairly marginalised. And, it is also pointed out, the *Life of Johnson* is not really a full Life at all. Boswell came late upon the scene and his attachment lasted for just over twenty of his subject's seventy-five years. The book runs to about 1400 pages: of these, under three hundred cover life-before-Boswell. And although Boswell claims to have 'run half over London, in search of a date' (and often actually did so), some of these pre-Boswell years are either blank or are rushed through in a couple of pages. Johnson's life between the ages of thirty and forty gets just over forty pages of the total 1400.

It is this imbalance towards Johnson the mature celebrity, and more particularly towards Johnson as he functioned in the hearing of James Boswell, that can stir professional Johnsonians to indignation: such as these wish us to read the master's books, not listen to his chat: 'it is

Boswell who must bear the responsibility . . . Boswell who forged the iron curtain which has fallen between the increasingly complex and sympathetic Johnson discovered by scholarship and the immutable Great Cham of the "intelligent general reader".' The words here are by Donald Greene, in a *TLS* review of John Wain's 1974 biography of Johnson. Greene goes on to propose a theory that Boswell's 'much-touted "hero-worship" of Johnson is a mask, disguising from himself and others an unconscious wish to cut Johnson down to size and to establish, in the end, the superiority of Boswell'.

'Unconscious' is the word to ponder here, and it need not be pondered for too long. Boswell was not so abjectly worshipful that he held back from itemising much Johnsoniana that was hard (even for him) to take: the 'uncouth' dress, the 'slovenly particularities' of his apartments, the 'disgusting eating habits', the prejudices and the inconsistencies (Johnson's 'varying of himself in talk'). But even here the biographer could plead that he was acting on orders issued from on high: 'If a man is to write a Panegyrick, he may keep vices out of sight, but if he professes to write a life, he must represent it really as it was.' This is the drift of all Johnson's pronouncements on the subject of biography, even those which pre-date Boswell. The author of the *Life of Savage* destroyed a mass of his own papers before he died and he knew pretty well what he had bequeathed to Boswell. He also knew what Boswell's verdict, conscious or unconscious, would turn out to be: that Johnson, 'great and good as he was, must not be supposed to be entirely perfect'. The burden of the *Life* is not, at any level, inconsistent with this verdict, and the verdict itself is one for which Johnson himself would happily have settled.

There is an irony in Donald Greene's evocation of 'the increasingly complex and sympathetic Johnson discovered by scholarship', an irony of which Greene himself is bitterly aware. What Greene sees as Boswell's 'preposterously inflated reputation' owes almost everything to the discoveries of modern scholarship or, as Greene describes them, to

the band of modern scholars who have invested their professional energies in the editing of Boswell's colossal hoard of 'private papers' (in whose acquisition by Yale University a very large sum of money, as well, was invested), and are understandably concerned that their investment should not depreciate. For those who believe – and who with any rudimentary sense of literary values can help believing? – that Johnson is a very great writer and Boswell a very minor one, it was disconcerting to learn recently that, unless funds were provided by private sources, the Yale edition of Johnson's works, less than half way to completion, would be terminated. We hear of no such threat to the Yale Edition of Boswell's papers, so that we can count on being regaled indefinitely with the details of Boswell's claps and hangovers.

The saga of Boswell's 'colossal hoard' is usually narrated from the point of view of the intrepid scholars who in the 1930s recaptured from an Irish castle and a Scottish country house a trove of Boswelliana, including his 8000-page Journal, the manuscript of the *Life* (mainly pages torn from the Journal and sent off to the printer), two or three thousand letters (to and from), unpublished sections of the Hebridean diary, plus proofs, family documents and details of the sorry state of the clan finances. On the basis of the discovery, Boswell's reputation, both as a biographer and as a 'minor writer', was substantially restructured: the *Life of Johnson* was shown to be not so much a marvel of eighteenth-century stenography as a work crafted with considerable literary cunning, and the Journal as a whole revealed Boswell as darker, funnier, more troublingly complicated than the buffoon-figure that had seemingly been set in marble by Macaulay's notorious 1831 review:

> a man of the meanest and feeblest intellect . . . He was the laughing stock of the whole of that brilliant society which has owed to him the greater part of its fame. He was always laying himself at the feet of some eminent man, and begging to be spit upon and trampled upon . . . Servile and impertinent, shallow and pedantic, a bigot and a sot, bloated with family pride, and eternally blustering about the dignity of a born gentleman, yet stooping to be a talebearer, an eavesdropper, a common butt in the taverns of London . . .

Macaulay's great paradox, that 'one of the best books in the world' had been written by a fool, is now – thanks to 'scholarship' – in ruins.

When Boswell died in 1795, his will appointed three literary executors: Edmund Malone, who had helped him with the *Life*, and two other trusted friends, William Temple and Sir William Forbes. Their instructions regarding the papers were 'to publish more or less' as they saw fit, and – although they derived 'rich entertainment' from the Journal – their conclusion was that dear old Boz had in it 'put down many things both of himself and others that should not appear'. It was agreed that any decision about the selection and possible publication of excerpts should be left until Boswell's 17-year-old second son had come of age. This son, James, had been Boswell's favourite: 'An extraordinary boy . . . He is much of his father.'

The new Laird of Auchinleck, and Boswell's heir, was Alexander, and he seems to have shared the family's general touchiness on the subject of his father's literary fame. According to Macaulay, Alexander was 'ashamed' of the Johnson *Life*, and 'hated to hear it mentioned'. Macaulay, as usual, overstates but Alexander was a proud young laird and, twenty years old at his father's death, was not yet embarked on his career as a songsmith and antiquary: he hated to see Boswell ridiculed, in satires and cartoons, as Johnson's whipping boy. Walter Scott probably summed up the Auchinleck view most accurately when he wrote that Boswell's book, 'though one of the most entertaining in the world, is not just what one would wish a near relation to have written'. This was indeed the attitude of Alexander's wife: she it was who sent Joshua Reynolds' portrait of Johnson to the saleroom. Boswell also bequeathed a few financial problems.

Altogether, there was a feeling that the Boswell name had suffered sufficient exposure to the public gaze. Consequently, the great cache of manuscripts was set to one side: some of it was at Auchinleck, some still in the hands of the executors and some with James, who lived in London. Alexander perhaps did not even open the boxes stored at Auchinleck; James showed an interest but never followed through in any systematic way. And then, in 1822, both he and Alexander died: James of a sudden illness and Alexander in a duel. Each was in his forties. And by this time, the three executors were also dead. Their original idea had been to collect the papers together in one place but Forbes, the chief executor, died ten years after Boswell and a load of manuscripts still languished at his Scottish home. Nobody at Auchinleck had ever shown any great interest in retrieving them and now, with James and Alexander dead, perhaps nobody knew that they were there. The new laird was another James, aged fifteen in 1822. He, with his mother's guidance, was also disposed to keep the lid on his ancestor's private writings.

The performance of Boswell's immediate heirs and executors is strangely unimpressive, considering their credentials and their tastes. Boswell's two sons were, in their different ways, both literary men. Alexander was a bibliophile and ran his own private press at

Auchinleck specialising in reprints of rare books, and he was active in Edinburgh literary circles (hyperactive, on occasions) where he tended to remind people of his father: according to John Gibson Lockhart, Alexander had all of 'Bozzy's cleverness, good humour, and joviality, without one touch of his meaner qualities' (which nicely encapsulates the then-current view of Bozzy). Maybe Alexander was too gregarious and impulsive to have taken on the job of sorting through a mountain of old papers: whatever the reason, he was busier in the service of Burns's posterity than of his father's. With Burns, it was anyway merely a matter of putting up a statue.

James – as Boswell anticipated – was a much likelier bet. He was a lawyer and a literary scholar and he was close to Malone: indeed such was his closeness that Malone chose him as *his* literary heir. James worked with Malone on his great edition of Shakespeare and, after Malone's death, it was James who inherited the task of completing the twenty-one volumes, adding prefaces, notes and even a glossarial index. Amusingly, in the circumstances, the edition became known as 'Boswell's Malone'. From the point of view of poor Bozzy's estate, we have the peculiar spectacle of his favourite son and the most literary of his three executors so busy with the Life and Works of Shakespeare (and of Johnson; Malone, helped by James, supervised four editions of the *Life*) that they had little or no time left over to attend to the after-fame of a biographer. Malone, as a matter of fact, could hardly have been busier, and might easily have entered our narrative by other routes. He was an indefatigable 'ferret in charter warrens' and did much important burrowing at Stratford (he also arranged for Shakespeare's bust in the church there to be whitewashed). He was toiling over a four-volume edition of Dryden, which included a biography, transcribing Spence's *Anecdotes*, defending the manuscripts of Aubrey and helping to expose the forgeries of Chatterton. He has been accused of neglecting his Boswell duties, but 'neglect' hardly seems the right word to describe any aspect of the man's career.

The first test of what, by default, had gradually become the Auchinleck position took place in 1829, when John Wilson Croker was preparing his edition of the *Life of Johnson* (an edition which would provoke Macaulay's wrathful words on Boswell, not to mention his even more wrathful words on Croker, whom he loathed). Croker wrote to Auchinleck, asking about any surviving Boswell papers, but got no reply. A prominent politician, he was greatly piqued and at once enlisted Walter Scott to act as go-between. Scott did his best but in spite of all 'importunities and influence' Croker continued to be shunned. In the preface to his edition, he complains about his treatment and not altogether face-savingly concludes that 'the original journals do not exist at Auchinleck: perhaps to this fact the silence of Sir James Boswell can be attributed.'

At the back of Croker's mind, the suspicion probably was that the Boswell heirs had had a bonfire and were reluctant to admit it; and he believed he had some other grounds for thinking so. Malone, in a footnote to the fifth edition of Boswell's *Life*, made reference to a letter having been 'burned in a mass of papers in Scotland'. The theory now is that 'burned' was a misprint for 'buried' and that it was this misprint, coupled with Croker's official-sounding statement in his preface, that started the myth which prevailed throughout the century: the myth that Boswell's papers were destroyed.

Nearly thirty years after Croker, in 1857, the announcement of a bizarre discovery in France should really have made Boswell scholars think again. A certain Major Stone, late of the East India Company, was out shopping in Boulogne and noticed that some of his purchases had been wrapped in a letter signed 'James Boswell'. The major asked where the wrapping had come from and was told that a bundle of paper had been bought from a hawker. Quite a lot of the bundle had already been used for wrapping but Stone managed to get hold of what was left: ninety-seven letters by Boswell to William Temple, the biographer's life-long friend and one of his three literary executors. The story of how the letters got to France is complicated (to do with Temple's eldest daughter marrying a debt-ridden clergyman who had been forced to flee across the Channel), but it is probably just as well that the material surfaced where it did: an English-reading shopkeeper might have thought twice about subjecting her customers to Boswell's true confessions. When the Temple letters were published, they were heavily expurgated – not heavily enough, though, to disguise their predominating flavour: the boozy, libidinous Boswell who wrote without inhibition to his chum was close enough to the Macaulay caricature for the family to feel thoroughly justified in its policy of silence. And in the England of 1857 no outsider was going to lament that material similar to this had been destroyed.

The Boswell family had in any case undergone a change. The James who had rebuffed Croker died in the year of the Temple letters' publication and his death marked the end of the direct male line: the Boswell papers were now controlled by women. There was the dowager, Alexander's widow (who lived on until 1864), there was James's wife (who died in 1884) and there were two daughters, Julia and Emily. Emily eventually married an Irish peer, Lord Talbot de Malahide, and it was after her death in 1898 that the contents of Auchinleck were gradually removed to Malahide Castle, near Dublin. The Talbots had one son, yet another James.

Between the death of Sir James in 1857 and the removal to Malahide (which was probably completed in 1915) there were three significant events in the great Boswell papers saga. In 1874, the Rev. Charles Rogers edited a collection of *Boswelliana* (based on papers which had once belonged to James, the biographer's second son). Rogers, having in mind the Malone footnote and Croker's preface, freshly underscored what was now the generally accepted view: 'Boswell's manuscripts were left to the immediate disposal of his family; and it is believed that the whole were immediately destroyed.' No contradiction was issued by the family and the myth was thus revitalised: so much so that when George Birkbeck Hill in 1887 published his acclaimed edition of the *Life*, he made no reference to the possible existence of any fugitive Boswelliana. Hill later revealed that he had in fact 'once tried to penetrate into Auchinleck, Boswell's ancestral home' but had been most rudely repulsed. Even in this grumbling testimony, though, Hill did not suggest that, had he been admitted, he would have discovered more than, at best, 'many curious memorials'.

When the Auchinleck collection was transferred to Malahide Castle, most of it was stored in an ebony cabinet of which Boswell himself had been particularly fond. In the process, some superficial sorting seems to have been done: enough, anyway, for Lord Talbot and his second wife (he had remarried in 1901) to begin speculating on the possible cash value of the hoard. Like all Boswells and sub-Boswells, the Talbots were seriously short of cash. At some point, Lord Talbot's brother, a distinguished colonel in the Royal Engineers, even went so far as to begin *reading* Boswell's Journals. For this alone, Milo Talbot earns his niche in literary history. It was by now more than a hundred years since Boswell's death and, so far as we know, not a single page of the Journals had been read by anyone since the original executors' examination.

Milo's verdict was that some sort of publication should be countenanced, and that handsome profits might well be afoot. In 1911, he sent a censored typescript of the Journals to John Murray. The firm of Murray had long been sensitive on the matter of private papers and (as we shall see) had recently been re-embroiled in the Byron controversy. Even so, it seems remarkable that the publisher should have reacted to Boswell as he did. Acknowledging receipt of what we now think of as one of the century's great literary *coups*, Murray reported to Lord Talbot that both he and his reader had, on reading the material, experienced both 'disappointment' and 'dismay'. Presumably, he said, Lord Talbot was familiar with Macaulay's 'poor opinion' of Boswell (an opinion now sixty years of age):

> But Macaulay had not seen these journals: had he done so he would have added that [Boswell] was an incurable sot and libertine: conscious of his own iniquities: sometimes palliating them as 'Asiatic satisfactions quite consistent with devotion and with a fervent attachment to my valuable spouse': sometimes making resolutions of amendment which were not carried into effect, but always lapsing into the slough of drunkenness and debauchery and indolence.
>
> The occasions on which he records that he was intoxicated, and even blind drunk are innumerable, and over and over again he notes that 'he ranged the streets and followed whores' or words to that effect.
>
> Many passages have been cut out, I presume on account of their immorality, but if they were worse than many which remain they must have been very bad indeed.

Murray could see that the Journals might conceivably be of interest to a Boswell biographer but publication would be to nobody's advantage: 'If we eliminate the passages which have already been published' – by which he meant any bits that had gone into the *Life of Johnson* – 'those which are unpublishable: and those which are too trivial for permanence, the residuum is I fear very small.'

After this, the Talbots decided to sit on their typescript for a while; more than likely, they accepted Murray's view. But the secret of the Journals' existence was now out, at least locally: dinner guests at Malahide Castle were shown the ebony cabinet and told what it contained. There were even occasional readings from the Journals. None of these goings-on, however, was reported in the English Department of Yale University where Professor Chauncy B. Tinker was working on a book about the young James Boswell, and preparing what he believed would be a definitive edition of Boswell's correspondence. In July 1920, nine years after the Talbots' overtures to Murray, Tinker placed an advertisement in the *TLS* requesting owners of any Boswell letters to get in touch with him. He got two replies, both directing him to Malahide. Tinker at once wrote off to Talbot and received this answer from the son: 'I am very sorry I am unable to give you any letters of James Boswell for publication. I regret I cannot meet your views in this respect.'

Astonishingly, Tinker accepted the brush-off and quietly proceeded with his work. His edition of the letters was by this stage well advanced and would be his *magnum opus*: he was, it seems, hungry for publication and (according to one of his distinguished colleagues) 'he was in fact consciously or unconsciously inhibited from vigorous and persistent enquiry by not really wanting to turn up a large new mass of Boswell letters.' Tinker's edition appeared in 1924 to the applause of academe. Only then did he brace himself for a second crack at Malahide.

By this date the Talbot personnel had somewhat changed. Lord Talbot had died in 1921 and his son succeeded to the title at the age of forty-seven. Three years later, he married an actress half his age, one Joyce Gunning Kerr. This new Lady Talbot was untouched by any lingering traces of Boswell family pride, and she had literary pretensions. Her husband, a racing man, had none. Thus, when Tinker made his second approach, it was Joyce Gunning Kerr who invited him to tea at Malahide and who chastised him for not having sought Talbot permission before issuing his 1924 edition of the *Letters*.

Tinker was then allowed to peek inside the ebony cabinet. What he saw there both amazed and sickened him. He wrote to a friend:

> I was led into an adjoining room, where I found myself standing in front of the famous 'ebony cabinet' – a sort of highboy with many drawers. The drawers which I was permitted to pull open were crammed with papers in the wildest confusion. I felt like Sinbad in the valley of rubies. I glanced – panting the while – at a few sheets. One was a letter from Boswell to Alexander, then a schoolboy. At once I realized that a new day had dawned for Boswellians, and that for C. B. Tinker there was a dreadful crisis, the resolution of which would alter the whole of his future life. (I did not sleep that night.)

Tinker was not allowed to take anything away, nor to copy any of the papers. He left Malahide 'feeling . . . that his life's work lay in ruins'.

Perhaps the kindest way of explaining Lady Talbot's conduct here is to remember that she was more of an actress than a scholar. Less charitably, it might be conjectured that she knew Tinker would soon spread the word; in Boswell matters, his authentication carried weight.

In a July 1925 postcard to A. Edward Newton, the eminent American book collector, Tinker cried: 'Everything here and nothing to be touched. I have been on the rack.' Within days, the rare book trade was alerted. Cables were fired off to Malahide. The Talbots, though, stood firm: the collection was not for sale.

Newton alone seems to have divined that the owners might need subtler handling. 'I'll bet a hat someone works this invaluable mine.' The someone did not take long to appear. Newton reported the Tinker mission and its aftermath to Lieutenant Colonel Ralph Hayward Isham, telling what he knew of the ebony cabinet, of Tinker's anguish, and of the Talbots' opposition to a sale. He may even have mentioned that the youthful Lady Talbot could be susceptible to Isham's legendary charm. For Tinker, the Malahide treasure trove spelled ruin. And so it did for Isham, although he did not recognise this at the time. As soon as Newton planted the idea, there was engendered in this amateur collector and part-time Boswellian an obsession which over the next quarter of a century would dominate his life, soaking up all his money, spoiling his marriages, even from time to time imperilling his sanity.

Isham had a curious background. A 35-year-old American of considerable wealth, educated at Cornell and Yale, he had served in the British Army during World War I and had by this means acquired an English accent and a range of upper-bracket British friends to go with his 'strikingly handsome physical appearance, [his] great charm of manner and formidable powers of persuasion'. A 'fascinating devil' was the common designation, supported now and then by rumours to do with his volatile temperament and his wicked way with women. Thus armed, Isham laid siege to Malahide Castle and after two years of silver-tongued negotiation, the million-word Boswell hoard belonged to him – at a price of around £35,000, which was low but a good deal more than he could actually afford. Page by page, with deletions *passim* in the Talbot hand, the collection was shipped to the United States. Isham at once appointed an editor, Geoffrey Scott, and set about constructing a monument to the 'new' Boswell, and to his own sterling conduct in the field: a de luxe eighteen-volume limited edition, on antique paper and with eighteenth-century typography. The idea was to finance the five-year project by advance subscriptions and by the sale of subsidiary rights.

From the start, Isham's scheme was plagued by irritations and setbacks: his editor died and had to be replaced, Lady Talbot was intent on censoring the Journal and was not pleased to learn that Isham's lieutenants were deciphering the words she had inked over, and the money was forever running low. Isham's personal funds had been exhausted by the purchase and after a time he was having to borrow from friends and even to sell off the odd manuscript. A further irritant, although one not wholly unwelcome in its substance, was Lady Talbot's habit of suddenly discovering new bundles of Boswelliana: for instance, an old croquet box was found to be stuffed with Boswell papers, including the manuscript of his Hebridean Journal. A hayloft would eventually yield further gems. Now and again, Isham found himself experiencing spasms of the Tinker syndrome; how much *more* would turn up after his edition was 'complete'? There were, after all, some gaps in the Malahide Castle haul: letters from several of Boswell's known correspondents (including Johnson), the complete manuscript of the *Life* and, most serious of all, the section of the Journal which recorded Boswell's arrival in London and his first encounters with Johnson. Isham assumed – and maybe even hoped – that such items had been lost.

What Isham did not know, as he rushed his 'definitive' edition towards a 1934 completion date, was that most of these items had already been discovered, not at Malahide, which might not have surprised him, but at Fettercairn House in Aberdeenshire. In 1930, an Aberdeen University lecturer, Claude Colleer Abbott, was researching the life of the eighteenth-century poet and philosopher James Beattie. Beattie's biographer had been Sir William Forbes, Boswell's chief literary executor. Searching for Beattie material at Fettercairn, Abbott started coming across odd items of Boswelliana: a fair copy of the London Journal (1762–3), letters from Boswell to Forbes, and to Boswell from several well-known figures of his day. There was a packet marked by Boswell 'Concerning Ladies' which contained notes to the biographer from his admirers and a lock of hair. Abbott did not at once know the significance of what he had found: for example, he believed that the London Journal had already been turned up at Malahide. It was evident, though, that 'the house must be systematically searched'. There were cupboards stuffed with papers and a large double attic 'tremendous with lumber of all kinds, the accumulation of generations. Boxes, small and great, abounded.'

With exemplary self-control, Abbott did keep to a system in his search so that, needless to say, the best find of all came last. On the fourth day, he finally reached 'the farther end of the right hand attic':

Nothing had been touched there for years, and of papers there was no sign. A great wooden box, extricated with difficulty, held nothing but rolls of wall-paper. But when I moved the next up-sided table I saw, wedged in between other furniture, a small sack, rather like a small mail-bag, with rents here and there from which letters were ready to drop. Quickly I dragged it out. A loose letter fell. It was written to Boswell. Down the winding stairs I hurried the sack, wondering whether all the contents could possibly concern Boswell. Before emptying the papers I drew out another loose letter. The omen was favourable. Soon I knew the truth. The sack was stuffed tight with Boswell's papers, most of them arranged in stout wads, torn here and there, and dirty, but for the most part in excellent order. Neither damp nor worm nor mouse had gnawed at them. My luck held. Almost to the last corner I have tracked the main find.

The Fettercairn haul ran to some 1600 items: two-thirds of these were letters written to Boswell. There were also over 300 drafts or copies of letters in Boswell's own hand, seven 'major manuscripts', and over 200 letters by Johnson – collected by Boswell for his *Life*. In addition to all this, there were many miscellaneous notes, lists and registers and a bundle of contemporary newspaper articles and cuttings.

Lacking this treasure, the glorious Isham edition of *The Private Papers* could hardly fail to seem somewhat diminished, although its editor – Frederick A. Pottle – had always been careful to point out that there were gaps. Isham and Pottle had good reason to feel annoyed that for five years, between 1931 and 1936, neither Abbott nor his prospective publisher, The Clarendon Press, had thought it correct to tip them off. The *sangfroid* of the Press seemed particularly impressive since – during this time – it had been negotiating with the Isham camp about an English edition of the *Private Papers* Index. The head of The Clarendon Press was R. W. Chapman who, since the 1920s, had been engaged on his own edition of Johnson's letters. Solidarity among scholars was not for him a rigid principle. Lord Clinton, the owner of Fettercairn, had asked for a policy of secrecy and Chapman was afraid that if he did not go along with this, he would lose access to the papers; both as a publisher and as a Johnsonian, he was unable to countenance a deprivation of this magnitude. Johnson letters were in short supply. Isham possessed but one; Abbott had scored an unbelievable 200.

Behind all this mild skulduggery, of course, was the fear that the Fettercairn haul might actually *belong* to Isham. He had bought from the Talbots the whole of their collection of Boswelliana, and this included any papers that had not yet, at the time of purchase, come to light. Since the Talbots were the heirs of the Boswell estate, the Fettercairn booty must, in law, be theirs and thus, by contract, Isham's. Between 1936 and 1938, Isham fought in the Scottish courts for recognition of his claim, and won. A combination of legal technicalities, disputes over costs, and – during the war – a nervousness about exposing priceless Boswelliana to a hazardous Atlantic crossing, postponed Isham's second, rather battered, Boswell triumph until 1948. Then, at last, the great collector's photograph appeared on the front page of the *New York Times*: 'The Boswell Papers discovered at Fettercairn House in 1931 and for twelve years in the custody of the Court of Session are now released and have reached these shores,' he said. A year later, Isham sold his entire collection, both Malahide and Fettercairn, to Yale for nearly half a million dollars.

Isham died in 1955, aged sixty-four, and Frederick A. Pottle, who worked with him almost from the start and was often exasperated by his 'histrionic' ways, wrote of him that 'he accomplished what was essentially desirable for Boswell's papers':

> he brought them together and then turned them over to a great institutional library where they could be expertly handled and made available to scholars and the general public. In a period of little over twenty years, working deliberately, adroitly, and with great courage, he reassembled Boswell's archives in the face of a complication of difficulties which no ordinary collector would or could have surmounted . . . He deserves the unstinted gratitude of posterity.

And so he does. And so, too, do several of the saga's supporting personnel. And yet, surveying the story from a distance, it is hard not to wonder why the whole thing took so long. The attitude of the Boswell family at the outset can readily be understood, and we can see too how the Malone misprint, the Coker preface, the Macaulay review, and so on, helped to perpetuate a bonfire myth. But with the entry of the scholars, we might have expected a speedier dénouement. It is particularly hard to fathom why, for nearly 150 years, nobody thought to take a look into the estate of Sir William Forbes. It was Forbes, after all, to whom Boswell first entrusted his great archive, and every Boswell scholar knew this, from the will. Even after Malahide, neither Tinker, Isham nor Pottle thought to ask the most obvious of questions: what did Sir William *do* about the papers during the ten years between his appointment as executor and his death in 1806? And after that, what did his family do? If any investigation on these lines had been begun, it would have led swiftly to Fettercairn, and Isham for one might have been spared – or denied – his twenty years of biblio-heroics.

# CHAPTER SIX

# THE FRAILTIES OF ROBERT BURNS

In April 1813, a librarian named William Upcott was invited by Lady Evelyn, descendant of the seventeenth-century diarist, to make a catalogue of the contents of the family library at Wotton House, in Surrey:

> Sitting one evening [Upcott says] after dinner with her Ladyship and her intimate friend Mrs Molyneux, my attention was attracted towards a tippet of birds' feathers which Lady Evelyn was then making: We have each of us our hobbies, said I. Very true, rejoined Lady E, and pray what may yours be, Mr Upcott? Mine, Madam . . . the handwriting, or autographs, of men who may have distinguished themselves in every walk of life. Handwritings, cried her Ladyship with some surprise, surely you don't mean old letters? at the same moment opening a drawer of her work table and taking out a small packet of papers, some of which had just been cut up by Mrs Molyneux as patterns for the body of a dress . . . The sight of these papers afforded me the greatest possible gratification in looking them over. Oh, added her Ladyship, laughing heartily, if you care for old letters like these, you shall have plenty, for Evelyn and those who succeeded him preserved most of their letters.

A maid was then sent to fetch 'a clothesbasketful of letters' and, as Upcott tells it, he was given permission to 'lay aside any that he cared to add to his own collection'. This he did, and thirty years later, when his own library came up for sale, it ran to some sixty-three lots (some of these containing hundreds of letters). As well as letters, there were books, engravings and manuscripts, all of them 'laid aside' from the library at Wotton. The Evelyn family was obliged to buy them back at a cost of several hundred pounds.

It makes a nice story, but how much of it can be believed? Would even the most myopic seamstress in 1813 not have been aware that the letters of the famous dead might be worth a lot of money?

Admittedly, John Evelyn's *Diaries*, on which his fame now largely rests, were not yet published, but in his day he had been notable for many curious pursuits (he was something of a proto-Green, in fact, with his treatises on air pollution, forest trees and modern architecture) and had numerous well-known associates.

If Lady Evelyn knew enough to have her library catalogued, she would probably have known too that the reading public, post-Boswell, was in the grip of a new appetite for literary trivia or 'remains': letters, memoirs, anecdotes, diaries, autographs. Upcott's home, where he stored his Evelyn booty, was actually called 'Autograph Cottage'. Twenty-five years earlier, Isaak D'Israeli's *Curiosities of Literature* had begun to appear and its six volumes of scholarly anecdotage were big sellers during the first two or three decades of the nineteenth century, helping to consolidate and extend a Boswell-inspired passion for biographical minutiae. To the high-minded, this was a sorry sort of passion: curiosity legitimised, or Boswellised. To its exponents, it invested the creative personality with human glamour. D'Israeli, picking up on Johnson's dictum that there is 'nothing . . . too little for so little a creature as man', defended his own wittily microscopic archivism by invoking the need to 'understand': 'Human nature, like a vast machine, is not to be understood by looking on its superficies but by dwelling on its minutest springs and wheels.'

We now tend to think of the ten or fifteen years at the end of the eighteenth century as if they were not really of that century at all. We speak of the period as 'pre-Romantic', as if literature all of a sudden decided that it ought to shift from (in Northrop Frye's evocation) 'a reptilian classicism, all cold and dry reason, to a mammalian Romanticism, all warm and wet feeling'. A similar opposition is assumed when it comes to discussing ways of 'understanding' human nature. Man in society yields, with a worldly shrug, to man alone. It can thus be felt as something of a jolt when we register that Boswell's *Life of Johnson* pre-dates *The Lyrical Ballads* by a mere seven years. Wordsworth was twenty-one when Boswell's *Life* appeared, and Coleridge was nineteen: the *Life*'s three-volume second edition appeared in 1793 and there was a third edition in 1799. The two young poets read Boswell with admiration, believing at first that he had inaugurated a new sort of biography that broke taboos which needed to be broken: the new age would indeed be an age of 'personality', 'character', and 'experience'.

It became evident early on, however, that there was necessary conflict between a Boswellian pursuit of the whole truth about the life of the biographee, and the Romantic writers' mythologising disposition. Wordsworth's rapturous memorial to Chatterton, the 'marvellous boy', would have found no favour in the Boswell camp, even though Boswellians might have concurred in the proposition that the literary life leads to 'despondency and madness'. Their objection would have been that there were other things to be said about Chatterton, not all of them particularly marvellous. So far as biography was concerned, the need for marvels typified a resurgent reverentialism, the old hagiography in secular dress. In the church, evangelism was newly on the march: so too in the world of letters. It was this compulsion to sanctify that would seek to expel Boswellism to the realm of gossip.

The idea of the poet as a type of saint, extraordinary, set apart, ablaze with mysterious sensitivities and insights, was of course essential to Romantic cultism. The creative genius, both privileged and penalised by his irresistible vocation, was available for homage from his kindred spirits and even for abuse from those whose ordinariness was the measure of his rarity, but there was something repellent in the spectacle of a man of inspiration being grounded, so to speak, by those who should be his disciples. Of course it was the duty of the biographer to tell the truth but the truth here was surely of a sort that transcended worldly data; the quest for it should gaze beyond quotidian deficiencies of conduct in order to celebrate the 'character' that really mattered: the *poetic* character. By this reckoning, Boswellian accumulation would always end up playing into the hands of the enemies of literature. A poet may have a duty to write about the common man; he also had a duty not to be one.

The conflict is well dramatised in the case of Robert Burns, the first important literary Life to come up for posthumous inspection since the *Life of Johnson*, and one in which Wordsworth had a particular involvement. Burns died in 1796, at the age of thirty-seven, leaving a widow and, by her, six children – one of these born on the day of his funeral. His last months had been an ordeal of sickness and financial worry. He knew that he was going to die and he spoke movingly to a friend about his prospects, after death:

he showed great concern about the care of his literary fame, and particularly the publication of his posthumous works. He said he was well aware that his death would occasion some noise, and that every scrap of his writing would be revived against him to the injury of his future reputation; that letters and verses written with unguarded and improper freedom, and which he earnestly wished to have buried in oblivion, would be handed about by idle vanity and malevolence, when no dread of his resentment would restrain them, or prevent the censures of shrill-tongued malice, or the insidious sarcasms of envy, from pouring forth all their venom to blast his fame.

He lamented that he had written many epigrams on persons against whom he entertained no enmity, and whose characters he would be sorry to wound; and many indifferent poetical pieces, which he feared would now, with all their imperfections on their head, be thrust upon the world. On this account he deeply regretted having deferred to put his papers into a state of arrangement, as he was now quite incapable of the exertion.

The woman Burns was here addressing, Maria Riddell, had been on the receiving end of one or two of Burns's 'unguarded and improper verses'. Married to the absent brother of the poet's friend and benefactor, John Riddell, Maria – a capricious eighteen-year-old – seems to have encouraged Burns in a flirtation; drunkenly, he had over-stepped the mark and, as a consequence, was banned from the Riddell household. Burns blamed Maria for the rift (having tried blaming himself) and for a period circulated scurrilous attacks on her, but had sought a reconciliation near the end. Maria would soon be writing a generous and intelligent obituary and, to the horror of Burns's drinking friends, there was even a passing thought that she might write the Life.

Unburdening to Maria, Burns naturally focused on the various injuries which he would not be able to repair. There were other worries, though, which he could easily have mentioned. In 1796, his 'image' – on which he had, from time to time, expended much subtle calculation – was in urgent need of re-arrangement. Had he died a few years earlier, during the six months or so in which he was the 'heaven-taught ploughman', courted by Edinburgh toffs, he might at least have gone out in some style at the height of his celebrity and with a pocketful of guineas. And had he held on for a few more years . . . well, who could tell?

Burns, at his death, was famous, but his was a complicated sort of fame, given to him, as it were, on loan – or, as some would later say, on false pretences. It had peaked ten years earlier with his Kilmarnock edition: poems presented to the world as the 'natural' effusions of an untaught rustic: 'Unacquainted with the necessary requisites for commencing Poet by rule, he sings the sentiments and manners he felt and saw in himself and his rustic compeers around him, in his and their native tongue.' It was this presentation that had caused the Ayrshire peasant to be taken up in Edinburgh, and there the literati who discovered him were further amazed to find that, in person, he was very far from being a straw-in-the-mouth yokel. Burns performed superbly in the salons, winning praise for the 'purity' of his 'turn of expression', and for avoiding 'more successfully than most Scotch-men the peculiarities of Scottish phraseology'. And this was in addition to a rather fetching pair of buckskin breeches, a disturbing intensity of gaze, and so on.

It was an act, but Burns for a period was in control. Robert Anderson, who talked to him about it, later filed a report to Burns's biographer: 'It was, I know, a part of the machinery, as he called it, of his poetical character to pass for an illiterate ploughman who wrote from pure inspiration.' Burns turned his back on Edinburgh because he began to feel that his control was slipping. He often felt, he said, 'the embarrassment of my singular situation, drawn forth from the veriest shades of life to the glare of remark'. The Kilmarnock volume was added to and a new 'Edinburgh' edition of his works turned out to be an Edinburgh triumph, netting him fresh plaudits and about £1200 in cash. He acquired connections, both literary and aristocratic, and the peasant-factor was beginning to recede: it was expected that Burns should now conduct himself as a distinguished gentleman of letters.

For Burns the question soon became: How can I keep this up? He knew which poems and songs he had *not* included in the Edinburgh volume and he knew also that those who condescended to admire the pious labourers of 'A Cotter's Saturday Night' might not regard Scotia's immortal bard so warmly were they to dip into the 'Merry Muses of Caledonia', his privately distributed anthology of raunchy drinking songs. That is to say, he knew himself: he knew his own randiness, his irascibility, his weakness for the bottle, his easily bruised vanity, etc. He wanted to get back to his 'men's men', to the wenching and the taverns, to the rural melancholia, the sense of grievance he was born with.

And in any case, Edinburgh might soon be having problems with *its* act. After the first few months of adulation, there were murmurings against the more 'robust' aspects of this peasant genius. With one mildly uneasy benefactress, Mrs Dunlop, Burns now and then allowed himself to blow a fuse: 'I know what I may expect from the world, by and by; illiberal abuse and perhaps contemptuous neglect; but I am resolved to study the sentiments of a very respectable Personage: Milton's Satan – "Hail horrors! hail infernal world!" ' He knew, and maybe Mrs Dunlop was beginning to suspect, that after a few drinks on a Saturday night, he was capable of a 'robustness' which even the most forbearing of his Edinburgh circle would find hard to overlook:

> I have long studied myself, and I think I know pretty well what ground I occupy, both as a Man & a Poet; and however the world, or a friend, may sometimes differ from me in that particular, I stand for it, in silent resolve, with all the tenaciousness of Property. – I am willing to believe that my abilities deserved a better fate than the veriest shades of life; but to be dragged forth, with all my imperfections on my head, to the full glare of learned and polite observation, is what, I am afraid, I shall have bitter reason to repent.

Burns's so-called Edinburgh period lasted for some eighteen months. In 1788, he left the city to set up as a farmer in Dumfriesshire and in the following year he accepted a position with His Majesty's Excise: his task, amusingly enough, would be to roam the country on the look-out for illegal stills, or 'searching auld wives' barrels', as he put it. This government job had been fixed for him by his Edinburgh connections and would cause him more than a few pangs of self-contempt. In the good old pre-Edinburgh days he had been able to write freely of the 'curst horse-leeches o' the Excise' and he was aware that, in accepting the appointment, he would surely 'stain' his 'laurels'. But he had finally married Jean Armour and he needed the money. Maybe he also needed to be on the move. His absences on excise duty meant that the farm business was not properly supervised and it eventually failed, as – it seems – he knew it would: 'Should my farm, which it possibly may, turn out a ruinous bargain, I have a certainty of an employment, poor as it may *comparatively* be, whose emoluments are luxury to any thing my first twenty-five years of Life could promise.' He wrote this four months after signing the lease at Ellisland.

The last few years of Burns's life can be made to offer a catalogue of rifts, embarrassments, showdowns, mostly fuelled by drink; or they can be presented as years in which, by his folk-song researches, the ploughboy achieved an authentic rediscovery of his native roots.

Looked at from the outside, by his contemporaries, the outline was depressing: in none of his roles did Burns seem quite to fit. The quarrel with the Riddells seemed to have in it most of the ingredients that were ruining his fame, and perhaps Burns thought so too. By 1788 – apart from *Tam o' Shanter* – his best poems had been written.

Burns's estate was handled by a committee of executors, headed by the most loyally adoring of his friends, John Syme, a colleague in the Excise and in the Royal Dumfries Volunteers (formed in 1795 to prepare against a French invasion): 'Nobody had more of the knack of getting along with the poet than Syme, and nobody did more on behalf of Burns to repair the broken fences of his relations with others.' Syme had been witness to several of Burns's drunken tempers, and knew all about his 'obstreperous independence' (on the trips they took together, 'Burns . . . would not dine but, where he should, as he said, eat like a Turk, drink like a fish, and swear like the Devil'.). But he was steadfast in his affection and felt privileged to have Burns's respect. Syme saw Burns on his death-bed and wrote at once to another of the poet's (and his) drinking cronies, Alexander Cunningham, in Edinburgh:

> I believe it is all over with him . . . today the hand of Death is visibly fixed upon him. I cannot dwell on the scene. It overpowers me – yet Gracious God were it in thy will to recover him! . . .
>
> My dear Cunningham, we must think on what can be done for his family. I fear they are in a pitiable condition. We will here exercise our benevolence, but that cannot be great . . . In the metropolis of Scotland, where men of Letters and affluence, his contemporaries and admirers, reside, I fondly hope there will be bestowed on his family that attention and regard which ought to flow from such a source into such a channel. It is superfluous in me to suggest such an idea to *you*.

And so it was. Cunningham, already knowing the gravity of Burns's illness, had formed a plan: '1st. a Subscription for his Wife and Infant family and *afterwards*, the sale of his posthumous works, Letters, Songs etc. to a respectable London bookseller.'

Syme agreed and, after Burns's funeral, they set to work immediately on the fund-raising and took the first steps towards organising the poet's papers. For the purposes of the fund, Cunningham took charge of Edinburgh and Syme of the national appeal. Already, though, Burns's obituaries had begun to appear, and nearly all of them managed to sneak in a mention of his 'frailties', 'irregularities', 'indigence', and so on. William Nicol, writing in August 1796, angrily summed up the prevailing atmosphere in Edinburgh:

> it gives me great pain to see that the encomiums passed upon him, both in the Scotch and English news-papers, are mingled with reproaches, of the most indelicate and cruel nature. But stupidity and idiotcy rejoice when a great and immortal genius falls; and they pour forth their invidious reflections, without reserve, well knowing that the dead Lion, from whose presence they formerly scudded away with terror, and at whose voice they trembled through every nerve, can devour no more.

Burns's family – principally his wife Jean and his brother Gilbert – stayed silent. The press notices were augmented by much word-of-mouth rumour-mongering and it was soon clear to Syme and his committee that it was going to be harder than they had thought to whip up moneyed sympathy for Burns. The rumours have been tersely summarised as follows: 'drinking excessively to the detriment of health; amours and tom-catting as a husband and father; proclivity to offend others with abuse of mouth or pen; and democratic or Jacobin sentiments and sympathies'. It did not help either when the English obituarists threw in a few sneers about the Scots having forced their greatest poet to become an exciseman. 'It was exceedingly unfortunate to make a Poet an exciseman,' wrote the London *Morning Chronicle*; 'poor Burns all his life time was but too apt to be led away *by the temptation of good spirits*. What then must have been the case when it became his daily occupation *to fathom the cask*?' And Coleridge wrote:

> Is thy Burns dead?
> And shall he die unwept, and sink to earth
> 'Without the meed of one melodious tear'?
> Thy Burns, and Nature's own beloved bard,
> Who to the 'Illustrious of his native Land
> So properly did look for patronage.'
> Ghost of Maecenas! hide thy blushing face!
> They snatch'd him from the sickle and the plough –
> To gauge ale-firkins.

Such laboured contributions from the South had the effect of tightening the Scottish purse-strings. In Edinburgh, enthusiasm for Burns had 'cooled with the corpse'. Cunningham's canvassing was being met with 'cold civility and humiliating advice':

The truth is, my dear Syme, the poor Bard's *frailties* – excuse this vile word – were not only so well known here, but often I believe exaggerated, that even the admirers of Genius cannot be prevailed on to do what we all ought – 'to forget and forgive'.

After eight months, Cunningham had raised less than £200 and believed that he could get no more. Syme had promises of about £500 but much of this had come from a handful of individuals. The overall response – particularly in 'Burns country' – had been thoroughly depressing: 'those friends in Ayr etc. whom the Bard has immortalised have not contributed a sou! By heavens, they should be d—d and a list of the d—d should be made out.'

The widow, then, could expect about £700 from the appeal: a decent sum, but not sufficient to secure her, or the children's, future. Phase Two of the Syme/Cunningham plan was now put into operation: a posthumous edition of the Works, to include unpublished songs and poems, some Letters and perhaps a Life.

The Dumfries executors' committee had already done some preliminary sifting and, fearing piracies, had advertised for any Burns material that was in private hands. The mass of papers they found at the poet's house was 'in utter confusion' but it took no more than a glance to determine that much of the collection ought probably to be destroyed: 'viz. such as may touch on the most private and delicate matters relative to female individuals'. When, in August, a bonfire was arranged, Syme was more hesitant: 'Avaunt the sacrilege of destroying them and shutting them forever from the light! But on the other hand, can we bring them into the light?' On this occasion, only a few 'unimportant' notes and cards were burned.

At least part of Syme's problem was solved by the prompt intervention of several of Burns's correspondents. For a time, there was something of a panic, with lady-friends and drinking buddies urgently pressing for the return of their letters to Burns and at the same time seeing to it that the letters they had had from him were 'lost'. Maria Riddell got hers back, and so did Mrs Dunlop. And Mrs McLehose, with whom Burns had conducted a steamily sentimental love affair by letter (the 'Sylvander' and 'Clarinda' correspondence: 'Clarinda' is the object of the famous 'Ae Fond Kiss'), 'preserved most of Burns's love letters, and in her later life used to exhibit them till they were torn to tatters, but her caution was as great as her vanity. Besides inking over many of the proper names, she used her scissors to remove the address, even when doing so mutilated the text overleaf, and once or twice seems even to have employed chemicals to obliterate every trace of writing from portions of a page.' There was more than one case where a batch of letters was exchanged for a contribution to the fund or where members of the family were persuaded to advise the committee of the disadvantages that might result from any indiscretion.

Unsure of his legal position, Syme was torn between wishing to protect the poet's reputation from the emergence of any new scandalous material and hating to see these one-time friends attempt to suppress the facts of an illustrious biography. Altogether, he and the committee soon began to feel out of their depth. None of them had the time or the expertise even to sort the papers, let alone arrange for publication, and Cunningham in Edinburgh was not keen to have the problem passed to him. It was at this point that Maria Riddell began to be thought of as a possible editor and biographer. Left to himself, the weary and exasperated Syme might well have handed her the job, although he had been distressed by her (as he saw it) too-candid obituary of Burns, and he shared the committee's horror at the idea of such delicate tasks being undertaken by a woman.

Almost from the start of his fund-raising campaign, Syme had been in touch with James Currie, an old college friend and now an eminent medical practitioner in Liverpool. Currie helped to orchestrate the English end of the appeal and when it became obvious to him that neither Syme nor any of Burns's Edinburgh associates was eager to take on the editing responsibilities, he rather half-heartedly proposed that he might make himself available. Syme, already impressed by Currie's contemptuous response to the slanderous obituaries, jumped at the offer. Currie tried to backtrack but was not allowed to. Eventually, after much pressing by Syme and much demurring and condition-making by Currie, the manuscripts were shipped to Liverpool in January 1797. Syme and his committee were, it seems, glad to see the back of them. Currie, a busy man for whom literature was but a hobby, wrote to acknowledge them as follows:

My dear Syme: Your letter of the 6th January reached me on the 12th, and along with it came the remains of poor Burns. I viewed the huge and shapeless mass with astonishment! Instead of finding, as I expected, a selection of his papers, with such annotations as might clear up any obscurities – of papers perused and approved by his friends as fit for publication – I received the complete sweepings of his drawers and of his desk (as it appeared to me), even to the copy-book on which his little boy had been practising writing. No one has given these papers a perusal, or even an inspection; the sheep were not separated from the goats; and – what has, perhaps, not happened before since the beginning of the world – the manuscripts of a man of genius, unarranged by himself, and unexamined by his family or friends, were sent, with all their sins on their head, to meet the eye of an entire stranger.

'With all their sins on their head' is an unconscious echo of the poet. 'With all their imperfections on their head', said Burns to Maria Riddell, meaning his unpublished poems; and he used the phrase again, to Mrs Dunlop, referring this time to the imperfections of his personality and conduct. What to Burns was an imperfection was to Currie more deplorable and it was indeed rash of Syme to expect from this 'entire stranger' a response to Burns – encountered on the private page – that would neatly chime with his own warm, complicated recollections. He based his trust in Currie on a letter the doctor had written to him six months earlier: it was more of a sermon than a letter, and in it Currie had held forth on the subject of literary genius:

> The very circumstance of Burns having pourtrayed himself in such vivid colours, is a decisive proof of his superior genius. It is not often that the real character of an authour appears in his works. Inferior minds shrink from a full exposure of themselves . . . It is only for men of the first order of genius to present themselves, without covering or disguise, in all the nakedness of truth and all the energy of nature. This fact may be easily explained.

The explanation follows. This was the letter in which Currie first suggested himself as the 'authorised biographer' and warned Syme that there was a danger that some other 'volunteer' may 'deform and disgrace' the subject. He also stated his view that 'the biographer of Burns has not many events to relate – the history of his life may be confined to a very few pages.' From Syme's point of view, all this sounded pretty good. He ought to have reflected, though, that Currie's homily was based simply on a reading of the poems: the doctor had met Burns once, for a few moments, in the street, and actually knew very little of his real character. He was shocked by the obituaries because he had no knowledge of their background. So far as he was concerned, the point of a biography would be to make the

Works more saleable and thus bring money to 'the fatherless children, for whom I would certainly be willing to make some sacrifices'. All this, however, was before he read the 'complete sweepings' of the poet's drawers and desk.

Before Currie began work, there appeared a *Memoir* by Robert Heron, who had known Burns rather well. Heron, although sympathetic and admiring, expressed his anger at those who had encouraged his hero into an early grave: literary hangers-on and brother excisemen, he called them:

> At last, crippled, emaciated, having the very power of animation wasted by disease, quite broken-hearted by the sense of his errors, and of the hopeless miseries in which he saw himself and his family depressed; with his soul still tremblingly alive to the sense of shame, and to the love of virtue; yet, even in the last feebleness, and amid the last agonies of expiring life, yielded easily to any temptation that offered the semblance of intemperate enjoyment, he died at Dumfries, in the summer of the year 1796, while he was yet three or four years under the age of forty.

Heron, of course, meant to do Burns's memory a favour: the effect of his *Memoir*, though, was to endorse the current rumours. Whatever else Burns did or did not do, one fact was now established: he had died of drink.

To Currie, this verdict may at first have seemed distasteful, but he was more than ready to be persuaded of its justice. Drink would satisfactorily make sense of all the horrors he was turning up in his perusal of the papers. Also, a diagnosis of alcoholism would bring a literary subject into his own area of expertise. In 1797, Currie had begun to publish his celebrated 'Observations on the Nature of Fever and on the Effects of Opium, Alcohol and Inanition'. He continued to work on this research topic throughout his writing of the Burns biography.

Currie's aim, no doubt, was for clinical, humane detachment. In selecting the Works, he was careful to avoid indecencies and he did not shrink from doctoring Burns's letters, so as to make them seem healthier. In composing the Life, he kept his own voice out of the actual narrative so far as he was able to: more impresario than author, he gave over the bulk of the story-telling to reminiscences solicited from Burns's friends. Even so, the doctor had a ploddingly ruminative streak and could not resist approaching the whole matter as a 'case'. Through his association with the poet William Roscoe, he had developed notions about the nature of creative genius: here was an opportunity to probe the connection between the mysteries of literary giftedness and his other speciality, the menace of alcohol abuse. Burns's life, he pronounced, was one 'in which virtue and passion had been at perpetual variance'. Thanks to alcohol, passion had triumphed in the end.

Poets, Currie insisted, should not drink. 'It is the more necessary for men of genius to be on their guard against the habitual use of wine, because it is apt to steal on them insensibly.' Indolent and melancholic by nature, poets are reluctant to take 'regular and healthful exercise': they tend to sit about, waiting for moments when 'the unbidden splendors of the imagination' might 'irradiate the gloom which inactivity produces'. If such moments fail to come unbidden, the bottle is resorted to – a big mistake; drink makes things worse:

> . . . because on them, its effects are, physically and morally, in an especial manner injurious. In proportion to its stimulating influence on the system (on which the pleasurable sensations depend) is the debility that ensues; a debility that destroys digestion, and terminates in habitual fever, dropsy, jaundice, paralysis or insanity. As the strength of the body decays, the volition fails; in proportion as the sensations are soothing and gratified, the sensibility increases; and morbid sensibility is the parent of indolence, because, while it impairs the regulating power of the mind, it exaggerates all the obstacles to exertion. Activity, perseverance, and self-command, and the great purposes of utility, patriotism, or of honourable ambition, which had occupied the imagination, die away in fruitless resolutions, or in feeble efforts.

After a dozen or so pages along these lines, with scholarly footnotes invoking precedents from literary history and current medical statistics, Currie seems to sense that he might perhaps have gone too far and to recall that this was, after all, supposed to be a literary biography. He quits the podium with a post-Boswell, pre-Romantic shuffle:

> To apply these observations to the subject of our memoirs, would be a useless as well as a painful task. It is indeed a duty we owe to the living, not to allow our admiration of great genius, or even our pity for its unhappy destiny, to conceal or disguise its errors. But there are sentiments of respect, and even of tenderness, with which this duty should be performed; there is an awful sanctity which invests the mansions of the

dead; and let those who moralise over the graves of their contemporaries, reflect with humility on their own errors, nor forget how soon they may themselves require the candour and the sympathy they are called upon to bestow.

Can Currie really not have known what damage he was doing? With one so bewitched by the sound, and soundness, of his own delivery it is extremely hard to tell. Did he really believe, when he came to offer his own description of the death of Burns, that he was discreetly veiling an unpleasantness?

> His temper now became more irritable and gloomy; he fled from himself into society, often of the lowest kind. And in such company that part of the convivial scene, in which wine increases sensibility and excites benevolence, was hurried over, to reach the succeeding part, over which uncontrouled passion generally presided. He who suffers from pollution of inebriation, how shall he escape other pollution? But let us refrain from the mention of errors over which delicacy and humanity draw the veil.

This, then, was the autopsy report: alcoholic poisoning plus maybe a touch of venereal disease had killed off Scotland's greatest poet. The Currie post-mortem was 'official' and would not seriously be challenged for a hundred years.

And yet there were flaws in the diagnosis which, with goodwill, might easily have been picked up at the time. In his narrative of the poet's final days, Currie makes frequent reference to a debilitating 'fever' and he mentions also an attack of rheumatism during which Burns's 'appetite . . . began to fail; his hand shook and his voice faltered on any exertion or emotion. His pulse became weaker and more rapid, and pain in the larger joints, and in the hands and feet, deprived him of the enjoyment of refreshing sleep.' From Burns's letters, we know that he himself was bewildered by his symptoms. In April 1796, three months before his death, he spoke of 'Rheumatism, Cold and Fever', in May of what he called 'a flying gout', and in July of 'my inveterate rheumatism' and of being 'tortured with an excruciating rheumatism which had nearly reduced me to the last stage'. This last letter was dated 7 July; he died on the 21st.

Reading these letters, we have to wonder what Burns's doctor was doing during these three months. Dr William Maxwell was a close friend of the poet and would supply Currie with medical information for the Life. In Currie we read that 'about the latter end of June,

[Burns] was advised to go into the country, and impatient of medical advice, as well as of every species of controul, he determined for himself to try the effects of bathing in the sea'. From Burns's letters, though, we get a different picture: 'The medical folks tell me that my last & only chance is bathing and country quarters and riding.' Where Currie says: 'At first Burns imagined that bathing in the sea had been of benefit to him', Burns himself records (on 18 July): 'I returned from sea-bathing today, and my medical friends would almost persuade me that I am better, but I think and feel that my strength is so gone that the disorder will prove fatal to me.'

Burns had no reason to lie to his friends about the sea-bathing cure: if it really had been his idea, he would have said so. Dr Maxwell, however, did have cause to fear that his drastic prescriptions might have fatally misfired. And Currie also had a special interest in playing down the water-therapy. In addition to his interest in the bad effects of alcohol, Currie had another speciality. The full title of his well-known work of 1797 was as follows: 'Medical Reports on the Effects of Water, cold and warm, as a Remedy in Fever and Febrile Diseases, whether applied to the Surface of the Body, or used as a Drink, with Observations on the Nature of Fever and on the Effects of Opium, Alcohol and Inanition'. The book had run into four editions by 1805. In Currie's entry in the *Dictionary of National Biography*, his Life of Burns is dealt with in half a dozen lines. The larger part of the entry pays tribute to his Medical Reports: 'The object of the book is to establish three rules of practice: that the early stage of fever should be treated by pouring cold water over the body, that in later stages the temperature should be reduced by bathing with tepid water, and what in all stages of fever abundant potations of cold water are advantageous.' If the fevered Burns had had the chance to attend Dr Currie's consulting rooms in the spring of 1796, we can be fairly certain that the pouring of cold water would have been prominent in the prescription.

It was not until 1925 that Burns actually got the second opinion he deserved. By then the posthumous notoriety he had feared was in some quarters thoroughly entrenched and was based largely on the Currie diagnosis. Luckily for him, though, there was on record a detailed description of his symptoms and this was now scrutinised afresh by a Dumfries-born psychiatrist, Sir James Crichton-Browne. Crichton-Browne had recently retired from his position as Lord Chancellor's Visitor in Lunacy, and many years earlier he had achieved some literary fame by his involvement in the Carlyle–Froude controversy (which we will come to later on). When literature needed a doctor, Sir James was the man to call and, in the case of Burns, there was an element of local pride at work: after all, the poet was said to have been destroyed by the low-life of Dumfries.

In a series of articles in the *Glasgow Herald*, Crichton-Browne re-opened the medical dossier and after much weighing of the available contemporary testimony he decided that Currie had allowed his medical neutrality to be corrupted by 'Calvinistic prepossessions'. In other words, he had had an obsession with alcohol abuse and had become determined to exhibit Burns as a dread warning. Thanks to the example set by the 'arch-calumniator' Currie, later generations had been further misled by 'the lucubrations of a legion of bio-graphical scribblers'. Crichton-Browne dismissed all the old charges of alcoholism and VD and pronounced his own verdict on the cause of death:

> heart disease of a rheumatic origin, which cut him off at middle age, and no doubt dated from childhood. In all likelihood it was in 'the auld clay biggin', in the damp Ayrshire climate and not very weathertight, some 'Janwar blast' blew in the germ of life-long perturbation.

On the basis of the Crichton-Browne findings, a new Robert Burns was born: cleaned-up, de-toxed and pitiably the victim of a life-long sickness contracted during his famously disadvantaged childhood. At long last the Burns Clubs could adore their hero without reservation. The author of 'O, my luve's like a red, red rose' did not have syphilis. 'Oor Rabbie' liked a dram and was perhaps a devil with the ladies, but why not? The peasant amorist was essentially restored to health. When Burns's *Collected Letters* appeared a few years later, the evidence of booze and lechery was easily assimilated to the new image of disease-free rakishness: 'A man's a man for a' that.'

Crichton-Browne's destruction of the alcohol/VD hypothesis has held good ever since, even though his own 'rheumatic fever' diagnosis has now and then been challenged. Over the years, Burns's death has been attributed to a dozen diverse agues: sinusitis, diphtheria, pneumonia, even 'depression'. Possibly the most engaging theory is the one published most recently, in a 1988 study by Richard Hindle Fowler. Fowler, who exhibits much medical and other scientific know-how throughout his entertaining book, has combed the earlier findings from Currie to the present day and found that none of them fits all the symptoms: fever, melancholia, fatigue, loss of appetite, wasting, liver enlargement (Burns was treated with mercury at some point), 'flying gout', muscle spasms, and so on. He asks: 'Can there be named a serious disease, uncommon today and unrecognised in the late eighteenth century' which covers such a 'melancholy grouping of features'? Triumphantly, Fowler answers Yes: the disease is called brucellosis. The reason we may not have heard of it before is that it is usually diagnosed by vets: brucellosis is 'a zoonosis; that is to say, a disease of animals transmissible to man'. Most often it is found in cows. How then did Burns contrive to catch it? The offered explanation may already have sent new shudders through the Burns Clubs. According to Fowler, 'consumed raw, infected milk can initiate human brucellosis'. In other words, Burns may have caught it from his porridge.

In 1800, this analysis would also have raised a laugh, even among those who had found the Currie book distasteful. Opinions varied on the statistics of Burns's drinking and of his sexual escapades but there was no doubt in anybody's mind that there had been frequent deviations from the straight and narrow. When Burns's brother Gilbert tried to play down the 'injurious representations of my brother's character which have been given to the world', even he had to concede, on the question of alcohol, that when Burns 'removed to the town of Dumfries, temptations to this indulgence became more frequent . . . He never was, however, that slave to drinking which has been represented, and never drank but when in company.' To Burns's sympathisers, though, the question that mattered was not 'how much did he drink?' nor 'how many ladies' reputations did he help to ruin?'; what they wanted to know, quite simply, was: Is it correct that his personal habits should be the object of such ferocious scrutiny, such 'iron justice'?

Gilbert wrote his defence of his brother for an 1815 *Review of the Life of Robert Burns, and of Various Criticisms of his Character and Writings*, by Alexander Peterkin, and would eventually reprint it – along with other Peterkin materials – as an Appendix to his own 1820 republication of the Currie Life and Works (Currie's 1800 copyright having expired in 1814). The Peterkin volume assembled some stout and heartfelt vindications but it might never have been put together at all if the post-Currie slanders had been confined to the salons and taverns or to the popular prints. By the early 1800s, however, there had appeared a significant new presence, or irritant, on the literary landscape: the periodical review. The *Edinburgh Review*, launched in 1802, had rapidly established itself as an authoritative shaper of opinion, and its Scotch reviewers' verdict on this most Scotch of poets might well carry lasting weight. Francis Jeffrey's 1809 review of R. H. Cromek's *Reliques of Robert Burns* delivered what amounted to a confirmation of the Currie diagnosis. It delivered other things as well but for Burns's supporters it was biography that mattered. The Peterkin collection was in the nature of a last-ditch attempt to enter new evidence, although for most readers, by this time, the sentence was already passed.

The eighteenth century had had its reviewing journals but the *Edinburgh* was the first such publication to be free of publishers' manipulation, or 'puffery'. In a period marked by an 'irrepressible passion for discussion', it caught exactly the note of enlightened severity, liberal but not too liberal, that was needed by British intellectuals at this Revolutionary hour: it was forward-looking but not headstrong, and its tone of judicious condescension gave readers the feeling that in a necessarily changing world all the right old things could yet be made to stay in place. The *Edinburgh* soon bred imitators, and rivals. The Tory *Quarterly Review* was founded (by John Murray) in 1809; *Blackwood's Magazine* in 1817, by which date there were at least half a dozen others in the field.

We have already seen how Macaulay on Croker's Boswell determined a critical prejudice for sixty years. By the time Macaulay came to power, he was addressing an audience already well-banqueted on killer notices. Croker himself is now more famous for his *Quarterly* review of Keats than for his Boswell; Lockhart, for some, is better known for his 'Cockney School' bloodbaths in *Blackwood's* than for his *Life of Scott*, and Jeffrey's lasting celebrity owes almost everything these days to what he did, or tried to do, to Wordsworth. From its earliest issues, the *Edinburgh* had it in for the so-called Lake Poets (the inventing of snappy names for 'schools' of writers was another habit of the new reviewers). Jeffrey attacked Wordsworth's language as 'rude and negligent', his politics as 'splenetic and idle discontent with the existing institutions of society' and his nature worship as effortful and mainly bogus: 'It is possible enough, we allow, that the sight of a friend's garden spade, or a sparrow's nest, or a man gathering leeches, might really have suggested to such a mind a train of powerful impressions and interesting reflections, but it is certain that to most minds such associations will always appear forced, strained and unnatural.' In 1807, Jeffrey reviewed *Poems in Two Volumes* and denounced the Immortality Ode as 'illegible and unintelligible'; in 1815, he opened his piece on *The Excursion* with the notorious 'This will never do' and in the same year *The White Doe at Rylestone* was mocked as 'the very worst poem we ever saw imprinted in a quarto volume'. Jeffrey's tone was often that of an assassin, or a hanging judge, but he sometimes liked to see himself as a physician, or a nurse:

> The case of Mr Wordsworth, we perceive, is now manifestly hopeless; and we give him up as altogether incurable, and beyond the power of criticism. We cannot indeed altogether omit taking precautions now and then against the spreading of the malady; but for himself, though we shall watch the progress of his symptoms as a matter of professional curiosity and instruction, we really think it right not to harass him any longer with nauseous remedies, but rather to throw in cordials and lenitives, and wait in patience for the natural termination of the disorder.

It was in this year that Wordsworth was sent a copy of Alexander Peterkin's book in defence of Burns. One of the book's contributors, James Gray, had been friendly with Burns in Dumfries. He wanted to know, on behalf of Gilbert Burns, what further steps might be taken to mend the poet's 'injured reputation'. Specifically, Gilbert sought advice on the matter of republishing the Currie *Life*. Wordsworth was known to admire Burns: in 'Resolution and Independence', he had coupled him with Chatterton, seeing the pair of them as types of the glorious, doomed artist, and in 1803 he had composed a touching graveside elegy.

> I mourned with thousands, but as one
> Most deeply grieved, for He has gone
> Whose light I hailed when first it shone,
>     And showed my youth
> How verse may build a princely throne
>     On humble truth.

'Glory', 'joy', 'princely', 'like a star', 'fresh as a flower': Wordsworth on Burns owed nothing to the seamy revelations of biography, and this was an opportunity to say so. It was also an opportunity to strike back at Jeffrey and the *Edinburgh*. 'As to the Edinburgh Review,' he liked to say, 'I hold the author of it in entire contempt.' But he was furious at the treatment he was getting: to guess *how* furious we need to bear in mind that the *Edinburgh*'s was a new sort of reviewing and that Wordsworth was its first and favourite target. The jaunty bad-mouthing of *The Dunciad* and its like could be seen as kindergarten stuff compared to the sombre, momentous 'placing' of a Jeffrey or a Lockhart. The new reviewers (for all the nursemaid metaphors of Jeffrey) saw themselves as keepers of *the* flame, custodians of the tradition: it was their 'duty' to discriminate against unworthy candidates. Most writers of the day would rather have been chortled at as 'dunces' than to be gravely found wanting by these magistrates. The anonymity, the constant use of the regretful 'we', the pervasive assumption that all aspirants to literary fame were somehow out to fool the readership: these added up to a fearsome disincentive for any young writer with a 'new' programme of his own. Not everyone had Wordsworth's solemn sense of purpose: if he could be ruffled, who could not?

Jeffrey, in his article on Burns, had cleverly praised the plough-man's 'authentic rustics' and his genuine 'fidelity' to the spoken language at the expense of Wordsworth's 'puny affectations', and had instructed the Lake School to 'submit to be admonished by a self-taught and illiterate poet, who drew from Nature far more than they can do'. This was meant to hurt, but Wordsworth's instinct told him that the same class-snobbery that inflamed Jeffrey against him was also essential to the critic's attitude to Burns. Both Burns and Wordsworth were, to Jeffrey, beyond the social pale; they functioned on the margins, and it showed. Burns lacked 'chivalry', Wordsworth lacked a sense of the ridiculous: each of them might have benefited from some long exposure to metropolitan sophistication, but each – by birth or by perverse decision – was excluded from the vital mainstream:

> An habitual and general knowledge of the few settled and permanent maxims, which form the canon of general taste in all large and polished societies – a certain tact, which informs us at once that many things, which we still love and are moved by in secret, must necessarily be despised as childish, or derided as absurd, in all such societies – though it will not stand in the place of genius, seems necessary to the success of its exertions.

In agreeing to help cleanse the reputation of Burns, therefore, Wordsworth would be able to repair his own bruised self-esteem; above all, though, he would be able to defend poetry itself against these dangerous new styles of reductivism: there was a connection, he perceived, between Boswellian biography and the *Edinburgh*'s ad hominem reviewing. The impulse in each was to de-sanctify; for Wordsworth, to de-sanctify was to destroy. In a pamphlet entitled 'Letter to a Friend of Robert Burns', he 'well remembers':

> the acute sorrow with which, by my own fireside, I first perused Dr Currie's Narrative, and some of the letters, particularly those composed in the latter part of the poet's life. If my pity for Burns was extreme, this pity did not preclude a strong indignation, of which he was not the object. If, said I, it were in the power of a biographer to relate the truth, the *whole* truth, and nothing *but* the truth, the friends and surviving kindred of the deceased, for the sake of general benefit to mankind, might endure that such heart-rending communication should be made to the world. But in no case is this possible.

Biographical 'truth' is always partial truth: what good are facts unless we can penetrate the motives? Wordsworth attacks Currie for disregarding the sensitivities of Burns's widow and children, and for the 'ill-selected medley of correspondence' which he had exposed to public view. Burns wrote differently to different people and without thought of future publication: how can we know what he would actually have wished to say? Would Currie have exhibited such private materials if Burns had been of higher social rank, if he had not been one 'whose birth, education and employments had placed and kept him in a situation far below those in which the writers and readers of expensive volumes are usually found'? And, anyway, what purpose does all this *revealing* serve? Surely 'silence is a privilege of the grave, a right of the departed':

> Penalties of law, conventions of manners, and personal fear, protect the reputation of the living; and something of this protection is extended to the recently dead, – who survive, to a certain degree, in their kindred and friends. Few are so insensible as not to feel this, and not to be actuated by the feeling. But only to philosophy enlightened by the affections does it belong justly to estimate the claims of the deceased on the one hand, and of the present age and future generations, on the other; and to strike a balance between them. Such philosophy runs a risk of becoming extinct among us, if the coarse intrusions into the recesses, the gross breaches upon the sanctities, of domestic life, to which we have lately been more and more accustomed, are to be regarded as indications of a vigorous state of public feeling.

Wordsworth concedes that there might be some point in investigating the private lives of public men, those who 'have borne an active part in the world': in such cases, a knowledge of character can enable us to understand 'not only their own public conduct but that of those with whom they have acted'. But 'nothing of this applies to authors, considered merely as authors':

> Our business is with their books – to understand and to enjoy them. And, of poets more especially, it is true – that, if their works be good, they contain within themselves all that is necessary to their being compre-hended and relished . . . It is delightful to read what, in the happy exercise of his own genius, Horace chooses to communicate of himself and his friends; but I confess that I am not so much a lover of knowledge, independent of its quality, as to make it likely that it would much rejoice me, were I to hear that records of the Sabine poet and his contemporaries composed upon the Boswellian plan, had been unearthed among the ruins of Herculaneum . . . The least weighty objection to heterogeneous details, is that they are mainly superfluous, and therefore an encumbrance.

A more weighty objection is that such details can actually 'sully' an appreciation of the works, that – in the case of Burns – the 'remorseless hunters after fact' may have inclined readers to detect a 'hollowness', a fundamental unsoundness, in his poems. Should his art not be protected from his Life?

But what *about* the Life? What if 'all which has been raked up to the prejudice of Burns were literally true'? Here Wordsworth gets into something of a tangle. He begins by pleading that it is the 'privilege of poetic genius to catch . . . the spirit of pleasure where it may be found' and he acknowledges that Burns could not have written 'Tam o' Shanter' without knowing plenty about drink. What surely matters, though, is that this knowledge is fed into a poem which overall has a 'salutary moral effect'. The hero of the work – 'a desperate and sottish drunkard' – is made all the more repulsive by the poet's privately earned expertise. There was indeed a conflict in Burns between the 'order of his life' and the 'clearness of his views' (more or less as Currie said), and perhaps he would have been a greater poet if 'he could have controlled the propensities which his sensibility engendered'. But let no one imagine that Burns *liked* being bad: he 'preached from the text of his own errors' and experienced much 'personal suffering' when-ever he thought of his own 'thoughtless follies'. And here we seem to have drifted perilously close to biographical conjecture: which follies? what suffering? how do we know?

At around this point, Wordsworth presumably becomes aware that his argument is not really against biography but against the existing biographies of Burns and – more specifically – against a certain idle and malignant reviewer who has presumed to 'anatomise' the poet's 'moral character' on the basis of a Life that is, at best, but half a life. And this brings us neatly to one Francis Jeffrey: 'and him I single out because the author of the vindication of Burns [he means Peterkin] has treated his offences with comparative indulgence, to which he had no claim, and which, from whatever cause it might arise, has interfered with the dispensation of justice'. Then follows the sustained blast which, we suspect, Wordsworth has been brewing for some weeks:

> When a man, self-elected into the office of a public judge of the literature and life of his contemporaries, can have the audacity to go to these lengths in framing a summary of the contents of volumes that are scattered over every quarter of the globe, and extant in almost every cottage in Scotland, to give the lie to his labours; we must not wonder if, in the plenitude of his concern for the interests of abstract morality, the infatuated slanderer should have found no obstacle to prevent him from insinuating that the poet, whose writings are to this degree stained and disfigured, was 'one of the sons of fancy and of song who spend in vain superfluities the money that belongs of right to the pale industrious tradesman and the famishing infants; and who rave about friendship and philanthropy in a tavern, while their wives' hearts, &c &c.

(Wordsworth cannot bring himself to finish Jeffrey's sentence; it actually concludes: 'that it is a vile prostitution of language to talk of that man's generosity or goodness of heart, who sits raving about friendship and philanthropy in a tavern, while his wife's heart is breaking at her cheerless fireside, and his children pining in solitary poverty.')

Wordsworth's 'Letter to a Friend of Burns' is now spoken of as a key document in the history of biography, and rightly so. The oppositions it proposed – art versus life; genius versus conventional morality – are still extant; if Wordsworth was in a tangle, so are we. But there is a vehemence in his essay that may not altogether be accounted for by his loyalty to Burns, his dedication to the sanctity of poetry, nor even by his need to wreak revenge on Francis Jeffrey.

There was, as he well knew, an aspect of Burns's life over which

Currie did draw a decent veil: his ways with women. Currie hints that the poet was something of a whoremonger in his final months and hints that he may therefore have become sexually diseased. Currie no doubt hoped that Burns's widow, Jean Armour, would not pick up the 'pollution' innuendo or that, even if she did, she would be grateful that the Life did not itemise specific misdemeanours: after all, the Burns marriage had a somewhat irregular background. It is now believed that Burns 'initiated a recorded five, possibly six pregnancies in unmarried girls and in two instances there are grounds for suspecting consequential maternal death.' Mrs Burns certainly knew about one of the 'bastard weans'; she adopted Burns's daughter by the barmaid Anna Park. The probability is that she knew most of what there was to know. Even so, she would hardly welcome a string of claimants to the Burns estate, such as it was.

There were rumours, though, and Wordsworth would have heard them; with alarm, perhaps, since there was a 'wean' ingredient in his own biography which he had so far managed to keep fairly secret. Even *The Prelude* makes no reference to Annette Vallon. Currie's *Life of Burns* appeared not long before Wordsworth's second visit to France in 1802, when it was finally decided that he and Vallon would not marry; it was the first official literary life even to hint at sexual scandal. Wordsworth, who, from the beginning, had hoped that he 'might leave/Some monument behind me which pure hearts/Should reverence', had felt 'acute sorrow' and 'strong indignation' on first reading Currie's book. He may also have experienced an early intimation that immortality was not quite what it used to be.

# CHAPTER SEVEN

# BYRON AND THE BEST OF FRIENDS

'What an antithetical mind! – tenderness, roughness – delicacy, coarseness – sentiment, sensuality – soaring and grovelling, dirt and deity – all mixed up in that one compound of inspired clay!' This was Lord Byron, saying of Burns in 1813 what everybody else was saying about the author of *Childe Harold*. A year earlier, with the publication of that book, Byron 'at twenty-four . . . found himself on the highest pinnacle of literary fame, with Scott, Wordsworth, Southey, and a crowd of other distinguished writers, beneath his feet. There is scarcely an instance in history of so sudden a rise to so dizzy an eminence.' And, as we all know, it happened overnight.

Or did it? Byron from an early age had had the knack of drawing attention to himself and, once he had set up as a poet, it did not take him long to develop a certain nervously manipulative contempt for the general run of his spectators. 'A reforming age is always fertile of imposters', said Macaulay, and although Byron in his *English Bards and Scotch Reviewers* had been jauntily disdainful of the machinery by which literary reputations were established or destroyed, he could never quite free himself of the suspicion that a measure of imposture, a degree of carefully pre-planned theatricality, was essential to any successful cultural performance. He was not to know that many of those writers who rivalled him in fame – Moore, Rogers, Campbell and the like – would turn out to have been merely of the moment, but he did have an instinctive grasp of the shallowness of the taste he was learning to beguile.

Byron realised, as Burns did not, that it was good showbiz to be 'antithetical', 'mixed up'. An eighteenth-century mannerist with a nineteenth-century temperament, a neo-classicist subverted from within by curious romantic troubles, a hard-up and yet magnificently lordly lord, a philanderer whose heart was breakable, an egalitarian snob, a liberal reactionary, a foul-tempered sentimentalist – antithesis was the very stuff of Byronism and it provoked, in the audience, a fervently antithetical response: a pitying sort of envy, a censorious style of adulation, a love-hate:

> All the fairies, save one, had been bidden to his cradle. All the gossips had been profuse of their gifts. One had bestowed nobility, another genius, a third beauty. The malignant elf who had been uninvited, came last, and, unable to reverse what her sisters had done for their favourite, had mixed up a curse with every blessing. In the rank of Lord Byron, in his understanding, in his character, in his very person, there was a strange union of opposite extremes. He was born to all that men covet and admire. But in every one of those eminent advantages which he possessed over others, there was mingled something of misery and debasement.

Burns's mystique had been to do with disadvantages surmounted; Byron's thrived on the allure of squandered privilege. Burns felt that he had to suppress or disguise his satanic melancholia; Byron put his on parade, allowed it to foster a cult of ecstatic woefulness: legions of young admirers, we are told, learned how to curl the lip, shadow the brow, and turn themselves into 'things of dark imaginings – on whom the freshness of the heart ceased to fall like dew – whose passions had consumed themselves to dust, and to whom the relief of tears was denied'. According to their parents, they also ran the risk of learning the 'two great commandments' of committed Byronism: 'to hate your neighbour and to love your neighbour's wife'.

If Burns was the first writer to be pilloried after death for his personal 'frailties', Byron was the first to make a gripping public drama out of his most private miseries. Post-1816, there can have been few readers who did not know how to decode this poet's work in terms of the acrimonious break-up of his marriage: a break-up that was known to columnists, cartoonists and reviewers as – in capitals – The Separation. Lady Byron, almost everybody knew, had left the poet after not many months of marriage, taking their baby daughter with her. Byron wanted them back, or so he said, but his wife was as notable for moral rectitude as he was for its opposite, and would not relent. She and her sundry advisers let the world know that his Lordship's marital offence had been so heinous that it could neither be forgiven nor described.

What might it have *been*? The question instantly became central to the Byron myth, at all levels of sophistication. Infidelity, homosexuality, incest (with his half-sister Augusta Leigh), venereal disease:

or was it something other, something worse, an occult nuptial-bed malpractice not even to be guessed at by ordinary brides and grooms? 'There is no vice,' said Lady Byron, 'with which he has not endeavoured to familiarise me.' Rumours became ever more exotic and were variously stoked, not least by Byron's Tory foes. The most glamorous poet of the day found himself ostracised in the salons and, with bailiffs closing in on his far-too-expensive London residence, he decided he had had enough: he would renounce an England that was in the process of renouncing him. He made an early-morning dash for Dover in his brand-new Napoleonic carriage, with faithful entourage (both man and beast) in tow, possessions more or less intact, and with head angrily, Byronically, held high.

From Switzerland and then from Italy, the poet fought his corner, bringing to bear on his estranged wife the complete Byronic box of tricks: rages, tears, insults, imprecations, satires, and so on. He wrote the lachrymose poem 'Fare Thee Well' and must have believed that, if anything could melt her Ladyship, this would: the piece activated his full armoury of lyric fire-power. But when it found its way into the public prints, Lady Byron was furious, seeing it as just another ploy, a blatant bid for public sympathy:

> Fare thee well! and if for ever,
>   Still for ever, fare thee well:
> Even though unforgiving, never
>   'Gainst thee shall my heart rebel.

Byron was not accustomed to the sort of woman who could respond to this most tenderly phrased onslaught by demanding to know what he meant exactly by the word 'unforgiving'. Lady Byron was a poet herself, in a small way, but she was also a mathematician. Mathematicians have no taste for antitheses, for things that don't add up. 'It is unhappily your disposition,' she told him very early on, 'to consider what you *have* as worthless – what you have *lost* as invaluable. But remember that you believed yourself most miserable when I was yours.'

For half a dozen years, the Separation was a hot item, kept alive by reports of Byron's continental goings-on, his association with the Shelley gang in Pisa, and not least by the poet's often provocative compositions, both in prose and verse. By the time Byron left for his Greek adventure in 1824, opinion at home had hardened against him

111

and – worse still, perhaps – there were signs of a falling-off in the public fascination. Byron 'fancied' that 'he had become *low*, that the *better* English thought him out of fashion, and voted him vulgar.' So far as the world could tell, The Separation was at stalemate; evidently Lady Byron's lips were now permanently sealed. And the news of his Lordship was that he was slowing down: the scandal of *Don Juan* was nearly two years old, the celebrated looks were fading, the money problems were under control (thanks to a sizeable inheritance resulting from his marriage contract), and there was even a regular girlfriend: a neighbour's wife, admittedly, but regular. The most scandalous thing Byron had done lately was to help start up a short-lived little magazine – with Leigh Hunt, of all people. The myth was in need of some grand revitalising gesture.

And then Lord Byron died, at the age of thirty-six. Some commentators have been tempted to write it as: and so he died. His demise in the swamps of Missolonghi transmuted image into icon and bequeathed one splendid last antithesis: the supreme egotist died for a foreign cause. This, at any rate, was the burden of most of the obituaries, both public and private, and although Byron was denied a niche in the Abbey, there was no failure of national homage when his body was shipped back to England. Only his worst enemies – like Southey – failed to 'squeeze tears to his memory'. 'Even detraction has been silenced at his tomb,' said Hazlitt, one of his detractors, and Carlyle – who would later refer to Byron as a 'huge sulky Dandy' – gave way to great moanings of personal distress:

> Poor Byron! Alas poor Byron! The news of his death came down upon my heart like a mass of lead; and yet, the thought of it sends a painful twinge through all my being, as if I had lost a Brother! O God! That so many sons of mud and clay should fill up their base existence to its utmost bound, and this, the noblest spirit in Europe, should sink before half his course was run! Late so full of fire and generous passion, and proud purposes, and now forever dumb and cold.

*The Times* was unable to forget altogether its editorial policy on the Byronic mode but, in trying to do so, it properly divined the public appetite:

> There were individuals more to be approved of for moral qualities than Lord Byron – to be more safely followed, or more tenderly beloved; but there lives no man on earth whose sudden departure from it, under the

circumstances in which that nobleman was cut off, appears to us more calculated to impress the mind with profound and unmingled mourning.

Byron's literary executor was John Cam Hobhouse (later on Lord Broughton), one of his oldest and most loyal friends; adviser, confidant, financial go-between, but remembered now for his contribution to English literature's best-known act of executive vandalism: the destruction of Lord Byron's memoirs. On paper, Hobhouse was indeed the ideal keeper of the Byron flame, or conflagration: a fiery enough radical in his youth and then a busily reformist Member of Parliament (in 1824 he was not long out of jail, having served a few months in Newgate for a so-called 'breach of privilege'; ie he wrote a pamphlet), he was generally regarded as having had a restraining, not to say dampening influence on his vulcanic friend. Four years older than the poet, Hobhouse had literary interests but no great personal ambition as a writer; he was privy to Byron's secrets but was temperamentally discreet; he was of sufficient rank not to be pushed around but not so highly placed that he might disdain the humbler duties of the keepership. Byron once called him his 'Alter Ego' and 'tantamount to myself during my absence – or presence – ', and this was pretty much how Hobhouse liked to see himself.

In life, Byron often leaned on Hobhouse and seemed to have enjoyed his company, in shortish bursts. He took Hobhouse with him on part of his 'grand tour' of 1808–11 and allowed him to write notes for the fourth canto of *Childe Harold*. He also had him as groomsman at the ill-starred wedding (Byron suggested that Hobhouse might get married also, on the same day, so that they could be 'like people electrified in company through the same chain'.) It was Hobhouse who helped to 'liberate' Byron from Caroline Lamb, and he served as his chief spokesman at The Separation. As a member of the London Greek Committee, it was Hobhouse who encouraged the poet-hero to pursue his last adventure.

Hobhouse's love of Byron had significantly coloured his young manhood. It was a modest, undemanding sort of love; a second-fiddle, Boswellian attachment from which the junior partner expected little for himself. Or so it seemed. Hobhouse, though, was not a natural subordinate; his devotion had a price. He wanted, above all, to be acknowledged not just as Byron's friend but as his *best* friend, the one who mattered to him most. There were, of course, numerous contenders for this office, as Hobhouse would readily concede:

'Byron's power of attaching those about him to his person was such as no one I ever knew possessed. No human being could approach him without being sensible of his magical influence.' But, in a way, the more numerous the better: to be chosen as the first from so many was a privilege to be fought for and held onto. Whenever Hobhouse's rank as chief disciple came under threat, his normal equilibrium went haywire.

As literary executor, Hobhouse became Byron's representative-on-earth. He possessed the unpossessable; Byron's love of him was made official. Or was it? Again, there seemed no way of being certain. There was always an unease, an anxiety that at some point Byron himself, the love-object, might prove treacherous, that in the great stack of papers which would now come into the keeper's keeping there might be something unnerving about *him*, something that would mock his loyalty, make his ardour seem ridiculous, one-sided. Byron was a bit like that in life; why not in after-life? 'His principal failing,' Hobhouse said, 'was a wish to mystify those persons with whom he lived, especially if they were in an inferior condition and of inferior intellect to himself.'

It seems fairly certain that Hobhouse, the sensible, judicious and dependable best friend, was unaware of any destabilising factor in his own make-up. The posthumous curiosity about Byron was in general vulgar enough for an executor to feel that a policy of resistance was both dignified and decent. It was safe to play it safe. Once or twice, though, and in ways that seem to have been 'out of character', Hobhouse performed with weird impulsiveness. Most notoriously, there was the matter of the Memoirs. The bulk of this 400-page manuscript was composed between 1818 and 1821, and not long after starting it, Byron outlined the project to John Murray:

> The *Life* is *Memoranda* not Confessions. I have left out all my *loves* (except in a general way) and many other of the most important things (because I must not compromise other people), so that it is like the play of Hamlet – 'the part of Hamlet omitted by particular desire'. But you will find many opinions, and some fun, with a detailed account of my marriage and its consequences, as true as a party concerned can make such accounts, for I suppose we are all prejudiced.

To Lady Byron, he described it with more feeling:

You will perhaps say *why* write my life? – Alas! I say so too – but they who have traduced it – & blasted it – and branded me – should know that it is they – and not I – are the cause – It is no great pleasure to have lived – and less to live over again the details of existence – but the last becomes sometimes a necessity and even a duty.

The first Hobhouse knew of all this was in 1821 when he heard that Byron had handed over the near-completed manuscript of the Memoirs to the poet Thomas Moore. So far as Byron was concerned, this handing-over had made perfect sense. He liked Moore, and Moore was short of money. By using the Memoirs to raise a loan from John Murray, against the proceeds of publication after Byron's death (then thought to be a long way off), Moore was able to get the £2000 he needed and to lodge the manuscript where it would be safe from loss, or theft. Hobhouse, though, was sorely needled by the whole transaction. 'Lord Byron,' he said, 'made a present of himself to Mr Moore. Mr Moore sold his Lordship to the booksellers.' It pained him to know that Moore, in his view a lightweight Irish chancer, had been the first to be allowed a sight of this most private document. And it further rankled that Byron had given 'Mr Moore the permission to show the manuscript to the "Elect". Whom his Lordship meant to designate by that epithet it is not very easy to divine.' Moore did indeed pass the manuscript around 'to many persons', but he did not offer it to Hobhouse: no one did. And when Hobhouse protested to his Lordship, seeking as usual to protect his friend's best interests, Byron was upsettingly dismissive:

With regard to 'the Memoirs'. I can only say that Moore acted entirely with my approbation in the whole transaction . . . Do you really mean to say that I have not as good a right to leave such a MS after my death as the thousands who have done the same? Is there no *reason* that I should? Will not my life (it is egotism – but you know this is true of all men who have *had* a name even if they survive it) be given in a false and unfair point of view to others? I mean false as to *praise* as well as *censure*. If you have any *personal* feelings upon it, I can say, as far as I can recollect, that you are mentioned without anything that could annoy you, and if otherwise it shall be cut out.

Hobhouse had plenty of 'personal feelings upon it', but Byron rather obtusely fails to guess what they might be – a costly negligence.

When Byron died, Hobhouse's first thought, 'after the first access of grief was over', was 'to lose no time in doing my duty by preserving all that was left to me of my friend – his fame'. His first act, more or less, was to begin arranging for the destruction of the Memoirs, and there was a mad exhilaration, almost, in the way he set about it. He had not read the Memoirs and could hardly have been surprised or shocked by what was in them (Byron's letters to Hobhouse are ablaze with bawdy) but he had a fixed, now thoroughly habitual, hostility to the *idea* of them. They represented to him Byron's soft spot for Thomas Moore and as long as Moore had access to these papers there was a good chance that he would end up using them as the basis for a biography. Hobhouse was against biography, and the notion of *this* one made his blood boil. (Indeed, he had told Byron that by giving the Memoirs to Moore 'you might appear to have bought a biographer under the pretext of doing a generous action.') One of his chief tasks as executor would be to stop Moore writing Byron's Life: in this he failed but not for want of trying, and some of Hobhouse's most poignant writings can be found pencilled in the margins of Moore's *Life*.

In 1824, though, he was determined that such horrors would not come to pass. He had managed to persuade himself, and would later swear that Byron, towards the end of his life, had changed his mind about the Moore transaction, that he had come to regret it and wished that he could, with delicacy, retrieve the Memoirs and suppress them. Thus the executor provided himself with a means of representing his passion for destruction as a passion for obedience. And yet for one so vocally sure of his ground, Hobhouse moved with suspicious swiftness. He learned of Byron's death on 14 May. On 17 May, in John Murray's Albemarle Street office, Byron's pages were fed to the flames.

In these three days, the grieving Hobhouse managed to lobby all the likely claimants to Lord Byron's relic. John Murray needed no lobbying: he had been advised by the *Quarterly*'s William Gifford that the Memoirs were 'fit only for the brothel and would damn Lord Byron to everlasting infamy'. Lady Byron, who had spurned her husband's offer to let her read the manuscript and, if so inclined, make alterations, had for three years been urging their suppression, so she too was no problem. Even so, Hobhouse painstakingly honoured the formalities. Augusta Leigh, rumoured to be the most likely victim if publication were allowed, fussed and flapped, took conflicting advice, fussed some more and then tamely acquiesced: surely all these authoritative men knew what was best? By the 17th only Moore remained to be persuaded – or over-ruled.

Moore protested that to burn 'without any previous perusal or deliberation would be throwing a stigma upon the work, which it did not deserve'. He had read the manuscript and judged it to be largely innocuous. What if he bought it back from Murray? To this purpose, he raised £2000 from Longmans, but Murray would not sell. Moore then pleaded that perhaps some extracts could be saved. Request denied. Or perhaps the Memoirs could be placed under seal, in a bank? Suggestion over-ruled. Hobhouse then reminded Moore of another suggestion he had made; namely that the manuscript should be given, unopened, to Augusta Leigh. Well, yes, said Moore. All right then, replied Hobhouse: Miss Leigh's 'wish and intention [was] that the Mss. should be destroyed'. To this, Moore had no answer: the best he could manage was to demand that it be put on record that 'I protest against the burning, as contradictory to Lord Byron's wishes and unjust to me.' 'Whatever you please,' said Hobhouse, 'but I protest against your protestation.'

A little scene in Hobhouse's rooms conveys a sense of the prevailing atmosphere of bullying and bluster. The interested parties had gathered there before setting off to Murray's office for the burning. A friend of Moore's, one Henry Luttrell, had come along to lend his counsel and rather diffidently ventured that 'he could see no harm in reading the manuscript':

> Mr Hobhouse insisted very strongly on the impropriety of such a proceeding. Mr Moore said that both Mr Wilmot Horton and Colonel Doyle, friends of Lady Byron and of Lord Byron's family, saw no objection to the perusal of the Memoirs. Mr Hobhouse remarked that he could hardly bring himself to believe that; and Mr Murray stated that those two gentlemen themselves were at this moment waiting at his house in order to be present at the destruction of the Memoirs.
>
> On hearing this, this whole party left Mr Hobhouse's rooms and proceeded to Mr Murray's house in Albemarle Street.

It was Doyle and Horton, in the end, who tore up the pages and put them on the fire. At one point Horton 'passed a handful of the papers to Hobhouse, thinking that, as Byron's executor, he might wish to share the responsibility; but Hobhouse declined since, though he was acting in accordance with Augusta's wishes, he was not formally empowered by her.'

We might have hoped that at the last moment Thomas Moore would have leaped forward and put a stop to the grotesque ceremony. He was, after all, still the only one present at the burning who knew exactly what was being burned. Moore's position, though, was complicated, if not undermined, by the money factor. He was already nervous that his too vehement pleas for preservation had been interpreted as mere financial greed. On this score, he was extremely touchy: a grocer's son from Ireland, he was susceptible to any appeal addressed to his 'gentlemanly sense of honour'. Hobhouse and Murray knew his weakness and exploited it – to the extent that Moore, after the burning, would feel obliged to repay the £2000 that Murray had originally advanced. It was Moore whom Murray was addressing when he delivered a last statement before the adjournment to Albemarle St. The transcription is by Hobhouse:

> I do not care whose the Mss. are; here am I as a tradesman; I do not care a farthing about having your money, or whether I ever get it or not; but such regard have I for Lord Byron's fame and honour that I am willing and am determined to destroy these Mss. which have been read by Mr Gifford, who says they would be damaging to Lord Byron's name. It is very hard that I, as a tradesman, should be willing to make a sacrifice which you, as a gentleman, will not consent to.

According to Hobhouse, Moore called on him several months after the burning and admitted that his protests had been misguided. 'He told me that his conduct had often been attacked, even by friends, but that he silenced them by saying that Byron told me his wishes that the Memoirs should not be published. After some more talk on Byron, and his saying several times, "You were much more his friend than I can pretend to have been" he went away.' On this, Doris Langley Moore has aptly, if colourfully, commented:

> If only Hobhouse had been given that comforting assurance just seven months earlier . . . Byron's autobiography might now have its place on our shelves beside Rousseau's *Confessions*: for what his heart, in the first throes of grief, revolted against . . . was that Moore should be enabled to advertise to the world an intimacy with Byron which might be thought to eclipse his own.

On the day after the bonfire at John Murray's, Hobhouse received a message from Lady Byron suggesting that he should appoint himself as the poet's official biographer. She and the family, she said, would be prepared to offer their co-operation; between them, they would be able to forestall 'all spurious efforts' that might be made by others. Hobhouse replied that he had neither the 'spirits' nor the 'inclination' for the task, and later on confided to his journal: 'Poor Byron! Here is his dear friend Tom Moore, his publisher, Murray, and his wife: the first thing they think of is writing his Life or getting it written. Such are the friendships of great authors!'

Hobhouse might briefly have imagined that he could protect Byron from the biographers, that he could keep him for himself. Certainly this was the position he adopted at the outset. Within a year, though, he was beginning to have second thoughts. From the moment that the news of Byron's death reached England, the presses had begun cranking out the quickie Lives. Between 1824 and 1825 there were: *Full Particulars of the Much Lamented Death of Lord Byron*; *The Life and Genius of Lord Byron*; *Anecdotes of Lord Byron from Authentic Sources*; *Letters on the Character and Poetical Genius of Lord Byron*; *Inquiry into the Moral Character of Lord Byron*, and half a dozen others. The burning of the Memoirs had precisely the effect that Moore predicted: it threw a 'stigma' on the suppressed manuscript and encouraged a new bout of speculation on the subject of the 'reality' behind the recharged poet-hero myth.

For example, Thomas Medwin's *Conversations of Lord Byron*, rushed out in 1824, was a catchpenny concoction, full of ludicrous inaccuracies, and based on but four months' not very close association with the poet, but it cleverly won notoriety by announcing itself to be in deliberate opposition to the Albemarle Street cover-up:

> 'A great poet belongs to no country; his works are public property, and his Memoirs the inheritance of the public.' Such were the sentiments of Lord Byron; and have they been attended to? Has not a manifest injustice been done to the world, and an injury to his memory, by the destruction of his Memoirs? These are questions which it is now late, perhaps needless to ask; but I will endeavour to lessen, if not to remedy, the evil.
>
> I am aware that in publishing these reminiscences I shall have to contend with much obloquy from some parts of his family, – that I shall incur the animosity of many of his friends. There are authors, too, who will not be pleased to find their names in print, – to hear his real opinion of themselves, or of their works. There are others – but I have the satisfaction of feeling that I have set about executing the task I have undertaken, conscientiously: I mean neither to throw a veil over his errors, nor a gloss over his virtues.

119

Medwin did indeed 'incur the animosity' of Byron's friends, and he was right to suspect that there would be those who might take exception to the discovery of Byron's 'real opinion of themselves, or of their works'. John Murray, in particular, was pained to find himself disparaged in these pages as a moral coward and a grasping profiteer. It so happened that Medwin had been in Pisa when Byron was feeling out of sorts with Murray because of the tradesman's pusillanimous attitude to the publication of *Don Juan* and was anyway, it seems, in one of his 'Everybody hates Everybody' moods. Murray, of course, *knew* that Byron had been cross with him around that time, but seeing the dialogue in print brought a different, harder-to-swallow, sort of knowledge:

> Mr Murray is tender of my fame! How kind in him! He is afraid of my writing too fast. Why? Because he has a tenderer regard for his own pocket, and does not like the look of any new acquaintance, in the shape of a book of mine, till he has seen his old friends in a variety of new faces; *id est* disposed of a vast many editions of the former works . . . It is not easy to deal with Mr Murray . . . the most nervous of God's booksellers. When 'Don Juan' first came out, he was so frightened that he made a precipitate retreat into the country, shut himself up, and would not open his letters. The fact is, he prints for too many Bishops.

And so it went on, for several pages. Murray wrote a reply in the *Gentleman's Magazine* and a bit later Hobhouse weighed in too, along with other Murray friends: Medwin's inaccuracies were exposed and ridiculed, his motives called in question, his reporting skills deplored, but the sour taste he left was hard to shift.

Hobhouse, with indignation, watched Murray suffer what he himself most feared, and it was this old fear – of Byron's treacherously slack mouth – that guided his negotiations in the first major challenge to his executor's authority – the case of R. C. Dallas (or 'Damn'd ass' and 'Dull ass', as Hobhouse soon would be describing him). Robert Dallas was a moralising bore from out of Lord Byron's adolescence. A cousin of the poet, thirty years older and something of a man of letters, he had got in touch with the nineteen-year-old Byron when his first book, *Hours of Idleness*, appeared. Byron at that stage was glad of senior attention and for a period adopted Dallas as his mentor and unofficial literary agent, giving him presents of one or two important copyrights. Byron soon tired of his kinsman's proprietorial demeanour and Dallas, sensing the decline of his influence, became ever more scolding of the poet's godless ways. By the time of Byron's exile, it had become possible for Dallas to let it be known that it was he who had withdrawn, disillusioned, from the friendship.

Hobhouse had met Dallas now and then, and knew Byron's opinion of him, but saw him as, at least, a figure of much rectitude. It was something of a shock, then, for him to read, in June 1824, a publisher's announcement promising the *Private Correspondence of Lord Byron including his Letters to his Mother . . . connected by Memorandums and Observations* by R. C. Dallas. Hobhouse at once protested both to author and publisher, pointing out that Dallas had no rights to these letters and that their publication could have damaging effects: 'in confidential correspondence, individuals might be slightingly wounded en passant and their feelings most sorely wounded.' He threatened to move an injunction against the book if the letters were not removed. The publisher shrugged: for him this was 'merely . . . a commercial speculation' and in any case the letters had, he said, been long ago handed to Dallas by Lord Byron, with permission to use them as he pleased: 'Some day or another they will be curiosities.'

Dallas himself was in poor health and his reply to Hobhouse was written by his son Alexander, a clergyman even more fiercely upright than his father: 'There is no man on earth, Sir, who loved Lord Byron more truly, or was more jealous of his fair name, than my father, as long as there was a possibility of his name being fair.' Evidently the book was to be a parable of moral disrepair, with Dallas portrayed as the guiding light whom Byron had wilfully ignored in his 'unhesitating abandonment to the blindness of vice'. Hobhouse was of course familiar with the Dallas line and would probably have stomached a routinely sanctimonious critique, but to overlook the unauthorised publication of the letters would be to create a dangerous precedent. He determined to take the case to law and this determination was no more than briefly ruffled by the sight of a letter that Dallas Sr had written to Augusta Leigh. Referring to Hobhouse's objections, Dallas maintained that he had already cut his manuscript by 'nearly a half' so as to 'avoid giving pain, even to those that deserve it' but that Hobhouse's 'insolence' had persuaded him to reconsider:

> If I restore any portion of what I have crossed out, shall I not be justified by the insolence of the letter I have received from a pretended friend of Lord Byron, and who seems to be ignorant that a twenty-year companionship can exist without a spark of friendship! I do not wonder at his agitation; it is for himself that he is agitated, not for Lord Byron.

The innuendo was of course disturbing but Hobhouse correctly guessed the Dallas strategy: for him to press for an injunction now would seem like self-protection. He decided he would take that risk and three days later he successfully applied for an interim block on the book. But the Dallas letter troubled him: what *was* it that Byron had said that had made it possible for Dallas to crow about 'twenty years' companionship without a spark of friendship'? Two weeks later, he knew the answer and was mightily relieved. Through a third party, he learned that in the Dallas book he 'was named several times in terms of praise' and that the only doubtful ingredient was a reported remark of Byron's to the effect that 'Hobhouse is going home. I am glad of it for I am tired of him', to which he had added, 'this is my fault, for I am grown misanthropical.' So *that* was all it was.

Hobhouse was now thoroughly emboldened to press for a permanent injunction: 'to put a stop if possible to publishing Lord B's private letters, as well as to protect the property – upon principle.' The case – and it turned out to be a landmark case in the history of copyright law – was heard in the Court of Chancery by Lord Eldon in August 1824. Eldon's judgment read, in part, as follows:

> The property in letters is . . . that if A writes a letter to B, B has the property in that letter, for the purpose of reading and keeping it, but no property in it to publish it.

He also opined that, although Byron's actual words were protected by copyright, the substance of the letters could be reported: the wily Dallases would later rewrite all the correspondence 'in the form of a third-person narrative'.

In the meantime, though, they were rattled by the judgment. Dallas Sr was now seriously ill in Paris (he died a few months later) and by this suppression he stood to lose his £500 publisher's advance. A change of tune was necessitated and in late August Alexander wrote to Hobhouse offering – said Hobhouse – to 'cut out *two* things that might hurt my feelings'. *Two* things? Hobhouse knew of one. But he refused to be blackmailed: 'I resolved after some consideration not to answer this letter, but I keep it. Had it not been for the sort of menace in the conclusion of it perhaps I might have given some reply to it.' Brave words. The Dallases, not hearing from him, defiantly issued a French translation of the letters, with biography attached. By the end of September, Hobhouse was able to read the second hurtful thing. And this time it *was* hurtful. Fifteen years earlier, Byron had written from Greece to his mother:

> The Marquess of Sligo, my old fellow collegian, is here and wishes to accompany me into the Morea. We shall go together for that purpose but I am woefully sick of travelling companions, after a year's experience of Mr Hobhouse, who is on his way to Great Britain.

Hobhouse could not so easily rationalise this new disparagement. The phrase 'after a year's experience of Mr Hobhouse' seemed, at a stroke, to cancel out a fondly remembered stretch of shared experience and from now on Byron's sneer would always trouble him. There is a touching annotation in Hobhouse's copy of Moore's *Life* (which came out in 1832). When the ever-genial Moore tries to explain away the Byron insult by suggesting that the poet had become so 'enamoured' of 'lonely musings, that even the society of his fellow-traveller . . . grew at last to be a chain and burden to him', Hobhouse irritably comments: 'On what authority does Tom say this? He has not the remotest grasp of the real reason which induced Lord B. to prefer having no Englishman immediately [or] constantly with him.' We now suspect that the 'real reason' mentioned here was that Lord Byron wished to intensify his unEnglish adventures with 'the youths of the Athens monastery'. Just as certain of the poet's ill-considered quips lingered unsettlingly in the imaginations of his friends, so this unguarded jotting by Hobhouse has left its own questionable mark on Byron's much-mauled after-fame.

Hobhouse's executive embarrassments would usually spring to life when he crossed the thin line between keeping and possessing and nobody was more likely to tempt him into such transgression than the not-always-innocent Tom Moore. If Moore had been permitted to go ahead with his biography of Byron when the idea of it was first broached there is a good chance that the Medwins and the Dallases would have been given pause. But Hobhouse was set against the project, against Moore, from the outset, telling him that he saw 'no good in a life of our late friend' and making it pretty clear that he thought Moore was in it for the money. Negotiations dragged on for three years, with much bickering between Hobhouse, Moore and Murray. It was only when Leigh Hunt's scurrilous memoir appeared in 1828 that the three of them agreed to bury their differences. Moore's

*Life*, when it appeared four years later, was generally agreed to be as diplomatic as could be hoped for in the circumstances. Even Hobhouse, for all his local annotations, had to agree that it was a passably accurate portrayal.

On the matter of the Separation, Moore had tried to be circuitous, but it was clear enough to Lady Byron, and to others, that he was fundamentally on Byron's side. The impression his book gave was that a moderately wronged wife, urged on by her family and her 'advisers', had behaved with some inflexibility and by innuendo and sustained refusal to negotiate had damaged an admittedly far-from-perfect husband's name. In other words, Moore had tried to be impartial but had failed. Lady Byron at once issued a fifteen-page pamphlet, ostensibly in defence of her maligned relatives (Moore had quoted a few choice Byronisms on the subject of her family): she was not, she said, going to provide 'domestic details' but she did wish it to be known that she had had the best, or worst, reasons for refusing to entertain Byron's offered reconciliation. There were facts 'utterly unknown' to Moore and to the world at large which, if revealed, would vindicate her. With this pamphlet, and its busy reception in the periodicals, the Separation controversy had come alive once more; this time, however, the chattering had a somewhat exasperated edge – why would she not tell all? 'She should speak,' said 'Christopher North' in *Blackwood's*, 'or someone for her. One word would suffice.'

Lady Byron died in 1860, with lips sealed, or so it was believed. And in any case, by then the controversy was more or less forgotten. In 1868, though, the aged Countess Guiccioli (Byron's last great love) published her adoring reminiscences. In these, Lady Byron was cast as an 'absolute moral monstrosity, an anomaly in the history of types of female hideousness' (Guiccioli also believed that Byron had never seduced a woman, did not drink and was of an essentially forgiving disposition). Most reviewers laughed off the book as love-sick but in America it provoked an extraordinary response from none other than Harriet Beecher Stowe, who reported to the readers of *Macmillan's Magazine* that shortly before her death Lady Byron *had* in fact unsealed those lips and that she, Stowe, had been her chosen confidante. Her Ladyship, said Stowe, had revealed to her 'with an intensity of repressed emotion . . . the great fact upon which all turned.' Byron, she reported: 'was guilty of incest with his sister!'

he said that it was no sin; that it was the way the world was first peopled;

the Scriptures taught that all the world descended from one pair; and how could that be unless brothers married their sisters? that, if not a sin then, it could not be a sin now.

I immediately said, 'Why, Lady Byron, those are the very arguments given in the drama of "Cain".'

'The very same,' was her reply. 'He could reason very speciously on this subject.' She went on to say that when she pressed him hard with the universal sentiment of mankind as to the horror and the crime, he took another turn, and said that the horror and crime were the very attraction; that he had worn out all *ordinary* forms of sin, and that he *'longed for the stimulus of a new kind of vice'*.

The Stowe article (later amplified to book length) whipped up a great storm on both sides of the Atlantic but was generally denounced as scandal-mongering, and probably mendacious. It was hard for most readers to imagine Byron saying to his wife – 'in the sneering tone which was common with him' – things like: 'The world will believe me, and it will *not* believe you. The world has made up its mind that "By" is a glorious boy; and the world will go for "By", right or wrong. Besides, I shall make it my life's object to discredit you: I shall use all my powers.' There was also an air of desperation in Stowe's raking around in *Manfred*, *Cain*, *Childe Harold* and elsewhere for incriminating lines and stanzas. Where was the documentary proof?

Forty years later, after the Separation controversy had undergone a second death, the 'proof' arrived, in the shape of *Astarte*, a privately printed 'Fragment of Truth Concerning George Gordon, Sixth Lord Byron – recorded by his grandson Ralph Milbanke, Earl of Lovelace'. Lovelace was the son of Ada, child of the dread Byron marriage. Ada had died young, and Ralph was largely brought up by his grand-mother, Lady Byron, who had it seems educated him in Separation-lore. Now, somewhat late in the day, he had determined to 'clear away once and for all the cloud of calumnies and injustices which had settled around certain facts'. The Lovelace case is essentially the same as Stowe's ('Astarte' is the name of the beloved sister in Byron's *Manfred*), but with documentation: letters between Byron and Augusta, papers relating to the Separation, details of Lady Byron's traffic with Augusta and vice versa. It is a tedious, intemperate presentation and on its first, furtive appearance was widely con-demned for mean-spiritedly digging up old enmities. In 1921, an enlarged version was published, on the open market, by Lovelace's widow in an attempt, she said, to defend *her* dead husband's honour.

This time round, opinion was divided: on the evidence, it was still possible to argue that Byron's passion for his sister was platonic – rather too much of the *Astarte* deposition hinged on a single love-letter of 1817 from which the addressee's name had been expunged. Lovelace said the letter was written to Augusta; others were not so sure. Incest or no incest, though, most readers were probably repelled by the spectacle of Byron's grandson so busy with the vitriol. The new edition of the book ran to over three hundred and fifty pages: all in order to document a 100-year-old passion.

The nakedly polemical intent of *Astarte* gave rise to suspicions that the documentation it presented might well have been rigged (and so it was). After all, Lovelace had sole access to the papers and when, after the death of his wife, they passed into the keeping of Judith, Lady Wentworth (the daughter of Ralph's sister, Anne), a strict embargo was imposed. Indeed, it was not until the mid-1950s, when Doris Langley Moore breached the Ockham Park defences, that the full story of the 'late Lord Byron' could be told. Moore's untidy but entertaining study accepts the incest accusation but awards few marks to Lady Byron and her pious retinue – or, for that matter, to the scattily disloyal Augusta Leigh. Byron is portrayed as a character far too complicated and oblique (and humorous) to be fathomed by any of his close associates – and was thus singularly ill-served by those who set themselves up as the custodians of his posterity. Too many second- raters wanted a piece of him: this, roughly speaking, was the verdict of Doris Langley Moore. And Byron, of course, used to say the same kind of thing himself.

When Doris Langley Moore made her first attempt on the Lovelace Papers in 1957, she was granted an interview by Lady Wentworth, Byron's great-granddaughter. Moore approached the meeting with much nervousness because Lady Wentworth 'had certainly been brought up to believe Lady Byron all saint, Lord Byron all sinner, and the idea that there was any other point of view to be expressed might be utterly unacceptable to her'. The quaking interviewer might have taken comfort, though, from a study of Lady Wentworth's own parental background. Ten years earlier, these paragraphs appeared in the letters columns of the *Listener* magazine:

> Not the least of [my mother's] incredibility was that in spite of her light-hearted vitality and the endowment of astonishing genius and artistic gifts

. . . she generously allowed these gifts to suffer almost total eclipse in order to enhance those of a uniquely outrageous husband . . . That she carried this subservience and self-obliteration such as no woman today would tolerate for a moment was so incredible as to lead to a complete misunderstanding by the outside world, a misunderstanding fostered by [my father] to cover up his own lapses by the very common 'erring husband's' fiction that his wild impassioned poetic nature was suffering frustration from a cold prudish unsympathetic partner . . .

In justice to him and his dupes I must add that his astonishing good looks from childhood on brought him such intoxicating incense as is given to few men. No one could overlook him or forget him. He had as a young man the face of a Greek God and always retained those chiselled features and those magnetic glowing eyes which drove women crazy. Truly was he unique. Even those who suffered most and realised to the full his heartless egoism never quite escaped that fatal magic but returned again and again to perish like a moth in the candle. To many, including myself, he was a glorious ideal which crashed into dust to their everlasting grief.

The magnetic villain here is Wilfred Scawen Blunt, poet, lover, orientalist, adventurer, champion of the underdog, etc. – a sort of Byron reincarnate, who ruined the life of Lady Anne just as Byron ruined the life of Anne's grandmother, Lady Byron – or so it was agreed in Lovelace circles. With Blunt, though, there was no incest, so far as anybody knew, and no controversial Separation. His wife did not spend a lifetime dreaming up reprisals. On the contrary, she seems to have behaved rather as Lord Byron would have wished *his* wife to behave: 'She worshipped blindly at his shrine. He might violate every principle of moral and other law, human and divine, and boast of it, but fascinated and overmastered, despised and insulted, she remained his adoring slave.' Reading this, written by Blunt's vengeful daughter, we are not surprised that it was she who would finally open the Byron archive to impartial scrutiny. Compared to *her* father, Byron had actually behaved not too badly. And in any case, Blunt had always been in favour of playing down the Byron scandals.

Blunt, it might be added, was less than Byronic in his attitude to his own posterity. When he died in 1922, he left behind a mass of secret papers. He did not, though, bequeath them to a hard-up poet friend. He had his Memoirs put under seal in the Fitzwilliam Museum in Cambridge, embargoed for a period of fifty years. There is a story that when, in 1972, the time came for them to be unsealed, the executors took one look and locked them up again.

# CHAPTER EIGHT

# AT THE SHELLEY SHRINE

In an 1830 debate at Oxford University, a visiting team from Cambridge tabled the proposition that one Percy Bysshe Shelley was a greater poet than Lord Byron. The motion was comfortably defeated, with Shelley bagging less than a quarter of the vote. His supporters, though, saw the tally as a breakthrough: before the debate, they said, Oxford had no memory of this 'poet' who in 1811 had been expelled from University College for preaching *The Necessity of Atheism*. Now, thanks to Cambridge, she at least knew how to distinguish Shelley from Shenstone. Shelley was the one 'whom Lord Byron patronised and who was drowned some years ago'.

When Shelley died in 1822, the obituarists jeered: 'Shelley, the writer of some infidel verses, has been drowned; *now* he knows whether there is a God or no.' And Byron wrote to Thomas Moore: 'There is another man gone, about whom the world was ill-naturedly, and ignorantly and brutally mistaken. It will perhaps do him justice *now* when he can be no better for it.' If Shelley's friends had seen this letter, they would have called it typical of Byron's self-absorption that he should scrutinise Shelley's ashes for traces of his own predicament. Byron *did* patronise Shelley: it was hard not to in the face of the younger man's self-humbling adoration, and even harder not to when that adoration started to turn sour ('I despair of rivalling Lord Byron . . . the sun has extinguished the glow-worm'). He also – and more consistently – patronised Leigh Hunt and Edward John Trelawney, each of whom would shortly write memoirs of both poets, memoirs in which the principal business was to elevate Shelley and cut Byron down to size.

Hunt and Trelawney had their own axes to grind and they also had to negotiate relationships with the surviving Shelley women: the widow Mary and her step-sister Claire Clairmont (the wronged mistress of Byron and, possibly, of Shelley too). At the outset, though, with his Lordship safely dead and Shelley not 'discovered', it was easy for those with grudges against Byron to pretend that, by backing Shelley, they were merely seeking to correct a literary-critical injustice. Later on, with Keats recruited to the cause, anti-Byronists could further argue that a pure poetry of spirit and sensation was being set against the corruptions of an earthbound knowingness. Pre-Tennyson, the way to promote 'sensitivity' was to thicken Byron's skin, to de-poeticise his temper.

But then Shelley's reputation was perhaps in need of special pleading. Mary Shelley was a pious keeper of her husband's flame – she edited his Works with, she fervently believed, a minimum exercise of censorship, and she put Shelley-like characters into her novels. She might have written the biography if she had been free to do so, but she and her son Percy were financially dependent on Shelley's father, the much-put-upon Sir Timothy, who decreed that so long as he drew breath there would be no dredging up of bygone Shelley scandals: nothing about the atheism, the expulsion, the elopements, the free love, the extra-marital offspring, the suicide of Shelley's first wife Harriet, and so on. Mary herself had no wish for any such disclosures, and was scathing about the poet's unofficial memoirists – 'in times past when a man died worms eat him, now in addition vile insects feed on his more precious memory, wounding his survivors by their remorseless calumnies' – but she would quite like to have penned her own archangelic version of the Life. As it was, she contented herself with discreet biographical annotations of the poems. Concerning Shelley's reputed 'errors of action', she said:

> I abstain from any remark on the occurrences of his private life; except, inasmuch as the passions which they engendered, inspired his poetry. This is not the time to relate the truth; and I should reject any colouring of the truth. No account of these events has ever been given at all approaching reality in their details, either as regards himself or others.

By the time Sir Timothy died – at ninety, in 1844 – Shelley's reputation as a poet was ascendant and Mary knew that 'the time to relate the truth' could no longer be postponed – or at any rate she knew that this would be the view of others. She felt isolated and got at by Shelley's friends and hangers-on. There were quarrels over the poet's legacies which were, in theory, now freed for distribution, and she was being harassed by forgers and blackmailers claiming to have this or that embarrassing love-letter. More than once she had allowed herself to be tricked or exploited. And Thomas Medwin, whose Byron book she had abhorred, was threatening a full-scale Life. When Medwin pressed Mary for details of Harriet's suicide and of the Chancery suit over custody of her and Shelley's children, Mary begged him to leave well alone. Medwin replied:

> I have found in the Record Office, and made extracts of the proceedings in Chancery regarding Shelley's children, which I have deemed an indispensable passage in his life. There are also other passages, I fear, whose discussion you would not approve of, but which justice to his memory has obliged me to dilate on.
>
> It pains me much that I could not at once, on receipt of your letter, suppress the 'Memoirs'. The book occupied me eight months, and I have an expensive journey back to Germany [where he now lived], to bring it out, and have now disposed of it for £250. You are, I am sure, too reasonable to ask me, poor as I am, to make this great Sacrifice. If you are desirous that the 'Life' should not be published, and will make me some indemnity for the losses I should sustain, I will give you up the Ms., stipulating at the same time never to write anything more about Shelley. This sacrifice of my own fame, and, in some degree, of Shelley's fame, I am ready to make, solely with a view of complying with your wishes.
>
> As we are going to press immediately, let me have a reply by return of post.

Medwin's book, when it appeared in 1847, was mauled by the critics for its inaccuracies, and turned out to be not at all the 'disgrace to Shelley's name' that Mary feared. But it seemed to suggest the shape of things to come. Sir Timothy, for all his faults, had at least kept the scavengers at bay.

Although his blackmail bid failed, Medwin had known where to apply the pressure. At the heart of Mary's anxiety about a Shelley Life was a specific recognition that any impartial account of her own most treasured wifely memories – the first meeting, the elopement, the early months in Europe – would necessarily be tinged with the pathos of Harriet Westbrook's suicide: Harriet – 'far advanced in pregnancy' – was found dead in the Serpentine two years after Shelley left her. For Mary the difficulty was how to honour her own most vivid experience without seeming to disdain its most dramatic consequence; and how to defend Shelley without seeming to defend herself. She died without having found an answer, or without having put anything on paper. Nonetheless, she did – perhaps inadvertently – assist in the contrivance of a posthumous solution to the problem.

In 1848, Mary met Jane St John (young widow of the great-grandson of Pope's 'guide, philosopher and friend') and found in her 'a prize indeed in the lottery being the best and sweetest thing in the world'. When Jane first laid eyes on Mary she said to herself, 'Who are you – you lovely being?':

> She must have seen my start of surprise, for, rising gently from the sofa she came towards me and said very softly, 'I am Mary Shelley.' You ask me what she was like. Well, she was tall and slim and had the most beautiful deep-set eyes I have ever seen. They seemed to change in colour when she was animated and keen. She dressed as a rule in long soft grey material, simply and beautifully made.

As Sylva Norman comments: 'It sounds exquisite. But as Mary was neither tall nor slim, we doubt even that long, soft grey material – the very stuff of vision and angel's wing. Mrs St John had fallen in love with Mary, and this is a lover's account.' A marriage was swiftly arranged between Jane St John and the equably directionless Sir Percy (he having inherited the title from Sir Timothy): Percy had been dabbling unsuccessfully in politics but all he was really good at was being a slightly dotty, well-liked country gentleman: his inherited distinctiveness expressed itself as a passion for amateur theatricals, photography and boat-building. He used to refer to the poet Shelley as 'me old father'. After the wedding, 'Mary accompanied the young couple wherever they went . . . acquiescent as a shadow'.

The 'shadow' survived Mary's death in 1851. For the next forty years or so, Lady Shelley made it her life's task to safeguard the 'memory' of her mother-in-law's marriage. When she and Percy moved into Boscombe Manor, she set up a Shelley sanctum in a bedroom alcove and there displayed precious relics of the poet she had never met: manuscripts, locks of hair, the poet's knife and fork, his baby-rattle, together with various busts and portraits – not just of Shelley, but also of Mary and, rather oddly, of Trelawney. It was a room, she said, 'built expressly to receive all that we hold most sacred . . . This same room is never entered but by kindred feet, or by those in whose hearts Shelley lives.' She also went in for commissioning ludicrously idealised statuary and – with Sir Percy's affable consent – watched over the Shelley papers with a fierce, possessive zeal.

Jane also, needless to say, took charge of the Biography. First of all, she approached Thomas Jefferson Hogg, the poet's somewhat madcap college friend. Hogg had been Mary's choice; in 1832 he had published a magazine memoir of which she had approved and there had been some Shelleyan intimacy between them in the early days. In appointing Hogg, Jane believed she was following her mother-in-law's wishes; trustingly, she gave him total access:

> All Shelley's journals, letters, fragments, every scrap of paper indeed relating to him or to his affairs, whether it was written by himself, or by other persons, have been placed in my hands and at my disposal by his family; my materials are at once authentic and abundant. This is much, but it will be far more, to write a living Life of the young Poet; to give him a breathing, moving, speaking portrait.

Unluckily, Hogg had a few Shelley-related secrets of his own that he was keen to eliminate from these abundant annals (he was always trying to get off with Shelley's women) and, with this in mind, he set about manipulating certain of the manuscripts. For instance, a letter of Shelley's which attacked Hogg for having tried to seduce Harriet was printed, with names changed, as a *Fragment of a Novel*. Also the Shelley Hogg had known and delighted in came over, in his lively telling, as a somewhat cranky, late-adolescent type, subject to weird fads and hypochondrias, more silly than spiritual:

> He was a climber, a creeper, an elegant, beautiful odoriferous parasitical plant; he could not support himself; he must be tied up fast to something of a firmer texture, harder and more rigid than his own pliant yielding structure; to some person of a less flexible formation: he always required a prop . . .
> He was altogether incapable of rendering an account of any transaction whatsoever, according to the strict and precise truth, and the bare, naked realities of actual life; not through an addiction to falsehood, which he cordially detested, but because he was the creature, the unsuspecting and resisting victim, of his irresistible imagination . . .

For Jane, this simply wouldn't do: was Hogg saying that the demi-god told lies? 'It was with the most powerful feelings of dismay,' she wrote, 'that we perused what we could only look upon as a fantastic caricature, going forth to the public with my apparent sanction – for it was dedicated to myself.' Having completed two volumes, Hogg was ordered to return the papers. His Volumes Three and Four never appeared, although for a time Lady Shelley feared they might: when dismissed, he was just about to report on Shelley's decision to abandon his first marriage. 'Our feelings of duty to the memory of Shelley left us no other alternative than to withdraw the materials which we had originally trusted to his early friend and which we could not but consider had been seriously misused.'

It seems unlikely that Hogg could have written a book that would have been acceptable to Lady Shelley: he was not the reverential type. Even so, a great opportunity was missed and she would never again be so obliging. Having, so to speak, exhausted Mary's specific requirements in the matter, she now felt free to organise a correct version of the sacred Life – or Lives, for it was always her belief that, without Mary, Shelley might not have added up to much. In 1859, with the help of Richard Garnett, she issued her own *Shelley Memorials*; her object, she said, was 'to give a truthful statement of long-distorted facts, and to clear away the mist in which the misrepresentations of foes and professed friends have obscured the memory of Shelley'.

On the Harriet Westbrook question – which by now had the same status in Shelley's memorials as The Separation had in Byron's – her strategy was to be bold, definite and merciless: in effect, to demolish, by power-scholarship, any suspicion that Shelley's noble love affair with Mary had had any damaging side-effects. Shelley's union with Harriet had from the beginning been a terrible mistake: 'in a sad and evil hour for both, this girl, "who had thrown herself upon his protection" and "with whom he was not in love", became his wife.' The quoted phrases, she said, were from letters, 'the authenticity of which I am not able to guarantee'. There were already a number of forged Shelley letters on the market and whenever possible the family had acquired them. If Lady Shelley liked what she read in a forged letter, she would tend to believe that, although not in Shelley's hand, it had been copied from a lost 'original'. She allowed her instinct to direct her in these matters, and in this case she was prepared to use 'quotation' to establish that Shelley's first marriage could not possibly have worked: the tender-hearted poet had taken pity on an impressionable schoolgirl, and their inevitable estrangement had been encouraged by the malign influence of Harriet's sister, Eliza, a long-established enemy of the family by now because Harriet, in her suicide note, had begged Shelley to allow Eliza to bring up their baby daughter.

Having discredited the marriage, Lady Shelley makes as if to move forward to the separation, but then stops: 'The occurrences of this painful epoch in Shelley's life, and of the causes which led to them, I am spared from relating. In Mary Shelley's own words: This is not the time to relate the truth . . .' She goes on to invoke Mary Shelley's 'firm conviction' that if Shelley's 'errors of action' were to be 'judged impartially', his character 'would stand in fairer and brighter light than that of any contemporary'. And to this, Lady Shelley merely adds:

> Of those remaining who were intimate with Shelley at this time, each has given us a different version of this sad event, coloured by his own views and personal feelings. Evidently Shelley confided to none of these friends. We, who bear his name, and are of his family, have in our possession papers written by his own hand, which few now living, except Shelley's own children, have perused.

In other words, we have all the proof we need, but we are not going to put it on display and some of it, of course, may – for all we know – be inauthentic. This would become Lady Shelley's standard ploy whenever her version of the Life was challenged, and it would land her in trouble later on. For example, when Thomas Love Peacock, enraged by Harriet's treatment in Lady Shelley's *Memorials*, gave his own account of the marriage, he was publicly rebuked by Richard Garnett. The family, Garnett said, had 'evidence' that 'most decidedly contradicts the allegations of Mr Peacock'. To this, Peacock delivered a most dignified response: 'A few facts in the order of time will show, I will not say the extreme improbability, but the absolute impossibility, of Shelley's family being in possession of any such documents as are here alleged to exist.' (Probably neither Garnett nor Peacock was aware that the family had been buying up forged letters.) Lady Shelley's riposte to Peacock's impertinence was to let it be known, semi-privately, that he and Harriet had been lovers, and that this was *another* reason why poor Shelley had become fed up with his altogether impossible first wife.

Later on, kindly analysts of Lady Shelley's character would contend that 'guided by the best of feelings' she 'filled up all the gaps' in Shelley's life 'with conjectures which time seemed to have altered into something like certainties'. No doubt something of this sort happened later on but at the time of the *Memorials* she seems to have been not so much deluded as unscrupulous. For example, the book's Chapter 6 concludes as follows:

> One mistake which has gone forth to the world, we feel ourselves called upon positively to contradict.
>
> Harriet's death has sometimes been ascribed to Shelley. This is entirely false. There was no immediate connection whatever between her tragic end and any conduct on the part of her husband. It is true, however, that it was a permanent source of the deepest sorrow to him; for never during all his after life did the dark shade depart which had fallen on his gentle and sensitive nature from the self-sought grave of the companion of his early youth.

And Chapter 7 begins – on the facing page – like this:

> To the family of Godwin, Shelley had, from the period of his self-introduction at Keswick, been an object of interest; and the acquaintance-ship which had sprung up between them during the poet's occasional visits to London had grown into a cordial friendship. It was in the society and sympathy of the Godwins that Shelley sought and found some relief in his present sorrow.

The casual reader, indeed the not-so-casual reader, might here easily gain the impression that Shelley's 'present sorrow' was the same 'deepest sorrow' with which Chapter 6 had closed: in other words, that Harriet had killed herself before he had even been *introduced* to Mary. As if to dissuade us from pondering the point, the narrative instantly intensifies:

> Godwin's daughter Mary, now a girl of sixteen . . . had been accustomed to hear Shelley spoken of as something rare and strange. To her, as they met one eventful day in St Pancras Churchyard, by her mother's grave, Bysshe, in burning words, poured forth the tale of his wild past – how he had suffered, how he had been misled, and how, if supported by her love, he hoped in future years to enrol his name with the wise and good who had done battle for their fellow-men, and been true through all adverse storms to the cause of humanity.
>
> Unhesitatingly, she placed her hand in his, and linked her fortune with his own; and most truthfully, as the remaining portions of these Memorials will prove, was the pledge of both redeemed.

This, or something like it, happened in June 1814. Harriet's suicide

135

was two years later. But when we come to 1816 in Lady Shelley's now-resumed chronology we are told merely that in this year 'Shelley's second marriage took place' and that he 'now had a sure refuge. Evil might be without; but by his hearth were sympathy, and encouragement, and love.'

The *Shelley Memorials* were furiously attacked by Shelley's contemporaries; elsewhere the book was seen for what it was, an interim whitewash. Lady Shelley, though, was stuck with it and was obliged to defend it from attack. Over the ensuing years she continued to leak anti-Harriet stories – most notoriously the suggestion that Harriet had been unfaithful to Shelley during their marriage and that in the months leading up to her death had drifted into prostitution – and to insist that there was evidence which, when viewed, would support these allegations. But viewed by whom, and when?

The Shelleys wanted Richard Garnett to take on the biography, but he said he was too busy. For a time, it looked as if Garnett might steer the job in the direction of William Michael Rossetti who, in 1870, edited the poems, with a Memoir. The pre-Raphaelites had temporarily settled the Byron–Shelley debate in Shelley's favour and William was the Brotherhood's 'keeper' and factotum: the sensible, non-creative one who worked for the Inland Revenue and had done good works on behalf of Blake and Whitman. But at Boscombe Manor it was sensed, no doubt correctly, that Rossetti would not readily submit to guidance. He was much attached to the idea of his 'integrity'. As it happened, he did rather worship Shelley and, on the Harriet issue, his inclination was to toe the family line: he revised his Memoir after being ticked off by Sir Percy. But a full-scale biography would have been a sterner test of his dedication to the myth and it was evident from his textual labours that his instincts were disturbingly inquisitorial. He wrote:

> I can't be two things at once – I can't be to the public a biographer and to the family a suppressor of published facts. Besides, I consider that the world, now nearly half a century after Shelley's death, has a full right to know whatever throws light upon HIM.

(Soon afterwards, William would be serving as executor of the estate of his brother and sister, Dante Gabriel and Christina: in both cases, he would prove almost as craftily suppressive as the Shelleys, keeping an iron grip on all editions, biographies and memoirs, and devoting the last thirty years of his life to promoting his tidied-up version of the family legend. He even set up a Rossetti museum in his house. Of his own sanctifying efforts, he confessed: 'A brother neither is nor can be the best biographer. Some readers . . . may be inclined to ask: "Have you told everything, of a substantial kind, that you know about your deceased brother?" My answer shall be given . . . without disguise: "No; I have told what I choose to tell; if you want more, be pleased to consult some other informant." ')

The Shelley family did not appoint a biographer until 1883, and their choice then was another friend of Garnett's, Edward Dowden, a Dublin university professor who said of his election to the task that it was equivalent to 'the offer of a Bishopric' – a formulation that might have made even Shelley raise a smile. Dowden's book, when it appeared in 1886, was something of an anti-climax: it made a great show of independence but – re Harriet – it came up with a compromise that seemed tailored to appease the family. Dowden defended Harriet's pre-1814 virtue but argued that Shelley genuinely believed that his wife had been unfaithful to him before he fell in love with Mary; thus the biographer was able to exculpate Harriet without needing to accuse Shelley of anything that was not easy to forgive:

> It is no part of this biography to justify Shelley in all his words and deeds. The biographer's duty is rather to show precisely what those words and deeds were, leaving the reader to pronounce such judgement as may seem just. Still less is it the part of Shelley's biographer to cast a shadow upon the memory of Shelley's first wife. In many instances Shelley erred in his judgement of men and things; he may have erred here.

It was pointed out in reply that none of the documents Dowden introduced to establish Shelley's belief in Harriet's infidelity in fact predated her eventual suicide: two letters of 1817 and a much-later testimony from the unreliable Claire Clairmont. If Shelley had all along thought that she had been unfaithful, why did he not make the accusation earlier: for example, when he was seeking custody of her children in 1816? And why did Mary – if she too believed that 'Harriet was . . . faithless to her bond of love' – make no mention of the infidelity in her journal or, come to that, in her novel *Lodore*, which is in parts 'an almost literal transcript of her life and that of Shelley.'

Dowden, in what Mark Twain called his 'cakewalk', asked none of these key questions; nor did he look too closely at certain of the other documents that Lady Shelley had been sitting on for years and darkly quoting from. Everybody knew that in the late 1840s the market had been flooded with spurious manuscript material and the unmasking, in 1852, of the notorious 'Major Byron' had reddened the faces of quite a few estimable literary figures. Even so, Dowden seems not to have found it alarming that Lady Shelley liked to show him 'transcripts' and 'excerpts' from her secret hoard rather than the manuscripts themselves. And he was only mildly ruffled when, after his book appeared, someone pointed out that one of his more poignant Shelley letters had in fact been written in the eighteenth century, by Lord Bolingbroke to Swift. In general, he seems to have been too polite to question Lady Shelley's firm belief that she could tell the difference between a 'forgery' and a 'copy made from a missing or destroyed original'. In years to come, her belief – and his ready acceptance of it – would be severely called in question.

Between the Shelley *Memorials* and the Biography there had been a period of some twenty-five years in which speculation and counter-speculation about the private life of Shelley became ridiculously intricate and vehement, with figures like Browning, Swinburne, John Addington Symonds and, of course, Rossetti, swopping clues and leads in the manner of juvenile philatelists. What it all came down to, much of the time, was a rehashing of the old insolubles: does poetic genius excuse or mitigate bad conduct; does/should knowing about the life have a bearing on how we read the work? When Matthew Arnold delivered his famous 'ineffectual angel' verdict, he had already been repelled both by Lady Shelley's determination to construct an 'angel' legend and – just as forcibly – by what he had come to know about the deeply unangelic goings-on in Shelley's circle: 'What a set!' he groaned, and there was something of this elementary exasperation in the way he responded to the poems. Shelley, it could be said, was made to pay for the ardent ministrations of his devotees.

The saga of Shelley biography is a mid-Victorian saga, typical in its essentials of the epoch: the Family embattled on behalf of an idealised portrayal, the biographer hopelessly trying to balance a regard for 'the truth' against a need to gain access to the archives. There are biographers today who would contend that the Shelley tale is timeless, that nowadays we would perhaps get more cunning in the Family's presentation and/or a greater ruthlessness on the part of the

138

biographer but that otherwise nothing much has changed. The Aspern Papers were the Shelley papers after all, and we do not think of Henry James's tale as antiquated. And yet the shock moment in James is when we learn that the papers *are* destroyed. We tend now to prize candour above decorum and to prefer the embargo to the bonfire, but when the Victorians set about fixing the record, they very often made sure that it stayed fixed. The would-be biographer in those days worked to the sound of snipping scissors and paper crackling in the grate – much of this done with an almost flamboyant disregard for the possible censure of a later age. What mattered was this generation, or the next.

Certainly, it was a rare custodian who took the line that some more distant posterity should inherit the evidence on which perhaps to judge the matter differently. When John Gibson Lockhart cut and re-arranged Walter Scott's letters in the 1830s, he was aware that 'the perhaps dismalest thing for me . . . is that very likely, when all [Scott's] letters are thrown open to an unscrupulous after-age, my manipulations may be thrown overboard entirely.' Lockhart did not try to cover his tracks; he was not ashamed of what he had done. As he saw it, he had paid his dues as Scott's genuinely admiring son-in-law and, in his literary capacity, he had tried to tell the truth without violating any meaningful proprieties.

'Proprieties', however, were severally defined. For some, it was improper even to mention the 'decay of [Scott's] intellectual vigour'; for others, it was scandalous that a man's financial anxieties should be mulled over for the public entertainment. Lockhart's understanding of Scott's life, its tragic curve, its triumph-in-defeat, obliged him not to duck these issues, but he had to tread with stealth. For example, Walter Scott may have been – probably was – incoherent on his deathbed: Lockhart sensed that by granting him a resonantly lucid exit he, the biographer, might be forgiven for his earlier medical disclosures:

'Lockhart,' he said, 'I may have but a minute to speak to you. My dear, be a good man – be virtuous – be religious – be a good man. Nothing else will give you any comfort when you come to lie here.' He paused, and I said, 'Shall I send for Sophia and Anne?' 'No,' said he, 'don't disturb them. Poor souls! I know they were up all night – God bless you all.' With this he sunk into a very tranquil sleep, and, indeed, he scarcely afterwards gave any sign of consciousness, except for an instant on the arrival of his sons . . . About half-past one a.m. on the 21st September, Sir Walter breathed his last, in the presence of all his children. It was a beautiful day – so warm, that every window was wide open – and so perfectly still that the sound of all others most delicious to his ear, the gentle ripple of the Tweed over its pebbles, was distinctly audible as we knelt around the bed, and his eldest son kissed and closed his eyes.

The Waltonesque deathbed scene had long been an established feature of the official or monumental biography but post-Lockhart the convention was often carried to laborious extremes. Dean Stanley's *Life of Thomas Arnold* is perhaps the classic of the genre, taking five pages to get us from Arnold's 6 am chest pains to a prayerful demise at 8 am. Doctors deliberate, relatives rush to the bedside, psalms are requested and supplied, and through it all the pain-racked Arnold acceptingly contemplates his imminent release. Rivalling Stanley is the death-scene of Charles Kingsley, as reported by Max Muller:

Never shall I forget the moment when for the last time I gazed upon the manly features of Charles Kingsley, features which death had rendered calm, grand, sublime. The constant struggle that in life seemed to allow no rest to his expression, the spirit, like a caged lion, shaking the bars of his prison, the mind striving for utterance, the soul wearying for loving response – all that was over. There remained only the satisfied expression of triumph and peace, as of a soldier who had fought a good fight, and who, while sinking into the stillness of the slumber of death, listens to the distant sounds of music and to the shouts of victory. One saw the ideal man, as Nature had meant him to be.

The dividing line between nineteenth-century biography and fiction was never narrower than when piety was the narrative mainspring. Somewhat in the manner of his subjects, the life-writer found in death-writing a kind of sweated-for sense of liberation and fulfilment. Unshackled at last, he was able to demonstrate that even official biographers could *write*.

Lockhart's *Scott* is disparaged nowadays for its huge length, its shameless editings and inventions, its dull accumulations. The book offers a case, perhaps, where the prestige of the biography has kept pace with the prestige of its subject: just as Scott wrote far too much, so his biography is far too long. But Lockhart was also disparaged at the time – for disloyalty, irreverence, excessive dwelling on the master's frailties, outspokenness on money matters and so on: a response famously derided by Carlyle:

One thing we hear greatly blamed in Mr Lockhart, that he has been too communicative, indiscreet, and has recorded much that ought to have lain suppressed. Persons are mentioned, and circumstances not always of an ornamental sort. It would appear that there is far less reticence than was looked for! Various persons, name and surname, have 'received pain'. Nay, the very hero of the biography is rendered unheroic; unornamental facts of him, and of those he had to do with, being set forth in plain English; hence 'personality', 'indiscretion', or worse 'sanctities of private life', etc. How delicate, decent, is English biography, bless its mealy mouth! A Damocles sword of *Respectability* hangs forever over the poor English life-writer . . . The English Biographer has long felt that if in writing his biography he wrote down anything that could by possibility offend any man, he had written wrong. The plain consequence was that, properly speaking, no biography whatever could be produced.

Carlyle went on to suggest that Lockhart would have written an even better book if Scott had not been so 'altogether lovely to him'. But this 'radical defect' had to be stomached; the point was that this biographer had dared to break at least some of the rules: 'They that will crowd about bonfires may sometimes very fairly get their beards singed; it is the price they pay for such illuminations; natural twilight is safe and free to all.' Carlyle, we cannot help noting, is rather more ahead of his time than the biographer he praises, but this was in 1837, the year of Victoria's accession: mealier mouths than Lockhart's were already waiting to be fed.

It has been suggested, by admirers, that Lockhart's *Scott* acts out a compromise between two warring theories of biography, that it embodies both theories in its own performance: Boswellism introduced into life-writing a new investigative curiosity even as Romanticism introduced into writers' lives a new propensity for 'scandalous' malpractice. The Romantics mistrusted the desanctifying tendencies of Boswellism and yet, in their private conduct, they supplied the opposition with all manner of alluring docu-dramas. The inevitable upshot was a new sort of highbrow journalese: a Medwinism, or Trelawneyism, purportedly 'first hand' or 'in conversation with' or based on 'documentary evidence' but actually almost impossible either to authenticate or to refute. Thus Cam Hobhouse described it in 1830:

The writers of Lives have, in our time, assumed a licence not enjoyed by their predecessors – for they interweave the adventures of the living with the memoirs of the dead; and, pretending to portray the peculiarities which sometimes mark the man of genius, they invade the privacy and disturb the peace of his existing associates.

Carlyle would have called this mealy-mouthed, and so it is, but Hobhouse had in mind a strain of biographical writing which was perhaps beneath Carlyle's notice or which in any case he might have seen as a healthily beard-singeing side-effect of the general access of candour he was pleading for. Lockhart, on the other hand, cited the peril of unreliability (not disrespectfulness) as his chief reason for rejecting a Boswellian approach; the method, he believed, was tainted.

The case of Byron – the case that Hobhouse had in mind – can perhaps be taken as inaugural. In the making of the Byron myth Boswellism and Romanticism are in conflict even as they are rather fondly feeding off each other's plates. On the one hand, Byron can be presented as the victim of what Peacock calls the 'small Boswells' of 'the eavesdropping genus', chroniclers ready to misreport for profit or in order to settle an old score. On the other, he can be seen as an arch-manipulator, bewildering his spectators with a surfeit of information, with calculated moodshifts and inconsistencies, leaving them stocked with a mass of 'material' but unable to make sense of it.

Either way, the Byron enigma put paid to biography's post-Boswell pretensions as a branch of science, or even as a branch of history. Witnesses, it was now perceived, were likely to be either mendacious or gullible, or both; letters were probably composed with publication in view and could anyway be forged; conversation was easily tailored to fit the susceptibilities of the stenographer. At the most mundane level, it was noted – with Byron – that there was not even agreement on the matter of his celebrated limp. He had a club foot, but which foot was it? For every witness who claimed it was the right foot, there was another who would swear it was the left. Tom Moore, in his biography, was undecided. And of course Trelawney, the great Romantic undertaker, testified that 'both his feet were clubbed and his legs withered to the knee – the form and features of an Apollo, with the feet and legs of a sylvan satyr'. (There is a similar problem with Shelley: did he have a 'little turnup nose' or was it 'firm and strong'; was he afflicted by a 'receding chin and protuberant larynx'; was his face overall notable for its 'firmness and

142

hardness' or was it 'feminine and artless'? Small wonder that Shelley's son took up photography.)

The unreliability of the various 'small Boswells' who swarmed around the glamorous Romantic poets did have two notable results. It liberated the biographer into a new view of himself as an imaginative artist, and it reinforced the defensiveness of those whose task it was to safeguard the posterity of the biographee. On the one hand, it produced Mrs Gaskell's biography of Charlotte Brontë, which compensates for 'correct' suppressions by 'colourful' inventions; on the other hand, it gave us Lady Shelley.

# CHAPTER NINE

# JOHN FORSTER, OF DICKENS FAME

'By the year 1840,' wrote Harold Nicolson in his *Development of English Biography*, 'the tide of Victorian biography was setting in . . . the Boswell tradition was dead: people reverted with relief to the old, unworthy origins of English biography.' Nicolson cited Mrs Kingsley on Mr Kingsley, Mr Cross on Mrs Cross (George Eliot), Lady Burton on 'her curious husband': these, he said, were typical of the 'innumerable widow or family biographies' that by mid-century had come to dominate the field. Hagiography was reborn at the hearth – or, very often, *in* the hearth.

A new Copyright Act of 1842 strengthened authors' control over their writings by granting a 42-year period of ownership from the date of publication or until seven years after an author's death ('whichever is the sooner'). This new legislation had the effect of intensifying the involvement of wives, sons and daughters in the administration of their loved-one's literary leavings. The prompt issue of a family-controlled biography would, it was perceived, both safeguard the biographee's good name (by forestalling unauthorised attempts) and also see to it that the good name was, so to speak, kept warm during the seven-year period of copyright control. A legend could be fed and milked. After the funeral would come the slamming of doors, the scrubbing of marble and then, within two years or so, the emergence of what Gladstone called 'a Reticence in three volumes'.

The suggestion sometimes is that the dead author might have wished for less protection from his kinsfolk. Thackeray, for example, is said to have thrown to the floor his copy of the reverential *Memorials of Thomas Hood* (put together by Hood's children) and to have then exclaimed: 'Let there be nothing of this when I am gone!' His daughter took the imprecation at face value: after Thackeray's death she locked up all his letters and vetoed all thoughts of a biography – engendering, in later years, much speculation about skeletons-in-cupboards. There was, it so happens, nothing much to hide: an insane wife (also locked up), a certain amount of boozing and whoring, a long, unsuccessful lusting after the wife of his best friend. Even so, ranks were swiftly closed. John Carey, reviewing a recent collection of contemporary Interviews and Recollections, reports that:

> At Thackeray's funeral . . . a crowd of garishly dressed women in scarlet and blue feathers gathered so quickly around the grave that 'true mourners and friends' could not get near. Unfortunately, none of these Jezebels has bequeathed us an Interview or Recollection, and of the dozen or so accredited friends in [these] pages only one gets round to mentioning that the urethral stricture that caused Thackeray such agony, and sent him so frequently to his doctor, resulted from a venereal infection.

Would the gossipy, red-blooded Thack have required his slate to be so disinfected? We doubt it: after all, he did once say, 'What care I to appear to future ages (who will be deeply interested in discussing the subject) as other than I really am?'

We might similarly wonder if George Eliot would have enjoyed the idea of being remembered for a deficiency of humorous self-deprecation. Her second husband, John Walter Cross, married her six months before she died and she was grateful for his earnest adoration. For Cross, though, George Eliot was first of all to be worshipped as a heavy thinker. She needed to be saved from pre-Cross failures of solemnity. Introducing 'Her Life as Related in her Letters and Journals', he boasted that 'no single letter is printed entire from beginning to end'. When his wife wrote 'it is raining blue devils', Cross struck out the blue devils; when she said of some mislaid proofs: 'I would rather have lost one of my toes', he altered 'toes' to 'fingers'. George Eliot's own view of such goings-on might be deduced from a letter in which she urged a friend:

> I wish you would burn my letters when you have read them once through, and then . . . there would be no risk of a critical third pair of eyes getting a sight of them, which would certainly be a death-blow to my reputation for gravity and wisdom – not that I am very careful in this matter – for this bump of cautiousness with which nature has furnished me is of very little use to me.

Thackeray died in 1863; George Eliot in 1880; Thomas Hood in

1845 – in each case, and there are many others, the family custodians were obedient to the inexplicit requirements of the Zeitgeist, the unchanging and unchangeable spirit of the age. They did not see anything shifty or underhand in burying a fellow's 'frailties' or 'foibles'. Indeed, to have done otherwise would have been to betray the dead in order to sell poison to the living. As early as 1814, we find the *Quarterly Review* fulminating against the publication of Nelson's letters to Lady Hamilton:

> It is with great regret that we undertake to give our readers some account of these volumes . . .
>
> In what we have to say, we shall not follow the example which we reprobate, nor contribute to spread the poison which, with a double malignancy, invades the reputation of the dead, and the tranquillity of the living. We should indeed not have noticed this publication at all, but that public justice and the peace and well-being of society require that we should visit such an attempt with the severest punishment that our literary authority can pronounce.

Severest punishment? The *Edinburgh*, on the same subject four months later, courted apoplexy in its effort to outdo the opposition:

> We scarcely remember to have seen a more reprehensible publication; or one in which the frailties of the Mighty Dead have been more wantonly and barbarously unveiled – without the possibility or indeed the pretext of any other motive than that of the sordid and miserable profit that may be made of the exhibition. The man who should violate the last hallowed retreat of his war-worn frame, and display, for hire, the naked and festering limbs of the departed hero to the gaze of the brutal multitude, would be guilty, we think, of a less profanation. The outrage against decency, and the offence to all generous feeling, would not at least be aggravated in such a case, as we cannot help fearing they are here, by the strangest ingratitude and the most incredible breach of confidence: for who but *the receiver* of these letters could have the means of giving them to the public? who but the *object* of this guilty, but ardent and devoted love, could have betrayed its follies and its frenzy to our gaze?

And so a certain tone was set. What was bad for Nelson could be even worse for the less Mighty Dead; after all, none came mightier than he. In the *Edinburgh*, some seventy-five years later, the tone is wearier, more mechanical, but the custodial standpoint is pretty much the same. The subject this time is Keats's fifty-year-old letters to Fanny Brawne (suppressed by earlier biographers and editors and first published, to great obloquy, in 1877):

> in common with many other admirers of the poet, we regard this publication and republication as a violation of the duties of the biographer – an act of sacrilege to the memory of Keats. No man, surely, should know more intimately than Mr Forman the abhorrence with which Keats would have viewed any such prostitution of the secrets of his love. As if this were not enough, we see while we write these words that the love-letters of John Keats to Fanny Brawne have been sold by public auction. This act of desecration – for such we hold it to be – is evidently a consequence of the publication of those feverish letters which certainly never were intended to see the light or to be sold at public auction.

(On the matter of Keats's supposed 'abhorrence', it is worth noting that in one of his letters to Fanny Brawne he tells her that he has been 'turning over two volumes of Letters written between Rousseau and two Ladies'. His reading prompts the question: 'What would Rousseau have said at seeing our little correspondence! What would his Ladies have said! I don't care much – I would sooner have Shakespeare's opinion about the matter.')

Between the blood-spitting fervour of the Nelson notices and the defeated-sounding disapproval of the Keats publication, there was a stretch – mid-century – in which a more balanced style of censure was in evidence: to protest against indecorous disclosure was to express the general will of the literary community. Between, say, 1840 and 1880 most intelligent readers took it for granted that the cover-up, the bonfire, the editorial sleight of hand, were obligatory procedures for coping with new, low-level habits of intrusiveness. The proliferating mass-circulation magazines and news sheets had turned authors into breakfast-table stars. The brutal multitude was taking coach trips to the Lake District or Burns Country; Americans in search of autographs were camping at the door. There were forgers and gossip-sleuths, relic-hounds and bibliomanes. It was easy enough for the owner of a literary property to think of biography in terms of burglary. Such is the thinking behind the relaxed facetiousness of *Blackwood's Magazine* in 1849. The writer here is at one with his readership; he neither splutters nor sermonises. He merely ventilates a settled prejudice:

We shudder at the thought of putting out a book, not from fear of anything that the critic can do, but lest it should take with the public, and expose us to the danger of a posthumous biography. Were we to awake some fine morning and find ourselves famous, our peace of mind would be gone for ever. Mercy on us! what a quantity of foolish letters have we not written during the days of our youth, under the confident impression that, when read, they would be immediately committed to the flames. Madrigals innumerable recur to our memory; and, if these were published, there would be no rest for us in the grave! If any misguided critic should say of us, 'The works of this author are destined to descend to posterity', our response would be a hollow groan. If convinced that our biography would be attempted, from that hour the friend of our bosom would appear in the light of a base and ignominious spy. How durst we ever unbosom ourselves to him, when, for aught we know, the wretch may be treasuring up our casual remarks over the fifth tumbler, for immediate registration at home?

The author, who is supposed to be reviewing William Beattie's *Life of Thomas Campbell*, rambles on in this half-jokey vein for several pages: we hear of 'Silas Fixings', the American, who will 'take down your whole conversation in black and white, deliberately alter it to suit his private purposes and Transatlantically retail it as a specimen of your life and opinions'; of 'McTavish' who, posing as a waiter at a 'bluestocking coterie', is 'in all probability a leading contributor to a fifth-rate periodical'; of three authors who 'meet at a dinner party':

> The conversation is very lively, takes a literary turn, and the three gentlemen, with that sportive freedom which is very common in a society where no treachery is apprehended, pass some rather poignant strictures upon the writings or habits of their contemporaries. One of them either keeps a journal, or is in the habit of writing, for the amusement of a confidential friend at a distance, any literary gossip which may be current, and he commits to paper the heads of the recent dialogue. He dies, and his literary executor immediately pounces upon the document, and, to the confusion of the two living critics, prints it. Every literary brother whom they have noticed is of course their enemy for life.

In other words, careless talk costs lives – literary lives. The atmosphere so jauntily evoked is of a war-zone, or of a city under occupation, with spies, fifth-columnists and traitors behind every arras – and all of them up to some biographical no-good. Who can be trusted with a 'sacred trust'? *Blackwoods*' final advice to the famous is to 'Drop all correspondence, if you are wise, and have any ambition to stand well in the eyes of the coming generation. Let your conversation be as curt as a Quaker's, and select no one for a friend . . . Perhaps the best mode of combining philanthropy, society and safety, is to have nobody in the house, save an old woman who is so utterly deaf that you must order your dinner by pantomime.' It is feeble stuff, but in a way the very feebleness is symptomatic, as if this is one subject on which the jocund scribbler need fear no audience-resistance.

In 1849, the pre-eminent literary celebrity was Dickens, who in fact spent that year writing the voluntarily 'veil-uplifting' *David Copperfield*, planning the launch of *Household Words*, in which he would soon be revealing to the world some spicey-ish domestic secrets, and firing off long letters from the seaside to his future 'beeograffer' John Forster, whose gossipy *Life of Goldsmith* had come out the year before. Neither Dickens nor Forster appears to have been much troubled by *Blackwoods*' emergency instructions. 'Remember that for my Biography,' Dickens would say, after he had done something particularly lovable, and Forster would obediently write it down. It was a kind of joke between them.

It was more of a joke, though, for Dickens than it was for Forster. To Dickens, Forster himself was often something of a joke, like Podsnap in *Our Mutual Friend* (a character described by the unknowing Forster as a 'vulgar canting fellow'); he was half-parasite, half-prop; he was the arch-facilitator, who knew how to dismantle a contract, to copy-edit and proof-read, to plan career-moves, birthday treats, memorial services, and so on. He was also, in spite of his booming actor's voice, the best listener in town. Well, Dickens evidently thought so, now and then:

> I hardly know why I write this but the more than friendship which has grown between us seems to force it on me in the present mood. We shall speak of it all, you and I, Heaven grant, wisely and wonderingly many and many a time in after years. In the meanwhile I am more at rest for having opened all my heart and mind to you.

This is touching, but just a shade impersonal. On all the big issues of the later Dickens life – the separation from his wife, his affair with Ellen Ternan, the self-destructive public readings – Forster's advice was brushed aside. Perhaps Dickens did not expect to be outlived by his beeograffer: they were the same age and Forster was famously sick much of the time, very often to be found, as Dickens put it, 'in a languid state of rheumatico-calico-hiccoughy-frowsy-aperient-medical mystery'. Maybe what most amused Dickens about his biography was that he thought it would never actually get written. Forster, 'long before' Dickens's death, 'ceased to believe that I [Forster] should survive to write about him'.

The son of a Newcastle cattle-dealer, John Forster came to London as a law-student in the 1830s and within weeks he had declared his true intent. He wished to be a 'man of letters' – a vocation which can best be defined by an aggregation of his subsequent activities: he wrote histories, biographies and essays, edited periodicals, advised publishers, campaigned for literary causes, and in general made himself unignorably important in the world of books. On top of all this, he had a small stable of literary heroes, for whom he performed all manner of services, from running errands to managing estates. His over-riding mission, he would say, was to nurture and sustain the 'dignity' of the literary profession: a function and a concept which Thackeray, for one, viewed with derision. Forster, he would say, 'is the greatest man I know. Great and Beneficent like a Superior Power . . . whenever anybody is in a scrape we all fly to him for refuge. He is omniscient and works miracles'.

Forster's first 'miracle' was the reconstruction of Leigh Hunt. When these two met, Forster was seventeen and panting with adoration of anyone who had actually met Keats, Shelley, Byron, the glamorous Romantic dead. To serve Hunt was the next best thing to serving *them*. As for Hunt, he was in his mid-forties and as usual short of guineas and of critical esteem: he made Forster welcome, and was much gratified by his exertions. Forster appointed himself Hunt's 'agent' (there were no such creatures in those days) and went around town extolling the merits of this 'veteran wit, poet, prose-man, partyman, translator'. He badgered publishers, reviewed Hunt's writings in the magazines (not always favourably, it should be said), solicited cash from the Royal Literary Fund, petitioned for a Civil List pension, arranged a pre-subscribed selection of the Works. As the years went by, Hunt became almost pitiably dependent on his champion, and Forster – as would become his habit in his later years – waxed dictatorial. By the 1850s, the battered eminent was afraid to make a literary move without checking first with his adviser: when Forster told him to cut *The Story of Rimini*, he cut it; when Forster urged him to write poems in dialogue, he did as he was told, and gratefully. The controller-bully in Forster was no doubt there from the beginning and with the hard-up, almost washed-up Hunt there was an open invitation to manipulate, to supervise, to condescend. Forster's later 'great patron king' demeanour presumably owed much to this early training.

Leigh Hunt, of course, had his uses as well as his grievances: he may not have had much ready cash but he did have dazzling connections. It was through Hunt that Forster in 1830 met his second hero-figure, the 55-year-old Charles Lamb. If Hunt perhaps proved something of a let-down, Lamb did not. There was nothing the great essayist particularly wanted from Forster, it would seem, apart from the fervour of his admiration. With this, Forster was unstinting; it was sufficient for him that Lamb 'quite realised the expectations of those who think that an author and wit should have a distinct air, a separate costume, a particular cloth, something positive and singular about him'. It was all there: the head as if by Titian, the face nobly lined with 'traces of sensibility, imagination, suffering, and much thought'. And Lamb had the character to match: his weakness for the bottle not to be wondered at in view of 'the great and peculiar sorrows he was fated to experience through life'. When Lamb died in 1834, the ideal was intact and Forster was able to cherish it in perpetuity: not only did he keep a loving eye on Lamb's posthumous reputation, he also used Lamb as a kind of touchstone in matters of taste (Forster's biographer has shown in detail the debt he owed, as a reviewer, to Lamb's influence) and in matters of professional deportment.

After Lamb died, there was Landor, whom Forster 'looked after' for what remained of that long, eccentric life (Landor died in 1864, aged eighty-nine) and among his contemporaries there were Browning, Bulwer-Lytton and, of course, Charles Dickens. As Forster grew in visibility – and grow he did, from willowy sensitive to corpulent personage – he picked up a hundred and one subsidiary labours: amateur theatricals on behalf of a hoped-for Guild of Literature and Art; fund-raising for various 'refugees from literary history' (Burns's sister, Southey's son, Johnson's god-daughter), for distressed actors, orphans of dead journalists; the getting up of petitions, testimonials, commemorations. On top of all this there were books to be written, quarrels to be seen through to a conclusion (Forster could be both aggressive and swift to take offence and he invariably had some 'falling out' in progress), champagne suppers to be hosted at his would-be Johnsonian chambers in Lincoln's Inn

Fields. By the mid-1840s, Forster was not just visible, he was impossible to avoid. There are few Victorian literary biographies in which he does not make an appearance in one or another of his several personae: these appearances on the whole are welcomed but there was often a good deal of ribaldry when he had left the room. Dickens once described an earthquake: 'I was awakened by a violent swaying of my bedstead from side to side, accompanied by a singular heaving motion. It was exactly as if some great beast had been crouching asleep under the bed, and was now shaking itself and trying to rise.' 'Ah, Forster!' cried the wits.

It seems clear that, in person, Forster *was* a little hard to take: 'Regarded by strangers, his loud voice, his decisive manner, his features, which in any serious mood were rather stern and authoritative, would probably have appeared anything but prepossessing.' Not only strangers recoiled from his distinctive presence: even those who could not do without him very often wished they could. Browning dedicated his *Collected Poems* to Forster, 'their promptest and staunchest helper', Landor penned a lyric in tribute to 'Forster! whose zeal has seized each written page/That fell from me', Thackeray confessed that neither *Pendennis* nor anything after it would have been penned but for the help of 'a kind friend' (Thackeray had been sick unto death, and it was Forster who had called the doctor), Bulwer Lytton hailed his 'nature solid and valuable as a block of gold'. Each of these friendships, though, was regularly in the balance, ever susceptible to sulks and storms. Forster's deep fund of well-meaningness was over-stretched; after a time, it was a rare dinner party at which he 'did not say a single rude thing the whole evening!'

With not-easy-to-bully types like Dickens and Carlyle, Forster seems to have been more even-tempered. The Carlyles, of course, patronised him but they enjoyed having him around. Jane at first took him to be 'one of those people who go about, that one likes, in moderation, without feeling them to be worth the pain of a particular study', but melted into more than respectfulness when Forster told her that she was 'little short of being as great a genius as my husband'. And the Sage summed him up with unaccustomed generosity as 'a most noisy man but really rather a good fellow (as one gradually finds), and with some substance in his tumultuary brains'. With testimonials like these, and with his near-ownership of Dickens there for all to see, Forster could put up with being laughed at as a toady, a butcher's boy, a strutting peacock: while dunces mocked, he supped with giants.

The Dickens friendship was, of course, the one that mattered most. In his *Life of Goldsmith*, Forster wrote of 'lion-hunting Boswell, more pompous and conceited than ever . . . pushing his way into every salon, inflicting himself on every celebrity and ridiculed by all'. This is, some of his readers may have registered, rather how Boswell had seen Goldsmith and how Forster was himself regularly seen: disciples do tend to be catty about co-disciples. Even Forster's own devotees, however, found it hard to view him separately from what-he-did-for-Dickens: 'As I look back,' wrote Percy Fitzgerald, 'I can never call up the image of Dickens without seeing Forster beside him; Forster seems always to interpose his bulky form. He was ever bustling about his friend, interpreting him and explaining him.' And making sure that nobody else got too close to him. Forster was unhappy when Dickens and Tennyson seemed about to become chums, and he failed to deliver some Dickens praise to Browning at a time when the poet was praise-starved (apart from Forster's own pioneering praise, that is).

Forster's agent-like efforts on behalf of Dickens have been widely chronicled, and deservedly extolled. They met in 1836, just as Dickens was about to score his big success, and a few weeks before the death of Mary Hogarth. It was the perfect moment for the forging of a bond. Forster was beginning to establish himself as dictator of taste at Chapman and Hall and he had not long become freed from an unhappy engagement to the poetess Letitia Landon. Ambition with a dash of heart-break was the common ground. By day, Forster threw himself into the business end of things and at night he was 'ready with comfort and consolation' as Dickens mourned his loss – a loss which Forster (again rather possessively, one feels) would forever insist was 'the feeling of his life that always had mastery over him'. As the business prospered, so further confidences flowed and for over a decade Forster was to Dickens all that he wished to be: masterful servant, heeded confidant.

In later years, the bond became less vibrant. Dickens came to need support rather than advice, and by then Forster had become quite fond of the sound of his own counsel. There was an inevitable distancing, more irksome to Forster than to Dickens, but there was no break. When Dickens died, Forster wrote to Charles Eliot Norton: 'To you only I say this, my dear Norton. I have not been able, nor shall be, to have speech on these matters with anyone. And to you for the present I will only further say that nothing in future can, to me, ever again be as it was. The duties of life remain, but for me all the joy of it is gone for ever more.'

This was 1870; Forster was fifty-eight, late-married, rich, and a great figure in the literary world. His always suspect health, though, had begun to fail and he was tired; tired, certainly, of being 'tireless'. He had not long completed the pious labour of compiling the biography of Landor, a task that had given him none of the pleasure which had no doubt been envisaged years before, when he agreed to take it on. Landor, in his protracted 'final days', had put a near-intolerable strain on Forster's rock-like attributes; indeed, there is a plausible theory that when the 84-year-old poet plunged into Italian exile to escape a cranky libel suit, Forster had done less than he could have to restrain him. Certainly, he would have got out of writing the biography if Landor had allowed him to. In one of his rages, the biographee had demanded that his papers be transferred to another writer but at the last moment changed his mind and begged Forster to accept a re-instatement: 'How often have I known you vindicate from unmerited aspersions honest literary men!'

It was indeed Forster's habit as a biographer to salvage ill-used reputations, and he was not fastidious about rules of evidence: such was his reverence for the idea of literary genius that when a Life did not fit as it ought to with the Work, he was prepared to make the necessary adjustments. The trouble was, as one of his friends put it, he 'could scarcely bring himself to recognise that moral meannesses could co-exist with majesty of intellect, or that a man who was a genius in his books could out of his line be inferior to ordinary mortals'. In the case of Landor, recognition had been forced upon him. This was the first time Forster had attempted the Life of a contemporary, a Life in which he himself had played a part, as had several of his likely readers. On the whole, he kept his distance, allowing Landor to do most of the talking (albeit with editorial elisions), but he was not tempted to suppress evidence of his own meritorious conduct in the field. When Landor had strayed from the high duties of his calling, it was more often than not because he had failed to follow his biographer's advice.

There is much of this same self-aggrandisement in Forster's celebrated *Life of Dickens*, on which he was obliged to set to work within weeks of his friend's sudden death. The Landor assignment had been difficult to handle: this one was straightforwardly intimidating. It was 'like a nightmare', he said, trying to cover all the angles: there was Georgina Hogarth, his co-executor; there was the banished Mrs

Dickens and her sympathisers; there were the children; there was Ellen Ternan; and, of course, there was the waiting readership for whom the beloved Dickens's passing had been a large-scale national calamity. Not least, there was the matter of his own by-now mixed feelings – or should one say, his faintly diluted adoration. His attitude to Dickens's 'fixed and eager determination . . . [his] restless and resistless energy' was no longer unequivocal: it was, after all, this same relentlessness that had driven Dickens first into callous error and from there into an early grave.

Although his main purpose was to honour an exemplary life, Forster also wanted to write a biography that Carlyle, his one surviving hero, would not be able to dismiss as mealy-mouthed. To this end, he adopted a method of what he called 'indications'. Thus, for example, he would say that Dickens 'cared little for money' and then print a long letter in which there are as many numerals and exclamation marks as there are words. He makes no mention of Ellen Ternan in his text but prints Dickens's will in which Ternan was left a not princely but sufficiently eyebrow-raising £1000. And when, on the conduct of the separation, Forster actually does come out with a few direct reproaches, these are cleverly couched in the language of routine biographer's decorum:

> The course taken by the author of this book at the time of these occurrences, will not be departed from here. Such illustration of grave defects in Dickens's character as the passage in his life affords, I have not shrunk from placing side by side with such excuses in regard to it as he had unquestionable right to claim should be put forward also. How far what remained of his story took tone or colour from it, and especially from the altered career on which at the same time he entered, will thus be sufficiently explained; and with anything else the public have nothing to do.

If we now feel that Forster's biography could have been a lot better than it is, we are not really wishing for more candour. In all the circumstances, he was about as forthright as we could reasonably hope for. The chief regret is that, by the time he came to write the book, Forster no longer had the energy it seeks to celebrate. He was a sick man when he began it and became steadily worse throughout the whole period of composition. Rather than hunt around for documentation, or attempt 'living witness' interviews, he depended almost exclusively on the letters Dickens wrote to him and on what had been confided to him during their years of intimacy. Like Dickens, we are rarely free of Forster – but our Forster is not the 'restless, resistless' companion with whom the novelist had dealings throughout the 1840s. Ours is bereaved, ill, tired, and has a book to finish.

Weariness, to be sure, can be discerned in Forster's treatment of the documents that were to hand. With the Dickens letters, he started out transcribing (albeit rather freely, so it seems) but when this labour got too much for him, he began snipping out the bits he wished to print; these he would paste into a manuscript book, ready for the printer. The unused sections were then thrown away (and so too was most of the manuscript book after publication). Of the almost one thousand letters that are quoted in the *Life*, a mere fifty-five have managed to survive. Forster's conduct here was not as outlandish as it now appears: in those days 'definitive' meant what it said, or tried to. But we might have expected a younger, happier John Forster to have dealt more reverentially with his friend's relics.

Dickens himself, of course, had organised two big bonfires of his papers, and had wished that they could have been much bigger, so Forster perhaps felt that he was under orders. His biographer's instinct, though, was to leave behind a narrative that would be hard to alter. It has often been noted that Forster's editorial inclination (in so far as it can now be fathomed) was usually to play up his own importance in the Dickens *Life*: to this purpose, he rewrote some of the letters, altered dates, even added new lines of his own. At least one reviewer of the *Life* (the first two volumes) complained that the book 'should not be called the Life of Dickens but the History of Dickens' Relations to Mr Forster'. Forster, of course, may not have understood there to be much difference between the two.

When Forster died in 1876, three years after the publication of his three-volume *Dickens*, he left instructions to his executors that 'generally it is my express wish that all letters coming under the denomination of merely private correspondence shall at once be destroyed, and I leave the decision of this absolutely to my said executors . . . on which judgement I also implicitly rely that such letters as shall . . . be retained . . . shall be those only which derive interest from the reputation and position of the writers, and which . . . may properly be preserved'. The 'non-private' letters were bequeathed to the South Kensington Museum, but under the tight control of Forster's widow, who survived him by almost twenty years

– twenty years, it has been said, in which her unbending vigilance ensured that his name disappeared from view. In some cases, Forster had marked the letters which he wanted destroyed, and one or two of his friends stepped forward at his death to reclaim their correspondence, but several boxes were in the end shipped to the literary executor, Whitwell Elwin, so that he could exercise his fine discrimination. Elwin promptly arranged for the whole lot to be set on fire, in his rectory garden. Years later, his son Warwick 'recalled . . . roasting chestnuts in the ashes of the great'.

# CHAPTER TEN

# FROUDE'S CARLYLE, CARLYLE'S FROUDE

'It has been the fortune of some persons who are in themselves alike unambitious and undeserving to have been connected with others who are destined for immortality. Instead of dispersing into mist they are dragged as satellites through the generations still attached to the orb.' This private jotting by James Anthony Froude was perhaps not intended to sound plaintive, but it does. The name Froude, for readers now, suggests at once another, larger name: Thomas Carlyle – rather as the name John Forster makes us think of Dickens. With Forster, though, we might also think of Lamb, Landor, Browning and the other names (Carlyle's included) to which he glued his own. We might even think of him as to do with the founding of the London Library, or with copyright reform, or with Chapman and Hall. Forster was a 'servant of literature'; Froude we can only think of as a servant of Carlyle. Certainly it is not for his scandalous novel, *The Nemesis of Faith*, or his twelve-volume *History of England*, nor for any of his numerous *Short Studies on Great Subjects* that this gifted writer now lodges in the literary histories. These works, along with several other achievements of a busy and important life, have long ago dispersed into the mist. We are left now with Froude's *Carlyle*, and Carlyle's Froude.

Froude became a Carlyle satellite in 1849, when he was first taken to gaze upon the Sage of Cheyne Row. Carlyle was fifty-four, Johnson's age when he met Boswell. Froude was thirty-one; once a satellite of Newman, and before that in thrall to a fierce vicarage upbringing, he was in this year newly famous as a 'heretic in distress' because of *The Nemesis of Faith* (he had been stripped of his Oxford fellowship and his novel had been burned in public). On the matter of the novel, Carlyle had already formed a view – 'What on earth is the use of a wretched mortal's vomiting up all his interior crudities, dubitations and spiritual, agonising bellyaches into the view of the public?' – and would not have been pleased to learn that it had been a reading of his own *French Revolution* that 'like a flash of lightning' had encouraged Froude to lay waste to his ecclesiastical career.

For Froude, who knew something of Carlyle's verdict on his book, the meeting was all that an amanuensis could have wished. Not only did the prophet's eyes have 'fire burning at the bottom of them' but also there was a properly dismissive grimness in his manner: 'I saw then what I saw ever after – that no one need look for conventional politeness from Carlyle – he would hear the exact truth from him and nothing else.' Froude was sent 'shortly and sternly . . . I cannot say unkindly' from the presence and for the next ten years, having retreated to North Wales, he exercised his discipleship by setting up as an unorthodox historian; his huge *History of England* evinces an attachment to recognisably Carlylean positions: antiPapism, great-man-ism, history-as-retribution-ism, and so on. Reviewers of Froude's first four volumes (which appeared between 1856 and 1858) were particularly riled by the author's reverence for the conduct and character of Henry VIII ('he made the Reformation – he saved England – he was a demi-god,' as Lytton Strachey later scoffingly reported it). Here too the background presence of Carlyle was spied:

> Mr Carlyle has a good deal to answer for in having been the means, by his splendid and dangerous example, of spoiling what might have been so good a book, and compelling its honest critics to say, that it may stand very high in the estimation of those who look in a history only for interest and excitement, but that it cannot stand high in the estimation of those who look in a history above all things for the truth.

Froude made replies to such attacks but he was perhaps not altogether displeased to have his occasional inaccuracies seen as a price paid for the essential creativity of his approach. Judgements of this sort bound him all the closer to his hero. Throughout the writing of his *History* Froude had been soliciting Carlyle's advice and was sent numerous annotations: 'for Froude, Carlyle was at once graduate school, professor of history, and seminar leader,' writes Froude's biographer, 'and he read the work of the younger man with minute care.' In the end, it did not matter much what the reviewers said; the important triumph, when it came, was to be told by Carlyle: 'there is such a generous breadth of intelligence, of manly sympathy, sound judgement, and in general of luminous solidity, promised in this Book, that I will gladly read it however it be put together.'

In 1860, Froude moved to London, where he would shortly take up the editorship of *Fraser's Magazine*, and it was around this time that the teacher–pupil relationship assumed a warmer aspect. According to Froude, Carlyle took the initiative:

> Late one afternoon, in the middle of winter, Carlyle called on me, and said he wished to see more of me – willed me in fact to be his companion, so far as I could, in his daily rides and walks . . . and from that date, for twenty years, up to his own death, except when either or both of us were out of town, I never ceased to see him twice or three times a week, and to have two or three hours of conversation with him.

In the course of these regular perambulations, Carlyle would amiably discourse on philosophy, history, politics, the passing scene, stopping now and then to enquire after the fortunes of a beggar-boy or to relocate morsels of stale bread for the better convenience of hungry birds. At home he was terrorising his wife and servants as he angrily slogged on with his 'unutterable' biography of Frederick the Great, a task he had already been wrestling with for some nine years – and hating every minute of, he said. Mrs Carlyle commented sardonically on her husband's 'lamb-like' demeanour as he rambled through the parks with Froude – she would like to have seen a bit more of this side of him at Cheyne Row.

Froude had not much access at this stage to the Carlyles' domestic life, although he was greatly taken by Jane Welsh Carlyle ('I thought her the most brilliant and interesting woman that I had ever fallen in with') and evidently knew something of the tensions of the marriage from Jane's confidante, the novelist Geraldine Jewsbury, another Carlyle satellite. Jewsbury and others regaled him with anecdotes of Carlyle's titanic self-absorption and of Jane's pert fortitude, and no doubt he was given an outline of the Lady Ashburton drama (in the 1850s, Carlyle had been taken up by that lady and her circle). He also knew of Jane's recent illnesses. 'She was in bad health and he [Carlyle] did not seem to see it.' Indeed, the master of the house was forever fretting about his own, largely imagined, ailments, 'as if he was an exceptional victim of the Destinies'. Neither Carlyle nor Jane spoke to Froude directly of such miseries, although Jane did give him a few hints: 'it was evident that her life was painful and dreary. She was sarcastic when she spoke of her husband – a curious blending of pity, contempt, and other feelings.'

Jane died in 1866 – on 21 April, when her husband was in Edinburgh, delivering his acclaimed rectorial address. Carlyle rushed back to London, in a state of shock, and it was a week or two before Froude spoke to him:

> Somewhere about in the first week of May, Carlyle, who had hitherto desired to be left alone, sent me a message that he would like to see me. He came down to me in the library in his dressing gown, haggard and as if turned to stone. He had scarcely slept, he said, since the funeral. He could not 'cry'. He was stunned and stupefied. He had never realised the possibility of losing her. He had settled that he would die first, and now she was gone. From this time and onwards, as long as he was in town, I saw him almost daily . . . In his long sleepless nights, he recognised too late what she had felt and suffered under his childish irritabilities. His faults rose up in remorseless judgement, and as he had thought too little of them before, so now he exaggerated them to himself in his helpless repentance. For such faults an atonement was due, and to her no atonement could now be made.

At the end of this same month, Geraldine Jewsbury sent to Carlyle a short biographical sketch she had written for private circulation. It was inaccurate in several details but to him immensely moving in its evocation of Jane's early life. There had always been a notion that Jane herself (who shared this notion) might have made a literary reputation and Carlyle knew from her letters that she had unusual gifts, gifts that had come to nothing – he would now say – because of what he had made her be: his 'wife and helpmate'.

Carlyle, in these first months after Jane's death, believed that his own life was at an end. Indeed, he hoped it was; he could not see what might be left for him by way of occupation: his loathed Frederick was finished, sent forever, he said, 'into the belly of oblivion' and there was no other cruel task in prospect. He was seventy, there could now be 'nothing of joyful' in his life: without Jane, without a punishing work-schedule, he might as well be dead. One thing perhaps he could do, though, before he died. He had been looking through Jane's papers, 'her notebooks and journals', and 'old scenes' had come 'mercilessly back to him in vistas of mournful memory'. He could, he said, 'write a memoir of the beautiful life which had gone at the side of his own . . . a testimony of his own appreciation'. This memoir would not be 'for the world'; indeed, when he finished it, Carlyle added a note to the last page of the manuscript:

161

I still mainly mean to burn this book before my own departure; but feel I shall always have a kind of grudge to do it, and an indolent excuse, 'Not yet; wait, any day that can be done!' and that it is possible the thing may be left behind me legible to inter[est]ed survivors – friends only, I will hope and with worthy curiosity, not unworthy!

In which event I solemnly forbid them, each and all, to publish this bit of writing as it stands here; and warn them that without fit editing no part of it should be printed (nor so far as I can order, shall ever be); – and that the 'fit editing' of perhaps nine-tenths of it will, after I am gone, have become impossible.

This act of penance done, Carlyle left for the South of France; friends had persuaded him that a sight of the Mediterranean, which he had never seen, would do him good. He went, Froude says, languidly, indifferently, 'expecting that in all probability he would never see England again'. On the Riviera, he composed another memoir, of the life of Edward Irving, a friend of his young manhood and Jane's first great love (she had renounced Irving when she heard that he was 'promised to another' and Carlyle had then stepped in). It was a further penance and so too, in their different ways, were the other portraits and reminiscences he wrote in that first year: of Francis Jeffrey and, more briefly, of Wordsworth and Southey. Some of these pieces he did in France and the rest when he got back to England in the spring of 1867. He saw them as mere 'rags', 'a mockery of work', and reckoned that he would probably burn them also pretty soon. He never did, of course, but he also never recognised that in ten 'empty' months following Jane's death, he had written a small masterpiece, a book that would outlive his *Frederick*, his *Cromwell* and even – except for flashes in it here and there – his *French Revolution*.

In 1867, this would have seemed to him a prospect to be laughed at. Returned to Chelsea, his main business was to brood on his devastating loss, and to lash himself for his blindness, his ingratitude, his tyrannical and – it now seemed – pointless obsession with his work. 'The shadow of his lost wife seemed to rise between him and every other object on which he tried to fix his thoughts': the shadow of her 'kindness, love and perfect unity of heart', 'her bright, cheery, beautiful face mirrored in the glass beside my own rugged, soapy one answering curtly to keep up her cheerful, pretty talk'.

Ah! and where is it now? Forever hidden from me. Forever? The answer is with God alone, and one's poor hopes seem too fond and too blessed to be true. Ah me! Ah me! not quite till this morning did I ever see what a perfect love, and under such conditions too, this little bit of simple spontaneity betokened on my poor Jeannie's part. Never till her death did I see how much she loved me . . . Nor, I fear, did she ever know (how could she have seen across the stormy clouds and eclipsing miseries) what a love I bore *her*, and shall always, but vainly now, in my inmost heart. These things are beautiful, but they are unutterably sad, and have in them something considerable of remorse as well as sorrow. Alas! why does one first see fully what worth the soul's jewel had when it is gone without return? Most weak creatures are we; weak, perverse, wayward, especially weak . . . Of late, in my total lameness and impotency for work (which is a chief evil for me), I have sometimes thought, 'One thing you could do – write some record of her – make some selection of her letters which you think justly among the cleverest ever written, and which none but yourself can quite understand. But no! but no! How speak of her to such an audience? What can it do for her or for me?

Carlyle had of course already written 'some record of her' but he now set to organising a possible 'edition' of her letters. Helped by his niece, Mary, who had come down from Scotland to serve him as a secretary-housekeeper, he wrote around to Jane's friends, asking for letters, and when he had got together a sizeable collection, he arranged them in chronological order, elucidating proper names, and from time to time adding his own notes – as if to make reply. It seemed to him that there was much that needed to be answered, answered for.

Jane, writing to her friends, had been as shrewd, as springily ironic, as he might have anticipated; he was able to register once more that he had been married to a writer of real talent. What he had not altogether bargained for was the letters' rich vein of unhappiness, the endless complaining, about aches and pains some of the time, but very often about *him*, about the near-unremitting nervous strain that he had put her through. The letters Jane addressed to Carlyle were full of minor grouses about servants, builders, travel arrangements, and the two of them had made it a habit in their correspondence to swap symptoms of their several and recurring ailments – he reported on his bilious crises, his lumbago, and she retaliated with details of her insomnia, her 24-hour head-aches, but direct reproaches against him were relatively few, and were usually brought on by some criticism he had made of her. To her friends, though, Jane was less inhibited: 'When one has married a man of genius, one must take the consequences'; 'all the while I must be standing between Mr C and a new bother'; 'the long worry and anxiety I have had with Mr C's nervousness had reduced myself to the brink of nervous fever'; 'it is like living in a madhouse on the days when he gets ill on with his writing'; 'I sometimes feel as if I should like to run away. But the question always arises: where to?'

And so it went on, in the later years especially, week in, week out. And to add to the pain of having to read this catalogue of recrimination, Carlyle was reminded of the strange period a year or so before she died when, critically ill after an accident, Jane had allowed herself to let go, to cling to him – 'Oh my husband . . . I am terribly alone.' Carlyle had responded, tried to mend his ways, but when she recovered he had, with some relief, resumed his familiar preoccupations. It was now heart-rending for him to learn how grateful she had been for that short passage of attentiveness: 'I cannot tell you how gentle and good Mr Carlyle is! He is busy as ever, but he studies my comfort and peace as he never did before.'

Carlyle's notes on the letters are terrible to read: 'Shame on me!'; 'My poor little wife'; 'Ah me! ah me! whither fled?'; 'stonyhearted, shame on me'; 'miserable egoist'; 'how miserable my books must have been to her'; 'my little heroine'; 'Oh was it not beautiful, all this I have lost forever'; 'Oh my dearest! my dearest that cannot now know how dear'; 'Alas! how little did I ever *know* of these secret wishes and necessities – now or ever!'; 'Oh her love to me; her cheering, unaffected, useful practicality of help'; 'Ah me! in vain, palpably in vain; and what a look in those bonny eyes vividly present to me yet; unaidable, and like to break one's heart.'

This 'pilgrimage through Hades' lasted for two years, 'night after night, and month after month', and by the end of 1869 Carlyle had three volumes' worth of Jane's letters organised and annotated. But he was uncertain what ought to be done next. He had taken his punishment, he had paid homage to Jane's literary gifts, he had apologised, but the ordeal (surely) had been private, between him and her. Even Froude, who was seeing him all the time, and with whom he spoke of Jane 'continually, always in the same remorseful tone, always with bitter self-reproach', knew nothing of his recent labours – neither the 1866 Reminiscence nor the annotated letters:

One day – the middle or end of June, 1871 – he brought, himself, to my house a large parcel of papers. He put it in my hands. He told me to take it simply and absolutely as my own, without reference to any other person or persons, and to do with it as I pleased after he was gone. He explained, when he saw me surprised, that it was an account of his wife's history, that it was incomplete, that he could himself form no opinion whether it ought to be published or not, that he could no more do it, and must pass it over to me. He wished never to hear of it again. I must judge. I must publish it, the whole, or part – or else destroy it all, if I thought that this would be the wisest thing to do. He said nothing of any limit of time. I was to wait only till he was dead, and he was then in constant expectation of the end.

Froude agreed to look over the material and 'the perusal', he said, was 'intimately affecting'. What Carlyle had done seemed to him breathtakingly courageous, 'something so beautiful, so unexampled in the whole history of literature, that I could not but admire it with all my heart'. And yet at the same time, he was appalled. He had known something of Jane's discontent, and of the ways in which Carlyle's 'irritable temperament . . . had saddened their married life', but he had not known the extent of the unrest: 'For the first time I realised what a tragedy the life in Cheyne Row had been – a tragedy as stern and real as the story of Oedipus. The quarrels, I found to my sorrow, had been no surface differences of married life, but fierce and violent. Surely enough the remorse was needed.' He was in particular shocked by a passage from Jane's diaries, quoted by Carlyle in his Memoir, which spoke of 'the blue marks which in a fit of passion he had once inflicted on her arms'.

What to advise, then, on the matter of future publication? Should he tell Carlyle not to publish and thus negate 'the bravest action which I ever heard of' or should he urge upon the world's attention 'the errors of the best friend that I had ever had'? What if he *did* burn the manuscript? Jane had been a voluminous letter-writer: someone else would collect other letters and broadcast them, but without her husband's grieving commentary.

I should then have done Carlyle's memory irreparable wrong. He had himself been ready with a frank and noble confession, and the world, after its first astonishment, would have felt increased admiration for the man who had the courage to make it . . . Sooner or later the whole truth would be revealed. Shall it be told voluntarily by him, or maliciously by others hereafter? That was the question.

In the end, Froude advised Carlyle that 'the letters *might* be published', but only if there was a change of mind about the 1866

Memoir. This memoir, Froude believed, ought to appear before the letters (maybe as a preface): in other words, the defence should be heard before the prosecution. Carlyle gave his assent and there and then, Froude says, revoked the prohibition which he had attached to the last page of the memoir – Froude's impression was that he had by this time forgotten that he had ever pencilled such a note. The timing of the publication was talked about and Carlyle proposed a delay of ten years from the time he had handed the manuscripts to Froude – that is to say, he agreed to publication in 1881.

This arrangement did not altogether put a stop to Froude's anxieties: 'I felt at the time that he was laying upon me a cruel test of friendship, though he did not mean to be cruel.' Before finally accepting the responsibility, he consulted John Forster, famously wise in matters legal and financial. Forster said that Carlyle should clarify the position in a will or 'trouble could come of it'; he promised to say the same thing to Carlyle, and no doubt did. In the course of his consultation, Froude was given a new slant on the Lady Ashburton *affaire*: Forster's version was that Lady A 'had fallen deeply in love with Carlyle' and that 'Carlyle had behaved nobly'. This was not what Froude had heard from others and in any case 'the idea that Carlyle would behave nobly under such extraordinary circumstances seemed extremely unlikely to me'. (It was perhaps at this moment that Froude realised what it was that had all along most repelled him about Carlyle's lordly treatment of his wife: Carlyle was a worker's son, Jane was middle-class. On the Lady Ashburton matter, Froude murmured, almost to himself: 'Lady Ashburton was a great lady of the world. Carlyle, with all his genius, had the manners to the last of an Annandale peasant.')

In 1873, Carlyle did make a will, and in it he confirmed what had been decided in his 1871 accord with Froude. Referring to the 'Letters and Memorials of Jane Welsh Carlyle', he said:

> Of that Manuscript, my kind, considerate and ever-faithful friend, James Anthony Froude (as he has lovingly promised me) takes precious charge in my stead; to him therefore I give it with whatever other fartherances and elucidations may be possible; and I solemnly request of him to do his best and wisest in the matter, as I feel assured he will.

On the matter of a biography, Carlyle added: 'I had really rather that there should be none.' There was, he said, 'a quantity of Autobiographical Record' in his notes to the letters and memorials; he himself put 'no value' on these jottings but, again, he left it to Froude to 'furnish a better judgement than mine can be'. Ownership of his papers – with the exception of what he had already passed to Froude – was bequeathed to his brother John.

Not long after drawing up this will, Carlyle suddenly changed his mind about the desirability of a biography. He had discovered, he said, that 'whether he wished it or not, a life, or perhaps various lives, of himself, would appear when he was gone.' He wanted Froude to take on the job of writing an authoritative version, and to this purpose he supplied a further box of 'letters, diaries, memoirs, miscellanies of endless sorts, the accumulations of a life' – with directions, as before, said Froude, 'to burn freely as I might think right'. Froude again felt both honoured and daunted, envisaging 'complexities which even at a distance looked sufficiently formidable', but he agreed to do it, 'provided I was left free to deal with the story exactly as I might think right, and that I was not to be interfered with'.

Froude's apprehensions darkened when he came to examine the material. From Carlyle's Journal he learned that 'there was a secret connected with him unknown to his closest friends, that no one knew and no one would know it, and that without a knowledge of it no true biography of him was possible.' Froude never questioned Carlyle about his secret and there was no further mention of it in the papers. An answer was volunteered by Geraldine Jewsbury:

> When she heard that Carlyle had selected me to write his biography she came to me to say that she had something to tell me which I ought to know. I must have learnt that the state of things had been most unsatisfactory; the explanation of the whole of it was that 'Carlyle was one of those persons who ought never to have married'. Mrs Carlyle had at first endeavoured to make the best of the position in which she found herself. But his extraordinary temper was a consequence of his organisation. As he grew older and more famous, he had become more violent and overbearing. She had longed for children, and children were denied to her. This had been at the bottom of all the quarrels and all the unhappiness.

In addition, Jewsbury was able to confirm that the 'blue marks were made by personal violence. Geraldine did not acquit her friend in all this. She admitted that she could be extremely provoking.'

Also in the latest cache of papers was Jane's diary and from this Froude found out more about the Lady Ashburton intimacy – it was as he had expected: the Scotch peasant had indeed 'sate at the feet of the fine lady adoring and worshipping, had made himself the plaything of her caprices . . . It was of course the purest Gloriana worship, the homage of the slave to his imperious mistress.' Jane's bitterness was now all the more understandable: 'Intellectual and spiritual affection being all which [Carlyle] had to give, Mrs Carlyle naturally looked on these at least as exclusively her own. She had once been his idol, and the imaginative homage which had been once hers was given to another. This had been the occasion of the most violent outbreaks between them.'

Froude was now seriously troubled: he knew more than he wanted to know. The impotence, the blue marks, Lady Ashburton, Carlyle's abject remorse: 'these things were communicated to me, and I was to be Carlyle's biographer. What was I to make of them? It was so weird, so uncanny a business that the more I thought of it the less I could tell what to do.' All these disclosures came to Froude in 1873; Carlyle still had more than seven years to live. Froude started work on the biography, as he had agreed he would, but concentrated his attention on the early years, the 'Scotch part', as he called it. As to the later, London years, he was no longer so firm in his conviction that the Letters and Memorials should be published as a separate book: after all, now that he was writing the biography, he would surely wish to make extensive (and selective) use of this material. Now and then he toyed with the idea of suppressing everything he knew, of resorting to the simple whitewash, but he had not forgotten Carlyle's words on Lockhart's *Scott*. Quite often, he wished that he could be rid of the entire business of Carlyle: he had had a plan of work mapped out for his old age which now would have to be abandoned. He would soon be sixty. None of these misgivings was reported to Carlyle. Froude was still nervous of his master; perhaps all the more so in their new relationship. And in any case Carlyle was not easy to approach: 'When any subject was disagreeable, it was his habit to thrust it away, and desire to hear no more of it. So these papers were thrust upon me, and so for seven years they remained.'

Meanwhile Carlyle himself, unknown to Froude, was having new domestic problems: minor stuff, but irritating. His niece Mary, after what she saw as long years of selfless service, had begun to fret about her future prospects. From this point of view, she was not in the least happy with the arrangement that Carlyle had made with Froude. Mary knew that Carlyle's papers were of value and she wanted to know what would become of them after her uncle's death. To whom would they belong; did Froude believe that what he had been given now belonged to him? In Carlyle's will, 'papers' were mentioned as part of the Cheyne Row property, along with the furniture, pictures, plate, and so on, and were bequeathed to Carlyle's brother John, but nothing had been itemised. Explicitly bequeathed to Froude was the manuscript of his 1866 Memoir – on this there was no room for doubt – but what about the mass of material that had been handed over in 1873? Mary had acquaintances in bookish circles and the advice of certain of these friends was that she should get the long-term legal situation sorted out: after all, her uncle John was also old and ailing. Carlyle seems to have equivocated. Mary would later say that in 1875 he gave her a verbal promise that when John died the papers would be hers. In 1878 – as a result of continued nudging on her part – a codicil was added to the will, making it clear that John's legacy would eventually go to her, but not making particular mention of the papers. John Carlyle died in 1879, a month after Mary was married to her cousin Alexander.

The first that Froude knew of Carlyle's negotiations with his niece was some time in 1880 when Carlyle told him: 'When you have done with those papers of mine give them to Mary.' Since he had years ago been told that he could 'burn freely', Froude was taken aback by this new twist. Carlyle assured him that, as literary executor, he would still have control over how the manuscripts were used, but he came away uneasy, knowing that he should have 'insisted on [Carlyle] defining precisely and with his own hand the respective positions in which we were to stand'. To cheer himself up, he 'concluded that [Carlyle] would himself have left in writing something that was to guide me. He left nothing.' And so it remained, until three months before Carlyle's death in 1881, when, Froude says, Carlyle reaffirmed his wish that the 'letters and memorials' should be published and asked Froude what his intentions were. Froude replied along the lines of their original 1871 agreement: he would first publish a book of Reminiscences, which would include the 1866 Memoir of Jane along with the essays on Irving, Jeffrey, Southey and others. Shortly afterwards, he would issue the Letters, with Carlyle's annotations. 'I briefly told him this. He was entirely satisfied, and never spoke about it again.' At some point, Froude proposed that Carlyle might like to supervise the presentation of the texts, since they were more or less ready for the press. Carlyle said that the effort would 'agitate and excite' him and that he had complete faith in Froude's editorial discrimination.

Carlyle died on 5 February 1881. Froude's last words to him were: 'Ours has been a long friendship; I will try to do as you wish.' On 14 February, Froude wrote to *The Times*, announcing the imminent appearance of the *Reminiscences*, and giving an account of Carlyle's final instructions. The essays, he said, would be 'printed exactly as Mr Carlyle wrote them', with the exception of the memoir of his wife – this, he said, contained 'many things obviously not intended for publication, and Mr Carlyle directed in strong terms that it was not to appear without careful examination and revision. I have, therefore, used my discretion in making large omissions.'

Not large enough, as it turned out, for most readers of the book. When *Reminiscences* appeared on 5 March, exactly one month after Carlyle's death, there was outcry on all sides: how could Froude have allowed Carlyle's remorse, his dark domestic secrets, to be advertised in such appalling detail; why had he not censored certain off-the-cuff acerbities (in particular those aimed at the living or the not-long-dead); why had he been in such a hurry to blacken Carlyle's name? Froude genuinely believed that he had cut out 'everything that could *injure* anybody' and he knew (as the readership did not) that he had suppressed secrets much darker than the ones he had revealed. Far from blackening his hero's name, he had presented a portrayal, a self-portrayal, which in his view was both 'true' and 'beautiful'. The swift appearance of the book was meant to put a stop to 'the rush of unmeaning adulation which burst out at his death'. Carlyle had foreseen 'that when he died there would be much written and said about him. He wished the world to have something authentic to go on.'

Froude had expected to be attacked – indeed he had made sure that he was out of the country when the book appeared – but he was both hurt and alarmed when, two months after publication, Mary and her new husband took up the offensive. In May 1881, Mary wrote to *The Times* to protest against Froude's conduct: she pointed out that in the note attached to his 1866 manuscript Carlyle had solemnly forbidden his friends 'each and all, to publish this bit of writing as it stands here'. She was aware, she said, of Froude's contention that these 'very clear directions were cancelled by subsequent oral communications to him by Mr Carlyle' but she, who had lived with her uncle for thirteen years and many times heard him speak of this same Memoir, 'was led to form an opinion entirely different from Mr Froude's as to his wishes regarding it; and was astounded when I learned by chance that it was in print'. She demanded the return of all the Carlyle papers in Froude's possession, so that they could be examined and assessed by a panel of Carlyle's 'friends'.

Carlyle now had two keepers of the flame, and Mary's letter to *The Times* was but the first round in a contest that would last well into the next century, outliving the two original protagonists – a contest, really, between two rival notions of the Carlyle personality and marriage, and two rival notions of biography. Froude wanted to write a Carlylean *Carlyle*; Mary wanted straightforward, old-style, mealy-mouthed commemoration. Froude, though, was rattled by Mary's sudden hostility: he had always, he thought, got on pretty well with her and, in another of his many promises to Carlyle, he had said he would treat her as a 'daughter'. And he was provoked almost to anger when, a few months later, she began sending him solicitors' letters requesting a bigger slice of the royalties from *Reminiscences* – the book she said ought not to have been published. Froude had in fact generously offered her most of the profits; she did not want his 'generosity', however – she was after what she believed was hers by legal right.

Even so, he proceeded with his master-plan, his sacred trust. He published the 'Scotch part' (Volumes 1 and 2) of the Carlyle *Life* in 1882, the *Letters and Memorials* in 1883, and the final two volumes of the biography in 1884: a total of nine volumes in five years: the *Letters and Memorials* came out in three volumes, the *Reminiscences* in two. As soon as he reached the end of his labours, he returned all the Carlyle papers – except the Memoir of Jane, which *did* belong to him – to Cheyne Row. With each new Froude publication, Mary's animosity intensified – encouraged, no doubt, by the tumult of excitement in the literary world. Even the most sophisticated judges did not know what to make of Froude's extraordinary indiscretions; rather like Froude himself they were torn between deploring Carlyle's conduct and admiring the intensity and courage of his self-reproach but, not being Froude himself, they could not be certain that this *Life*, these sensational disclosures, really were what Carlyle would have wished or had actually requested.

On the whole, Froude was more depressed than dismayed by the public reception of his work. Even when it was praised, he did not feel that the complicated, tragic point of it had quite been grasped. He wrote in 1884 to his sister-in-law, Mrs Charles Kingsley (who had eight years before published her rather different *Life* of Kingsley):

> the more intimately I knew Carlyle, the more I loved and admired him; and some people . . . after reading the *Life*, can tell me that their opinion of him is raised rather than diminished. There is something *demonic* both in him and her which will never be adequately understood; but the hearts of both of them were sound and true to the last fibre. You may guess what difficulty mine has been, and how weary the responsibility. You may guess, too, how dreary it is to hear myself praised for frankness, when I find all the world fastening on Carlyle's faults, while the splendid qualities are ignored or forgotten. Let them look into their own miserable souls, and ask themselves how *they* could bear to have their own private histories ransacked and laid bare. I deliberately say (and I have said it in the book), that Carlyle's was the finest nature I have ever known. It is a Rembrandt picture, but what a picture! Ruskin, too, understands him, and feels too, as he should, for *me*, if that mattered, which it doesn't in the least.

It was this 'fastening on Carlyle's faults' that so enraged Mary Carlyle: to her this was nothing to do with truth and beauty: it was slander. Froude's Carlyle – tyrannical, violent, demonic and then nobly broken by remorse – did not accord with her recollections of the man, nor with what she had seen of his memorabilia, much of which she had transcribed. Froude, she believed, had been bewitched by Jane and had told *her* life-story, not Carlyle's. The 'remorse' passages were intended to ennoble her, not him. To this end, Froude had rigged the evidence, she reckoned.

When the Carlyle papers were returned to Chelsea, Mary was for the first time in a position to analyse Froude's editorial procedures, to find out what he had used, what he had chosen to ignore. Her suspicions, as she saw it, were confirmed: it seemed to her that, on the basis of these same documents, a very different narrative could have been contrived, a narrative in which the great and splendid prophet had found himself shackled to a neurotic malcontent whose gifts and virtues he had, with characteristic magnanimity, exaggerated and then, after death, impetuously glorified. There *were* no faults to be fastened on, unless great generosity of spirit should be deemed a fault. Mary and Alexander (her husband was by now taking an active part in the anti-Froude campaign) became convinced that the evidence had indeed been tampered with. Froude must be exposed.

For scholarly support, the Carlyles turned to the American Charles

Eliot Norton. Norton had attached himself to Carlyle when he was in London and had from the outset taken against Froude – 'an accomplished flatterer', 'his face betrays the cynical insincerity of his profession'. Invited now to 'supervise' the Carlyle papers, he threw himself into the commission with some gusto, re-editing the *Reminiscences* and compiling an edition of Carlyle's early letters. The main thrust of his endeavour, though, was to discredit Froude. He knew, as did almost everyone, that Froude had an Achilles heel: he 'suffered from constitutional inaccuracy, made strange blunders even in copying from plain documents and often used his authorities in an arbitrary and desultory fashion'. As an historian, Froude had many times been caught napping and there were even those in his field who would call him 'not merely untrustworthy but mendacious'. On the matter of textual fidelity, Norton did an almost indecently thorough job, discovering straightaway a wealth of wrong transcriptions in Froude's edition of the *Reminiscences* ('consciously' for 'censoriously', 'about 1720' for 'about 1727', 'centres' for 'cinctures' and so on – many scores of them). Froude's defence was sorrowing and near-apologetic: he said that the master's hand was badly palsied when he wrote and had become both tremulous and microscopic ('I worked through his manuscripts with a magnifying glass') and that, because of Mary's insistence that the papers be returned, there had been no opportunity to revise the book's later editions – from which, he added, she had silently accepted the proceeds. Surely Norton and/or the Carlyles might have had the courtesy to point out the mistakes to him instead of parading them in public? (In fact, Froude was not alone in taking this attitude to Norton's gleeful emendations: Ruskin wrote to the American – who was a friend of his – to protest against his 'niggling and naggling'.)

Even as Norton chipped away on the accuracy front – denouncing Froude as 'a Mephistopheles', 'a continental liar', 'a moral equivalent of Warburton' – Mary was busily formulating new accusations of malpractice. She claimed that Froude had deliberately misread Carlyle's will (the clause about 'seven or ten years' meant 'as from his death' and not 'as from the writing of the will') and she said that she had found a further note in Carlyle's hand in which he had vetoed the publication of his own love-letters (one or two of these appear to hint that, as a lover, he is not as other men); Froude was again obliged to argue that the veto had been later on revoked; again he had no written proof that this was so.

Between them, Mary and Norton compiled a detailed case against the *Life*: Froude, they said, had exaggerated Jane's regard for Edward Irving and her unhappiness at Craigenputtock, where she and Carlyle spent the early years of their marriage on a drearily isolated farm; Froude's account of the Lady Ashburton episode, which the biographer himself believed had been tactfully played down, was 'gratuitous and inexcusable . . . not only untrue but the opposite of the truth'; Froude had made far too much of the couple's supposed class differences (it was claimed here that the Carlyles were descended from King Duncan – but who wasn't?) and by unscrupulously selective quotation he had suppressed evidence of Jane's mental instability.

Froude's public stance throughout all this was silent and aloof, but privately – and semi-privately – he was indignant. More than once, he cursed Carlyle: 'he ought to have known his own mind. If he trusted me at all, he ought to have trusted me altogether. Of course had I known that after I had done my best the persons into whose hands the papers were to pass were to be at liberty to vilify me and what I might do, I would have had nothing to do with it. Nor would anyone in such a situation.' In 1886, he asked his co-executor, Sir James Stephen (High Court judge, brother of Leslie, uncle of Virginia Woolf and, some have said, father of Jack the Ripper) to set down 'wholly and completely' his narrative of the background to the Mary Carlyle operation, so that 'there is an authoritative statement in existence to which, if circumstances make it necessary, an appeal may hereafter be made'. Sir James complied, composing a lawyer-like but persuasive statement of all the pro-Froude arguments, and his letter was distributed privately in pamphlet form.

A year later, Froude wrote his own pamphlet, 'My Relations with Carlyle', addressed to posterity and not to be published unless, after his death, the assaults on his 'honour and good faith' became too much for his family to bear. In this document, Froude set out all the 'evidence' he had omitted from the *Life*: the 'blue marks' entry in Jane's diary, the complete Lady Ashburton story, and – in his view, the key to the whole saga – Geraldine Jewsbury's report of Carlyle's impotence. He could have used this evidence already, in self-defence, but had decided not to: his intention had been that the Jewsbury story would die with him. Perhaps even now the truth need not come out. He had been pushed, though, to the limit. He was determined that 'those who care for me may have something to rely upon'.

Froude died in 1894, Mary Carlyle in 1895. The anti-Froude campaign continued, though, and could now strike a shriller, even more vindictive note. In 1903, Alexander Carlyle published a *New Letters and Memorials of Jane Welsh Carlyle*, with his own annotations, and with an introduction by Sir James Crichton-Browne (the doctor who had rewritten Currie's verdict on the death of Burns). Alexander's annotations exposed many more Froude errors, and Crichton-Browne supplied a medical man's diagnosis of Jane's mental health: she was a congenital neuropath, subject to bouts of hysterical mania, suffering – in short – from 'masked insanity'. Froude's biography, said Crichton-Browne, 'began with hero-worship and ended in a study of demoniacal possession', but Froude had wilfully misidentified the demon.

In response to this formidable two-pronged attack, Froude's children decided that the time had come: they published *My Relations with Carlyle*, blue marks, impotence and all. Crichton-Browne struck back with vigour (the controversy at one point getting into the pages of the *British Medical Journal*, where Crichton-Browne clearly believed that it belonged): the blue marks, he said, came about when Carlyle thwarted one of his wife's suicide attempts, the remorse was not remorse at all but an example of that 'poignant grief in which noble natures so often upbraid themselves with imaginary misdeeds and defaults and magnify their foibles into grievous sin. Remorse indeed!' And as for the impotence: this was self-evidently an invention by the also-not-entirely-stable Geraldine Jewsbury: how could Froude have taken her word for it? Why did he not seek confirmation from the Carlyles' doctors? Froude believed the tale because he wanted to believe it.

As Augustine Birrell commented, the Froude *Life* of Carlyle had 'managed to divide the Carlyle reading public into two classes – husband's men and wife's men' and, looked at in this way, the debate might be said to have lived on. The details of the controversy, however, are now pretty well forgotten and, without the details, it is not easy to register the pathos of Froude's situation. His story can be seen as a parable of the disciple who got in too deep. And yet if Froude's *Life* of Carlyle is now valued as the most heartfelt and compelling of Victorian biographies, this is largely because of the bewildered conscientiousness that went into the making of it. Froude was perhaps too anxious to write the one book that his uncompromising master might have cherished, but the anxiety pays off: in the end, we are grateful that, as narrator, he was driven forward by a need to fathom the Carlyles' strange, perhaps unfathomable, misalliance. Even so, Froude's last years ought not to have been made as wretched as they were. Who was to blame? Sir James Stephen, in his judicial summing-up, was in no doubt:

> Of him I will make only one remark in justice to you. He did not use you well. He threw upon you the responsibility of a decision which he ought to have taken himself in a plain, unmistakable way. He considered himself bound to expiate the wrongs which he had done to his wife. If he had done this himself it would have been a courageous thing; but he did not do it himself. He did not even decide for himself that it should be done after his death. If any courage was shown in the matter, it was shown by you, and not by him. You took the responsibility of deciding for him that it ought to be done. You took the odium of doing it, of avowing to the world the faults and weaknesses of one whom you regarded as your teacher and master. In order to present to the world a true picture of him as he really was, you, well knowing what you were about, stepped into a pillory in which you were charged with treachery, violation of confidence, and every imaginable base motive, when you were in fact guilty of no other fault than that of practising Mr Carlyle's great doctrine that men ought to tell the truth.

# CHAPTER ELEVEN

# KEEPING HOUSE:
# TENNYSON AND SWINBURNE

'In the absence of other evidence, her sudden collapse seems like a mute call for help, a stifled cry from a woman who had for a quarter of a century choked the expression of her own emotions in order to preserve a calm atmosphere for a husband always on the edge of a nervous disaster.' This is not Froude writing about Jane Carlyle but Robert Bernard Martin – one hundred years later – on the subject of Emily, the wife of Alfred Tennyson. 'Mute', 'stifled', 'choked': both Emily and Alfred would have been horrified by the idea that posterity might thus summarise their famously successful love-match. Emily's horror would no doubt have outweighed her husband's. She would have borne the extra burden of having to worry about how Ally might respond to such a slur.

Emily took a long time making up her mind to marry Tennyson and he himself was in no hurry to resign his bachelor torments. The two of them fell in love in 1836 and were married in 1850, the year of *In Memoriam* and of Tennyson's accession to the Laureateship: he was forty-one, she thirty-seven. *In Memoriam*, it seems, had persuaded Emily that Tennyson's unquiet soul was savable and for the next forty years she did indeed strive to 'preserve a calm atmosphere' in which he could wrestle with his demons. She managed the money, the business of two households, the children, the entertaining, the letter-writing, the repelling of unwanted company – and, at the end of a long wifely day, she would more than likely be expected to listen to a reading of her husband's latest work and, if necessary, find ways of indicating that this or that line perhaps fell short of the celestial norm.

By all accounts, Emily was at first more than equal to these tasks. Even though she was fashionably out of sorts much of the time, her fragile health seemed to contribute to the ethereal competence with which she carried out her duties. But then, in 1874, she cracked. The details are not known. In her Journal, she wrote:

> I had to answer many letters from unknown correspondents, asking advice from A. as to religious questions, and desiring criticisms of poems, etc., and I became very ill, and could do but little, so my Journal ends here.

And Tennyson wrote to a friend:

> She has overwrought herself with the multifarious correspondence of many years, and is now suffering for it. I trust that with perfect quiet she will recover; but it will never again do for her to insist upon answering every idle fellow who writes to me. I always prayed her not to do so but she did not like the unanswered (she used to say) to feel wroth and unsatisfied with me.

As Robert Martin suggests, it takes more than a heavy mailbag to bring about a physical breakdown of the sort Emily seems to have experienced: for the rest of her life she was a semi-invalid. She gave up the letter-writing; she did not resume the Journal, thus robbing Tennyson's future biographers of an invaluable day-to-day account of his elderly activities. Post-1874, her personal letters are few and far between. She outlived Tennyson by four years, the difference in their ages, but her presence is shadowy – the shadow of a shadow, some would say.

As a victim-wife, Emily has affinities with Jane Carlyle. Emily, though, was more genuinely self-effacing than Jane, and altogether less subversive of her master's power. And Tennyson – along with all other living creatures – was less temptestuous and irascible than Carlyle. The Tennyson marriage functioned mostly in bucolic settings, so that from time to time Emily could look up from her secretarial chores and observe the great man ministering tenderly to shrubs and baby trees. The childless Jane had no such compensations – for her the best that could be hoped for was total silence from an upper room. But in their different ways, the two wives were engaged in the same losing battle when it came to laying on the atmosphere in which genius was meant to prosper. Carlyle was phobic about noise and noise could not – in Chelsea – be eliminated. Tennyson was phobic about critics and they too were indestructible. Just as Carlyle always had an angry ear cocked for the sound of – well, in one famous case – his neighbour's cocks – so Tennyson's was fine-tuned to pick up the vibrations of even the most far-off, faintly murmured disparagement. Even if he ignored the quarterlies – which he didn't – he could be thrown off balance for weeks by a crank letter from 'yours in aversion . . . I hate you, you beast!' It was Emily's job to shield him from admirers (the short-sighted Tennyson was once gravely startled by a flock of sheep; he had mistaken them for an invading horde of fans), from non-admirers and from semi-admirers, those awkward customers who liked some poems and not others. It has been argued that she did the job too well, for her own good and for his, and that as a poet he would have been better off married to some 'jolly Woman who would have laughed and cried without any reason why', or not married at all. But there is no evidence that Emily or Alfred believed this to be so; in their experience, the Laureate needed all the over-protection he could get.

When Edward Fitzgerald quite early on expressed doubts about something Tennyson had written, a desperation in the poet's response made it clear that more was at stake than simple vanity: 'Don't abuse my book,' he begged. 'You can't hate it more than I do, but it does no good to hear it abused; if it is bad, you and others are to blame who continually urged me to publish. Not for my sake but yours did I consent to submit my papers to the herd – d—m 'em! and all reproach comes too late.' Tennyson's fear of criticism was also a fear of his own hard-to-manage vehemence, the Tennysonian 'black blood' which had driven so many of his relatives into asylums, drug addiction, drink: 'don't make me angry' could be translated as 'don't make me remember that I too might easily go mad'.

And in any case, Tennyson had good reason to feel threatened and badly used. In 1833 – Tennyson's worst year, it might be said, the year of Hallam's death – his *Poems* (1832) had been brutally maltreated in the periodicals: most notoriously by Croker in the 'Hang, Draw and *Quarterly*' (Croker had deliberately set out to 'make another Keats of him'), but more woundingly, perhaps, by Edward Bulwer in the *New Monthly Magazine*. The foppish Bulwer sneered at 'a want of manliness . . . a eunuch strain' in the new poems. Tennyson was no good at either striking back or sucking up – although in the case of one powerful assailant he made rather shaming efforts to do both: mostly, he fumed and squirmed and made vows never again to submit his papers to the herd. In 1839, he wrote (but did not publish) a lengthy rumination on the subject of voluntary publication, asking why – 'in these dark ages of the Press' – any sane man would seek the imprint of the 'public thumb' upon his 'honest thoughts', his 'children of the silence':

> I today
> Lord of myself and of my ways, the next
> A popular property, nauseate, when my name
> Shot like a racketball from mouth to mouth
> And bandied in the barren lips of fools
> May yield my feeling organism pain
> Thrice keener than delight from duest praise . . .

Tennyson of course went on to publish and be praised, praised more lavishly and comprehensively than any other poet of his epoch. But he never really dropped his guard; if anything, the more famous he got, the more edgily he glanced about for hidden foes. And this fear of criticism soon turned into, or merged with, a fear that was somewhat easier to voice: a fear of biographical intrusion. There is always something pitiful in the protests of a writer who feels himself to have been diminished by his critics; to protest against biography, however, can be passed off as proudly leonine. When Tennyson in 1848 wrote his now well-known 'To ——, after Reading a Life and Letters', he presented himself as the defender of Keats's posthumous privacy but we suspect that the assassination attempts of John Wilson Croker were not altogether absent from his thoughts:

> For now the Poet cannot die
>   Nor leave his music as of old,
>   But round him ere he scarce be cold
> Begins the scandal and the cry:
>
> 'Proclaim the faults he would not show:
>   Break lock and seal: betray the trust:
>   Keep nothing sacred: 'tis but just
> The many-headed beast should know.'
>
> Ah shameless! for he did but sing
>   A song that pleased us from its worth;
>   No public life was his on earth,
> No blazon'd statesman he, nor king.

> He gave the people of his best:
>   His worst he kept, his best he gave.
>   My Shakespeare's curse on clown and knave
> Who will not let his ashes rest!

This is grave, sonorous, considered and in Tennyson's best public voice. Privately he could sound a mite less stable on the subject, railing against the way in which 'the lives of great men' were treated 'like pigs to be ripped open for the public'. He knew, he said, that 'he himself should be ripped open like a pig' and he 'thanked God Almighty that he knew nothing of Jane Austen, and that there were no letters preserved either of Shakespeare's or Jane Austen's, that they had not been ripped open like pigs'.

How to forestall and outwit the pig-surgeons became a serious preoccupation of the poet's later, grander days. 'The worth of a biography', he came to pronounce, 'depends on whether it is done by one who wholly loves the man whose life he writes, but loves him in a discriminating way.' In his immediate circle, he could see quite a few candidates for the post of biographer-elect and it became his habit to nurture the discipleship of figures like William Allingham, who for forty years kept a diary of Tennyson's conversation, and the architect-journalist James Knowles, who boasted that 'from time to time and bit by bit he read over to me almost all his poems, commenting on them as he read, and pausing to dictate a few words here and there for me to take down from his lips.' Friends used to refer to Knowles as 'Tennyson's keeper' and 'A.T.'s new Bozzy'. The true keeper, though, was Emily. Her Journal dated from the first days of their marriage and would provide the factual basis for a 'responsible' commemoration. Only she could be trusted, in death as in life, to keep the 'many-headed beast' at bay.

When Emily collapsed in 1874, Tennyson recalled their son Hallam from Cambridge to serve as his secretary/amanuensis. No one, least of all Hallam, seems to have found anything odd in this arrangement, and it was a natural next step for him to be groomed as the official author of the Life. He was faultlessly in awe of father's gifts and rank and seems to have shared his views on the need for total reticence. In the 1880s, these views – along with those of several other prospective literary biographees – were concentrated into determination by the appearance of Froude's Carlyle publications. Tennyson was rumoured to have said that Froude (an old acquaintance and soon to serve, oddly enough, as pall-bearer at the poet's funeral) had betrayed his master for 'thirty pieces of silver'. When Froude protested, it was Hallam who issued a denial and Froude was understandably put out by the rebuff. He did not know enough about the contents of the Laureate's own closet to understand what nightmares his biography had set in motion.

Post-Froude, Tennyson would stand over Hallam as he scissored his way through the archives: it was at Tennyson's direction that the bulk of his early correspondence with Emily – ie 'the many passages which would show . . . intensity of feeling' – was put to the torch. From a letter to Gladstone of 1883, we get a pretty clear idea of how the son would have perceived the father's biographical house-rules. Tennyson is here describing the exploits of Mrs Procter, widow of the celebrated songsmith 'Barry Cornwall':

> I heard of an old lady the other day, to whom all the great men of her time had written. When Froude's Carlyle came out, she ran up to her room and to an old chest there wherein she kept her letters, and she flung them into the fire. 'They were written to *me*,' she said, 'not to the public', and she set her chimney on fire, and her children and grandchildren ran in – 'the chimney's on fire', 'never mind' she said and went on burning. I should like to raise an altar to that old lady and burn incense upon it.

Tennyson died on 6 October 1892. Five days later, Emily wrote: 'I had been joyful in the hope of going with Him but my Hallam tells me that I can be a help in the work to be done.' The work to be done was, of course, the biography, or *Memoir*: the remaining four years of her life would be devoted to helping Hallam shape the Life. And there would never be any doubt about the shape she had in mind. When James Knowles, the ousted Boswell, published a reminiscence three months after Tennyson's death, she was shocked by the author's 'treachery': 'we must forgive the grievous wrong he has done and try to repair it as best we can.' Knowles's grievous wrong had been to mention, in an otherwise laudatory article, the matter of Tennyson's extreme sensitivity to criticism: 'He was hurt by it as a sensitive child might be hurt by the cross look of a passing stranger, or rather as a supersensitive skin is hurt by the sting of an invisible midge.'

For Hallam's convenience, Emily produced an 'epitome' of her 25-year Journal (the originals were later destroyed) and she was at hand throughout the writing of his book. Not even the faintest whiff of treachery was countenanced. The 'black blood' preoccupation was thoroughly suppressed: so too were the bad reviews, the hesitation about getting married, the broken friendships, the melancholia, the vanity, the rough manners – everything indeed that was irregularly human or that seemed not to fit with the Prime Minister of Poetry status of his later years. Instead, there are lengthy encomia from well-known friends, lists of social engagements, travel notes, domestic cameos, pearls of wisdom, and so on. To achieve the perfection of this 'smooth bust of rosy wax' there was much tampering with documents: inkings out, excisions, alterations, disappearances.

The two-volume upshot would soon enough be mocked as 'the enduring model of the official or family-approved, late Victorian biography' but even at the time there were readers aplenty who had actually met Tennyson and knew something of what had been done 'on his behalf'. The book was received with, on the whole, awkward politeness. Emily Tennyson died when it was at proof stage and eulogies to the 'saintliness of her spirit' and the 'sweet movements of her soul' were still audible on publication day. Rebuking the biographer for reticence would have been unseemly – as unseemly, almost, as it would be to look for ambiguities in Emily's resonant last words to Hallam. 'I tried to be a good wife,' she is said to have said. And when Hallam reassured her, she replied: 'I might have done more.'

*Alfred, Lord Tennyson: A Memoir* by his Son appeared in 1897 and one of its most enthusiastic welcomers was the poetry critic of *The Athenaeum*. Theodore Watts-Dunton had a year earlier eulogised Emily as the perfect poet's-wife and now he hymned the son, without whose 'tender care' Tennyson 'could never in his later years have done the work he did'. The relationships between poet and biographer had been, he said, 'those of brother and brother rather than of father and son':

> In the story of English poetry these relations held a place that was quite unique. What the biographer says about the poet's sagacity, judgement and good sense . . . will be challenged by no one who knew him. Still, the fact remains that Tennyson's temperament was poetic entirely. And the more attention the poet pays to his art the more unfitted does he become to pay attention to anything else. For in these days the mechanism of social life moves on grating wheels that need no little oiling if the poet is to bring out the very best that is within him.

Watts-Dunton here spoke with unusual authority and his use of the word 'oiling' would have raised a few chuckles around town. Eighteen years earlier, the pious reviewer had performed one of the great rescue acts in literary history: it was his tender care that had saved Algernon Charles Swinburne from the bottle.

The story is well known. By 1879, Swinburne was prostrate, the victim of alcoholic dysentery, and largely despaired of by his relatives and friends. Several rehabilitation schemes had been attempted in the past but a general feeling had by now set in that Swinburne *needed* to be drunk most of the time: he had a 'thirsty Muse', his outbreaks of violence and blasphemy, his mad cavortings, his endangered health, were all part of the price that must be paid if this poet was to 'bring out the very best' that was within him. Those who were in the know took a similar view of his regular visits to 'a mysterious house in St John's Wood where two golden-haired and rouge-cheeked ladies received, in luxuriously furnished rooms, gentlemen whom they consented to chastise for large sums'. Swinburne was rich but not rich enough in this case for 'the price that must be paid'. Again, though, it was believed 'that these scourgings were in some extraordinary way a mode by which the excessive tension of Swinburne's nerves was relieved'.

When the poet could not afford St John's Wood, he was to be found browsing in Lord Houghton's 'interesting' library, or spouting de Sade, or dashing off memoirs of the birchings he had had, or wished he'd had, at Eton. On the one occasion when some well-meaning chums managed to direct him towards more orthodox felicities, he had simply not known what to do. The obliging Adah Menken, an 'actress' who used to 'get carried around the stage in tights bound to the back of a very tame horse', reported that after several attempts she had failed to coax poor Swinburne 'up to scratch': 'I can't make him understand that biting's no use' was her lament. Swinburne's lament was that Adah insisted on reading out her poems: he may have been a glutton for punishment but this 'Lady of pain', it seems, knew not where to draw the line.

After Adah, it was back to the old ways: the flogging block, the fallings-over, the trampling of toppers at the Arts Club, the crazed enmities and adorations. After a couple of glasses of brandy, there was no holding him: he would invariably start reading out *his* poems, at top volume, and well before the main course had arrived. 'He was like a person who had taken laughing gas': and the effect was often laughable, not least because of Swinburne's personal appearance – five feet four with tiny hands and feet and an enormous dome-like head, the dome haloed by eruptions of red hair. There has been disagreement over the details, but most people thought he had the look of one who was, well, merely passing through:

> He carried his large head very buoyantly on a tiny frame, the apparent fragility of which was exaggerated by the sloping of his shoulders, which gave him, almost into middle life, a girlish look. He held himself upright, and, as he was very restless, he skipped as he stood, with his hands jerking or linked behind him while he talked, and, when he was still, one toe was often pressed against the heel of the other foot. In this attitude the slenderness and slightness gave him a kind of fairy look, which I, for one, have never seen repeated in any other human being.

In some this 'fairy look' aroused maternal feelings but by 1879 even his mother had more or less given up on him. He needed a new mother; he needed Theodore Watts-Dunton.

Watts-Dunton, walrus-moustached, frock-coated, humourless, was an ex-lawyer, hanger-on of the pre-Raphaelites, and by this date an influential, if not hugely esteemed, book reviewer. A year earlier he had written a strange notice of Swinburne's *Poems and Ballads – Second Series* in which he had contrived to decode the book's scandalous component as 'a wail from a bed of vice . . . a jeremiad on the misery of pleasure'. In other words, a cry for help. It was a review to warm a mother's heart and when Watts-Dunton shortly afterwards proposed to Lady Swinburne that her son be moved from his Bloomsbury lodgings to the Watts-Dunton residence in Putney (soon to be the famous No. 2, The Pines), she was sorrowingly grateful: £200 a year would take care of Swinburne's bed and board, and Watts-Dunton would take care of his physical and spiritual reconstitution. It has been told by Edmund Gosse (Swinburne's first biographer) that the poet was carried off 'by force'; in fact, he went quietly, and for the next thirty years showed no signs of wishing to escape.

Once installed in two first-floor rooms, Swinburne allowed Watts-Dunton to handle everything: the money, the visitors, the bits and pieces of his fame. In return, he was obedient to his keeper's therapeutic regimen. Watts-Dunton started out by attacking the booze problem. Brandy, he declared, was a medicine, it stank of the sick-room. A great poet ought to drink a poet's drink: the noble port, for instance, which Tennyson was known to quaff. 'They tell me,' he said, 'that Tennyson never drinks less than a bottle of port a day, and that its generous, life-giving qualities make another man of him.' Swinburne switched to port. After a month or two, Watts-Dunton began to mutter about tiredness and back-pains and to wonder aloud 'if you and I are not perhaps such tough and hardy Berserkers as old Tennyson'. Port was perhaps a trifle heavy for such nimble sprites as they: was it not 'brain-firing' burgundy that had kept D'Artagnan on his toes? – not to mention Athos, Porthos and Aramis: 'you are half a Frenchman, you tell me – it is the wine of your own La Belle France. I picked up a case the other day, and I propose we sample a bottle at lunch, if only to drink to Dumas and the immortal three.'

For the next few weeks, the Putney musketeers touched nothing but burgundy. 'The poet and the child in Swinburne' sipped away contentedly, it seems, but never, glass by glass, getting anything like as plastered as they used to. He was almost ready for Stage Three of the Watts-Dunton Cure:

> after a month or so, Watts-Dunton achieved his final triumph, delivering himself as follows: 'There is a theory of mine, a pet theory, that I want to ask your opinion about. It is this, that wherever you are, you should drink the "wine of the country". If one is in Scotland, one drinks whisky, Scotch whisky; if in Ireland, Irish whiskey; if in Germany hock or German moselle; if in France, Graves, Sauterne, Claret, Burgundy or champagne; if in Spain or Portugal, port; in Italy, chianti. Why, whether drunk out of the cool depths of a pewter or china mug, in some quaint old English inn with diamond-paned windows, sanded floors and oaken benches, or out of a silver tankard from His Lordship's sideboard – the most refreshing, appetising, stimulating, healthiest, best and most natural of all drinks for an Englishman is Charles Stuart Calverley's "beverage for feasting gods", Shakespeare's brown October, our own glorious and incomparable British beer!'

And so it came to pass that Swinburne, every morning at 11 am, was wrapped up and sent off for his morning walk to Wimbledon, where he feasted on a bottle of pale ale at the Rose and Crown; then it was briskly back to Putney for luncheon and a glass of Bass. He was not allowed to speak until he had eaten up his mutton and in the afternoons he was packed off to bed for a siesta. From now on, awe-struck friends from long ago observed, he 'ate like a caterpillar and slept like a dormouse' and never strayed from the Watts-Dunton timetable (to make sure he didn't, Watts-Dunton in the evenings hid his shoes). Instead of brandy and tyrannicide, it was beer and babies; in Putney, Swinburne developed a strange new interest in humans smaller than himself: on his morning walks he was forever peering into prams and fluttering delightedly at what he found therein (Robert Graves has claimed that in babyhood he was once coochie-cooed by Swinburne on Wimbledon Common). One of Watts-Dunton's few custodial panics resulted from the poet taking a rather *too* strange new interest in Bertie, Dunton's six-year-old nephew – writing ardent love poems to the nipper and missing him heart-brokenly when he went off on his hols – but in the end the attachment was fondly diagnosed as puppy-love.

As the days ticked regularly by, the Sixties rebel put on weight, got deaf, grew a beard, wrote metronomic landscape verse, adopted patriotic rightwing views, and settled into studying the works of obscure Jacobean playwrights. Certain of the old preoccupations lingered, but in an academic way: he continued to weave fantasies of delicious schoolboy swishings but his personal disciplinary requirements seem to have been satisfied by an agreement made with his new prefect that he, Swinburne, should be addressed as 'Minor'. Watts-Dunton was called 'Major'.

'It is because of his helplessness that I love him so much,' affirmed Watts-Dunton. To be certain of sustaining Swinburne's baby-like dependence, he fed him not just beer and mutton but regular plattersful of praise. Each new poem that Swinburne produced – and needless to say he produced plenty – was hailed as the best thing he had ever done. An addiction soon took hold. 'I really believe,' Swinburne said, 'the stimulus of your criticism has come to be generally necessary to salvation if not to creation in my case.' Watts-Dunton has been blamed for quenching something 'luminous and vivid' in the poet's nature, but it could also be argued that by 1879 Swinburne was well-numbed into a mechanical effusiveness, that his best poems were written even before the brandy had begun to work its spell, when he was actually as young as he wished his poetry to sound. And even those who jeered at Watts-Dunton as a 'dingy old nursemaid' who had transformed this 'most cosmopolitan of poets into the most parochial' could not deny that, without him, Swinburne would not have reached his fifties.

As it was, he died aged seventy-two in 1909. Appropriately enough, Swinburne managed to exit while Watts-Dunton was, so to put it, on the blink, trapped by influenza on a sick-bed of his own. The poet's funeral on the Isle of Wight (where he had spent most of his childhood) was a comically controversial affair with Watts-Dunton, too ill to attend, having to fire off telegrams to the local vicar, reminding him that Swinburne had decreed that there should be no formal burial service. The vicar rather naughtily smuggled a 'Requiescat in Pace' into his graveside address and there was a brief fuss about the matter in the press until *The Times* supplied the necessary cold compress: 'a fitting and beautiful end to a noble and beautiful life, and though in their love for the dead man his closest friends may feel aggrieved that his wishes were not carried out to the letter, there can be no doubt that, to all intents and purposes, the spirit of them was faithfully observed.' (The bit about 'a noble and beautiful life' was too much for the Vice-Dean of St Paul's who, from the pulpit some days later, thundered that 'it required but little knowledge of souls to know that there was no more deadly poison than the portrayal of corrupt passions in flowing and artistic language.')

Watts-Dunton was named in Swinburne's will as sole executor and beneficiary of the estate – a matter of some £25,000, in addition to whatever might be forthcoming from the poet's copyrights and relics. Now that Swinburne was no longer being 'kept alive', the gossips were free to reckon up what Watts-Dunton had got out of the thirty-year liaison. It had been evident for at least a decade that his nursing duties had been doing as much for him as for Swinburne; indeed they had worked a rejuvenating magic. In his sixties, Watts-Dunton had begun publishing poetry and fiction in which a bizarre obsession with gypsy girls found colourful expession; with the novel *Aylwin* (orig. 'The Renascence of Wonder') he had in 1898 scored a dizzying popular success. Seven years after that, at the age of seventy-three, he had married, not a gypsy but perhaps the next best thing: the twenty-one-year old Clara Reich, a Putney girl with whom he had for many years fostered a Ruskinesque attachment. This match was viewed sourly by Watts-Dunton's live-in sisters but Swinburne was not at all disturbed. On hearing of the marriage, he had fluted: 'You know, I think all this is very jolly.'

And so, apparently, it was – Clara was no less ardent for the marriage than her ancient mate. She had revered Watts-Dunton since their first meeting, when (she said): 'A magnetic arrow invisibly thrilled us both' – in *Aylwin*, interestingly enough, magnets are used to exorcise hysteria – 'I was profoundly conscious that I would never be the same again.' Clara's adoration, plus the hit novel, plus the gypsy thing, plus (now) the Swinburne riches: added up, they offered to the world an altogether new Watts-Dunton, barely recognisable as the dreary do-gooder who had plucked a drunken poet from his 'bed of vice'. Someone who visited The Pines not long before Swinburne's death, reported having met a 'bright-eyed, vampire-like little man who had saved Swinburne's life and now derived his own strength from it'. The blood-sucking image, or some similar depiction, would, from the mid-1890s, crop up fairly often in Pines' bulletins. Watts-Dunton had saved Swinburne, to be sure, but he had also earned himself a second childhood.

Watts-Dunton lived on for five years after Swinburne's death and from what we know of these years they were largely spent coping with administrative tasks for which he had no taste or flair. He soon 'began to imagine himself overburdened with literary and business affairs' and altogether the jumble of papers and manuscripts caused him 'to shrink with dismay from the thought of tackling the onerous task'.

All around Swinburne's sitting-room there were discovered after his death unsightly rolls of parcels tied up in old newspaper, some of them looking as if they had not been opened for half a century. These parcels were found to contain proofs, bills, letters, prospectuses and every species of rubbish, together with occasional MSS. in prose and verse . . . For many years Swinburne was in the habit of allowing miscellaneous material to gather on his table, until a moment came when he could bear the pressure of it no longer. He would then gather everything up, tie the whole in the current newspaper of the day, and then delicately place it on a shelf, where it never was again disturbed. A fresh heap would then begin to grow, till the day when the poet suddenly pounced upon it, and doomed it to the recesses of another newspaper. Through a great part of his life, Swinburne seems to have carried out this curious plan, and in earlier days, when he wandered from lodging-house to lodging-house, he must always have carried with him his carpet-bag of newspaper parcels.

The Swinburne estate was indeed a model of complication: rival keepers, ugly secrets, a mass of unpublished, perhaps unpublishable, writing. Watts-Dunton from the start was outclassed by the various contenders who closed in on him during these last years. There was the Swinburne family, in the shape of the poet's sister Isabel (who held the 'family letters and papers touching on the poet's early life') and his cousin, the novelist Mary Disney Leith (née Gordon, reputedly the 'lost love' of the early poems and secretly a co-student of the Sadean delights): these two formidable ladies were determined that a deeply sanitised Algernon should be offered to posterity. There was Edmund Gosse, would-be biographer and possessor of much spicy information on the drinking, the St John's Wood forays and much else; it was Gosse's conviction that Watts-Dunton had sat on Swinburne's talent and plundered his finances. And there was Thomas Wise, book-dealer and bibliographer, many years later to be unmasked as the prince of literary forgers, and already a well-known expert in the packaging of literary detritus.

Not surprisingly, it was Wise who was first on the Pines' doorstep in the spring of 1909, with Gosse (in spirit, at any rate) not far behind. Wise and Gosse in fact had a cosy professional relationship: the idea was that the eminent, if famously fallible, man of letters would supply a 'seal of approval' to the various pamphlets and limited editions that Wise concocted for the market. In return for some light editing duties and a brief, authenticating preface, Gosse would get a free copy of each astoundingly rare item and also, of course, access to materials on which to base a *Life*. When the bibliomane possibilities were exhausted, Wise and Gosse would go on to co-edit, for the open market, a 200-page volume of Swinburne's *Posthumous Poems* (1917), a two-volume edition of the *Letters* (1918), and eventually a 20-volume collection of the *Works* (1925–7). First, though, the manuscripts had to be acquired.

Wise was always careful to buy the copyrights of the manuscripts he marketed and he was never happier than when he ran across an executor who knew nothing of the law. Not long before he got his teeth into Swinburne, he had been deep in Brontë studies – this time in association with the critic Clement Shorter. Shorter, in 1895, had tracked to Ireland Charlotte's widower, Arthur Bell Nicholls, and persuaded him to part with numerous letters, diaries and books together with 'all copyright of future Brontë letters and manuscripts'. In the Brotherton Library at Leeds there is a touching, half-finished letter from Nicholls to Shorter in which the executor agrees to 'sign a form giving you the exclusive right to publish all manuscripts I send you', and then – as if in afterthought – 'What is a "Literary Executor"? What are his rights and duties?' There is no evidence that he ever found out; certainly it was not the business of Wise and Shorter to enlighten him.

In the same library there is also a long correspondence between Wise and Gosse, with Wise reporting at regular intervals on his campaign to wrest Swinburniana from the nervous but possessive grasp of the executor. The first letter is dated as early as 10 May 1909. Swinburne had died in April. Wise tells Gosse that the bereaved Watts-Dunton is planning to move to the South of France and therefore wishes to dispose of various accumulated papers:

> he wants to know if I would like to buy the books and MSS. 'I would' . . . He wishes to bring out a vol. of *uncollected prose*, and one of *uncollected verse*, and asked me to tell him what exists in uncollected form. This I will do. He is S's sole Legatee as well as sole Executor, and seems to be 'on the move' . . .
>
> He is without the idea of anyone writing about S. save himself. Thinks it is poaching on his preserves. Says he'll write an authoritative 'Life and Letters' – which he certainly will *not*. Says he'll stop a single letter being published . . .
>
> The old chap is shockingly feeble and helpless, but amazingly *wide awake*!

Wise was soon to know how wide awake. By 28 June, after more than one further trip to Putney, he has managed to bag only a few items. The old chap was no pushover. Watts-Dunton, Wise complains:

> is *terribly* slow to deal with: brings out one item at a time, and talks over it for half an hour on end, with the idea of increasing my desire for it, and consequently my notion of price.
>
> I have utterly lost all respect and regard for him, as I have found him to *lie* to me consistently. To see an old man, tottering on the brink of the grave, piling lie upon lie on the off-chance of squeezing an extra pound or two is pitiful in the extreme.
>
> Until yesterday I did my utmost to act fairly, and told him candidly what I considered the value of such items as he was ignorant of. Yesterday I knew him to be a liar and I ceased to consider his interests at all, and sought to buy as cheaply as I could.

When Wise came to call, Watts-Dunton, it seems, sat with a list in front of him of 'valuations for probate' and every time the dealer 'named a figure, the miserable old reptile pretended to consult his list and topped my offer'. The Wise theory was that Watts-Dunton habitually added a percentage to the listed price – that is to say, he *lied*. All this is recounted by Wise to Gosse in tones of moral outrage. Wise can now see, he says, 'the reality of [W–D's] affection for ACS . . . it strikes me that their "beautiful friendship" which has moved the public to tears was a very one-sided affair after all. Swinburne was *loyal* to it: W–D was not.'

The haggling dragged on throughout the summer and, inter-mittently, for several years thereafter. Read in sequence, the letters offer a richly comic narrative: the shady relic-hunter gradually breaking down the avaricious but increasingly uncertain legatee, with each casting himself in the role of keeper of the Swinburne flame, and each viewing the other as a grasping opportunist. And on the sidelines there was Gosse, one eye already on the biography, encouraging his useful friend in his delusions of piety: 'I lose all power of speech when I think of the gluttony and shamelessness of the old toad. I only hope that you will succeed, some day, in wiping the slime of T. W–D off the pure marble of Swinburne's memory. You are surely going to prevent that he go down to posterity as the Hero-Friend.' And Wise was of course playing a double-game with Gosse, feeding him horror tales of the reptile's greed and cunning while making sure that his own invitations to The Pines did not dry up.

On 30 June, Wise reports: 'I went to Putney last evening and bought a few more MSS. I got the old chap down a trifle for the single sheet poems and bought them. He will not take less than £5 for a sonnet.' On 2 July: 'He does not know what he possesses . . . I saw one day a large drawer full of unsorted blue sheets . . . I took up one or two myself, but could get no price put upon them. "I will reflect," said the old boy . . . He asks the highest cent he thinks he can get, and if only his information was a bit more up to date, the prices would be higher still,' and on 5 July: 'I spent the whole of yesterday afternoon and evening at The Pines, so you may guess I have got some treasures. As a matter of fact, I have brought away some *glorious* treasures . . .' A busy seven days, and not untypical of Wise's comings-and-goings during the summer of 1909. Wise made the most of his booty – over the years he put out 'some 70 pamphlets all from unpublished Swinburne letters and manuscripts'. Watts-Dunton never got to France. He died in 1914, his final years a blur of executive bewilder-ment, it seems.

The row over the Swinburne biography did not properly get going until 1912, when Edmund Gosse published a reticent but not wholly reverential entry on Swinburne for the *Dictionary of National Biography*. In it he happened to make one of his famous blunders, attributing to Swinburne some poems that Wise had come across, signed 'A.C.S.', in an old copy of *Fraser's Magazine*. Swinburne would have been eleven at the time of the *Fraser's* publication. The actual author of the verses was one Anthony Coningham-Sterling. Before the error was exposed, Wise had published the pieces as Swinburne's *Juvenilia*. It was Gosse, though, as the 'literary' member of the team, who came in for the greater ridicule and Isabel Swinburne, incensed by Gosse's *DNB* 'insinuations', seized on the howler as a discrediting last straw. From then on she did everything she could to block progress on a Gosse Life of her brother.

In this enterprise she had a formidable ally in Mrs Disney Leith, the cousin. Leith's position on the Swinburne legend was that Algernon, far from being irreligious, 'was in communion with the Church of England all his life', that he was 'never intoxicated' and that it was nonsense to suppose that Adah Menken (and not herself) was the model for 'Dolores': 'Algernon was far too well bred a gentleman ever to speak to a woman of that class.' Poor Watts-Dunton, terrified of the two old ladies, was caught in the middle. He did not wish to offend the family and he was in any case just as keen as the ladies were that Swinburne's secrets should be buried. On the other side, he was under pressure from Wise, who was pushing the Gosse interest and had allowed it to be known that there were incriminating Swinburne letters which, in the event of total non-cooperation, might have to be released. Something of the flavour of the situation is captured in the Wise–Gosse correspondence:

> if only the old chap really can be brought to entertain feelings of friendliness towards you, much good would result.
>
> But I must say this – that it is the 'Fear of God' we have managed to instil into his heart that has done the trick: he is under the impression that Gosse is another Jove, and holds a good handful of thunderbolts in the shape of 'bad' letters of Swinburne. Thinking this, he would argue to himself – 'We must not worry the rat too much in his corner: he may turn in desperation and bite . . .'
>
> . . . he said: 'Cannot you induce Gosse to destroy those *bad* letters?' I replied: 'No; and after Isabel's attack upon him, would you not yourself think him a fool if he destroyed anything that supported his statements?' 'Well, yes, I suppose so: but give him my kind regards and tell him I consider his article in the Quarterly very good indeed.'

When Isabel Swinburne made it clear that, if Gosse were to write the Life, she would 'forbid any reference' in it to herself, Watts–Dunton said to Wise (or so Wise has it):

I do hope Gosse will make proper reference to me, unlike our lady I *wish* to be mentioned *fully*. In fact any book about Swinburne that had not a very great deal to say about me would be a book to be laughed at. All, or very nearly all, that Swinburne became he owed to me. I can quite understand that once a woman has taken a dislike to anyone nothing can change her views. But *I* am not a woman . . . I hope you showed [Gosse] my letter, and made it clear to him that it was not possible for me to say anything more. Of course you understand that he *will*, very properly, acknowledge my rights when making selections to quote. I'm sure you can perceive why I am unable to give a formal permission for them to be made.

'Poor devil!' comments Wise. 'He's between the "two horns", and the position is not a comfortable one.'

Both Isabel and Watts–Dunton were dead by the time Gosse got down to serious work on the biography in 1915, but the opposition of Mrs Disney Leith had all along been more energetic and intense than anything the other two could muster, and she was resolute in her refusal to relax her opposition. Mrs Leith's involvement in the Swinburne presentation was, it is now perceived, not in the least straightforward. Although she would eventually destroy a mass of family correspondence, letters have survived which make it clear that she shared – and early on perhaps stimulated – the poet's taste for flagellation. And the novels she wrote were, in any case, packed with squirming Swinburne types: like Freddy in *Undercliff* who was 'massively flagellated at every turn of his boyhood – on one page 18 times in 43 days'. And this was no schoolgirl silliness. *Undercliff* came out in 1890, when Mary was in her sixties. And at this same late age she and Swinburne were busily exchanging flirtatious, lightly coded letters on the subject of '*old fashioned* methods of discipline', picking up where they had left off some thirty years before, when Mary had, it seems, renounced the love of her mad poet-cousin in order to marry the dashing (and, it so happened, rather intriguingly *wounded*) Colonel Leith. Colonel Leith died in 1892.

To Edmund Gosse in 1915, however, her opposition was – as we have seen – traditionally moralistic. Was Gosse perhaps too much of a gentleman to have retaliated with – at the very least – an exegesis of her novels, or had he not been able to bring himself to mug up on the trials of Freddy? In the event, his biography does refer to Swinburne's youthful collaboration with his cousin on a story called *Children of the Chapel* but does not record, as a modern biography feels bound to, that the story 'contains the sort of flagellation scenes that appealed to both of them'.

But then Gosse's *Life*, when it finally appeared in 1917, was agreed – even by the biographer's close friends – to have feebly glossed over Swinburne's weaknesses. The ladies, it was said, had won. 'The shadow of fear hangs over the whole book,' wrote A. C. Benson, 'fear of critics, fear of relations, fear of press-cuttings. The result is that S. is buried – and by the one man who might have made him live.' Gosse knew that he had caved in, that he had suppressed the drunkenness, the flagellation, Adah Menken – indeed, anything at all that might have stirred the wrath of Mrs Disney Leith. 'The family,' he would later plead,

> actuated by an intense determination to reduce the poet to a respectable commonplace, offered me a resistance that was quite formidable . . . Not only did they refuse to help me in any degree, but they sent me a message that if I published anything 'unpleasant' they should denounce the whole of my narrative as 'a pack of falsehoods' . . . there was a sort of conspiracy that Algernon should be presented to posterity as a guileless and featureless model of respectability.

In the Preface to his biography, however, he refers to the 'extraordinary and almost universal kindness' with which he has been treated by 'Swinburne's representatives and friends'.

It was a timorous performance, if not – as Ezra Pound sneered – 'the kowtowing' of 'a silly and pompous old man' (the book, for those who knew, did manage to send out some signals). To make amends, Gosse prepared a document in which – out of, he said, a sense of 'duty to posterity' – he set down all the ugly stuff he had been forced to censor from the *Life*. 'Swinburne . . . was a drunkard'; 'he not only liked to be whipped, but he experienced an ecstatic pleasure in letting his mind rest on flagellation, and to conjure up scenes of it'. This so-called *Confidential Paper* Gosse in 1920 lodged in the British Museum (where it remained unpublished until 1962) but he first sent copies to a number of his friends. The replies he got covered an interesting range of contemporary opinion. A. E. Housman was intrigued: 'It is curious that though Sade is the author who most influenced Swinburne and though Swinburne's writings are full of Sadism properly so-called, his own propensities were those of Rousseau and Sacher-Masoch. It is true that these are cheaper to indulge, but that does not seem to have been the reason.' Max Beerbohm recoiled in comic horror: 'How dreary and ghastly and disgusting the whole thing becomes. Why should anyone in posterity *know* that Swinburne did those things?' And Sir Walter Raleigh gamely occupied the middle ground: 'I suppose A.C.S. was impotent. The flowers of the human mind grow in queer soils . . . Adah Menken comes very well out of it. She was a gentleman, so to speak.'

# CHAPTER TWELVE

# ROBERT LOUIS STEVENSON AND HENRY JAMES

Most writers have more than one keeper of the flame. Edmund Gosse deplored Watts-Dunton for having transplanted Swinburne from the destructive element, for having levelled out the poet's tragi-farce. He, Gosse, liked to perform as Mr Steady, and he saw the Watts-Dunton intervention as a sort of theft, or kidnap. And he was not alone in seeing it this way: when Swinburne took off for The Pines he left behind him a small troupe of thwarted literary nursemaids – friends for whom the mad drunkenness, and their indulgence of it, had been the stuff of a reborn romanticism, a renaissance of wonder, so to speak. The Swinburnians' resentment of Watts-Dunton, though, was far from being just to do with poems: W-D was reviled also as the new wife who had broken up the bachelors' long night out.

When Robert Louis Stevenson's newish wife took him off to America and then to the South Seas, there was a similar commotion. Sidney Colvin, W. E. Henley, James Baxter and a few other associates (including Gosse) of Stevenson's young manhood made all the correct noises at the time – their tubercular comrade needed a warm climate and all that – but they also felt as if they had been robbed; and in the case of the magnetic Stevenson, this was a loss that hurt. Stevenson's marriage had been hard enough to take. The roistering Edinburgh days, the boozing and the wenching, the sub-Bohemian male camaraderie: all this would certainly have had to stop and had anyway been something of a pose. But the boyish R.L.S. should surely have stayed boyish, unattached. And now the wife who had already semi-suburbanised him was stealing him away – for one winter, it was said, but of course she never brought him back.

The wish to look after Stevenson was felt powerfully, it seems, even by friends whom he (in money terms) frequently looked after. Swinburne excited a similar possessiveness but Swinburne was

197

thought to be a freak; Stevenson, by all accounts, was loved. And yet, of those who loved him, only Henry James loved him well enough to concede wholeheartedly that he *ought* to be away from England, from his friends, from the temptations of the Savile Club, of Shepherd's Bush and the so-called Henley Regatta. Good company was bad for him and James feared that Stevenson's next haemorrhage would be his last.

For the whisky-toping Henley, himself crippled in youth by tuberculosis (he had lost a leg), a sort of razor's-edge ebullience was the creative source, or so he liked to say. Just as there were two Swinburnes to be cared for – pre and post Watts–Dunton – so for the likes of Henley there would be two Stevensons: 'the Stevenson who went to America in '87, and the Stevenson who never came back'. There would be the ragged original: 'riotous, scornful . . . unmarried and irresponsible', and the smartened-up successor: the 'brilliant and distinguished' man of letters, 'authorised and acceptable'.

Stevenson met Fanny Osbourne (née Vandergrift) in 1876, when he was in his mid-twenties and she was thirty-six, an American about-to-be divorcée fled to Paris with her children to become a painter. They married four years later. According to a friendly witness, Fanny was 'both physically and mentally the very antithesis of the gay, hilarious, open-hearted Stevenson and for that reason perhaps the woman in the world best fitted to be his life comrade and helpmate'. To most of his chums, though, hers was the face that did not fit: 'stalwart, swarthy and determined' was one of the more flattering descriptions. They were repelled by her busy managerial efficiency, her new-woman lack of winsomeness and most of all by her flintily unenchanted attitude to *them*. 'For no one in the world,' she wrote, 'will I stop in London another hour after the time set':

It is a most unhealthful place at this season, and Louis knows far too many people to get a moment's rest . . . Company comes in at all hours from early morning till late at night, so that I almost never have a moment alone, and if we do not soon get away from London I shall become an embittered woman. It is not good for my mind, nor my body either, to sit smiling at Louis's friends until I feel like a hypocritical Cheshire cat, talking stiff nothings with one and another in order to let Louis have a chance with the one he cares the most for, and all the time furtively watching the clock and thirsting for their blood because they stay so late.

The smiles seem to have fooled no one. Sidney Colvin was diplomatic – 'a build and character that somehow suggested Napoleon', he said of her – but then Colvin had been ready enough to have Stevenson's romantic ardour directed away from his own wife-to-be, Mrs Fanny Sitwell, to whom R.L.S. had been paying somewhat over-florid court for several years. Colvin doted on Stevenson and had got him started as a writer but even his vastly amenable disposition had been stretched to the limit, one would think. There was no great warmth between him and Fanny Stevenson but each saw the other's point.

Not so with Henley. Before Fanny came along, Henley was central to the Stevenson affections; he had been agent, mentor and collaborator and it was Stevenson's admiration for his 'maimed strength and masterfulness' that had 'begot' the character of Long John Silver. 'We have lived, we have loved, we have suffered' more or less summed up the aimed-for tone of the relationship, pre-Fanny. 'Marriage often puts old friends to the door,' wrote Stevenson, and when in 1888 he and Henley had their celebrated falling-out, the immediate issue was Henley's attitude to Fanny. The quarrel has been heavily documented – in brief, it was to do with a suggestion of Henley's that a story written by Fanny was 'borrowed' from a mutual friend – and it could easily have been patched up. The two friends desperately wanted to make peace, but the outraged, insulted Fanny would not let the matter rest: 'I am not likely to change in my feelings of resentment. The wrong can never be condoned, nor do I ever wish to see England again. It is most probable that I never shall.'

Even before the quarrel (which was conducted by mail between London and Samoa), Fanny had managed to persuade Stevenson to drop his original intention that Henley should one day be the author of his Life. Before leaving England, Stevenson had added a codicil to his will:

If my wife shall find herself able and willing to undertake my life with her own hand, I desire that this shall be left to her, and should so have arranged it from the first if I had not understood her to refuse: at the same time I request her to allow my formerly designated biographer, W. E. Henley, to give his own account of matters that he knows best, and to share emoluments with him in proportion.

A touching attempt to bring the 'two Stevensons' together. If Fanny were to decide not to write the book, the codicil goes on, then Henley should be re-appointed – but with a proviso which perhaps tells us why he had been pushed aside:

> I beg Henley, suppose my wife shall desist from her present profession of willingness to execute the task, to carry along with him in his work the counsels of my wife and of my friend Sidney Colvin; and I beseech him to remember that whereas I do believe an entertaining and not unuseful book may be made of my biography, it is never worthwhile to inflict pain upon a snail for any literary purpose; and that where events may appear to be favourable to me and contrary to others, I would rather be misunderstood than cause any pang to anyone whom I have known, far less whom I have loved.

After the great quarrel, Henley had to be removed from the picture altogether. In December 1888, Stevenson wrote a second statement of his wishes. This he put into a sealed envelope and handed to his stepson, Lloyd Osbourne. The statement did not explicitly revoke the 1885 codicil – indeed it barely mentioned Henley – but it named Sidney Colvin as 'the boy to do' a short sketch of his life, which might serve as preface to 'a popular volume . . . made of my reliquiae, little verses, certain of my letters, etc.' Again, a proviso or caution was added. Stevenson feared that Henley might prove to be an impetuous, if not malicious, biographer: 'it is never worthwhile to inflict pain upon a snail'. With Colvin, the worry was that *he* would turn out to be snail-like:

> Another caution I must give you; and have no hesitation in shewing it to Colvin: this is quite a public letter. You must beg Colvin not to run away with all the profits by incessant alteration and delay: that is the danger of S.C.; but for my sake and my family's, he will make an effort and conquer his besetting sins.

Stevenson died in 1894, without leaving further instructions, although in 1892 he did write to Colvin: 'It came over me the other day suddenly that this diary of mine to you would make good pickings after I am dead.' Within days of his theatrical Samoan burial, Fanny was arranging for advertisements in the British newspapers, requesting that R.L.S. letters be sent to her for an edition. She invited Henry James to be literary executor, but he declined. She offered to send Henley the Union Jack that had been laid over Stevenson's body before burial, but he said he did not want it. In the end, she turned to Colvin, as her husband would have wished. The Stevenson papers were bundled up and sent to him in London, and it was agreed that he should write the Life.

Fanny was not keen on the idea of Colvin as biographer. He had opposed the decision to settle in Samoa, and she suspected that he would insufficiently glorify this all-important aspect of the legend. She may also have known, or suspected, that Stevenson had confided to his friend that during its last two years the marriage had been under strain. She had suffered more than one 'neurasthenic' breakdown during this period, complete with tantrums, hallucinations, violent jealousies, etc., and had generally been making it hard for the great writer to get on with his work – work from which, in any case, she had felt increasingly estranged. The revived 'Scottishness' of Stevenson's thinking in his final years had been, for her, a sinister development. So too had been her husband's deepening reliance on the companionship and secretarial acumen of his step-daughter (and, of course, her daughter) Belle. If Colvin knew anything of all this – and he did – there was a danger that he might be lured into a Henley-ish interpretation of the Exile. And Fanny was not above considering the money angle. With his death, Stevenson shares were riding high, and prompt nourishment of the South Seas idyll legend was required. She had by now read her husband's words about Colvin's besetting sins.

In fact, Colvin at first seemed to move into action fairly smartly. He was already (with Charles Baxter) editing the Edinburgh Edition of Stevenson's Collected Works, but even so, within a year of his friend's death he had put out a selection of *Vailima Letters* (the 'pickings' Stevenson had urged him to preserve). These, Fanny might have been relieved to find, were heavily edited and did no damage at all to the evolving myth:

> They tell, with the zest and often in the language of a man who remained to the last a boy in spirit, of the pleasure and troubles of a planter founding his home in the virgin soil of a tropical island; the pleasures of an invalid beginning after many years to resume habits of outdoor life and exercise; the toils and satisfactions, failures and successes, of a creative artist whose invention was as fertile as his standards were high and his industry unflinching. These divers characters have probably never been so united in any man before.

So far so good. Colvin was also preparing the unfinished *Weir of Hermiston* for publication and was known to be gathering in Stevenson's scattered correspondence. A busy man – he worked full-time at the British Museum – Colvin could hardly be accused of dragging his feet.

And yet, after four years of seeming zeal, there was no sign of the promised Life. In 1898, Fanny made a trip to Europe and began to push Colvin for a report on progress:

> I want something definite . . . to look forward to and hope for. Can you not give me that? I have waited long and patiently. If I can be of any help to you – I mean if you want me at hand to answer any questions, or explain things, I will take rooms near the Museum and stay there all summer and all winter until the work is finished; and any moment you call me I will be there.

Even this terrifying prospect failed to panic Colvin into hasty promises. He wrote back, murmuring agreeably about 'limitations of leisure and health' and of 'the labour I have had already in your interests the last three years' and requesting that Fanny 'trust me in patience'. If she could not trust him, he would have to 'give it up':

> the sense of pressure, – or of being expected to hurry, of your hungriness and waiting (which I can perfectly well understand and sympathise with) would simply paralyse me, and drive me into a nervous condition when I should be unable to work at all, or do any duty in the service by which I gain my bread, or in that of the memory which is so dear to us both.

Fanny decided to back off but nine months later Colvin was still dithering: 'my head has quite broken down again, and I cannot go on with the biography at present.' He suggested that perhaps a two-volume edition of the letters, plus commentary, might be enough to be going on with. But he was not surrendering his commission: 'how could I forego the hope of linking my name with Louis' and doing something for him, and for you that would be worthy of him and be a joy forever.'

To this, Colvin got a reply not from Fanny but from her son Lloyd Osbourne, making it clear that the family's patience had run out: 'let me say in all frankness that you must give up the task – we have waited and I think you will admit how patiently and generously – for more than five years; we can wait no longer.' Colvin, irked by Osbourne's tone, struck back with threats that, if the Life were taken from him, a number of powerful literary friends would refuse to co-operate with his successor (at this point thought most likely to be Lloyd himself). And he would of course feel obliged to hang on to his own treasures, against the day when he might well, at his own pace, complete 'what had been the great hope and interest of my life'.

Lloyd, who 'had an unlucky way of putting things', got combative, and began to haggle about Colvin's share of the proceeds of the Letters. For a few weeks the whole thing seemed likely to turn ugly. In the end, though, Colvin – no great fighter – stepped aside, promising limited assistance to the family's appointee, who eventually turned out to be one Graham Balfour, a lawyer-cousin of Stevenson's. Balfour had no writing experience but he had served time in Samoa. Colvin did not altogether yield his ground. He would, he said, tell the story of R.L.S. 'my own way at some future time'. Balfour, though, was welcome to take over the official Life.

Sidney Colvin never did write his Stevenson biography. The nearest he got to it was an anodyne *Memoir* of some thirty pages, published in 1921. Reading these pages, we might wonder why he found it so hard to get to grips with the biography. Their determined inoffensiveness is comfortably in line with Henley's jokey prediction to Stevenson in 1881 that 'If you have a chance of reading Colvin's biography of you, you will see him veiling (in print) his blushing cheek and passing over certain of your earlier years – the years of Jink – in a manly and sorrowful silence.' To this, Stevenson had replied: 'Chapter Two "Youth in Edinburgh" is likely to be a masterpiece of the genteel evasion.' It is not known that Colvin ever read this exchange – but what if he did? And what if he was stung by the revelation that Stevenson had picked him as biographer because he could trust him to blush and draw the veil? In a letter to Lloyd Osbourne, concerning the Letters, Colvin wrote: 'I am afraid it is not possible, with any regard to eventual truth, to avoid upsetting the idyllic fictions about Louis' Edinburgh days.' For Colvin, this was fighting talk.

But it was only talk. Having resolved to be candid (if he did so resolve), Colvin would immediately have come up against a major inhibition of his own: how to characterise Stevenson's long wooing of his, Colvin's, mistress in the 1870s? (Colvin and Mrs Sitwell were not free to marry until 1903, when Mr Sitwell at last died; thus, at the time when Colvin was worrying about how to do the Life, the connection between them was not public.) Luckily, perhaps, Stevenson had destroyed Mrs Sitwell's letters to him, but his own side of their correspondence made it clear 'that the relations between them in the years 1873–6, while almost certainly held within the bounds of propriety, were intimate and emotional'. Everything in Colvin's situation and temperament would have constrained him to play down the whole episode. But, if he did, how could he elsewhere make a pretence of being fearless? How could he tell all, or anything, about the Edinburgh 'years of Jink', about Stevenson's quarrel with his father, about the pre-marriage relationship between Stevenson and Fanny Osbourne (their 'mutual anticipation of the parson'), about the disintegrating last months in Samoa? It must have seemed to Colvin that, if he did write the biography, he would be forced back into the very reticence which everyone expected of him, forced to write the book that Henley was waiting to make mock of.

When Graham Balfour's *Life of Robert Louis Stevenson* appeared in 1901, it was generally agreed to be a skilfully diplomatic performance. Fanny certainly was pleased by it. The Edinburgh years were buried under a heap of avuncular generalities ('the fiery pace of his age and temperament; his senses were importunate'), the quarrel with father was presented as a stimulating conflict of ideas, the Stevensons' long pre-marital interlude was deftly made to seem much shorter than it was, and the Samoan period was given a triumphant, culminating prominence – it occupied four-fifths of the text. On the subject of Mrs Sitwell, Balfour trod with a delicate surefootedness that Colvin must have both envied and been grateful for. The biographer spoke gravely of the 'solace' and 'strength' that Stevenson had got from the friendship during his 'troubles of youth', his 'passing moods of immaturity':

> It is the good fortune of some to receive in this crisis that service which it is generally beyond the power of man to bestow, and which is possible only for the few women who combine a quick intelligence and a knowledge of the world with charm of temperament and intuition heightened by sympathy.

On publication, Colvin told Balfour: 'I am sure there could not be a more faithful and exact chronicle, or one more excellent in taste and temper. If anything it seems to me you have a little overshirked the Bohemian aspects of his early life . . . (and I still have the fear that

Henley will come charging in on that subject)'. In all the circumstances, Colvin's condescension was impressive. On the matter of Henley, though, his fears turned out to have substance. In the December issue of the *Pall Mall Magazine* the 'assassin' delivered his soon-to-be-famous verdict on the Balfour portrait:

> 'Tis as that of an angel clean from heaven, and I for my part flatly refuse to recognise it. Not, if I can help it, shall this faultless, or very nearly faultless, monster go down to after years as the Lewis [*sic*] I knew and loved, and laboured with and for, with all my heart and strength and understanding. In days to come I may write as much as can be told of him. Till those days come, this protest must suffice. If it conveys the impression that I take a view of Stevenson which is my own, and which declines to be concerned with this Seraph in Chocolate, this barley-sugar effigy of a real man . . . suffice it will.

It was a breathtakingly venomous performance, aimed not really at Balfour or Colvin (for whose 'forthcoming' Stevenson biography, it was rumoured, the piece was first prepared) but at Fanny. For Henley, the Balfour book and all the legend-mongering it fostered and endorsed, represented a Samoan victory, a victory for Fanny's theft of Stevenson. It was she who had stopped Stevenson putting any sex into his books; it was she who had turned him into a prayerful moralist, a picturesque South Seas romancer. Henley 'wanted to savage Fanny, and he wanted to wound her in her love for R.L.S. as harshly as he believed she had wounded him in his love'. Balfour's book, he would have noted, made no mention of the famous quarrel. Henry James condemned the review as 'a strong and lurid – and so far interesting – case of long discomfortable jealousy and ranklement turned at last to posthumous (as it were!) malignity', but he would not have been surprised that the phrases 'Seraph in Chocolate' and 'barley-sugar effigy' were powerful enough to outlive the Balfour *Life*.

Fanny's post-Stevenson career – from 1894 to 1914 – makes rather dismal reading: the travelling about, the house-buildings, the string of 'protégés', the spiritualism, the long-running vendetta launched against her by Lloyd's wife (a mad 'Stevensonian' who blamed Fanny for just about everything and who eventually had to be bought off). The professional widow, Fanny had literary ambitions of her own, but even in her last weeks she was still writing about Stevenson – about Stevenson and Mrs Stevenson, that is. In 1915, her ashes were transported to Samoa and given a burial that was a near-replica of Stevenson's: the mountainside procession, the assembled island chieftains, even a bronze casket 'fitted in and cemented over by the same half-caste mason who had built the tomb for Louis'. 'An old chief said to Belle in his own tongue: "Tusitala is happy now. His true love has come back to him!" ' Shortly afterwards, Fanny's children were rushing Stevensoniana to the London sale-rooms. And so too, to everyone's surprise, was Colvin (now Sir Sidney), the biographer who couldn't.

In 1960, a pair of articles appeared in *The Times Literary Supplement*: 'How the Biography of Robert Louis Stevenson Came to be Written' by Michael Balfour, son of the biographer. Drawing on a number of unpublished letters, Balfour Jr gave the background to the Colvin dilemma and to his father's recruitment by the family. It was Balfour Jr who first suggested that the Mrs Sitwell problem was at the heart of Colvin's dithering; although he did allow that there was something in the man's personality which might in any case have brought him to a halt: 'he was a hesitant man given to procrastinating who was being pulled in contrary directions by his friends and by his own inclinations.' The two Balfour articles provoked a letter to the paper from Alan Osbourne, son of Lloyd, in which a further interpretation was proposed – an interpretation less complicatedly human than Balfour's but one which – incidentally – helps to explain Sir Sidney's recourse to the sale-room:

> The relations between Sidney Colvin and Stevenson were very strained shortly before Stevenson's death. Stevenson wrote Colvin a very sharp note which was not included among the collected letters. My father told me that Colvin had earlier found himself in certain financial difficulties and had appealed to Stevenson for help. Stevenson, to help Colvin, had ordered his publishers to pay the royalties on a certain book to Colvin. Stevenson had expected this to be a temporary expedient but Colvin went on collecting these royalties for some time. Stevenson one day discovered this when going over his accounts. This misunderstanding had most to do with Colvin's not getting the right to prepare a Life of R.L.S. . . . My people did not want Colvin to 'do' the Life. My father felt that the easiest way out was to let Colvin start on a life of R.L.S. but hang himself, due to his great tendency to become over-meticulous and to procrastinate. I am not defending my people in this matter, but they got what they wanted.

When Stevenson died, Henry James wrote a letter of condolence to his widow. James's way of comforting Fanny in her loss was to evoke the legendary aspects of her husband's life, to play up the ways in which he had not died. James spoke of 'that splendid life, that beautiful, bountiful being' now 'converted into a fable as strange and romantic as one of his own, a thing that *has* been and is ended'. Ended, and yet not ended; the pain of his absence, James delicately hints, is or might be soothed by the continuing vigour of his legend. 'He lighted up one whole side of the globe, and was in himself a whole province of one's imagination . . . He has gone in time not to be old, early enough to be generously young and late enough to have drunk deep of the cup.' James writes in the hour of his distress, and his purpose is elegiac and consolatory. It is evident, though, that he himself has begun to be moved by the myth he has conjectured, to thrill somewhat to a certain *rightness* in this hard-to-bear calamity. There would now never be a not-young R.L.S. The narrative achieves its closure; it is known 'what happens next'.

James was, of course, fascinated by the subject of literary com-memoration. *The Aspern Papers* had come out in 1888 and during the 1890s he published several stories and reviews that focused on what he called 'the greatest of literary quarrels . . . the quarrel beside which all others are mild and arrangeable, the eternal dispute between the public and the private, between curiosity and delicacy'; 'Nothing comes up oftener today than the question of the rights of privacy; of our warrant, or want of warrant, for getting behind, by the aid of editors and other retailers, certain appearances of distinction . . . the general knot in the business is, indeed, a hard one to untie.' The Stevenson case he found particularly gripping, and not just because of his personal involvement. He had backed away from Fanny's proposal that he become R.L.S.'s literary executor and had similarly shrunk from getting drawn into the Lloyd Osbourne dispute with Colvin. From his chosen distance, though, he monitored the progress of his friend's posthumous celebrity, and seems to have found in it – and in his response to it – a provocation.

On the one hand, James was spellbound by the myth of Stevenson, the myth – as he saw it – of the 'moribund' adventurer, the active contemplative, the man 'launched into the world for a fighter with the organism of, say, a composer', whose life had hung 'but by a thread'; 'it all hung, the situation, by that beautiful golden thread'. On the other hand, he hated to see his friend taken over by the mob, the world of 'newspapers and telegrams and photographs and interviews'. And yet if Stevenson had not been vastly popular, had not lit up one whole side of the globe, would he now so powerfully occupy a province of the discriminating Jamesian imagination? It was all very well to deplore, in the mass audience, a curiosity about the real Stevenson but what was it that legitimised one's own appetite for revelation? And was not this (of course, far finer) appetite sharpened somewhat by the immensity of the general, vulgar 'wish to know'?

In the end James would decide that here, as with so many other varieties of human experience, it was a matter of 'knowing where to stop'. Thus, when Colvin's edition of Stevenson's *Letters* appeared in 1899, James had no qualms about intrusiveness. Indeed, what he enjoys about the *Letters* is, he says, that they 'positively make for revelations. Stevenson never covered his tracks, and the tracks prove, perhaps, to be what most attaches us. We follow them here, from year to year and from stage to stage, with the same charmed sense with which he made us follow one of his hunted heroes in the heather.' In other words, the revelations act in concert with the work; thanks to Colvin's discreet presentation, there is nothing in them to subvert or diffuse our literary apprehension of the myth. On the contrary, they reinforce it, by offering 'real-life' support. Stevenson can now pass 'ineffaceably into happy legend', and can even – thanks to his fame – become 'something other than the author of this or that particular beautiful thing, or of all such things together':

> It has been his fortune (whether or no the greatest that can befall a man of letters) to have had to consent to become, by a process not purely mystic and not wholly untraceable – what shall we call it? – a Figure. Tracing is needless now, for the personality has acted and the incarnation is full . . . This case of the figure is of the rarest, and the honour surely of the greatest. In all our literature we can count them, sometimes with the work and sometimes without. The work has often been great and yet the figure nil.

How the 'Figure' differs from what Henley calls the 'effigy' is not explored. When James came to read the Balfour biography his objections were not, as Henley's were, that R.L.S. had been prettified. James's disappointment was to do with a different sort of diminution. Writing to Balfour, he praised the book's 'infinite taste, discretion, happiness of touch and sense of proportion' and added, with tranquil irony, the hope that 'you feel that you have put up a very fair and shapely monument. Fanny Stevenson and Lloyd O must feel it and I enter deeply into all it must be for you to know that you have gratified *her*.' Then came the 'but':

There are other thoughts, other and different consequences (of all the cumulative publicity and commemoration) that make the critical spirit in me put a question . . . whether Louis's work itself doesn't *pay* somewhat for the so complete exhibition of the man and the life. You may say that the work was, or *is*, the man and the life as well; still, the books are jealous and a certain supremacy and mystery (above all) has, as it were, gone from them. The achieved legend and history that has *him* for subject has made, so to speak, light of their subject, of their claim to represent him. In other words you have made him – everything has made him – too *personally* celebrated for his literary legacy. He had of course only to be then himself less picturesque, and none of us who knew him would have had him so by an inch. But the fact remains that the *exhibition* that has overtaken him has helped, and that he is thus as artist and creator in some degree the victim of himself. I speak as from the literary vision, the vision for which the rarest works pop out of the dark of the inscrutable, the untracked.

Balfour may well have been puzzled by these fine discriminations: where had he gone wrong? Or was James merely saying that formal biography is the enemy of legend because it partakes so avidly of the mundane? James often based his own fictions on real people but it became hard for him to do so when he knew too much about his models – close up, they got blurred. With Colvin's *Letters*, the reader had been able to marvel at the legend from a distance.

The key word of course is 'mystery'. It was one of James's favourites. 'Out of no mystery now do they issue, the creations in question,' he wrote to Edmund Gosse, a few days after his letter to Balfour, and then added: 'and they couldn't afford to lose it.' Was there always a touch of envying condescension in James's view of Stevenson's success? In the Henry James career, 1894 marked the beginning of the end of his own bid for mass acclaim. A year later, after the humiliating failure of his play, *Guy Domville*, he would give up all notions of finding himself transmuted into a 'figure' of popular legend, of the Stevenson type. Removed to Rye, he would begin to work even harder than before at perfecting an opposite style of distinctiveness. If 'mystery' was what mattered, he would see to it that his own was unassailable.

Not that James was ever in any real danger of having the secrets of his art superseded or overlaid by exhibitions of his personality. The James life is now thought of as a highly mannered composition, an enterprise of style at the cost of passion, of decision at the cost of accident, and yet harbouring – just as his later writings do – a core of darkness, something inscrutable, untracked, an undeciphered 'figure in the carpet', a not entirely tamed 'beast in the jungle'. In about a dozen stories of the 1890s, James has 'legendary' authors as objects of awed and baffled scrutiny and in each story there is a strangely intense savouring of the thwartedness of those who would wish to penetrate and/or appropriate the Master's mysteries, to solve him and explain him. The Master is usually himself thwarted in the grave and secret business of his lifetime's work; his own grasp of what he is up to is no more assured than that of his disciples. Nonetheless, he is the Master – and as long as there are disciples to bewilder, he'll remain so: mystery *is* mastery.

James was always careful to inject some 'operative irony' into his Neil Paradays, Ralph Limberts, Hugh Verekers and all the other 'super-subtle fry' whose genius these tales take so easily (too easily?) for granted. Such flawed magicians are the best that can be offered as retaliation against the age's new-style inquisitors and celebrants. And even the most bewitched disciples have to be kept guessing, for they too are likely to be tainted by the contagion of 'newspaperism'. More than once, in James's literary tales, the disciple-figure is a hard-up young journalist.

In *The Aspern Papers* we were offered a parable to do with 'that most fatal of human passions, our not knowing where to stop'. The Aspern relic-hunter persuades himself that he is somehow 'serving' the great poet: 'There's no baseness I wouldn't commit for Jeffrey Aspern's sake.' The hero of another, later story called 'The Real Right Thing' is similarly self-deluding. Three months after the death of the writer Ashton Dyne, George Withermore is hired by the widow to research Dyne's Life. The widow is in a hurry; she installs Withermore in Dyne's old study and gives him free access to the archives:

> These materials – diaries, letters, memoranda, notes, documents of many sorts – were her property, and wholly in her control, no conditions at all attaching to any portion of the heritage, so that she was free at present to do as she liked – free, in particular, to do nothing.

(The literary widow who chooses to 'do nothing', is, in James's reckoning, the rarest of rare birds.) Withermore begins his researches and after a bit receives visits from none other than the ghost of the dead author. At first the biographer takes these appearances as a sign that Ashton Dyne is 'with him', is approving and abetting. Soon, though, the ghost becomes less friendly. Withermore fears that he, the biographer, must be getting something wrong: 'Had he taken, on some important point – or looked as if he might take – some wrong line or wrong view? had he somewhere benightedly falsified or inadequately insisted?' It then emerges that the ghost is actually opposed to the whole project, that Dyne doesn't *want* a Life. Withermore reports back to the widow:

> 'in my original simplicity, I was mistaken. I was – I don't know what to call it – so excited and charmed that I didn't understand. But I understand at last. He only wanted to communicate. He strains forward out of the darkness; he reaches towards us out of his mystery; he makes us dim signs out of his horror.'
> 'Horror?' Mrs Dyne gasped with her fan up to her mouth.
> 'At what we're doing.'

Withermore resolves not to proceed with his assignment but the widow persuades him to have one more try. She wants, she says, to do 'the real right thing'. When Withermore revisits the Dyne study, he finds the ghost waiting at the door, barring his way. That does it: he abandons the biography. And James spells out the message:

> What warrant had he ever received from Ashton Dyne himself for so direct and, as it were, so familiar an approach? Great was the art of biography, but there were lives and lives, there were subjects and subjects. He confusedly recalled, so far as that went, old words dropped by Dyne over contemporary compilations, suggestions of how he himself discriminated as to other heroes and other panoramas. He even remembered how his friend, at moments, would have seemed to show himself as holding that the 'literary' career might – save in the case of a Johnson and a Scott, with a Boswell and a Lockhart to help – best content itself to be represented. The artist was what he *did* – he was nothing else. Yet how, on the other hand, was not *he*, George Withermore, poor devil, to have jumped at the chance of spending his winter in an intimacy so rich?

On the matter of his own biography, James was haunted by the fate of Flaubert. Here was a writer for whom he had the strongest fellow-feeling, a writer for whom the 'ideal of dignity, of honour and renown, was that nothing should be known of him but that he had been an impeccable writer . . . he kept clear all his life of vulgarity and publicity and newspaperism.' In the end, though, to what purpose?

With the posthumous publication of his *Letters*, Flaubert was now – this was in 1893 – 'dragged after death into the middle of the market place, where the electric light beats fiercest'. He had been delivered to the Philistines 'with every weakness exposed, every mystery dispelled, every secret betrayed'.

This was the horror above all to be avoided. But, in times like these, was it avoidable? The publication of Flaubert's *Letters* 'indeed brings up with singular intensity the whole question of the rights and duties, the decencies and discretions of the insurmountable desire to *know*. To lay down a general code is perhaps as yet impossible, for there is no doubt that to know is good, or to want to know, at any rate, supremely natural.' The strength of James's meditations on the subject of biography – in his tales and in his criticism – is that he knows what biographical curiosity feels like, he has experienced that voyeuristic thrill. He was a voracious gossip, an energetic, note-taking tourist of literary tombs and birthplaces, a habitual watcher from the sidelines. He loved reviewing biographies and collections of letters, even as he chastised himself for his intrusiveness – there is a relish as well as a recoiling in his response to the unmasking of Flaubert. He would even, in 1903, fulfil a commission to write the Life of a recently dead artist – the expatriate American sculptor William Wetmore Story (Withermore? Wetmore? The dates *do* fit.) A promise to do the Story Life had been 'gouged' out of him years before by the family:

> a promise first to 'look at' the late W.W.S.'s papers and then to write a memorial volume of some sort about him . . . But there is no *subject* – there is nothing in the man himself to write about. There is nothing for me but to do a *tour de force*, or try to – leave poor dear W.W.S. *out*, practically, and make a little volume on the old Roman, Americo-Roman, Hawthornesque and other bygone days, that the intending, and extending, tourist will, in his millions, buy . . . to do all that and Please the Family too! Fortunately the Family is almost cynically indulgent – and I hope not to be kept Pleasing it more than three or four months. But my lamp burns low.

James had known Story for some years but neither liked him nor admired his work. The two-volume Life was dashed off in two months and was every bit as sketchy – re Story – as he said it would be.

A similarly cavalier attitude to the biographical craft was evinced in James's *Notes of a Son and a Brother*. Here the chronicler tampered with letters by his brother William so as to make these childhood reminiscences 'a reflection of all the amenity and felicity of our young life of that time at the highest pitch that was consistent with perfect truth – to show us all at our best for characteristic expression and colour and variety and everything that would be charming'. When William's son (later to be Henry's literary executor) protested at his treatment of the letters, James blithely and revealingly replied:

> when I laid hands on the letters to use as so many touches and tones in the picture, I frankly confess I seemed to see them in a better, or at all events in a different light, here and there, than those rough and rather illiterate copies I had from you showed at their face value . . . It was as if he had said to me on seeing me lay my hands on the weak little relics of our common youth, 'Oh, but you're not going to give me away, to hand me over, in my raggedness and my poor accidents, quite unhelped, unfriendly; you're going to do the very best for me you *can*, aren't you, and since you appear to be making such claims for me you're going to let me seem to justify them as much as I possibly may?' And it was as if I kept spiritually replying to this that he might indeed trust me to handle him with the last tact and devotion – that is to do with him everything I seemed to feel him *like*.

Throughout the 1890s, James reviewed several collections of literary Letters, many of them French, and time and again found himself grappling with the 'greatest of literary quarrels'. Reading Balzac's letters he feels like a burglar; confronting the spill-all approach of Zola and George Sand he feels straightforwardly repelled, or so he says: 'there is clean linen and soiled'; life would be 'intolerable' if there was no 'forbidden ground'. Perusing the Goncourts' *Journals*, he is baffled: 'What would have been thought of a friend or an editor, what would have been thought even of an enemy, who should have ventured to print the Journal of MM de Goncourt?'

It was when wincing at the revelations of George Sand that James evolved his now famous declaration of resistance. Since it was natural, he mused, for artists to wish to protect themselves against intruders, and just as natural for biographers to 'wish to know', why should there not be some intelligent *organisation* of the conflict? Whenever we 'meet on the broad highway the rueful denuded figure' of an eminent biographee, we recognise that 'mystery has fled with a shriek'. We also note that it is always as if the biographee has been taken by surprise, as if some unforeseen, unforeseeable accident has taken place.

Surely this need not be so:

The reporter and the reported have duly and equally to understand that they carry their life in their hands. There are secrets for privacy and silence; let them only be cultivated on the part of the hunted creature with even half the method with which the love of sport – or call it the historic sense – is cultivated on the part of the investigator. They have been left too much to the natural, the instinctive man; but they will be twice as effective after it begins to be observed that they may take their place among the triumphs of civilisation. Then at last the game will be fair and the two forces face to face; it will be 'pull devil, pull tailor', and the hardest pull will doubtless provide the happiest result. Then the cunning of the inquirer, envenomed with resistance, will exceed in subtlety and ferocity anything we today conceive, and the pale fore-warned victim, with every track covered, every paper burned and every letter unanswered, will, in the tower of art, the invulnerable granite, stand, without a sally, the siege of all the years.

Thus it was that Henry James became his own keeper of the flame. During the Nineties, his one or two glancing contacts with the world of scandalous disclosure made him all the more determined to see to it that his own tracks would be covered. In 1894, his friend Constance Fennimore Woolson died in Italy, probably by suicide. She had been vaguely pursuing the reluctant James for years but in the end had tired of his granite-like impersonality and had settled on her own in Venice. James was shaken by the violence and indeed by the mystery of her demise and – as we might deduce from his great story, 'The Beast in the Jungle' – was inclined to blame himself. What if she *had* killed herself because of him? When he heard of her death, he hastened to Italy and, according to Fennimore's sister, 'never left us until all her precious things were packed and boxed and sent to America'. It is presumed that James's purpose was to recover his own letters. He and Fennimore had agreed to destroy their correspondence, but what if she had not kept her side of the bargain? In all probability, the letters – if there were any to be recovered – would have been innocuous, exhibiting, at worst, an elegant equivocation. Even so, the mystery of Fennimore, and the remorse, were *his* – to be made into invulnerable art, perhaps, but not to be kept as materials for a biography.

A year later, with Stevenson's death intervening, there was the Oscar Wilde imprisonment, an event which had obvious repercussions for literary men nervous of their reputations, both current and posthumous. The year of Wilde's downfall was the year in which *Guy Domville*, booed from the stage, was replaced at the St James's Theatre by *The Importance of Being Earnest*, a triumphant hit. James had never liked Wilde – indeed he once described him as 'an unclean beast' – and the *Guy Domville* fiasco had cut deep. But it was more than professional jealousy that prompted James's attitude to the great scandal, an attitude both prim and prurient. James refused to sign a petition for clemency and his off-the-cuff remarks in letters were fairly consistently unsympathetic. Wilde had handed *himself* over to the Philistines. He had not known where to stop. And there was now 'a certain general shudder as to what, with regard to some other people, may possibly come to light'. The celibate James's own sexual inclinations seem to have been of the sort which he, at any rate, would hardly dare to name, but in practice he had nothing much to fear. 'It would have been almost as embarrassing to have had to tell them how little experience I had had in fact as to have had to tell them how much I had had in fancy.' Thus spake the narrator in *The Sacred Fount*, a few years later on, and it sounds like a fair description of the author's own predicament. Even so, there was an unsettling new electricity abroad; a new atmosphere of accusation and exposure. Writing to Edmund Gosse (who had his own good reasons to feel nervous), James is in a turmoil of excitement about Wilde:

> it has been, it is, hideously, atrociously dramatic and really interesting – so far as one can say that of a thing of which the interest is qualified by such a sickening horribility. It is the squalid gratuitousness of it all – of the mere exposure – that blurs the spectacle. But the *fall* – from nearly twenty years of a really unique kind of 'brilliant' conspicuity (wit, 'art', conversation – 'one of our two or three dramatists, etc.') to that sordid prison-cell and this gulf of obscenity over which the ghoulish public hangs and gloats – it is beyond any utterance of irony or any pang of compassion! He was never in the smallest degree interesting to me – but this hideous human history has made him so – in a manner.

Oscar Wilde was living James's nightmare: and in a court-room, where biographical interrogation is compulsory and spectacularly public, and liable to result in gruesome punishment if the audience happens not to like what it is told. Small wonder that the great self-effacer was transfixed; small wonder also that, essentially, James had nothing but contempt for Wilde – a 'fatuous fool', a 'tenth-rate cad'. No true artist would have brought *this* on himself.

In the space of two years – 1894–5 – James had witnessed the making of two literary legends – the sentimental adoration of Stevenson and the hate-filled tearing down of Oscar Wilde. And he had faced his own audience on the stage of the St James's Theatre, where the applause of his discriminating friends had been drowned out by the hissing of the mob. 'All the forces of civilisation in the house waged a battle of the most gallant, prolonged and sustained applause with the hoots and jeers and catcalls of the roughs, whose roars (like those of a cage of beasts at some infernal zoo) were only exacerbated by the conflict.' This was January 1895; it was three months later that Wilde (the playwright no one booed) was brought to face *his* jeers and catcalls.

Of the two legends – Stevenson's and Wilde's – James felt closer, in the public eye, to Wilde's. He had never been vastly adored but he did now have an idea of what it felt like to stand in the dock: 'these discordant notes tonight,' he told his rowdy jurors, 'have hurt me very much. I can only say that we have done our very best.' He would never again direct his 'very best' at *them*. In that same January he wrote to William Dean Howells: 'I have fallen upon evil days – every sign or symbol of one's being in the least *wanted*, anywhere or by anyone, having so utterly failed. A new generation that I know not, and mainly prize not, has taken universal possession. The sense of being utterly out of it weighed me down, and I asked myself what the future would be.'

This, then, was the beginning of the Final Years; the middle period was done. At fifty-five, James withdrew from London; he was 'in retreat'. 'That's right – *be* one of the few!' he soon would say. In Rye, he bought a typewriter, hired a secretary, and let himself dictate, no longer minding if 'scarce a human being will understand a word, or an intention, or an artistic element or glimmer of any sort'. He evolved a new, 'difficult' prose style in which he could luxuriate, let go: from now on, he said, his work would be allowed to unfold itself 'wholly from its own innards', independent of the 'childishness of publics'. He shaved off his beard, affected sage-like airs and orotundities, welcomed young pre-Bloomsbury devotees and encouraged them to call him Master, cher maître, maestro and the like; he even permitted himself the odd feelingful dalliance with certain of his better-looking male disciples – nothing physical, we understand ('I can't, I can't, I *can't*!' cried James, when young Hugh Walpole offered himself to him), but, expressed in letters, more unguardedly frolicsome than might have been expected – expected, that's to say, even by James.

But then James was not *really* in retreat. Reading of his final years, we get no sense, except intermittently, that he had given up; rather, he seems to have forever been regrouping for a fresh assault. On what, though? Not mass popularity, although he did continue to dabble in the theatre, and would not have said No to some cheap triumph. Current acolytes aside, the new audience was of the future. Certain of his own genius, of its magical immensity, James wanted to be sure that he had served it well, that he would leave it to the world in the best possible state of polish and repair – he was not going to hand over his life's work in its 'raggedness and . . . poor accidents, unhelped, unfriendly'. Just as he planned to forestall the biographers, so he would forestall the critics. He would grant himself the rebirth, the 'second existence' so yearned for by the failing eminent in his tale 'The Middle Years'. And of course, if it so happened that his present audience got bigger, he would no doubt be able to take that in his stride.

In 1903, James began to rewrite all his earlier work. The pretext was the issuing of a sumptuous, 24-volume New York Edition of his writings. By extensive, sometimes radical revisions, the old James could be of wise assistance to his younger self. 'How sickly I used to write!' he said, with relish. He could also provide, in Prefaces, a 'private history' of his fictions, 'the story of a story', and at the same time enter 'a sort of plea for Criticism, for Discrimination, for Appreciation on other than infantile lines – as against the so almost universal Anglo-Saxon absence of these things'.

It was an extraordinary undertaking, and occupied four years of James's writing life. It was to be his monument. It was also, he hoped, to be his pension. In 1909, when he began to get the first dismal sales returns, he was cast low; they were far worse than even he had dared to fear. 'I have been living in a fool's paradise,' he said; his first royalty cheque was for $211, his second not much bigger. Retreat or no retreat, this was for James his second major audience rejection – and worse than the *Guy Domville* setback, in a way, because this thumbs-down was from his reading public, and the spurned offering was a complete edition of his *Works*. The New York Edition turned out to be 'the most expensive job of my life'.

During the early months of 1909, James seems to have had a kind of nervous breakdown; he was 'worried and depressed' all the time and believed that at any moment he might be felled by a 'cardiac crisis'. The doctor he consulted has recorded that the writer was suffering from what we would probably now call 'stress-fibrillations' and that he, the medico, had merely tapped his patient's chest and said: 'It is the mystery which is making you ill.' If this is true, James might with justice have withheld payment of the bill. (We now know that the doctor had lately been reading 'The Turn of the Screw' and that during the consultation he got from James a small lecture on how literary, and indeed some medical mysteries are made: 'So long as the events are veiled the imagination will run riot and depict all sorts of horrors, but as soon as the veil is lifted, all mystery disappears and with it the sense of terror.')

James was nearing seventy and his theories about biographical disclosure, although expounded frequently enough, had not yet spurred him into action on his own behalf. The New York Edition monument, whatever the financial loss, was now in place; elsewhere all was raggedness and accident – and time, it seemed, was running out. From 1909 until his death in 1916, we find James readying himself for posthumous inspection. In spite of Edith Wharton's kindly machinations – she tried to get James a Nobel Prize and secretly subsidised Scribner's offer of a large advance for a new novel – fiction would no longer command the centre of his working days. With the death of his brother William in 1910, he would be free to permit himself a re-vision, so to speak, of his own, and William's, history: the autobiographical *Notes of a Son and a Brother* was published in 1914 and, if James had lived, would have been followed by *The Middle Years* (the story of that title had been printed in 1893).

The year 1909, though, was a turning point – the last such point in a life which, more than most, moved from one definable sequence to the next. In that year, James performed a curious literary errand which may well have helped to jolt him into a new autobiographical resolve. The Byron marriage had once more been under discussion in the salons, as a result of the publication of *Byron, the last phase* by one R. Edgcumbe. In this book, yet another theory about Byron's sex-life was proposed; namely, that his Lordship *had* consummated a liaison with his famously unattained and unattainable first amour, Mary Chaworth. Lord Lovelace, whose *Astarte* had caused a stir four years earlier, was now dead, but his widow had in her possession Byron's pre-marital letters to Lady Melbourne and these letters would, in her view, disprove Edgcumbe's thesis and corroborate *Astarte*'s. Her husband had not been allowed to print the letters in his book. In December 1909, Lady Lovelace invited James and the novelist John Buchan (who was married to her niece) to view the documents in question. James had once before been consulted by the Lovelace family and when *Astarte* appeared had written one of his too-fulsome-to-be-true letters of praise to the author. This latest 'urgent appeal on the part of Lady Lovelace' was 'at much cost to my convenience' but he agreed to visit her and do his best. John Buchan has left an amusing description of the episode:

> An aunt of my wife's, who was the widow of Byron's grandson, asked Henry James and myself to examine her archives in order to reach some conclusion on the merits of the quarrel between Byron and his wife. She thought that these particular papers might be destroyed by some successor and she wanted a statement of their contents deposited in the British Museum. So, during a summer week-end, Henry James and I waded through masses of ancient indecency, and duly wrote an opinion. The thing nearly made me sick, but my colleague never turned a hair. His only words for some special vileness were 'singular' – 'most curious' – 'nauseating, perhaps, but how quite inexpressibly significant'.

In the James–Buchan opinion (drawn up in April 1910), the novelists were able to 'bear witness that [the letters] afford weighty corroborative evidence of the truth of the story told by Lord Lovelace' – that is to say, Byron, during the period Edgcumbe claimed him to be paying court to his first love – was indeed 'otherwise occupied': 'at this very time he was . . . expressing contrition as to that connection of which he himself said that it had an element of the *terrible* which made all other loves seem insipid.'

Within days of returning home from this perusal of the Byron papers, James destroyed his own archive – forty years' accumulation of papers: letters, manuscripts and notebooks. He had now, he said, 'made tolerably absolute . . . the law of not leaving personal and private documents at the mercy of any accidents, or even of my executors! I kept almost all letters for years – till my receptacles would no longer hold them, then I made a gigantic bonfire and have been easier in mind since – save as to a certain residuum which *had* to survive.' According to Leon Edel, James did hold back 'a handful of cherished letters':

> In a number of instances he saved one trivial letter from each correspondent – as if to preserve one little part of them from complete obliteration. From these little snippets of letters we can deduce to a degree the pattern of James's destruction. But each relic serves also as an unintended mockery: it tells us that there were other letters which we shall never see, that in this given case or that there has been a victory for the private life.

219

Overall, though, there was not much of a victory; the 'great thing' he had done was not so great. Edel himself, at the time of writing the above (1956), spoke of having located some seven thousand of James's own letters – which of course had not been his to burn – 'and every year more turn up'.

The publishing scoundrels, in other words, would still have lots to go on. But James evidently felt that he had made a start. A few years later, he instructed Harry James, his executor, on the matter of whatever literary remains he had not been able to destroy. Like Tennyson in his verses 'To ——', James makes reference to the lines on Shakespeare's tomb: 'Blest be ye man yt spares these stones/A curse be he yt moves my bones.'

> I am greatly touched, dear Harry, by your interest in the other question you speak of – that of my own 'literary remains' and my liability to the invading chronicler. It has often occupied my mind – though never yet to the effect of my trying to provide against it (and, much less, to provide *for* it) by some anticipatory clause. My sole wish is to frustrate as utterly as possible the post-mortem exploiter – which, I know, is but so imperfectly possible. Still, one can do something, and I have long thought of launching, by a provision in my will, a curse not less explicit than Shakespeare's own on any such as try to move my bones. Your question determines me definitely to advert to the matter in my will – that is to declare my utter and absolute abhorrence of any attempted biography or the giving to the world by 'the family', or by any person for whom my disapproval has any sanctity, of any part or parts of my private correspondence. One can discredit and dishonour such enterprises even if one can't prevent them, and as you are my sole and exclusive literary heir and executor you will doubtless be able to serve in some degree as a check and a frustrator.

Shortly after writing this – in 1915 – James made another, final bonfire of his papers.

Oddly enough, though, he did not in his will 'advert to the matter' of biography and we have only to look up the name Leon Edel in the bibliographies to discover how wholeheartedly his injunctions have been overlooked: a five-volume *Life*, a four-volume edition of the *Letters*, and various other subsidiary items. James is one of the most visible biographees of modern times. For twenty or so years after his uncle's death, Harry James made efforts to keep the invading chroniclers at bay; he refused, says Edel, 'requests for publication of certain of James's letters unless they contained material of distinct literary interest, and he stipulated that the archive he gave to Harvard should be available only to post-doctoral researchers.' In 1920, the estate did sanction Percy Lubbock's two-volume selection of *Letters*. Lubbock printed a mere 400 – some of them extracts – and two-thirds of these were from the magisterial last years. He cut out endearments like 'dearest, dearest, darlingest Hugh' and suppressed all reference to that 'hideous affliction' which Hemingway and others would later take to signify some castrating childhood injury (in fact, James was talking of his constipation and the childhood injury, we now know – thanks to Edel – was not of the sort mentioned in *Fiesta*).

Lubbock was a disciple of the later James and he became a sort of keeper of the flame – seeing James's unfinished novels into print and editing a selection from his Prefaces – and he was more than happy to report, as to the *Letters*, that 'a close reader must still be left with the sense that something, the most essential and revealing strain, is little more than suggested here and there.' And he was right – and, although we now (thanks again to Edel) have many thousands more of James's *Letters* to pore over, our conclusion might be much the same: there are more mysteries than glimpses. Did it work then, that checking and frustrating, or was there nothing *to* check and frustrate? This mystery, if mystery it is, remains inviolate.

# CHAPTER THIRTEEN

# REMEMBERING RUPERT BROOKE

Henry James's last published writing was in praise of Rupert Brooke. Like many others who in 1915 were moved to commemorate the 'Apollo golden-haired', James did not have a lot to go on, but what he did have seemed to be enough. He had been shown Brooke's celebrated 'war sonnets' a few days before hearing of their author's death and had been polite about them to Brooke's friend Edward Marsh (the 'circumstances,' he said, 'have caused me to read them with an emotion that somehow precludes the critical measure'.) His appreciation of Brooke, though, was chiefly to do with how the poet *looked* and, after he had died, with his totemic splendour.

James had met Brooke in Cambridge in 1909. Brooke had played up to him – had pulled, he said, his 'fresh, boyish stunt' – and the old novelist had been bewitched. When Brooke died, it was not the war sonnets, nor *Poems* (1911), that made James declare that a 'wondrous, heroic legend' had been born; it was what he remembered of the poet's 'insidious' handsomeness, his 'simple act of presence and communication'. Rupert dead had turned into 'the ideal image of English youth':

> What it first and foremost really comes to . . . is the fact that at an hour when the civilised peoples are on exhibition, quite finally and sharply on show, as they absolutely never in all their long history have been before, the English tradition . . . should have flowered at once in a specimen so beautifully producible.

James's ornately maudlin essay was written when he was sick and near to his own death. He had, just a few days earlier, been made a naturalised Briton. It is clear enough from his other pronouncements of the time that he knew very well what Brooke actually stood for: 'the destruction, on such a scale, of priceless young life . . . poisons and blackens one's whole view of things, and makes one ask what the end,

222

*anywhere*, will be.' He also knew – and for him this was a similarly horrifying knowledge – that the war had 'used up words':

> they have weakened, they have deteriorated like motor car tires; they have like millions of other things, been more overstrained and knocked about and voided of the happy semblance during the last six months than in all the long ages before, and we are now confronted with a depreciation of all our terms, or, otherwise speaking, with a loss of expression through increase of limpness, that may well make us wonder what ghosts will be left to walk.

And yet James was moved – and privileged, he said – to be involved in the war effort, to be part of 'English life wound up to the heroic pitch'. If gilded rhetoric could help, then let it.

In April 1915, when Brooke died, it was still possible to talk of enlistment as a happy sacrifice, an escape from peacetime tedium, from 'a world grown old and cold and weary', into an elevated other-world of duty, honour, courage, comradeship. A few weeks before Brooke's sacrifice, Dean Inge had recited 'The Soldier' ('If I should die . . .') from the pulpit of St Paul's. Now that the poet had, so to speak, fulfilled his promise, it was natural that his image should be seized on. 'He is the youth of our race in symbol,' said the *Daily News*. For recruitment purposes, Brooke was a godsend; a Greek godsend. If physical beauty of this calibre could be 'joyfully laid down', the ill-favoured need not drag their feet. Death – who could tell? – might make them pretty too.

Winston Churchill (whom Edward Marsh served as Private Secretary and who had fixed Brooke's commission in the Royal Naval Division) was swift to consolidate the possibilities:

> The thoughts to which [Brooke] gave expression in the very few incomparable war sonnets which he has left behind will be shared by many thousands of young men moving resolutely and blithely forward into this, the hardest, cruellest and the least-rewarded of all the wars that men have fought. They are a whole history and revelation of Rupert Brooke himself. Joyous, fearless, deeply instructed, with classic symmetry of mind and body, he was all that one would wish England's noblest sons to be in days when no sacrifice but the most precious is acceptable, and the most precious is that which is most freely proffered.

It was the death of Byron all over again, but this time with no incubus of scandal. Brooke was cleaner, fresher, more embraceably unspoiled than bad Lord B. There was nothing seamy or contentious about him; he was – as someone said (admiringly) – more a creature than a man, to do with golden limbs, fresh water, sun. Even D. H. Lawrence liked to think that Brooke (who was actually felled by a Port Said mosquito bite) had been 'slain by bright Phoebus' shaft – it was in keeping with his general sunniness'.

Another advantage Brooke had over Byron was that most of those who mourned him knew nothing much about his work; he was not a literary star, in spite of the efforts of Dean Inge. He had published one book and had appeared in Edward Marsh's *Georgian Poetry* and in literary circles was mildly notorious for a piece about being sea-sick in the English Channel. For the majority, however, he was first heard of as a Dead Young Poet. The man himself might as well have been made out of marble.

A myth so unencumbered by prosaic data is in time likely to produce its warty progeny, its counter-myth, its legend of the 'real', and even in 1915 Brooke's family and friends were not unaware of the dangers of backlash. The dirtier the war became, the more they had reason to fear for the prospects of a reputation based on clean-limbed warrior-heroics. And yet even those who 'really knew' Brooke had, like James, been more sensible of his presence than of his achievement as a poet: if the five war sonnets were to be discredited, what would be left? 'Clouds', possibly; 'Tiare Tahiti', at a pinch; 'Grantchester', well . . . And as for the famous presence: that too had been looking a bit ragged when last viewed.

In 1912 Brooke, having got himself into a complicated sexual tangle, succumbed to a nervous breakdown and fled to the South Seas. On his return a year later, he had been looking more rubicund than golden, perhaps as much from embarrassment over the emotional havoc he had set in motion before leaving as from the Pacific ministrations of friend Phoebus. And his old Cambridge friends were not quite as they had been. Before his crack-up Brooke had for years been an equivocal figure on the Cambridge and post-Cambridge scene. Being a golden boy, gaped at as hungrily by James Strachey as by Frances Cornford (she who penned the 'Apollo' quatrain), he found it difficult to decide where to direct *his* admiration. One week he was to be found with earnest Fabians and William Morrisites, the next with the sardonically effete Apostles, and then – for rather longer stretches – with the dew-dabbling neo-Pagans ('Bloomsbury under canvas', they were called) whose romantic-progressive creed of youthful beauty had in it, tormentingly for Brooke, stern precepts against youthful fornication.

When Brooke collapsed in 1912, the Cambridge verdict – in all factions – was that he had been driven mad by sexual frustration or sexual indecision, or, most likely, by a fifty-fifty combination of the two: 'your nakedness and beauty . . . your mouth and breasts and cunt – shall I turn in a frenzy and rape James [Strachey] in the night?' Brooke's ailment was by no means foreign to young dreamers of his epoch; the tantrums he threw, however, were reckoned to be unusually babyish and unattractive. When over-heated, he was wont to wax abusive; particularly so when a girl let him have his uncertain way with her – which at least once, from pity and exhaustion, a girl did. When the poet died, more than one of his love-objects had a bundle of crazed, nastily worded letters to remember him by – letters, it might have been thought by their recipients, more vividly hard-hitting than anything he wrote in verse.

Brooke returned from his South Seas rehabilitation in June 1914. It was Edward Marsh who met him at the station, and Marsh who, during the months leading up to his enlistment, helped him to maintain a correctly sheepish distance from his Cambridge chums. While Brooke was away, Marsh had been working hard to build up his reputation as the poet 'who seemed to have everything that is worth having'. Now he was able to introduce his protégé in poetry circles (in which, thanks to the success of *Georgian Poetry*, Marsh had become impresario-in-chief) and – via his day-job with Churchill – in the country houses and drawing rooms of high-up politicians on the brink of war. From plotting new verse magazines with Lascelles Abercrombie, Brooke would now speed off to weekend with the Asquiths. It was from this Marsh-contrived ambience that the war sonnets would soon issue.

Marsh's attachment to Brooke was of the Jamesian variety. Fifteen years older than Brooke, his adoration had been ignited a decade earlier, at a Cambridge University production of Aeschylus's *Eumenides*: Rupert had a small part, as a trumpet-bearing herald, but Eddie was entranced by his 'radiant youthful figure in gold and vivid red and blue' and never quite recovered. When Marsh died, in 1953, his executors found among his things a 'Rupert Trunk' containing Brooke's tie, handkerchief, sprigs of olive from his grave and 'several copies of a pamphlet called *Sexual Ethics*'.

When Brooke went off to war, there were several likely keepers of his flame. There were the girlfriends – chiefly Katherine ('Ka') Cox, the one he had been most stormily involved with. There was Marsh, his literary mentor. There were his Georgian poet friends, like Abercrombie and Walter de la Mare. And, most formidably, there was the poet's widowed mother, Mary Brooke – known to Brooke and his friends as The Ranee (because of a fancied connection with the Victorian White Rajah of Sarawak).

The Ranee had watched over her son's development with some-what bewildered disapproval. His schooldays at Rugby were fine. Rupert's father had also been his housemaster (he did not die until after Rupert had left school), so Mrs Brooke had a close-up view of her boy's several triumphs, with both book and ball. Brooke himself tended to think of his time at Rugby as the high point of his life, from which all else must be felt as a decline: 'As I looked back at five years, I seemed to see almost every hour golden and radiant, and always increasing in beauty as I grew more conscious; and I could not (cannot) hope for or even quite imagine such happiness elsewhere.'

Later on, Brooke would lament that those years had perhaps turned him into an 'Infantile Paralytic', but for the Ranee they were very heaven. As she saw it, they were the years in which her son's conduct had been most in harmony with his 'true self'. Thereafter he would be subject to the perils of 'influence': the influence of Cambridge, of fast women (although Brooke somehow managed to keep from his mother the causes of his breakdown: not easy, since she rushed to his side and stayed there during the worst of it), and – in his final months – of Edward Marsh and his grand friends. Brooke, like his father before him, was just a bit afraid of Mrs Brooke. Although he mocked her to others in his letters, he was always too anxious for her thriftily dispensed approval. The Ranee had one other son, Alfred, who was killed in action just a few weeks after Rupert died. On hearing about Alfred, Henry James – who barely knew Brooke's mother – wrote to Marsh: 'One's soreness of soul for that poor tortured woman is beyond all speech – and I feel the vision of her as a nightmare within the nightmare.' It would not be long before Marsh, in a different spirit, would similarly speak of her.

Brooke seems to have thought that, if he should die, his mother would not long survive him. In a letter written to Dudley Ward from the troopship that was taking him to the Near East, he asked his old Cambridge friend to take care of a few things for him, 'in the event of

226

his death'. There were letters to be burned, or not burned – although Brooke said: 'I don't care what goes . . . Indeed, why keep anything? Well, I *might* turn out to be eminent and biographiable. If so, let them know the poor truths.' And in the same letter, he half-jested: 'It's odd, being dead. I'm afraid it'll finish off the Ranee.'

Shortly afterwards, he wrote to Marsh:

> You are to be my literary executor. But I'd like mother to have my MSS till she dies – the actual paper and ink, I mean – than you . . . You must decide everything about publication. Don't print much bad stuff.

And on the same day, he wrote also to his mother, setting out rather more formally his last wishes (he had made no will). He named three poets as his heirs: Abercrombie, de la Mare and Wilfred Gibson. They were to get the royalties from his literary works: 'If I can set them free, to any extent, to write the poetry and plays and books they want to, my death will bring more gain than loss.' (By all accounts, this bequest did make a significant difference to the lives of all three legatees.) He confirmed Marsh's appointment as literary executor but, in granting his mother lifelong possession of his papers, he was also granting her a measure of control over how the papers (and, by inference, his reputation) should be managed: 'Of course [Marsh] will consult you and you will tell him what you want.' In the absence of any clearer instructions, the Brooke copyrights indeed belonged to her. No doubt Brooke reckoned that, if she did survive, his mother would take no interest in his literary affairs – she took none when he was alive. But he did not want to hurt her feelings nor cause her to be upset with him in any way. The question of copyright probably never crossed his mind: he let the Ranee have the manuscripts for as long as she needed them, as keepsakes (which is perhaps how he regarded them; although he told Marsh that the papers would go to *him* after his mother's death, he also told Ka Cox: 'I'm telling the Ranee that after she's dead, you're to have my papers').

At first, there seemed to be no difficulty. In May 1915, Mrs Brooke wrote to Edward Marsh: 'He wishes you to look after the publication and be literary executor, to decide which of his writings, including, if necessary, letters are to be included. Rupert asks that you will consult me in the matter.' And in another communication that same month she told him: 'as one of his legal heirs I empower you to deal with the copyrights on the assumption that he died intestate.' This was what

Marsh had wanted, and expected – a more or less free hand. He moved into action at high speed. Brooke's *1914 and Other Poems* was in the shops by June and various other publications were arranged: a pamphlet of the war sonnets, Brooke's *Letters from America* (to which Henry James would contribute his essay, as a Preface), an essay on Webster and the Elizabethans. Most important of all, as Marsh saw it, was the compilation of a biographical Memoir, which he planned to print as an Introduction to Brooke's *Collected Poems*. This, he believed, must be assembled with a special urgency; it should appear, he said, 'before the glamour has had time to wear off and before the inevitable jealousies have begun'; Brooke's 'fame . . . should be *immediately* established'.

For the Ranee, there was something tasteless in all this. She heard stories that Marsh was going around the offices of periodicals in search of anonymous Brooke contributions; that he was securing the copyrights in certain photographs. She was also now and again chancing upon bits of information about her son's private affairs. 'Do you know who Cathleen Nesbitt is?' she asked, and was not thrilled to learn that this actress had been introduced to Brooke by Marsh. The more she found out about Brooke's London period, the less warmly she viewed his executor, he who had been (in her words) almost the poet's 'Second Self' throughout those final months. Like Marsh, she was afraid that there would be a reaction against the current adulation – 'I greatly fear a change from the whole-hearted praise I have heard of him lately' – and she was indignant when she read an article by E. J. Dent, another Cambridge friend of Brooke's, in which the poet's 'sudden and factitious celebrity' was called 'grotesquely tragic'. Dent's point was that the war sonnets were untypical of Brooke's writing; they had been composed 'in a phase that could only have been temporary'. This view was shared by several of Brooke's younger friends and when *Poems 1914* appeared in June, there was a certain amount of murmuring in the weeklies against the myth that had 'grown around the imaginary man very different from the real man'.

For Marsh, this kind of talk confirmed the need for speedy action. For the Ranee, it represented the beginning of a process which would only be hastened by the early issue of a Memoir. She knew nothing of poetry, and there were pieces in *Poems 1914* which she would rather not have read. If the war sonnets were what people liked, why confuse them by putting out these other, earlier, much less uplifting pieces – some of them written, alas, during Rupert's mysterious breakdown of

1912? As Marsh got busier, she got more defensive; by August she had come to view her co-executor as an intruder and an opportunist. And Marsh had come to fear her as a 'dragon' in his path – a dragon, moreover, who had to be approached protectively: as Marsh's biographer has put it, the Ranee – after Alfred's death – was 'elevated into a sublime region of sorrow where no ordinary mortal could converse with her on equal terms'.

It was in August that Marsh announced the completion of his Memoir. Instead of letting Mrs Brooke read it and form an opinion, he nervously chose to send her a letter in which he tried to anticipate her possible objections: 'I am very anxious that you should *in the main* like the way I've written about Rupert . . . I'd rather shoot myself than bring a shadow of shame to his memory.'

> But we must remember that *if* anyone wants to criticise, there is no way of preventing them. If any little faults or absurdities are admitted, they can criticise those; if none, they would say I was a slavish admirer making my hero into a prig or plaster saint . . . R. would have *wanted* the truth told about him . . . it would be a pity to leave out things because of the fear that aunts or schoolmasters might shake their heads.

Aunts, schoolmasters, or mothers. Marsh went on to assure Brooke's mother that he had 'made scarcely any reference to love affairs' and had throughout referred to Cathleen Nesbitt as 'X'. Mrs Brooke, reasonably enough, was on her guard. Marsh's letter, she told him, 'has certainly frightened me . . . it is evident you feel pretty sure that I won't like the memoir.' And what was all this talk of showing Rupert 'as he really was'? She knew more about her son than Marsh did and for her the truth was simple: Rupert had been 'a happy natural schoolboy full of life and fun and influencing others for good'.

When Mrs Brooke eventually read the Memoir, she found that *her* Rupert was barely discernible: he had grown up and become a friend of Edward Marsh. The Memoir, she pronounced, 'doesn't represent Rupert as he really was at all. It is too evidently written by someone who knew him for a comparatively short time and even for that time quite a small part of him.' And to Frances Cornford, she commented: 'Eddie always seems to be thinking of Rupert's *fame* and I can't stand it.' Marsh's idolatrous approach, she feared, would almost certainly stir up the E. J. Dents (Dent, she was enraged to find, was respectfully treated in the Memoir); she spoke, she said, 'as Rupert's mother, who

229

hates the idea of her son's name being almost derided'. So far as she was concerned, the whole thing should be postponed 'for at least a year', and in the meantime ought to be re-done. Best of all would be if it were cancelled altogether.

Marsh was severely rattled by this 'buffeting'. Without Mrs Brooke's approval, he could not proceed: the Memoir made extensive use of Rupert's letters, in which she held the rights. And in any case he wanted her to like him; he was hurt. Rupert had trusted him; why couldn't she? But he had had (or so she said) her final word: 'You and I who knew very little of each other before Rupert's death were suddenly placed in somewhat intimate relations towards each other as regards his affairs; perhaps both of us have been more or less used to having our own way . . . You must write and say that you forgive me and then we will dismiss the Memoir.' By this stage, Marsh was in no mood to do either but, as had become his habit during the past year, he turned for guidance to the Master. Henry James's advice was in his most delicate and decent vein – a model, really, of how such things should be done or, as James would have it, how they should be *seen*:

I found the Memoir and all its contents in the highest degree interesting and vivid and for the most part very *right*, in the degree in which your materials impose rightness. But to express the matter thus crudely, hastily and provisionally, the perusal of it all has had a signal effect – and a rather unexpected one – that of making me understand better poor Mrs Brooke's actual wincings and waverings. It's an account of her son which must make in her the impression of taking him totally away from her and breaking her links with him, taking him altogether out of her world of association of thought and credibility, the moral of which is that you must give her time *to get used* to that. She *will*, probably, but there are meanwhile too many notes of paradox and 'sophistication' that must simply bewilder and scare her. Those notes probably played no part in *their* intercourse (there were others for mother and son). Coming at her in the brilliant onset of your pages all at once they make her repudiate connection with them. Some graceful bridge could be constructed with art – though I can't tell you how to construct it. It's a rather curious but to *me* comprehensible case – but then I'm a battered old novelist and it's my business to comprehend. This isn't *half* all, dearest Eddie, and we must talk as soon as I am fitter. The great thing to my mind is that waiting a while does seem indicated.

To be buffeted by the Ranee was one thing: under her lash, Marsh could present himself as the champion of Brooke's literary legacy. To have even the faintest disapproval beamed at him by Henry James was an altogether more serious deterrent. 'I have a vague dread,' he wrote to James, 'not from anything you *say* – that I have ever so slightly disappointed *you* about Rupert.' He agreed to set the Memoir to one side: to wait and see.

A year later, he seems to have felt that he had waited long enough. He sent Mrs Brooke a second version of the Memoir. At first, she gave the impression that she liked this one better than the first, but she wanted Marsh to include contributions from other sources: A. C. Benson, she believed, could well represent the 'older' view and, of the young, what about Dudley Ward and Geoffrey Keynes? Marsh drew the line at Benson, much as he loved this 'comic figure in literature, always popping up everywhere', but he agreed to try the others. According to Geoffrey Keynes, the Ranee had already 'turned to Dudley Ward and myself to undertake the task; but both of us had to refuse our help at the time, owing to our wartime commitments'. Keynes, a Rugby schoolmate of Brooke's and by 1916 serving as an Army doctor, seems to have been a particular favourite with the Ranee; he would later testify that she 'treated me almost as a son' and it was his refusal to contribute to the Memoir that she gave as her reason for once more vetoing the publication: no Keynes, she said, no Memoir. Marsh protested that it was not his fault if people she wanted would not co-operate; surely she was being just a bit unfair. In reply to this, Mrs Brooke discharged 'the most tremendous broadside'. Marsh, she said, had all along been trying to rush her and 'couldn't bear me taking my stand as [Rupert's] mother'. She should have locked the study door at the beginning.

Poor Marsh was now thoroughly bewildered and he no longer had Henry James (who had died earlier that year) to tell him what to do. He turned to Edmund Gosse but Gosse, characteristically, could only suggest putting the Memoir out as a limited edition; he had no answer to what was becoming, for Marsh, the leading question – what was it that made the Ranee get so *cross* with him? All he wanted was to publish a near-worshipful portrait of her son; he had delayed negotiations for a year; he had made numerous alterations and additions at her bidding and – if she were to be nice to him – he could probably make more. Why did she persist in believing him to be the wrong man for the job? 'How Rupert could be produced by a woman without sense of humour or beauty, and narrow to that degree, I shall never understand.' This would be how he talked of her to friends but privately it was her attitude to *him* that he could 'never understand'. Geoffrey Keynes, writing much later, has suggested that the Ranee herself was not fully aware of what the matter was:

> Brooke's unmanly physical beauty was often taken as an indication that he was probably a homosexual and therefore to be despised. His patriotism was regarded as sentimentality and his talents as a brief efflorescence which would soon have been quenched by the realities of life. It had, of course, been far from Marsh's intention to produce any such impression. He had been deeply attached to Rupert, as he was to many young men, but lived himself in a sexual no-man's-land whose equivocal aura pervaded the Memoir and contributed to the Brooke 'legend'. Mrs Brooke had probably sensed this even though she might not have been able to put it into words.

After his 1916 buffeting, Marsh again put the Memoir to one side. A year later, in July 1917, it was Mrs Brooke who re-opened the discussion. Other 'memoirs' of Brooke were by then beginning to appear; perhaps, with a few more alterations, something could be done with Marsh's essay. For a third time, the manuscript went off to Rugby. Marsh was weary of it all and ready for almost any compromise. His letters to Mrs Brooke were now much more to do with his own piled-up resentment than with Rupert Brooke. In the end, after some more petty haggling, it was agreed. The Memoir saw print, along with Brooke's *Collected Poems* (the Ranee thought this was a 'swindle' since most people already *had* most of the poems) in April 1918, three years after Brooke's death. It had two Prefaces, one by the Ranee saying that the book had been delayed because she had wanted 'to gain the collaboration of some of [Brooke's] contemporaries at Cambridge and during his young manhood, for I believe strongly that they knew the largest part of him'; the other by Marsh, regretting that 'circumstances' had prevented earlier publication – since the piece had been written so long ago he would have liked to 'rewrite it in the changed perspective and on a different scale' but this had been 'impossible for several reasons'.

As to the actual *Memoir*, it was by now more a collection of letters and friendly affidavits than the biographical/literary-critical narrative that Marsh had originally hoped for. He had won one or two small victories: he was allowed to mention Brooke's early affectations of 'decadence' (ie silk shirts and Beardsley pictures on his study wall), his Fabianism and even his nervous breakdown, although this was put down to overwork and, in the Ranee's quoted testimony, 'sitting up most of the night' with his serious young friends. Cathleen Nesbitt was named but with no explanation; indeed, Marsh's suppression of Brooke's sexual entanglements provoked one coy reviewer to suggest that the poet had 'missed the uplifting education that the passion of love would have afforded him'. The South Seas episode was a blur of local colour, London the stage on which – post-1913, in the months of Eddie Marsh – Brooke became a serious grown-up, gripped by a fierce new moral idealism: 'goodness' had become 'the most important thing in life'.

The Ranee could also count her gains: there was nothing in the book of her son's gloomy, flippant or sardonic sides, there was no offensive language, no girlfriends. The politics had been toned down and so too had Marsh's sentimental fulsomeness. One story had it that where Marsh wrote 'Rupert returned from the South Seas in a blaze of glory', the Ranee struck out 'a blaze of glory' and put 'June'. From her point of view, the *Memoir* was still unsatisfactory; Marsh, she would say, had stampeded her into an agreement. The reviewers, though, were kind; no one was yet ready to assault the legend. Even Virginia Woolf reviewed the book with caution. It was, she wrote anonymously in the *TLS*, 'inevitably incomplete'; Marsh had had to overcome 'enormous difficulties' and had

> done his best to present a general survey of Rupert Brooke's life which those who knew him will be able to fill in here and there more fully, perhaps a little to the detriment of the composition as a whole. But they will be left, we believe, to reflect rather sadly upon the incomplete version which must in future represent Rupert Brooke to those who never knew him.

Privately, Woolf called the book 'one of the most repulsive biographies I've ever read . . . a disgraceful sloppy sentimental rhapsody, leaving Rupert rather tarnished'. Brooke's other Cambridge associates felt much the same and for a time plotted to produce a counter-blast – there was talk of James Strachey digging out some of *his* correspondence with the poet. (Brooke used to enjoy tormenting Strachey with accounts of his sexual adventures, such as they were.) It was not that these friends wanted to discredit Brooke; their fear – like the Ranee's – was that there would be a price to pay for Marsh's starry-eyed portrayal.

And of course we now know that there was. After the war, the work of front-line poets like Sassoon, Rosenberg and Owen would be used to make Brooke seem almost criminally foolish. Marsh's *Memoir*, appearing when it did, set up an easy target. Written in the spirit of 1914, it was largely read by an audience for whom that spirit had become repugnant. Marsh treated the war sonnets not as a 'temporary phase' which Brooke would surely have renounced, or wished to play down if he had had to fight, but as a culmination, a spiritual maturing. If Marsh in 1918 had revised the *Memoir*, he might at least have added to it that when Brooke was writing the sonnets (in December 1914, on Christmas leave) he, like everybody else, was being told by the staff-people at the front that there would be a 'sudden cracking on the part of the Germans, and peace in April'. In fact, Brooke found this upbeat prediction hard to swallow: 'I think we should do it by August.'

Mrs Brooke lived long enough to see literary opinion turn against her son. She died in 1931 and in her will she took revenge on Marsh, dismissing him as literary executor and appointing in his place her own chosen quartet: Keynes, Ward, de la Mare and Jack Sheppard, Provost of Brooke's Cambridge college, King's. There was much anguish and embarrassment all round. The Ranee had, in death, rescued Rupert from the clutches of her rival and put him back where he belonged, in the company of his schoolfellows. Geoffrey Keynes, it was assumed, would be the new executor-in-chief, and so it proved. For a short period there was a pretence of keeping Marsh in touch with Brooke developments but by the mid-1930s he had given up. His Brooke material was deposited at King's; it had become, he said, 'a constant reminder of the disagreeable way in which Mrs Brooke has seen fit to treat me'. Keynes was now free to 'discredit the Rupert Brooke legend and to establish a truer valuation of his wholly masculine character and mind'.

Not everyone would agree that Sir Geoffrey, as he became, succeeded in his mission, in spite of his heroic efforts with Brooke's *Collected Letters*, a publication which left nobody in any doubt that Rupert fell in love with girls. In fact, Keynes's selection barely did justice to Brooke's voluminous romantic correspondence; to this day, 'love-letters' continue to turn up from one source or another. And so too does material 'equivocal' enough to have earned for Brooke a small foothold in Gay Studies. If sexuality really was at the heart of Edward Marsh's battles with the Ranee, we can be glad that each of them was spared a sight of a July 1912 letter in which Brooke tells in some detail how he lost his virginity to a Rugby chap called Denham Russell-Smith:

> Intentions became plain; but still nothing was said. I broke away a second, as the dance began, to slip my pyjamas. His was the woman's part throughout. I had to make him take his off – do it for him. Then it was purely body to body – my first, you know! I was still a little frightened of his, at any too sudden step, bolting; and he, I suppose, was shy. We kissed very little, as far as I can remember, face to face. And I only rarely handled his penis. Mine he touched once with his fingers; and that made me shiver so much that I think he was frightened. But with alternate stirrings, and still pressures, we mounted.

And so it goes on, for three closely printed pages of Paul Delany's *The Neo-Pagans, Friendship and Love in the Rupert Brooke Circle*. Delany calls this 'probably the most revealing letter he ever wrote'. Brooke's current executor, Jon Stallworthy, is a Keynes appointee and reckons that the described incident may have been invented; addressed to James Strachey, the letter was meant to cool the Strachey lust. Who can tell? Brooke was twenty-eight when he died and was no closer to knowing who he 'really was' than we are, or than his friends were at the time. Jon Stallworthy nicely illustrates this truth with an account of Geoffrey Keynes' adventures with the *Letters*. Over a period of twenty years, Keynes assembled his selection, edited it and passed it to the publisher. When galleys arrived he thought it an act of courtesy to send them out to all the Brooke friends who had contributed:

> and he was amazed when people started saying: This is terrible. The letters to *me* show the real Rupert but what will people say about the other letters – all this posturing, it's extraordinary – you can't publish this. Eddie Marsh, Frances Cornford . . . all Brooke's friends said 'You can't publish it'. Keynes was absolutely flabbergasted. So he wrote to them all and said to X, Y and Z that you have *all* written in to say that only the letters to *me* are the real Rupert and that all the rest are posturing, attitudinising, sentimental. There is surely something we can all learn from this. We all have many faces and show different faces to different people. So let's have no more talk about, You can't publish it. They all said, Over my dead body. They forbade him. So, at his own expense, Geoffrey kept the galleys in type, paid the type-rent, and resolved to *outlive* the lot of them. The type remained in storage for nearly fifteen years. And when the last of Brooke's friends died, Keynes published.

When Rupert Brooke's war sonnets were re-read in 1918, it was not 'The Soldier' that attracted most displeasure – after all, if Brooke was ready to donate his Englishness to 'some corner of a foreign field', so be it: he had had his wish. Harder to forgive were the sentiments of Sonnet No. 1 – called 'Peace' – in which not only had he welcomed the Great War as offering an escape route from the humdrum but also had allowed himself a passing sneer at those who were not as keen as he was to rally to the flag:

> Leave the sick hearts that honour could not move
> And half-men, and their dirty songs and dreary
> And all the little emptiness of love.

In 1915, when the sonnets appeared, few of Brooke's friends were in much doubt about which 'half-men' the poet had in mind: the lines were aimed at the homosexual-pacifist wiseacres of the Bloomsbury set – and in particular at Lytton Strachey. Rupert had had it in for Lytton for some time, and not just because he was brother to the ardent James. Brooke was convinced that his affair with Katherine Cox had been sabotaged by Lytton Strachey. In brief, the Brooke idea was that Strachey had helped the painter Henry Lamb to make a play for Katherine (Strachey wanted Lamb, Lamb wanted Cox, etc.). Brooke's ensuing crack-up had been the consequence of Lytton's serpentine arrangements. Brooke wrote to Cox in February 1912:

> You told me – in the first flush of your young romance – of the whole picture – Lytton 'hovering' (your word) with a fond paternal anxiousness in the background, eyeing the two young lovers at their sport – it was the filthiest filthiest part of the most unbearably sickening disgusting blinding nightmare – and then one shrieks with the increasing pain that it was *true*.

According to Paul Delany, who was the first to get this and several other such unstable Brooke letters into print, Lytton saw his encouragement of the Lamb–Cox liaison as 'a rational compromise in which he settled for the biggest share in Henry's life that he could get: Rupert saw it as pimping.' And in 1914, Rupert saw Lytton's conscientious objections to the war as a similar opting-out of the main action – Strachey was 'pro-German', he was on the other side, half-man. As for Strachey, he was seven years older than Brooke, his brother's 'friend' – in his view, the poet was an intellectual light-weight. Even the famous looks he found too girlish. All in all, there was a pitiable failure of finesse; about the Lamb–Cox business – Brooke's hysterical rancour was 'too stupid'. Strachey rather hoped that he and Brooke might patch things up, and in the end felt mildly wretched that they hadn't.

When Lytton Strachey heard the news of Brooke's death, he was working on an essay about Florence Nightingale – about the 'real Miss Nightingale' who was 'more . . . interesting than the legendary one' and 'less . . . agreeable'. He was having trouble with it; was indeed worried that Eddie Marsh might find it boring (the worst imaginable literary shame). The Nightingale essay would, of course, eventually appear as one of the four counter-legends that make up Strachey's *Eminent Victorians*, a book which, in all the circumstances, can readily be seen as the half-man's riposte to the war-hero's jibes. *Eminent Victorians* was published in May 1918, just two months before Marsh's exhausted but still-smiling *Memoir* finally appeared, and the coincidence could not have been more telling. Although Marsh's version of Brooke's 'Life and Letters' did have a 'becoming brevity', in no other respect did it conform to the rules for a new sort of biography which Strachey set out in his Preface, and implied in his performance: the new biography should have 'freedom of spirit . . . lay bare the facts of the case' – 'je ne propose rien, j'expose.'

The Brooke–Marsh–Ranee saga was just the kind of thing that Strachey wanted to make mock of. Great passions had been expended on both sides of the conflict between Edward Marsh and Mrs Brooke but the two warring parties were essentially agreed, took it for granted, that nothing should be told of Brooke that might dim his fabricated reputation as the flower of England's patriotic youth. For Strachey – who knew things about Brooke that were unknown to Brooke's mother and to Marsh – the *Memoir* might have seemed to afford a ready-to-hand illustration of his belief that the art of English biography had 'fallen on evil times'. It is unlikely that Marsh and Brooke (or even Gosse's *Swinburne*, which had come out the year before) were on Strachey's mind when he composed his Preface; he was out to nail the big late-Victorian biographies like Hallam Tennyson's:

> those two fat volumes, with which it is our custom to commemorate the dead – who does not know them, with their ill-digested masses of material, their slipshod style, their tone of tedious panegyric, their lamentable lack of selection, of detachment and design.

But in 1918 it was not possible to use the phrase 'evil times' and pretend merely to be speaking of a literary genre.

*Eminent Victorians* was a book about the war, although Strachey did not intend it to be so (originally his plan was to present twelve 'Victorian Silhouettes' – six to be admired, six to be deplored: the good chaps were to have been mostly men of Science, 'of selection, of detachment and design'). In addition to the war-healer Florence Nightingale, Strachey settled on an educationist (Thomas Arnold, shaper of Brooke's Rugby), a churchman and a military chieftain: not a bad cross-section of the 'mouthing bungling hypocrites' whose influence might be held responsible for the death-lists that lengthened daily as he wrote. *Eminent Victorians* started out as an amusing portrait gallery – 'it might be entertaining, if it was properly pulled off' – and ended up as a tribunal. Michael Holroyd tells us:

> as the war got under way, [Strachey's] indignation mounted, and the Victorians he had elected to portray grew more and more to resemble 'those queer fishes that one sees behind glass at an aquarium, before whose grotesque proportions and sombre menacing agilities one hardly knows whether to laugh or shudder'.

Strachey was in his late thirties in 1918 but his book was widely applauded as youth's revenge on age. Hungry for culprits, a war-weary readership rejoiced in the pacifist's drawling, iconoclastic manner of address. And if there was a hint of the 'half-man' in Strachey's spite-filled reassessments, that simply added to the un-heroic mischief: it was fun. The tone was officer-class; the sentiment was other-rank.

Lytton Strachey is now routinely credited with having altered the course of English biography with his four portraits and a Preface: he is said to have made the genre more candid, more novelistic, more scurrilous, more psycho-analytical, more like Science, more like Art. Everything that has happened since can be traced back to him – to that first act of disobedience. Certainly, Strachey did spawn a battalion of small Stracheys in the 1920s, not all of whom we can be grateful for. Names like André Maurois and Richard Aldington spring un-appealingly to mind. Did Strachey read Freud and thus pave the way for a generation of psychographers? It seems that he did, and that Freud in his turn read Strachey (and we know that brother James did become Freud's English translator). But we also know that Freud, a year after the appearance of his near-namesake's *Life of Carlyle*, 'almost completed an undertaking which a number of people, still unborn but fated to misfortune, will feel severely': he – like so many others in 1884–5 – had made a bonfire of his papers. 'Let the biographers labour and toil,' said Freud, 'we won't make it too easy for them.' As we have already seen, it was not Lytton Strachey who first made biography seem fearsome.

Perhaps the least we should grant Strachey, though, is that he accelerated a process towards brevity, craftsmanship and candour that was already under way. E. F. Benson was not the only one who believed that John Morley's *English Men of Letters* series (launched in 1877) was guilty of 'stripping the mystery off anything that is lovely' or that when Leslie Stephen's *Dictionary of National Biography* (1882) said 'no flowers by request' it was allying itself with the sinister new taste for 'raking up . . . unsavoury trifles in the lives of the immortals':

> no one is safe. No degree of eminence, no feeling of compassion, may appeal, for the greater the man in the halls of fame, the more touching his struggles on the slopes of Parnassus, the busier are the rakers upon the ashes of his past. They have done their best with Shakespeare. They tried their hands on Keats – but fell away sadly routed by the pure brilliancy of that dazzling memory. They have always had their fangs in poor Shelley; he can never rest in peace! They have flung their slobber over the bust of Wagner, they fairly shattered that of Poe. They destroyed, for a time, the might of Carlyle. And hosts of the other great ones have suffered from their sorry depredations; George Eliot, the Brontës, Rossetti, and so one might go on.
>
> They rake up all the old details that might well have been left safely buried – for who among us has lived a life that would be flawless in the limelight? All the old scraps and letters and tittle-tattle are collected; they add to them and replenish, giving an altogether unnecessary polish; it is like the rolling snowball, and the conglomerate mass of gossip and fact and imagination grows until it assumes huge proportions – or, at least, enough for a volume!

This was written in 1911, the year before a 'spiritual revolution' transformed G. L. Strachey: book reviewer, into Lytton Strachey: demon-biographer. 'I had feared that after thirty one didn't have these things,' he said, referring to his 'revolution'.

In fact, Strachey was always more like a reviewer than a biographer. He had no worries about access to estates, permission to quote letters, no need to negotiate with relatives and friends. His method required someone else to have already done the leg-work. He was gleefully unauthorised; writing at one remove, he could talk down to the high and mighty. If it is true that Strachey steered biography away from first-hand investigation into realms of psychography, fictionalisation and debunkery, his influence may have been more peaceable than is usually supposed. For most keepers of the flame, a cartoon-style irreverence or a fanciful hypothesis is more readily tolerable than a straight-faced perusal of the facts. On the other hand, of course, a plodding sleuth – armed with a Stracheyesque contempt for old habits of decorum and respectfulness: well, he might turn out to be the worst development of all.

# CHAPTER FOURTEEN

# AUTHORISED LIVES: HARDY AND KIPLING

A year after the publication of *Eminent Victorians*, Thomas Hardy reported to a friend: 'I have not been doing much – mainly destroying papers of the last thirty years & they raise ghosts.' Six months later, he was at it again: 'I have been occupied in the dismal work of destroying all sorts of papers which were absolutely of no use for any purpose, God's or man's.' Was Hardy stirred into defensive action by fears of a new tribe of Stracheyesque debunkers? The suggestion is fanciful. This 1919 clear-out was the culmination of a lifetime's habit of excision and concealment. He had been planning it for years.

Hardy was almost eighty in 1919 and the biographers *were* closing in. But he had nothing to fear because he had already blue-printed the ultimate deterrent: a master-scheme designed to arrest, incapacitate and nullify an inquisitive posterity. Other writers talked about wishing to 'frustrate as utterly as possible the post-mortem exploiters' and now and again some of them made bonfires, but in the end they all tended to entrust their posthumous repute to others, to the goodwill of family and friends. Hardy was not the trusting kind. What better way to 'authorise' a biography than actually to author it oneself, and then have it put out, post-mortem, under someone else's name?

It was the sort of idea that might well have crossed the mind of a Tennyson or a Henry James, but neither of them could have been bothered to arrange it. Hardy could be bothered. With his wife Florence he toiled on his grand deception for ten years. When he died in 1928, the *Life of Thomas Hardy* had reached the year 1920 and was but two chapters short of a conclusion. The first volume of the 'biography' – *The Early Life* – was published within months of its subject's death and Florence Emily got respectable reviews. It was not until 1940 that the subterfuge was publicly exposed.

There is a pathos to be found in several aspects of the Hardy stratagem, and not least in the role played in it by Florence, Hardy's collaborator-typist. But then there was a pathos in her situation from the start. In 1917, when the notion of a secret biography was put to her by Hardy, she welcomed it almost as a lifeline, writing enthusiastically to friends: 'I have a tremendous job in hand – literary.' Being 'literary' meant a lot to Florence and she may have imagined that she would at least be co-author of the biography that would eventually bear her name. A journalist and story-writer, she had first endeared herself to Hardy by penning for the *Evening Standard* an article about him called 'Our Greatest Writer'; thereafter he more than once helped her by polishing her stories and getting them placed with magazines. Semi-clandestine meetings were contrived and for a time (*c.* 1910) Florence was the focus of an old man's romantic wistfulness. For the sake of literature, she played up to him, was flattered. Her own bona fide love interest, a youngish consumptive called A. H. Hyatt, was after all author of *The Pocket Thomas Hardy*. And the seventy-year-old novelist – Florence was in her late twenties when they met – was known to be locked into an impenetrably miserable marriage.

In 1912, Emma, the first Mrs Hardy, died – and so did Hyatt. Florence moved into the Hardy house – the famously grim and bathroomless Max Gate – as a sort of secretary-companion and on that day, she later on recalled, 'I seemed suddenly to leap from youth to dreary middle age.' After a few months, by force of apathy, local gossip and black looks from the Hardy clan, she consented to a marriage. She was 'lonely and helpless', she said. 'He wanted a housekeeper who could be a companion and read to him – etc. – so I came in.' Hardy appears to have taken it for granted that they would marry but gave no signs of believing that he had captured a great prize. People who observed the newly-weds together remarked on how wretchedly unhappy they each looked.

For Hardy, of course, unhappiness had long ago become his occupation: it was what he did. Florence, although herself no mean grumbler and sigher of sighs ('Life is altogether so sad, so infinitely sad'), had livelier designs upon the marriage than he did: social and literary designs, mostly, but also she rather expected to be seen as a helpmate more suitable than the cranky, embittered Emma had been, or had wished to be. 'I am never so happy as when I have someone to look after.'

She knew quite a lot about Hardy's first marriage, or she thought she did. During her time as Hardy's enchantress she had now and then worked at Max Gate as a secretary and Emma had rather fallen for her too. As writer to writer (Emma also had literary aspirations) she had given Florence a run-down on Hardy's principal character-defects: 'Don't you think he looks a bit like Dr Crippen' was the kind of thing she used to say. Florence was half-persuaded: perhaps Emma's essentially generous spirit and her lively way with words *had* been blocked by her mismarriage.

This view was altered, though, when Florence read Emma's '*awful* diary . . . full of venom, hatred and abuse of him [Hardy] and his family'. Not long after Emma's death she wrote to Edward Clodd:

> Mr Hardy looks very well and seems cheerful. Indeed his youngest sister tells me that he has regained the same happy laugh that he had when he was a young man. But, all the same, his life here is lonely beyond words, & he spends his evenings in reading and re-reading voluminous diaries that Mrs H. has kept from the time of her marriage. Nothing could be worse for him. He reads the comments upon himself – bitter denunciations, beginning about 1891 & continuing until within a day or two of her death – & I think he will end by *believing* them.

Florence was now confident that a second Mrs Hardy could hardly fail to do better than the first: she, at any rate, would not go around, Bible in hand, telling people that she had married beneath her, that it was she who had inspired and tidied up the Hardy novels, that *Jude the Obscure* ought not to have been written (although Florence *was* a bit uncertain on that score).

The actual turn of events is well-known. It was the dead Emma, and not the live Florence, who became Hardy's night-and-day preoccupation, his new Muse. Instead of turning with gratitude to his young bride, Hardy preferred to stand vigil by his dead wife's grave, consumed by the most terrible Carlylean remorse – remorse more difficult to fathom than Carlyle's, since Emma had for years been at her husband's throat, but no less overwhelming. For a year after Emma's death, Hardy poured out some fifty poems in her memory – love poems addressed not to an Emma anybody else had seen or could remember but to some long-ago lost beauty whom the poet had culpably ill-served. These poems were published in book form in 1914, the year of the new marriage, and it was generally agreed that in them Hardy's characteristic melancholy had become 'if anything, yet more intense' (G. L. Strachey, *New Statesman*):

Woman much missed, how you call to me, call to me,
Saying that now you are not as you were
When you had changed from the one who was all to me,
But as at first, when our day was fair.

Can it be you that I hear? Let me view you, then,
Standing as when I drew near to the town
Where you would wait for me: yes, as I knew you then,
Even to the original air-blue gown!

For Florence the book, *Satires of Circumstance* (or, to take the title of the 'Emma section', *Veteris vestigia flammae* – 'ashes of an old flame') was an almost unbearable humiliation; it seemed to advertise a serious deficiency in her. 'I read it with a horrible fascination,' she said; 'it seems I am an utter failure.' For three years after her marriage, Florence's letters are bulletins of gloom. 'Sometimes I feel eighty,' she complains: she hates the house, she spends 'literally thousands' of evenings alone because Hardy is up in his study brooding about Emma, there are few visitors or guests and the only journeys Hardy likes to take are to Cornwall, to hunt up the graves of Emma's relatives and ancestors: he was obsessed with these 'Emma sites' and seemed surprised that Florence was not always eager to help him seek them out.

Florence did her best to keep up appearances, to pretend that poems were poems and that the real Hardy was 'very well and amazingly cheerful . . . I wish people knew that he was really happy, for strangers must imagine that his only wish is to die and be in the grave with the only woman who ever gave him any happiness.' The 'diabolical diaries' were now burned and if Florence tried to remind Hardy of their contents, he would murmur indulgently: 'sheer hallucinations in her, poor thing.' By 1917, before the biography proposal, nothing much had changed: 'All I trust is that I may not, for the rest of his life, have to sit and listen humbly to an account of her virtues and graces.' To be asked to help Hardy with his Life was an important reinstatement.

It seems odd that Hardy had not begun earlier to attend to the construction of a Life. The question of 'how he would be seen' had always nagged at him and there were areas of his *curriculum vitae* which he habitually censored or embellished: lowly origins, poor education, ill-aimed infatuations. Even the record of his early relationship with Florence was a matter for unease – it was important to each of them that their secret meetings should stay secret. When, in 1910, Hardy had gone to stay with his friend Edward Clodd in Suffolk, it was sometimes arranged between them that Florence should also happen to be visiting. Clodd later on declared that he was working on *his* memoirs, and there was much panic at Max Gate.

Now and again, Hardy would be asked for biographical information and his usual response was to refer applicants to 'the barest of known facts (which would be, roughly speaking, those that appear in *Who's Who* or other such annuals)'. If anyone tried to push harder, to suggest – for instance – that Hardy used to speak in Dorset dialect, that his cottage birthplace did not have seven rooms, a paddock and various outbuildings, that his education had not been crowned by a sojourn at King's College, Cambridge, or that the architect heroes of his fiction were not born of pure invention, there would be sharp protests against 'prying', 'vivisection', 'pseudo-biographical analogies'. In 1922, he and Florence were able to suppress the translation into English of a University of Paris thesis (*Thomas Hardy, Penseur et Artiste*) on the grounds that it attempted a 'dissection' of Hardy's 'supposed personality' and proffered 'personal surmises from chapters in the books'.

Much of Hardy's reticence was intuitive, a rural or small-town self-protectiveness or 'closeness', but it had become empurpled, so to speak, by his various collisions with metropolitan sophistication – and in particular, with the reviewers of his novels. When critics railed at him, as they did most ferociously with *Jude the Obscure*, as 'degenerate', 'decadent' and 'grimy', it seemed to him that so-called criticism was actually biography in thin disguise: 'he underwent the strange exprience of beholding a sinister lay figure of himself constructed by them [the critics], which had no sort of resemblance to him as he was and which he, and those who knew him well, would not have recognised as being meant for himself if it had not been called by his name.'

Perhaps it was the circumstances of Emma's death that prompted Hardy to systematise his defence against such terrors and resentments. It has been suggested that he could have saved Emma's life if he had noticed that for several months before she died she had been 'in such pain that she was weeping before relatives'. He always made out that she died suddenly, having seemed 'distinctly unwell' from time to time but never 'seriously ill'. (The cause of death was 'impacted gallstones' and not – as was believed – a heart attack.) Or perhaps it was a reading of her diaries, the knowledge that such malign 'hallucinations' *could* be entertained. The poems, although offered as an act of 'expiation', would not secure for him much posthumous forgiveness: expiation for *what*? would surely be the cry. Some more soberly pre-emptive manoeuvre might have seemed to be required.

It was in 1914 that Hardy appointed his literary executors. Florence of course had to be one of them but to support her Hardy needed a more aggressively organisational type, someone to protect his copyrights and show the door to any 'impertinent or unmannerly' intruders. Sydney Cockerell, director of Cambridge's Fitzwilliam Museum, was well known for his 'forceful' administrative methods and when he bullied Hardy (whose works he had not read) into surrendering some important manuscripts for the museum, the timid novelist was so impressed by his show of philistine straightforwardness that he at once adopted him as a kind of manager, or agent. Cockerell would turn up at Max Gate and sit at Hardy's feet but he would also arrange for the re-hanging of his pictures and advise him to stop waxing his moustache. 'No nonsense' was the Cockerell creed: he got things done.

Perhaps Cockerell's most significant act of ingratiation was in 1913, two years after he and Hardy had first met for the manuscript transaction. In this year, he brought Hardy an out-of-the-way gift, a book entitled *Memoir of Thomas Hardy*, which turned out to be 'an autobiographical account of the public life of a namesake of Hardy's who had figured largely in certain religious controversies at the beginning of the nineteenth century'. The book was written in the third person, so as to 'obviate' – the author said – 'the necessity of calling the great *I* so repeatedly to my assistance.' Michael Millgate believes that Cockerell's gift may have 'had a special significance for Hardy':

> Given the circumstances in which the chronicle of his own life was written . . . it would have been an easy step from the idea of a third-person autobiography to that of an authorised biography written by the subject himself but intended for publication after his death over the collaborator's name.

The theory is entirely plausible. Cockerell was soon afterwards asked to serve as an executor, but he would not be let in on Hardy's scheme for a ghost-Life. So far as Cockerell knew, the Hardys were jotting down notes, memoranda, reminiscences, so that, after Hardy's death, an 'authentic' biography might 'be contemplated by her'. These materials would be 'at hand to do what you like with: eg to use if any preposterous stories should require contradictions, or as you choose'; he told Cockerell, 'I do not, in truth, feel *much* interest in posthumous opinions about me, or estimates, and shall sleep quite calmly at Stinsford whatever happens.' To this, the stout Cockerell replied: 'I will act loyally and faithfully to you and your memory if called upon to do so.'

By 1918 the secret biography was under way, and Florence's 'collaborative' duties had come to be defined. First, she had to arrange Hardy's notebooks and letters in chronological order (Hardy had for years kept drafts and carbon copies of his outgoing correspondence). Using these documents Hardy wrote his narrative by hand and Florence typed it up. The typed copy went back to Hardy for revisions, which he did in a fake calligraphic hand. Florence then typed up a final script. All the documents and anything that was in Hardy's genuine handwriting were destroyed. The 1919 clear-out was of materials which had already been made over into notes for the 'biography'.

The elaborate secrecy with which the plan was carried through suggests that Hardy – both Hardys – believed it would succeed. Florence told nobody (not even the book's eventual publisher, Macmillan's), and the few Hardy friends who, after his death, had their suspicions, were too kind to challenge Florence's claimed authorship. Nobody commented in print on the book's faintly antiquated style; nor was it found particularly odd that the first volume came out so quickly after Hardy's death – no doubt the novelist had supervised or, here and there, corrected his wife's manuscript, which in any case was perhaps 'founded on memoranda of his own composition'. Most reviewers found the biography dull, reticent and admirable.

Hardy died in January 1928 and within days of his death there was friction between his co-executors. Cockerell wanted a grand Westminster Abbey burial but Florence knew that Hardy had expected to 'sleep calmly at Stinsford'. (In 1924, Hardy had written to the vicar of Stinsford: 'Regard me as a parishioner. Certainly I hope to be still more one when I am in a supine position one day.') A somewhat macabre compromise was made: Hardy's ashes were deposited at the Abbey and his heart, removed and casketed by surgeons, was laid to rest at Stinsford. There was a clash too on the question of a Hardy monument, with Cockerell pressing for a great obelisk to be raised in open country and Florence (after some dithering) determined on a more modest construction – a life-sized, seated sculpture – in Dorchester's town centre. Florence won this argument, although later on some Americans took up the Cockerell plan. There was disagreement also about the projected publication of a book of Hardy's letters. Florence asked Gosse to edit a selection, Cockerell made haste to urge Gosse to take no notice of her rash request, and Gosse – who would have been Hardy's executor if he had been younger; he too died in 1928 – agreed to give up the job on condition that no one else got the opportunity to do it. By the end of the year, Florence was complaining about Cockerell's intolerably bossy manner and Cockerell was describing her as 'an inferior woman with a suburban mind'.

Unhappily, Cockerell was not the only one of Thomas Hardy's devotees to feel that there was no longer any need to be polite to Florence; over the years, as Cockerell took command of the detail of the estate's management, she would find that 'many literary people had tolerated her not for herself but as an adjunct of Hardy'. And even those who stayed friendly with her took it for granted that in Hardy matters it was Cockerell, not she, who called the tune – as, in fact, he did, most of the time.

As Florence saw it, the modest prestige which she had won with the publication of *The Early Life* was brutally stripped from her in 1930, with the appearance of Somerset Maugham's *Cakes and Ale*. In Maugham's novel, an ex-peasant writer called Edward Driffield has matured into a hugely eminent old age. Driffield used to be an outrageous, rip-roaring sort of fellow but his second wife, an inferior, suburban type ('not quite, quite a lady') has turned him into a grand literary personage; she has instructed him in the ways of the genteel and fussily protected him against unsuitable associates. She has also tried to suppress all traces of his roguish past. Driffield dies, and the widow wishes to arrange for an appropriately 'delicate' biography. Although Maugham did not know Florence and had never visited Max Gate, he had been well supplied with cattily observed minutiae of the Hardys' private life (he probably got it all from Siegfried Sassoon, whom Florence thought of as a trusted friend), and – in spite of authorial denials – nobody was left in any doubts about which writer, which widow, he had had in mind. J. B. Priestley (writing in America, out of range of Britain's libel laws) declared: 'If Somerset Maugham did not intend his readers to be reminded of Hardy, then he acted with strange stupidity (and a less stupid man than Somerset Maugham never put pen to paper).'

Luckily for Florence, in a way, the oily would-be biographer in *Cakes and Ale* was so blatantly modelled on Hugh Walpole that, in the ensuing controversy, the Maugham–Walpole hostilities took centre- stage. Maugham *did* know Walpole; indeed, poor Walpole had thought that they were chums: 'It is the stab in the back that hurts me so. He has used so many little friendly things and twisted them round . . . it's a caddish book.' Nonetheless, Florence was sufficiently outraged and embarrassed: 'There are moments,' she said, 'when I want to shake my fists at the sky, or shriek aloud in rage.' In October 1930, she was asked to unveil a Hardy memorial window in the Stinsford church but, post-Maugham, she could not face it: 'In a recent novel some very bitter things are said of a wife who "exploits her husband's fame before and after his death".' Cockerell, Maugham, the reviewers (many of whom found *Cakes and Ale* 'excellent comedy' and saw it as a useful corrective to 'the humbug and nonsense which is talked about established literary reputations'): it was a sneering sort of world in which to seek a role that could be played out with humility and style. Florence was now a rich woman, with several upmarket connections of the sort she prized, but in no sector of her widowhood did she feel genuinely cherished or esteemed: the Dorchester locals viewed her with suspicion and the London sophisticates made fun of her. Her predicament was getting to be unnervingly like Hardy's, as he had perceived it thirty years before.

Even so, she *was* the Hardy widow and the author of his *Life* (*The Later Years* also appeared in 1930). And for all her passivity in the day-to-day making of that *Life*, she had in the end been able to manage one or two small interventions of her own. Hardy may in truth have written his own biography but in granting Florence the nominal authorship he also granted her the opportunity, once he was dead, to make her own adjustments to the narrative, the record. In the *Early Years* volume, she trimmed 'nearly every one' of Hardy's favourable mentions of his first wife. As Florence Hardy's biographers describe it:

> as she read through the concocted work, her 'temper', as she called it, rose over Hardy's eagerness to record in its pages every single incident favourable to his first wife, her courage, her decision, her help, her social

successes, together with examples of his own affection for Emma. She red-pencilled out of the typescript nearly every one of these incidents and expressions. Out went a long passage describing Emma's bravery in rescuing Hardy from a street-attack by thieves in Rome, during the Hardys' visit there in 1887. She deleted equally long descriptions of successful lunch-parties given by Emma. Any sign of Hardy's retrospective tolerance of his first wife's religious beliefs was likewise removed, including the innocuous sentence, 'his wife was an old-fashioned Evangelical like her mother.'

In *The Later Years*, Florence was irked to find herself repeatedly described as 'Miss Dugdale, a literary friend of Mrs Hardy's' and to read that 'Mrs Hardy, accompanied by her friend Miss Dugdale' took this or that excursion. It had been agreed that Hardy should pretend that he and Florence had never made those pre-nuptial visits to Clodd's house in Suffolk, but did he also have to make out that in those days, the high days of their 'romance', he had known her only as his wife's 'literary friend'? The red pencil went to work again. In *The Later Years*, as published, Florence's first appearance is on page 363, where it is written: 'In February of the year following [1914] the subject of this memoir married the present writer.'

Having put the first Mrs Hardy in her place in the biography, Florence also made sure that Max Gate became thoroughly *her* place, as it had not been when Hardy was alive. She set about purging the house of all Emmabilia, so to call it. During the thirteen years of her marriage, Florence had longed to break into the 'two locked attic boudoirs' which had once been Emma's, but Hardy had always insisted that the rooms be left exactly as they were when Emma died. In 1928, 'with the help of a gardener', Florence emptied both rooms and dumped their contents in the garden. Clothes, toiletries, literary works, accumulated bric-à-brac, all the little personal relics that would surely have brought tears to the dead Hardy's eyes: 'Everything, including Emma's old corsets, is remembered as going up in flames.' This was the last of Max Gate's several bonfires. There had always been a first wife but there would be no second widow.

There *would*, of course, always be a first author of *The Life*, but Florence died in 1937, three years before the bibliographer Richard Purdy revealed the truth, with exemplary diffidence, in a centenary lecture in New York. Purdy had been very fond of her and he may well have been following instructions. By the time of her scholarly unmasking, Florence was sleeping safely in the Stinsford churchyard, next to the remains of Emma, and the Hardy heart.

In 1888, the novel *Robert Elsmere* by Mrs Humphry Ward sold 100,000 copies in the United States. This figure was 'estimated', as it had to be, because the book had more than one American publisher – indeed, it seems to have had several. According to Mrs Ward's biographer, the 'transatlantic pirates had a field day . . . competing with each other as to who could bring out the cheapest (and nastiest) edition'. In some stores, it was 'being given away free with every cake of Maine's "Balsam Fir Soap", a newly launched product which wished to impress on consumers the literal truth of cleanliness being next to godliness' – which, on a brisk thumb-through, might have seemed to be the novel's theme.

Mrs Ward was not amused: for her 'to tap into such a large readership and not be able to market one's literary property was torture'. Although her sales figures were unusually high, she was not the only British author to be set fuming by reports of profitless American successes. The Berne Union, agreed three years before, was a notable first step towards establishing international copyright protection, but the Americans had not put their names to it; and the British, wishing to press for their own copyright reform (their aim, eventually successful, was to extend the period of protection to fifty years from the date of an author's death), found it hard to work up much energy for the domestic struggle so long as the US side of things remained unsettled.

The Americans' Chace Act of 1891 would shortly grant foreign authors a measure of protection. In the late 1880s, though, the Anglo-American atmosphere was fairly tense. As John Sutherland explains, speaking of Mrs Ward, there were at that time but three courses open to British authors whose books sold in the United States:

> (1) to grin and bear it – as had generations of British authors before her; (2) to publish first in America – or at least to make her primary contracts with an American publisher who could then lease the copyright to a British co-publisher . . . (3) to wait for an equitable copyright agreement which would enable her to collect American royalties.

Writers who believed that (3) was imminent were in the meantime ready to put up with (1). Some, like Thomas Hardy, had profitable serialisation deals with American magazines, like *Harper's Monthly*, which were owned by book publishers. When the young Rudyard Kipling poured scorn on *Harper's* for publishing in book form an unauthorised collection of his tales, Hardy's instinct was to spring to the Americans' defence: his view was that 'reputable' firms like Harper's were themselves not happy with the prevailing injustices and ought to be exempt from scorn, an argument which earned from Kipling the memorable sally: 'Does he steal with tears when he buccaneers? 'Fore Gad, then, why does he steal?' Hardy was right, though, to prefer some Americans to others: after all, a few transatlantic publishers *did* from time to time send their British victims the odd £100 of conscience-money and – with a Copyright Bill before Congress – why give offence to influential allies?

For several distinguished British authors of that day, the best way to be American was to be like Wolcott Balestier. Balestier had lately set up in London as agent for the New York firm of John W. Lovell. Lovell's general objective was to anticipate the Chace Act by striking 'equitable' agreements with the British authors he already published (of whom Mrs Humphry Ward was one) and with any other likely-looking talent that Balestier could manage to recruit. As for Balestier, he shared Lovell's vision of cornering the British market in advance of legislation, but he also had one or two short-term incentives of his own. The author of three novels, he suggested to Mrs Ward that he and she might 'co-author' her next book and thus register for her a US copyright. To other writers he proposed that Lovell should buy up sheets of their new works as they came off the presses, and ship them to New York for simultaneous American publication. Lovell would by this means 'steal a march upon the pirates' by mopping up 'the cream of the sales'.

For the exploited British literati, this was the stuff of dreams, and the 'admirably intelligent and acute young Balestier' (H. James) clearly knew how to put himself across. In no time at all, the salons were a-quiver: 'As I look back upon that evening and ask myself what it was in the eager face which could create so instant a thrill of attraction, so unresisted a prescience of an intimate friendship ready to invade me, I can hardly find an answer.' Not for the first time, Edmund Gosse had his finger on the London literary pulse. Mrs Ward, Henry James, Thomas Hardy, Austin Dobson, Jean Ingelow, J. H. Shorthouse: some of these names are nowadays difficult to fit a book to, but in 1890 Balestier's list of conquests seemed brilliantly comprehensive. 'He was not merely as we used to tell him, "one of our conquerors", but the most successful of them all.'

It was through the over-animated Gosse that Balestier achieved his most significant and, in its effects, most lasting victory. Kipling, newly famous in a cultural milieu that was both strange and unappealing, was grumpily holed up in his Villiers Street apartments and already nurturing a near-Byronic contempt for publishers, both English and American. On the strength of his Indian tales, literary figures of all factions were pressing to adopt him, and he could afford to bide his time: 'this is only the beginning of the lark. You'll see some savage criticism of my work before spring. That's what I am playing for.' Of London's current groupings, the wrathful Henley set probably had most appeal – but Henley was *too* keen; he scented a replacement for his worshipped, newly estranged Stevenson. Kipling's stance was watchful, aloof, tending to the surly, and when Balestier's assistant, Arthur Waugh, arrived to sound him out, the response was 'kindly but a little querulous': 'Extraordinarily importunate person, this Mr Balestier . . . Tell him to inquire again in six months.'

Balestier, of course, was not to be kept waiting. When Kipling published his broadside against *Harper's*, the good American instantly 'leapt into the breach'. In a matter of weeks, he and Kipling were 'fast friends'. The House of Lovell was authorised to issue a new selection of Kipling's stories (including those which *Harper's* had pirated) and had secured permission to publish his first novel, *The Light that Failed*, complete with a new, happier ending aimed at the US market. And Balestier had found the English co-author he had been in search of. Incredibly, for those who knew him, Kipling agreed to collaborate with his new buddy on a novel-length East-meets-West romance, *The Naulahka*, of which Balestier would write the American scenes, Kipling the scenes set in India. 'No other man,' says one Kipling biographer, 'ever exercised so dominating an influence over Rudyard Kipling as did Wolcott Balestier during the eighteen months of their intimacy.'

*The Naulahka* was almost finished when the two friends separated. Kipling left England for a long sea-voyage in the summer of 1891, leaving Balestier to celebrate the Chace Act and to pursue several other mighty schemes: a tie-up with William Heinemann, a liaison with S. S. McClure, an English-based version of the popular Tauchnitz editions. Balestier was flying high; too high, perhaps. His health had always been fragile. In December, on a business trip to Dresden, he fell ill (with typhoid, it was thought) and died, aged twenty-nine. When Kipling heard the news, he hurried back to London, arriving too late for the funeral.

Eight days after Kipling's return, a few of Balestier's mourners were invited to attend another ceremony: the wedding of Kipling to Wolcott's sister, Carolyn – or Carrie, as she was generally known. The event provoked astonishment all round. Carrie was three years older than Kipling, and no beauty: 'a good man spoiled' was the verdict of Rudyard's not normally acerbic father, by which he meant that she was too brisk, too competent, too Yankee. And Henry James, who attended both funeral and wedding, called her 'poor little concentrated, passionate Carrie . . . remarkable in her force, acuteness, capacity and courage – and in the intense – almost manly – nature of her emotion . . . a worthy sister of poor dear big-spirited, only-by-death-quenchable Wolcott' but even he would have wished her to be less obviously 'unattractive'. 'An odd little marriage', was his summing-up.

Biographers still puzzle over the speed with which Kipling scurried into wedlock. Was he in love with Carrie before he left England in the summer: was she the 'dear lass' whom he invokes in his shipboard composition 'The Long Trail'? Or is it hugely significant that in an early draft of that poem the 'dear lass' is written as 'dear lad'?

The Lord knows what we may find, dear lass,
And The Deuce knows what we may do –
But we're back once more on the old trail, our own trail, the out trail,
We're down, hull-down, on the Long Trail – the trail that is always new!

Certainly, those life-writers who have declared themselves baffled by Kipling's subservience to Wolcott Balestier evince none of the same difficulty when required to get to grips with the saga of Carrie's 46-year domination of her husband. Like Fanny Stevenson, Carrie is portrayed in the histories as neurotically possessive, over-protective, bossily managerial, stifling of the later work, and so on. And it is amusing to note that, on his wedding day, Kipling felt obliged to write a note to Henley. He must have known that, to Henley and his crowd, it would seem that the Stevenson folly was happening again: a small, sallow, Yankee shrew had captured another of our boys.

And so it can be made to seem. Kipling *was* whisked off to the

United States (where, oddly enough, one of his recurrent dreams was that he would some day rendezvous with R.L.S.), but even after he and Carrie returned to live in England, 'no trespassers' was the order of the day. Carrie took charge of everything: she managed the money, the publication deals, the running of their not-easy-to-visit Sussex home, and she was always anxious to promote the stuffier, more 'official' features of her husband's eminence. She opened his letters and usually dictated the replies, she fussed over his health, she repelled visitors. 'Kipling handed himself over bodily, financially and spiritually to his spouse.' 'A dragon on guard', she 'built up a Maginot line around Rud', was one family description, and even the Kiplings' loyal daughter Elsie had moments when her mother's protectiveness seemed stifling and excessive: 'My mother introduced into everything she did . . . a sense of strain and worry amounting sometimes to hysteria . . . My father's much exaggerated reputation as a recluse sprang, to a certain extent, from her domination of his life.'

A fair account of Carrie's usefulness to Kipling would, at the very least, have to include an account of her steadfastness during several family crises: Kipling's near-to-death illness of 1899, the death in that same year of daughter Josephine, aged seven, the 1915 death in battle of son John. And there were other, lesser dramas in which even non-admirers had to acknowledge her competence and the near-absolute dependence of her spouse. But even so, man-management can get to be a habit, and so too can nursery compliance. Carrie does seem to have had something of Mrs Stevenson's volatile fearsomeness: unstable nerves coupled with a ferocious strength of will. Boyish types often end up with wives like this. Kipling's childhood was spent mostly in a state of fear and secrecy and so too, by all accounts, was his middle to late-middle age. During the last twenty or so years of his life, he was in almost constant pain. The cause was actually gastritis but some of his friends reckoned that his anguish was more to do with fear, misery and boredom, that he was suffering in truth from an overdose of wifely care. And in the very last years before his death (aged seventy) in 1936, his wife

> strengthened her control over the minor details of his life. When he went out for an evening walk she was there to see that he came back. When there were guests, her eyes followed his every movement. The only telephone in the house was situated in her bedroom . . . He was driven in upon

himself, and was now too often denied access to the outside world. He had become a guarded flame.

When Kipling died, Carrie was decisive in her interpretation of his posthumous requirements. After all, had he not bequeathed for her guidance an 'Appeal' to those who might disturb his bones?

> If I have given you delight
> By aught that I have done,
> Let me lie quiet in that night
> Which shall be yours anon:
>
> And for the little, little span
> The dead are borne in mind,
> Seek not to question other than
> The books I leave behind.

Also, three weeks before he died, Kipling had completed an auto-biography that made it clear how little of himself he wanted to be known. *Something of Myself* was the perfect title for this short study of 'his life from the point of view of his works'. Splendidly readable though it is, the book has nothing in it of Kipling's early, unrequited loves – Flo Garrard and Edmonia Hill; nothing about Wolcott Balestier nor about his madcap brother Beatty, with whom Kipling had publicly and rather shamingly quarrelled during his post-marriage sojourn in Vermont; no mention of the deaths of his two children (of the sorely-missed John we hear only that he 'arrived on a warm August '97, under what seemed every good omen'). As with his most disturbing stories, there is a sense in which the autobiography reveals 'by not telling' but if *Something of Myself* were all we had to go on we would know more about Mrs Bathurst than we do about Mrs Kipling – or 'the wife', as Mr Kipling calls her. Kipling's account of his wedding day – 'and then to London to be married in January '92 in the thick of an influenza epidemic, when the undertakers had run out of black horses and the dead had to be content with brown ones' – seems unprovocatively cryptic, something between 'mind your own busi-ness' and 'who cares?' But then *Something of Myself* was written under Carrie's watchful eye and in those circumstances Kipling's natural caginess was unlikely to be ruffled.

The book is not, like Hardy's ghost-Life, an effort to forestall biography, although Kipling shared Hardy's distaste for what he called 'the "Higher Cannibalism" . . . the exhumation of scarcely cold notorieties'. The Kiplings assumed that there would be various attempts upon his Life and they had 'made arrangements'. In 1911, Kipling had burned his correspondence with his parents – perhaps, biographically, the saddest loss of all. His sister commented: 'If Rud had been a criminal, he could not have been fonder of destroying any family papers that came his way – especially after the parents died.' And Carrie had from the start of their marriage made it her practice to destroy incoming letters.

As Kipling's executor, his widow saw it as her task to tidy up anything that seemed ragged and left-over, or that did not fit with the main facts of his Life as reported in *Something of Myself*: drafts, manuscripts, her husband's 'notion books', which contained sketches and ideas for future work – all were got rid of, along with the letters she and Kipling had written to each other. Carrie also kept an eye on the salerooms and on dealers' catalogues; whenever Kipling material came on the market she would attempt to buy it up. Most notoriously, she purchased a collection of Kipling's letters to Edmonia Hill, the married woman he had been fond of in India during the mid-1880s. These letters Carrie burned, not knowing that the dealer she bought them from had taken copies. As the editor of Kipling's letters recently observed, this was a costly oversight: in the absence of any letters to Carrie, Mrs Hill is now lodged as a key presence – warm, respected in the Kipling life – whereas Carrie herself remains shadowy, a sort of identikit portrayal, made up of others' not always charitable bits of reportage.

On the matter of a Kipling Life, Carrie's practice was to appoint a biographer and then give him such a hard time that he would soon despairingly resign: before her death in 1939, two appointees had been routed and she was getting ready to take on a third. Significantly, her choices were not literary men. At his death, Kipling's reputation in critical circles was at its nadir. He was not just out of fashion; he was widely seen as the enemy of all that was healthily progressive, both in politics and in the literary culture. It would not have been easy to find a non-decrepit man of letters who did not feel obliged to apologise on his behalf. Safer by far, and more in accord with how Carrie wanted Rudyard to be seen, to select a chronicler untainted by bookworld sophistication. First she chose Hector Bolitho, a low-powered social historian and author of respectful royal lives: had not Ruddy been a friend of George V? When Bolitho backed out, she turned to Taprell

Dorling, who was well-known for sea stories put out under the name 'Taffrail': he would surely be able to handle the ocean-going, machine-mad, man's man side of Kipling, and be responsive also to the lovably puerile ingredient which, in 1937–8, was somewhat lost from view.

Carrie did not live to see, or see off, another appointee. In 1939, the running of the estate was taken over by her daughter Elsie. Relations between mother and daughter had not always been tranquil. Carrie had opposed Elsie's 1924 betrothal to Captain George Bambridge and had then made 'constant, dangerous and uncalled for interferences' in the couple's married life. And before that she had been jealous of Kipling's occasional tendency to seek Elsie's guidance and advice. When Elsie later on wrote an autobiographical memoir, she found it hard to be altogether pious about mother: 'Her possessive and rather jealous nature, both with regard to my father and to us children, made our lives very difficult, while her uncertain moods kept us apprehensively on the alert for possible storms.'

Even so, as executor, Elsie's performance would have made Mrs Kipling proud. Certainly, Carrie could not have bettered the contract that her daughter drew up with *her* choice of biographer, the unfortunate Lord Birkenhead. Birkenhead had met Captain Bambridge in 1943 and soon afterwards applied to write the Kipling Life. He had already written a biography of his father, F. E. Smith – no friend of Kipling's – but the Bambridges seem not to have researched the political background of their appointee: young Birkenhead himself had been PPS to Lord Halifax at Munich, and it can be guessed what Rudyard would have thought of *that*. As for Birkenhead, he was keen to get the job and seems also not to have asked questions; his trust, presumably, was that Bambridge – an old-school country gent – would make sure that he was treated decently.

Birkenhead's contract of appointment gave Mrs Bambridge full editorial control: 'the Author,' it said, 'shall submit his work to Mrs Bambridge in convenient sections as he proceeds and shall omit from the completed work such passages or documents (if any) as Mrs Bambridge may desire.' Moreover, 'the copyright in the work shall be the property of Mrs Bambridge' and 'arrangements for the publication and exploitation of the work in any material form whatever shall be subject to the approval of Mrs Bambridge who shall have the entire control of the work when completed.' In return, Birkenhead would get one-third of the book's royalties plus certain travelling expenses and, of course, access to the Kipling archive. And there were other clauses that might have given him a flavour of what lay ahead: 'the Author will (if requested by Mrs Bambridge to do so), visit at his own expense the United States of America'; 'the Author will also if he considers it desirable and Mrs Bambridge consents visit (a) India . . . and/or (b) South Africa . . . The amount of the Author's personal expense of any such visit shall be borne as to Two Thirds by Mrs Bambridge and One Third by the Author'; 'the Author will visit at an early stage Earl Baldwin and Mrs Fleming and such other persons as Mrs Bambridge may indicate.'

In 1943, before the contract was drawn up, Captain Bambridge had died of pneumonia, leaving Elsie in charge of a 2500-acre estate, a huge Georgian mansion, numerous employees and a sizeable fortune. George Bambridge had been 'the light of her life and organiser of every common round and daily task'. With his sudden death, she found herself 'plunged into responsibilities and duties of which she had little or no knowledge whatever'. And indeed the contract with Birkenhead does have a hostile, self-protective tone. Perhaps Elsie never shared her husband's estimate of Birkenhead but felt obliged to honour it; perhaps she hoped that this biographer could be scared off like Bolitho and Dorling.

Birkenhead signed and, when the war ended, got down to his research. In 1948 he delivered to Mrs Bambridge a first draft of his biography, some 160,000 words. Elsie, who had by now developed a rather crusty style of widowhood – a 'seemingly hard veneer', as friends described it – was ruthless and absolute in her rejection: 'It is very unpleasant for me to have to tell you that I consider it so bad as a book that any attempt at palliative measures . . . rewriting here and altering there is not feasible.' Birkenhead, understandably, was horrified; a number of his important friends made overtures on his behalf but Elsie was unshakeable: the book was no good, it must not be published, and so on. Her precise objections were unclear, but then for her to have spelled out her reasons would have been to encourage Birkenhead to have another try, and this she vehemently did not want.

In an effort to buttress her objections, Elsie – via the agent A. P. Watt – had taken soundings in the literary world. T. S. Eliot was consulted and he reported back that he found the book 'pedestrian' and that it would 'not do as it stands': there was too much about Kipling's 'public activities' and not enough about the work – although Eliot rather doubted Birkenhead's literary-critical prowess. Most damagingly, he judged that the biographer had dealt unfairly with the 'public Kipling':

> what is important about Kipling in relation to politics and public affairs is his prophetic insight, and not his intemperate and sometimes silly utterances both public and private. I am not asking that a biographer should make the character of his subject more agreeable than he finds it to be, but that he should not leave us unable to reconcile the character he depicts with the literary works which we know. Possibly Lord Birkenhead might have his attention drawn to the importance and curiosity of Kipling's religious affinities – his sympathy with Islam, his attraction to Mithraism and masonic ritual, and his interest in the borderland of hysteria and insanity.

The manuscript was shown also to the once-eminent John Squire – Sir John, in fact: the Edmund Gosse of the 1920s but by now somewhat on the skids, although his name would have had a ring for Mrs Bambridge. Squire thought the biography far too long and far too badly written – he and Eliot seem not to have been told that they were reading a first draft – and that Birkenhead did not 'quite comprehend Kipling and his passions'. Altogether, though, the book was 'about as good a first standard Life as we are likely to get. It merely needs licking into shape.'

In September 1948, William Watt wrote to Mrs Bambridge, summarising the Eliot and Squire verdicts and suggesting that she pass them on to Birkenhead with instructions to cut and revise: 'the only alternative seems to be to say to Lord Birkenhead that you are not prepared to go any further in the matter and arrange to pay him some sum which would compensate for his work and disappointment.' This was what Elsie wanted to hear: she offered Birkenhead £3500 as compensation and a further £1500 'on condition that he made an undertaking never to publish or cause to be published any biography of Kipling'. Birkenhead took the cash, and immediately the 'banned' biography became notorious. It remained so for a further thirty years. What *was* it that Elsie had recoiled from? What 'something in the book' had 'shocked her deeply'? Birkenhead claimed to be mystified and Mrs Bambridge had nothing more to say.

In 1951, Elsie appointed her second official biographer of Kipling: the historian of Empire, Charles Carrington. Carrington's pedigree and bibliography seemed perfect: a vicar's son, schooled in New Zealand, he had served in both wars, rising to Lieutenant-Colonel in

World War II, and was now working as an academic publisher; he was author of a regimental history (as Kipling himself had been), a book about T. E. Lawrence and, most recently, a study of *The British Overseas*. Most important of all, though, in Carrington's own view, was that he and Elsie belonged to the same generation, the right generation, as they each believed:

> We had been brought up in Edwardian England, when the values now associated with 'Kiplingism' were the commonplaces of the British peoples. To us, Duty, Loyalty, Service and Efficiency were virtues not jokes. We did not doubt that British India was something to be proud of, that the Boer War was fought against a racialist oligarchy (strange how the lefty-trendies have swung backwards and forwards on that issue).

Elsie was not told, when she hired Carrington, that he had once before tried to write a life of Kipling. In 1936, he and a friend called Archie Lyall had co-authored a synopsis and submitted it, unsuccessfully, to A. P. Watt. The synopsis was not so much an outline for a Life as notes towards a 'lefty-trendy' diatribe against Kipling the 'fossilised schoolboy', the neurotic proto-fascist:

> R.K. [it said] had the complete Fascist–Nazi mentality: violent patriotism and insular nationalism; a contempt for intellectuals, internationalists and individual thinkers; a strong sense of the duty owed to the State, a belief in, and a fine capacity for coining, phrases and catchwords while at the same time despising and bitterly attacking democracy.

It is hardly to be wondered that A. P. Watt did not encourage further action on the project nor that Carrington, presenting his credentials in 1951, did not see fit to remind him of that earlier rebuff. (The synopsis is now in Carrington's papers, with a note attached, dated 1971, dismissing it as 'quite inadequate and unsympathetic, a typical love–hate reaction in that manner of the 1930s'.)

Elsie knew nothing of all this; the pair of them, it seems, got on extremely well: 'We argued powerfully but we never quarrelled. Her contributions to my book have been much praised by the critics and I asked her to put her name on the title-page as co-author. A Kipling to the end, she retained her independence.' Carrington's *Life* appeared in 1954, and it was indeed respectfully noticed. Many readers, though, scrutinised the text for clues that might help to solve the mystery of its predecessor's fate. It was now known what Mrs Bambridge *approved*, but of course the real excitement would be to know what she and Carrington had agreed to cover up.

When Mrs Bambridge died in 1976, she left orders for the destruction of Carrie Kipling's diaries – thirty-five notebooks covering the period 1892–1936 – together with her own diaries and those of her husband. It seems that she had already got rid of the manuscript of Birkenhead's biography (Birkenhead had died a year earlier but in the 1960s had substantially revised his book, still hoping for a 'thawing in Mrs Bambridge's attitude'.) Carrie's diaries, it so happens, were not entirely lost. Carrington took notes on them when researching his *Life* and from these it would appear that the originals were perfunctory, mere factual jottings:

30 Jan 1896. On reflection he finds *Kim* quite wrong.
1/2 Feb 1896. Taken with pains at midnight. Baby born at 3.20. All well.
4 Feb. We think of calling the child Elsie. '*Kim* must be revised by the Pater'.
9 Feb. Stuck dead over *Kim*.

Now and again there is a snatch of Kipling's speech, and from Carrie one or two lines of local description, but to judge from Carrington's notes the journals would have been chiefly valuable as a means of confirming what was already known: that Carrie was in charge of all practical arrangements, that Kipling rarely went anywhere without her, that there was something maternal in her attitude to his hobbies and enthusiasms – including the writing of his books – and that she took pride in his great fame. ('Somerset Maugham asks us to tea to meet the King and Queen of Siam. We refuse.') The portrayal is of a stable, efficient helpmate. On the known-about great miseries of Kipling's life – the death of daughter Josephine, for instance, or the quarrel with Beatty Balestier – the entries are stoically terse:

9th [May 1896]. Sat. A very warm day and so far the most wretched and unhappy of my life. Beatty arrested on a charge of threatening to kill Rud.
10th. Rud settles down to his singing. I am occupied with accounts.
11. Uncle John comes 10 p.m. We sit up till midnight attempting to discuss matters.
12. Beatty's trial comes on in the a.m. and lasts until 5 p.m. leaving Rud a wreck. The lawyers play to the reporters. Beatty held for $800 which he raises.

13. Rud a total wreck. Sleeps all the time. Dull, listless and weary. These are dark days for us.

It would, however, be unwise to characterise the diaries on the basis of what Carrington preseved. He was, after all, in continuous negotiation with Elsie and would not have seen much point in transcribing what he could not use. Birkenhead had also had access to the diaries and may have copied very different extracts.

Elsie Bambridge's diary-burning decrees put a final wintry touch to her image as a fierce keeper of the family secrets, but the real interest when she died was in the banned Birkenhead biography. 'WHAT DID KIPLING'S DAUGHTER WANT TO HIDE?' asked the *Sunday Times*; 'KIPLING SECRETS MAY BE REVEALED' (the *Sunday Telegraph*). By each of these newspapers, a few thin speculations were advanced: when Birkenhead penetrated 'the dark recesses', he had found evidence which 'called into question . . . the very basis of [Kipling's] conventional appeal' – in other words, the great Empire-builder had had moments of self-loathing and despair and his 'hasty marriage' to Carrie had been 'inspired by the guilt he felt over the death of her brother Wolcott' with whom 'Kipling had quarrelled'. And the stories were padded out with background on the Bambridge/Birkenhead dispute and denials from Charles Carrington: 'the secret in the Kipling archives is that there is no secret.'

They were, of course, non-stories, but they were prominent enough to refurbish the glamour of Birkenhead's banned book. The publishers stirred into action and in 1978 the biography finally appeared, to further headlines: 'REVEALED . . . THE KIPLING HIS FAMILY SUPPRESSED' (the *Daily Mail*). Carrington had at the same time brought out a 'new and revised' edition of his *Life*, so it was possible for reviewers to study the two books side by side. Philip Mason in *The Times* expressed the general sense of bathos when he wrote: 'They are both good biographies. They describe the same man; they tell the same story.' There were no important facts in Birkenhead that were not in Carrington, no new slants, no scandals. But then of course Birkenhead's manuscript *had* been revised. Could it be that he had eventually censored his own text?

Robert Blake was one of the few who had read Birkenhead's original submission, which he admired as 'one of the finest biographies written in modern times'. In 1948, along with John Betjeman, he had made representations to Mrs Bambridge on

Birkenhead's behalf. Reviewing the published book in 1978, he could find 'only two episodes which are not in the Carrington version and might have offended Kipling's daughter': one of these involved a Westward Ho! schoolmaster who had accused the boy Kipling of homosexuality (in rebuttal, Kipling was obliged to boast of his rompings among 'the fishgirls of Appledore'); the other told of Kipling's failure to fit in with Lahore club society because of his loutish manners and his 'caddishly dirty tongue'. Neither revelation seemed sufficient, in Blake's view, to have provoked the Bambridge veto.

Angus Wilson got closer to fathoming the ban, perhaps because he had published his own Kipling biography a year earlier and had all the materials to hand. Writing in *The Observer*, he too found 'very little that is new, only one thing of unusual interest, and nothing whatever that is scandalous'. The 'one thing' of interest was a 1901 fragment from Carrie Kipling's diary:

> July 18. Down and down I go . . . 20. Still down . . . 26. I remain empty at the bottom of my collapse. Aug. 4. Dreadful night trying to think out the black future. 5. Rud means to stop longer away. 6. A night of mental agony leaves me down in the bottom of the pit and well nigh hopeless for the black future. 7. Rud arrives at 6 p.m. Great rejoicings.

Birkenhead comments: 'This strange passage is the first indication in Caroline's diaries of the emotional instability that was to grow upon her with the years, and finally to cloud the relationship between her and Kipling.' He offers no other diary entries in the same vein, nor does he seem to know anything of the background to Carrie's three weeks of distress. Rudyard, it should be said, was 'away' on a quite innocent visit to his parents.

It does seem probable that one of Birkenhead's offences was in his bleak portrayal of the Kipling marriage but again, even on an issue of such sensitivity, some compromise could surely have been sought. As we know from her own *Memoir* Elsie was never starry-eyed about her mother. There had to be something else as well, something pervasive, uncorrectable and difficult for Elsie to describe. Robert Blake's theory was that, since the two episodes he singled out occurred very early in the book, 'Mrs Bambridge saw all the rest . . . with a jaundiced eye'. So jaundiced, perhaps, that she had not been able to read on?

In fact, she did read on. Notes on the manuscript, made by her in

1948, have survived. They run to several pages, and a selection will signify the general drift:

— no description of him at work, methods, nor description of his study . . . his *great* love of the Bible, English & French literature not mentioned.
— His position in England and abroad as a writer . . . his delightful and brilliant personality & talk, his vivid interest in the world and people are hardly mentioned.
— His worldwide reputation as a man of letters is ignored.
— His great admiration for and knowledge of Shakespeare.
— No mention of R.K.'s friendship with children and young people and his kindness to them.
— Great affection for his children and the trouble he took to answer their questions and to direct their reading and to read poetry to them.
— Friendship with George V, speeches, visits to Balmoral, *degrees*, Sorbonne and Strasbourg, visits with family, other degrees.
— no mention of his very vivid blue eyes.
— Enormous translation of books in all languages – collection in British Museum.
— Boy Scouts and Baden Powell.
— R.K.'s drawing of crests and selecting mottoes for new ships is not mentioned.
— No mention of his fellowship of Magdalene College.

There are criticisms also of the book's style and structure 'slipshod, careless and clumsy sentences', 'a jerky patchwork'. In general, though, the notes deal with specific errors of omission. The nearest Elsie gets to an overall appraisal is when she writes: 'R.K. represented as an acid, vehement personality, more interested in politics than in anything else.'

It is a poignant document, representing as it does an outmoded species of bewilderment. Without fully knowing it, Elsie is engaged in an argument about what biography is *for*, an argument that has long before been settled in favour of the opposition. When, late in her life, she was asked for the umpteenth time why she had so angrily suppressed the Birkenhead biography, she said that she could not remember. What she probably meant was that she could no longer remember a time when it was plausible for the relatives of a dead hero to expect him to be honoured by the writer of his Life. On another occasion, she told Carrington that she 'disliked' Birkenhead because he was so obviously 'allied to the "Bright Young Things" '. Nobody quite knew what or whom, in 1948, she would have had in mind.

In the same way, reviewers in 1978 could find nothing in Birkenhead's thirty-year–old book that might have caused such deep offence. But the offence itself was thirty years old and the offended party was born in 1896. She was eighteen at the outbreak of World War I, and she was Kipling's daughter. 'Kipling's constant dirty language becomes boring'; 'a streak of vulgarity in his nature'; 'bound up with this coarse streak was the abuse of dialect'; '[he was] like a hearty extrovert in the locker-room of a provincial golf-course'; 'there was something in him that made him repellent to many intelligent people'. Jibes like these are scattered throughout Birkenhead – they are usually thrown off in passing and are the less noticeable because they chime in with the author's customary tone. By the 1970s, this kind of casual biographical disparagement was commonplace, taken for granted. In 1948, to non-literary types like Elsie Bambridge, it still had a repugnant novelty – intolerably so, when it was aimed at a dead father's reputation.

And this may be the true, dull answer to 'one of the great literary controversies of our time'. It was not any dark revelation by Birkenhead that set Elsie's teeth on edge, nothing to do with Carrie's insanity or Rudyard's sexual guilt. The real irritant was the biographer's as-from-above *inspection* of a personality he ought to have looked up to. Angus Wilson talked of Birkenhead's 'unconscious Stracheyism'. Elsie Bambridge was not a great reader but she would surely have agreed with her father's verdict on Strachey and on the upstart-analytical new manner of biography his book helped to engender. Kipling called *Eminent Victorians* 'downright wicked in its heart' and would happily have kept *it* out of print for thirty years.

# CHAPTER FIFTEEN

# JAMES JOYCE'S PATRON SAINT

'Few people will love him, I think, in spite of his graces and his genius, and whosoever exchanges kindnesses with him is likely to get the worst of the bargain.' Stanislaus Joyce was eighteen when he wrote this in his diary: three years younger than his brother James, whom it describes. The boys' mother had died just a month before, aged forty-four. The two sons were at her bedside during her last hours and when an uncle told them to kneel down and pray, they both refused – or rather James refused, and Stanislaus did too.

This was in 1903. James had already broken with Catholicism, abandoned his plans for a medical career and had a first taste of his 'vagabond' destiny in Paris. He was committed to a life of separateness and disobedience; he was, he liked to say, a hunted deer – hunted, but defiant and uncatchable: 'Let the pack of enmities come tumbling and sniffing to the highlands after the game. There was his ground and he flung them disdain from his flashing antlers.' This disdain was flung chiefly at the 'trolls', the 'rabblement' of Ireland's lumpen middle class, all those who failed to honour the 'holy office' to which James Joyce was lately self-elected. But some of it, from time to time, was flung at Stanislaus, the transfixed acolyte. Stani's subservience was taken for granted; his attempts at self-assertion were made fun of. From boyhood, he was given to understand that his future would be decided by his brother's. The prospect was not unalarming:

[James] has extraordinary moral courage – courage so great that I have hoped that he will one day become the Rousseau of Ireland. Rousseau, indeed, might be accused of cherishing the secret hope of turning away the anger of disapproving readers by confessing unto them, but Jim cannot be suspected of this. His great passion is a fierce scorn of what he calls the 'rabblement' – a tiger-like, insatiable hatred . . . He has a distressing habit of saying quietly to those with whom he is familiar the most shocking things about himself and others, and, moreover, of selecting the most shocking times for saying them, not because they are shocking merely, but because they are true.

When Stani showed this paragraph to Jim, the Irish Rousseau's only quibble was with the phrase 'moral courage' – it failed, Joyce said, to convey the degree of intellectual severity with which he proposed to set about his tasks. He seems to have feared that it made him sound less chillingly high-destined than he knew himself to be; it made him sound – well, *nicer* than he really was. Stani would not make the same mistake again.

Joyce was at first meant to serve the Catholic priesthood; a habit of vocational boasting was ingrained. His first novel, *A Portrait of the Artist as a Young Man*, was to do with intentions, undertakings, journeys of 'error and glory' about to be embarked on, and yet Joyce also wished the book itself to be seen as an arrival, a fulfilment of the promise whose difficult formation it narrates. For him, as for the book's hero Stephen Dedalus, there would be no anxious conflicts between life and art. To be a creator of art was to be more god than priest, more god than man, but human gods must live in a dungheap human world, and must equip themselves with superhuman powers of dedication:

> I will tell you what I do not fear. I do not fear to be alone or to be spurned for another or to leave whatever I have to leave. And I am not afraid to make a mistake, even a great mistake, a lifelong mistake, and perhaps as long as eternity too.

A monkish novitiate might talk this way, but Stephen 'will not serve that in which I no longer believe'. Joyce neither: having spurned one possible 'lifelong mistake' he was eager for what might turn out to be another – but this time the error would be of his own devising.

It is earlier in this same speech that Stephen Dedalus vows to try to express himself 'as wholly as I can, using for my defence the only arms I allow myself to use – silence, exile and cunning'. Hearing this, his friend Cranley laughs: 'Cunning indeed! Is it you? You poor poet, you!' But the laugh freezes when Stephen boasts that he will be journeying alone:

> – Alone, quite alone. You have no fear of that? And you know what that

word means? Not only to be separate from all others but to have not even one friend.

– I will take the risk.

Joyce's exile from Dublin was indeed lifelong and it never turned into a repatriation. His preferred resting places were the hotels and furnished rooms and restaurants of European cities: none of these could, except fleetingly, be mistaken for a second home. And his failing eyesight would be like a steady, symbolic curtailment of any treacherous responsiveness to what was going on around him: the 'sights' of Paris or Trieste or Zurich were always indistinct.

As to the promised cunning: here too Joyce could be said to have delivered, although perhaps not in the ways that Stephen would have wished. As envisaged by Dedalus, an artist's craftiness – his priest-craft, so to speak – ought to support, defiantly, his willingness to walk alone. Joyce, in the day-to-day running of his life, rarely did anything without the assistance of a small team of admirers. And yet few of those who served him would have claimed that, in his genius, he was not awesomely 'alone'; and few did not detect in him a strong element of self-protective guile. 'Few will love him,' said Stanislaus, but then Joyce did not want to be loved by his literary helpmates. For 'love', he had his earthy, unenchantable Nora, who found it hard to read his books. From the disciples, he required merely an unflagging reverence.

Exile and cunning were to be used, by Dedalus, as arms in defence of a liberated mode of self-expression. What he meant by 'silence' is open to debate. Joyce's own relationship with that property was rarely, shall we say, harmonious. For long stretches, he was 'silenced' by official censorship and when, after great transcontinental struggles, he obtained a hearing, he chose to speak in a language few could understand. But then gods create what they happen to create: 'The mystery of esthetic, like that of material creation, is accomplished. The artist, like the God of creation, remains within or behind or beyond or above his handiwork, invisible, refined out of existence, indifferent, paring his fingernails.'

Well-manicured they may have been, but often Joyce felt as if his hands had been nailed to a cross. In each of the two main phases of his literary career – the *Ulysses* phase and the *Finnegans Wake* phase – he was able to cast himself as victim, a god crucified. He had an unrelenting sense of having been unjustly used. Leon Edel called him 'the injustice collector'. Over the years, Joyce compiled a mean dossier of grievances: there were the priests, the Irish, the censors, the publishers, the trolls. There were long-ago Dublin associates who did him wrong or talked against him or claimed to have once dallied with his wife; there were money-people who backed him and then stopped or who seemed to think that they had bought the right to tell him not to ride in taxis or buy drinks; there were sympathisers who spoke of him too sympathetically behind his back; there were the 'friends' of *Ulysses* who could not similarly love his *Work in Progress.* And when he, Joyce, tried to play the role of protector, what help did he get from those who claimed to be protecting *him*? Why couldn't his supporters admit that John Sullivan was an operatic genius, another victim of the general ignorance? And why was everyone so keen to persuade him that he was wrong to deny that his daughter Lucia was incurably insane? As Joyce saw it, the persecution, the betrayals, were incessant: surely no writer of comparable gifts (if such could be imagined) had been treated as he was.

Joyce left Ireland in 1904 and set up as a hand-to-mouth teacher of English in Trieste. He had persuaded Nora to elope with him, and Stani was in tow, but there was no money and, for ten years, no recognition. Throughout this first punishing decade, Joyce's book of stories, *Dubliners*, was in the hands of publishers who were demanding impossibly extensive expurgations. Enraged by their timidity, and generally undermined by lack of funds, he found it difficult to concentrate on the novel he had begun just before he had left home. The high scorn that had propelled him towards Europe was becoming edged with irritation, vengefulness, self-pity. As Richard Ellmann describes it: 'His letters home reveal that . . . he was struggling for a hold on the meaning of his exile. The letters were already set in the three modes that he held to throughout his life: the assertive, the plaintive and the self-exculpatory.'

It had been easier, more fun, to be rebellious in Dublin, where the shockable queued up to be shocked. In Trieste, working on *A Portrait of the Artist*, Joyce could bitterly re-savour that past time when a community took notice of his grand delinquencies, when 'A.E.' wrote to Yeats that 'of all the wild youths I have ever met he is the wildest' and when Yeats himself, having asked the young Joyce for a reading of his work, was told: 'I do since you ask me but I attach no more importance to your opinion than to anybody one meets in the street.' (When, at this same meeting, the talk turned to Yeats's own most recent verse, the stripling followed up with: 'We have met too late. You are too old for me to have any effect on you.' The 37-year-old Yeats commented: 'Never have I seen so much pretension with so little to show for it.') In Trieste it was more difficult to flash the antlers. Joyce could merely give Stanislaus a bad time, write indignant letters to publishers (and on one notable occasion to King George V), cling jealously to Nora, and spend his leisure poring over numerous unsettled bills, unsettled scores. If the world indeed owed this artist a living, the world was seriously in arrears.

In 1909 and 1912, Joyce briefly revisited his native land. On each trip, he was able to rack up a fresh supply of injuries and indignities; and, as was his wont, 'he saw his private quarrels writ large on a symbolic screen'. To have returned to Ireland in triumph might have made these journeys tame and bearable, but to go back penniless and with his stories still unpublished was merely to replenish his armoury – and the armouries of his opponents. He was asked more than once: Why don't you employ your undoubted gifts for the betterment of your own people? According to his mood, he would either wax altitudinous about the forging of the 'uncreated conscience' of his race, or he would sulkily wish it to be known that 'I was the first person to introduce Irish tweeds in Austria although that business is not in the least in my own line.' (The tweeds were actually no joke. During a phase of would-be business wizardry, Joyce did have the Trieste agency for Irish homespuns – a scheme which was about as successful as his other financial brainchild: persuading a group of Trieste merchants to bankroll the introduction of 'cinema theatres into Ireland, and especially in Dublin'. The cinema project got off the ground but failed within a few months. Joyce would later claim that by means of it he had 'deflected' 150,000 francs of 'continental money into the pockets of hungry Irishmen and women since they drove me out of this hospitable bog six years ago'.)

Joyce's 1912 visit would be his last. The crowning Irish insult came from the publisher Maunsell and Co., who three years earlier had taken over the *Dubliners* procrastination from the London firm Grant Richards. Maunsell's had agreed a contract and had even set the book in type; then, on legal advice, they began to demand major alterations – in particular, they wanted all proper names to be fictionalised. Joyce refused; the contract was broken and when the author indicated that he might attempt a private publication he was told that the printer's sheets had been destroyed. Years later, Joyce's approved biographer was probably echoing his subject's suspicions when he wrote: 'There has never been any valid explanation for this crude sacrifice and wanton destruction on the part of the printer. It may be pointed out here that the printers were Falconer and Company who did a lot of work for various Roman Catholic societies.' On the journey back to Trieste, Joyce penned a seething farewell to his country, to be spoken by the errant printer:

> Who was it said: Resist not evil?
> I'll burn that book, so help me devil.
> I'll sing a psalm as I watch it burn
> And the ashes I'll keep in a one-handled urn.
> I'll penance do with farts and groans
> Kneeling upon my narrow bones.
> The very next lent I will unbare
> My penitent buttocks to the air
> And sobbing beside my printing press
> My awful sin I will confess.

By 1913, Joyce was in the depths; his flame needed to be kept, but so did he. Haughty though he was, he had never proposed that his splendid odyssey should reject subsidy from outside sources. When, in his pre-exile years, he heard that the poet Padraic Colum was being financed by an American millionaire on condition that he 'live among country people and write', Joyce walked fourteen miles to seek out the philanthropist, with some proposal of his own. Ever since, he had been on the look-out for the 'patron [saint] of men of letters' so that he could 'remind him that I exist: but I understand that the last saint who held that position resigned in despair and no other will take the portfolio.'

It was in December 1913 that Joyce received his now-celebrated first approach from Ezra Pound. Pound was almost penniless himself but he had an impresario's appetite and flair. Already he was a notoriously shrill presence on the London literary scene, rounding up Imagist poets, pouring out manifestoes, running other people's magazines. By the time of his momentous letter to Trieste, he was in the early stages of taking over the literary section of a faintly dotty feminist periodical, *The New Freewoman* (later to be called *The Egoist*) and it had been Yeats – whom Pound served on and off as secretary – who had put him on to Joyce:

Dear Sir: Mr Yeats has been speaking to me of your writing. I am informally connected with a couple of new and impecunious papers . . . I also collect for two American magazines which pay top rates . . .

I am bonae voluntatis – don't in the least know that I can be of any use to you or you to me. From what W.B.Y. says I imagine we have a hate or two in common.

There was a 'severity' and 'clarity' in Joyce's writing that could be made to fit with Pound's Imagist propaganda of the day, and – as a movement-maker – he was anxious to recruit new names. But he was chiefly excited by what he soon learned about the Irishman's travails with publishers. Pound was an outsiderist but he was also a consummate gatecrasher. He railed against the literary establishment but he knew how to pull its strings. Having adopted the Joyce cause, he was unstoppable. On the money side, he hustled for grants – from the Royal Literary Fund and (via Eddie Marsh) from the Civil List – and he opened up an American outlet for Joyce's manuscripts. This last was something of a coup, considering that Joyce was still more or less unpublished, but again Pound had the right connection. (The American collector John Quinn half-employed Pound as a European scout, and had an admirable faith in his hunches; a faith which handsomely paid off in years to come.)

While raising the ready cash, Pound was also busily marketing the wares. He fixed for Joyce's just-completed novel to be serialised in *The Egoist*, he put his poems in the well-publicised anthology *Des Imagistes*, he wrote articles in praise of the new writer's 'clear, hard prose', its 'hardness and gauntness'. An exile himself, Pound found it easy to glorify Joyce's flight from Celtic provincialism to the centre, or near-centre, of Europe's new Renaissance:

Let us presume that Ireland is ignorant of Mr Joyce's existence, and that if any copy of his work ever reaches that country it will be reviled and put on the index. For ourselves, we can be thankful for clear, hard surfaces, for an escape from the softness and mushiness of the neo-symbolist movement, and from the Fruitier school of the neo-realists, and in no less a degree from the phantasists who are the most trivial and most wearying of the lot. All of which attests the existence of Mr Joyce, but by no means the continued existence of Ireland.

In January 1914, Grant Richards agreed to publish *Dubliners* (and six months later did); in February, the *Egoist* printed a first extract from *A*

*Portrait of the Artist*; in March, Joyce started work on *Ulysses*. Not quite an *annus mirabilis* – other events in Europe would soon force him to move from Trieste to Zurich – but certainly, thanks to the 'wonder worker' Pound, his most effective year so far.

The *Egoist* serialisation was Pound's idea. He thought the novel 'damn fine stuff' but he warned Joyce that the ladies who ran the magazine might 'jibe at one or two of your phrases'. He need not have worried. The editor, Dora Marsden, was about to stand down in order to pursue her private researches into the mysterious couplings of space and time, and she rarely read the literary pieces that Pound had begun to bring in to the magazine. In any event, Joyce's battles with the censorship had made him sound like a worthy cause: an 'egoist', as defined by Miss Marsden, was 'a free man, or woman, unamenable to pressures directing him towards what he ought to be, but fully alive to what he is'. Pound may have been more nervous about the response of Marsden's treasurer and soon-to-be-successor, Harriet Shaw Weaver. Where Miss Marsden was abstracted, highly strung and quarrelsome, the 38-year-old Miss Weaver (Joyce was now thirty-two) seemed demure, watchful, unpretentious – tending even to the 'hard and clear': qualities more welcome in prose styles than in prospective publishers. Pound probably already knew that it was Miss Weaver's money that – anonymously – kept the magazine alive.

Both Pound and Joyce were to be agreeably, and lastingly, surprised. By accident, they had found a patron saint – or, at any rate, a saintly patron. When Harriet Weaver took over the running of *The Egoist* in June 1914, she had already decided to 'look after' Mr Joyce. Rich, childless, idealistic, she saw in the predicament of this far-off victim genius of letters the great cause she had been hoping for, and yet had not quite found, when she joined up with Dora Marsden's 'interesting' circle of feminists, theosophists and freethinking self-fulfillers. Joyce's experience, she perceived, was not unlike her own. She too had broken free; she too was in a sort of exile.

A doctor's daughter, she had inherited Lancashire cotton money from her mother's side and early on decided to rebel against her strict Evangelical upbringing. Her parents had moved from Cheshire to Hampstead when she was fifteen and, inspired by a liberal-leaning governess, she had taken to sneaking off to the public library, there to soak up the thoughts of Emerson, Walt Whitman and John Stuart Mill – incendiary stuff for a young woman of her time and place. She came to believe that 'to live on inherited wealth was to live on usury'; denied the prospect of any further education, she took up social work in the East End of London and in her spare time went to lectures on topics like 'Sex Oppression and the Way Out' and 'The Abolition of Domestic Drudgery'. It was through these that she had met Dora Marsden and – as it then was – *The Freewoman*. The magazine, she thought, 'must have been edited on a mountain-top, it breathed so deeply of the spirit of freedom – a wide, deep freedom, not the noisy counterfeit which will clamour for advantage and shy at responsibilities, but the genuine sort which is prepared to count the costs, and, finding them heavy, agree to pay.'

One of Harriet's most tenacious childhood memories was of being caught, at home, with her nose in a novel by George Eliot. The vicar was summoned, to explain to her what was wrong (a) with the 'adulterous' G. Eliot and (b) with *Adam Bede*. The book was confiscated and at that moment, Harriet later recalled, she became a member of the literary avant-garde. She was determined that no one should confiscate James Joyce. Moved by what she now read of Joyce's long battle to get *Dubliners* into print, she soon came to regard her tutelage of *A Portrait of the Artist* as a symbolic, sacred trust. When the *Egoist*'s regular printers blue-pencilled Chapter 4, her response was to look for a new printer – even though certain of the controversial words (like 'fart' and 'bollocks') were 'not familiar to her'. She saw it as her duty to protect, in every detail, Joyce's text. From time to time, she had to give way to the printers' 'naughty minds', and wartime communications made it hard for her to keep her author abreast of what was going on, but Joyce was used to fighting against expurgations; what he was not used to was an editor who appeared to loathe them just as much as he did. 'I can but apologise to you,' Miss Weaver wrote to him in August 1915. 'I hope you will not have this annoyance when the novel comes to be printed in book form.'

The printing of *A Portrait* in book form did not, as was hoped, followed naturally from its appearance in the *Egoist*. Half of dozen London publishers, including Grant Richards, turned it down and in the end Miss Weaver resolved to publish it herself. But how? No printer would touch an uncut version. Ezra Pound proposed that blanks should be left, so that he could paste in the offending material by hand, and no one doubted that the offer was in earnest. But Pound, with John Quinn's help, had been active in America. The New York publisher Ben Huebsch agreed to take a risk, and the newly formed

Egoist Press undertook to buy a batch of sheets from him. By February 1917, after a year of complicated dealings, the novel was reviewed and advertised in English. Joyce wrote to his proud new publisher: 'I thank you again and very gratefully for all the trouble you have taken and hope it will be rewarded in some way.'

*A Portrait of the Artist* would remain Harriet Weaver's favourite of Joyce's writings. When chapters of *Ulysses* began to arrive at the *Egoist*, her response was not always as wholehearted as she would have wished. She was alternately enchanted, bewildered and repelled. But she was now committed to the entire Joyce enterprise, 'overwhelmingly convinced of his genius', and more than ready to take up arms for his new novel, which even Pound nervously called 'obscene, as life itself is obscene'. What Joyce wrote, she would back. Again, though, it would not be easy to deliver. The *Egoist* printed a few extracts but it was soon evident that the text was not getting any cleaner as it went along. The recent prosecution of Lawrence's *The Rainbow* had made printers even edgier than usual. A double censorship was now in play:

> we have in working practice in England a printer's censorship much more drastic than that of the official censorship itself. So it comes about that an intelligence abnormally acute and observant, an accomplished literary craftsman who sets down no phrase or line without its meaning for the creation as a whole, is faced with a situation in which the very possibility of existence for his work lies at the mercy and limitations of intelligence of – let us say – the printing-works foreman!

This was Harriet Weaver's last magazine editorial. In 1919, she suspended publication of the *Egoist*; from now on, she said, she would devote her energy to getting *Ulysses* published in book form.

Miss Weaver, as viewed by the smart London literati, was an unlikely-looking enemy of censorship. When she approached the Woolfs' Hogarth Press for help with the printing of *Ulysses*, Virginia at once took to her diary:

> I did my best to make her reveal herself in spite of her appearance, all that the editress of the Egoist ought to be, but she remained unalterably modest, judicious and decorous. Her neat mauve suit fitted both soul and body; her grey gloves laid straight by her plate symbolized domestic rectitude; her table manners were those of a well bred hen. We could get no talk to go. Possibly the poor woman was impeded by her sense that what

she had in the brown paper parcel was quite out of keeping with her own contents. But then how did she ever come in contact with Joyce and the rest? Why does their filth seek exit from her mouth? Heaven knows.

And it was not only the smart set who found it hard to grasp what she was up to. Her family was quietly aghast. Everything else in her life seemed so primly buttoned-up: her tiny flat in Gloucester Place, her carefulness with money, her austere personal habits, and so on. Said one close relative: 'How could she? How could she? An enigma! An enigma!'

Joyce and his patron had not met, and – as each of them came to believe – this was maybe just as well. From Europe, Joyce could issue regular bulletins of gloom; he could tell about the shortage of teaching work, the cost of the eye operations he now had to have, the hopelessness of trying to compose his great work with creditors banging on the door, the sacrifices endured by his 'wife' and two young children (he and Nora did not marry until 1931). As she imagined Joyce, he did nothing except work and suffer. It was unfair that she, so ungifted, should have money and good health when he, who had so much to give, was half-starving and half-blind. Here, if anywhere, there was a correctable injustice. Joyce would have said the same. In 1919, Harriet made over £5000 of war bonds to provide him with a quarterly income. A year later, when she was given money by some aunts, she arranged for it to go to Joyce. And she was also ready to help with extra medical expenses. The artist, she told herself, could now write on with dignity during his 'best and most productive years', and she could resume her modest efforts to place *Ulysses* before an undeserving world:

> Harriet felt strongly that she had no need for and no use for more money than she had already inherited. She intensely disliked the idea of possessing any more than she required for the simple life and the interests she had chosen for herself; and she disapproved, on grounds of her socialist principles, of wealth not proportionate to personal need.

Virginia Woolf might well have smiled about all this. Just as it was hard to understand Miss Weaver savouring certain passages of *Ulysses*, so it was almost impossible to picture her enjoying a night out in Zurich or Trieste with her adopted genius. There was so much that she did not know. For one thing, she was unaware that Joyce already had a private income, courtesy of a Mrs McCormick, a Swiss-based American disciple of Carl Jung. Mrs McCormick, not long before, had granted him 1000 francs (£60) a month. Harriet also never knew that, with this newfound wealth, he had been helping to fund a dramatic troupe, the English Players, nor that this latest showbiz wheeze would land him in some costly and wearying litigation. Like many other congenital irregulars, Joyce was a great one for the letter of the law. As Richard Ellmann has observed, the starveling was always ready to swell into the seigneur.

Miss Weaver had seen photographs of Joyce and had been mightily impressed; there was nothing in them to tell of his expensive tastes. He liked to dress nattily, buy fur coats for his wife, and tip big in fashionable restaurants; also, he rather fancied himself as a connoisseur of wines – to be sure, he did a lot of tasting. The god-artist was indeed a victim, but he was also a natural aristocrat – when he was fed, he liked to be well-fed. Miss Weaver's subsidies were welcome but her principal largesse was frustratingly tied up in stocks and bonds; the income was all too easily lived above, and it would not be long before Joyce was looking for ways of plundering the capital. As Miss Weaver's biographers have noted: 'Neither of them liked keeping money. They both preferred to get rid of it, although in very different ways and for very different reasons.'

In 1920, on Pound's advice, Joyce moved to Paris, where the seigneurial side of him could be indulged more lavishly than in Zurich or Trieste. In Paris, there was a flourishing, self-conscious avant-garde, for whom the author of *Ulysses* was seen to be a major prize. Joyce's still-unfinished novel was being serialised in the American *Little Review* and was about to be the subject of a famous prosecution. It was the book everybody couldn't wait to read. In response to the general curiosity, Joyce developed a new, sibylline demeanour; in the salons and cafés, they hung on his silences and marvelled when he pronounced that he could find little evidence of talent in the works of Marcel Proust or when he advised some budding wordsmith to 'write what is in your blood and not what is in your brain'. The stuff of greatness was there for all to see. Not surprisingly, when the bookseller Sylvia Beach gushed up to him at a poetry reading with the words: 'Is this the great James Joyce?', he played it cool. 'James Joyce,' was his more than adequate reply. For her, the 'light of genius' shone from his eyes: 'He gave the impression of sensitiveness exceeding any I had ever known.'

The next day, Joyce called in at Miss Beach's shop, Shakespeare and Co., liked what he saw, and settled in as an habitué, to be gawped at in the afternoons by Hem, Fitz, and all the other incoming literary expats. The myth of Paris in the 1920s was beginning to take shape. Miss Beach could barely contain herself. Shortly afterwards, Joyce told her that *Ulysses* had been banned in the USA:

> It was a heavy blow for him, and I felt, too, that his pride was hurt. In a tone of complete discouragement, he said, 'My book will never come out now.' All hope of publication in the English-speaking countries, at least for a long time to come, was gone. And here in my little bookshop sat James Joyce, sighing deeply.

What to do? On 1 April, Sylvia wrote to her mother: 'Mother dear . . . soon you may hear of us as regular publishers and of the most important book of the age . . . shhhhhh . . . it's a secret, all to be revealed in my next letter and it's going to make us famous rah rah!'

If Harriet Weaver felt at all put out by the emergence of a rival keeper, she did not show it – although she *was* somewhat troubled when Joyce, reporting to her the news of his Sylvia Beach contract, requested an immediate advance on Harriet's 'English edition' of the book. She paid up, though, and was soon in correspondence with Shakespeare and Co. about the possibilities of importing sheets of their edition. She was able to advise the novice Beach on subscription openings, booksellers' discounts, publicity handouts and the like. There was no awkwardness; so far as Miss Weaver was concerned, any new supporters Joyce managed to collect were to be regarded as allies.

Even so, there was at this time a different sort of awkwardness, and it was preying on her mind. From Wyndham Lewis, she had had a report of Joyce's astounding prowess as a drinker. Lewis had told her, admiringly, of 'uproarious all-night sittings' which ended up with Joyce dancing drunkenly around the room – and, it so happened, usually picking up everybody's bill. Harriet was, it seems, 'shattered' by this information; her 'whole nature and upbringing revolted against over-indulgence in drink'. After some hesitation, she decided she would have it out with him. She wrote a letter which has not survived but which reportedly tried to explain 'what she thought about drink – a great evil – and how much disturbed she was that he allowed it to get the better of him'.

279

This was the first time she had ever presumed to make judgements on her hero's private life. Joyce reacted instantly, and in a state of some alarm; he'd been found out. In reply, he penned a witty little essay, describing the peculiar 'legends about me' that were in circulation. He was rumoured, he said, to have been a cocaine addict, a lunatic, a cinema mogul, a spy (for both sides) during the war. Worse than these, he cleverly implied, was 'the rumour that I am extremely lazy and will never do or finish anything (I calculate that I must have spent 20,000 hours in writing *Ulysses*)':

> The truth probably is that I am a quite commonplace person undeserving of such imaginative painting. There is a further opinion that I am a crafty simulating and assimulating Ulysses-like type, a 'jejune jesuit', selfish and cynical. There is some truth in this, I suppose, but it is by no means all of me (nor was it of Ulysses) and it has been my habit to apply this alleged quality to safeguard my poor creations.

It was skilfully done. There was a natural anxiety to win over Miss Weaver, to win her back – not just as a money supply, but as a valued admirer – but Joyce was angry too: with her, with Lewis, with the whole business of having to defend himself in Harriet Shaw Weaver's court of law. He took care not to deny the Lewis story and made no non-ironical apologies. Drink was not mentioned in the letter; there was more than a hint of 'mind your own business' to be read between the lines:

> I now end this long shambling speech, having said nothing of the darker aspects of my detestable character. I suppose the law should now take its course with me because it must now seem to you a waste of rope to accomplish the dissolution of a person who has not dissolved visibly and possesses scarcely as much 'pendibility' as an uninhabited dressing gown.

In a practical way, Joyce was seriously troubled. He arranged for Robert McAlmon (who really was a drunk, and was also himself a backer of Joyce, to the tune of $150 a month) to explain to Harriet that Mr Joyce did indeed like to take a drink from time to time 'but in moderation' and that he was always able to 'hold his drink properly and as a gentleman'. Joyce also went to great lengths to retrieve and destroy a letter he had written to his friend Frank Budgen asking for advice on how to handle the Weaver/Lewis allegation. Budgen had told him he should make a joke of it.

And there *was* something humorous about it: timid temperance zealot ticks off unfettered genius for spending her money on white wine. Miss Weaver, in her way, was as secretive as Joyce, and she too had been exposed. The episode was an important breaking of the ice – a breaking too of the rules of distance and detachment which both parties had so far been careful to observe. For Harriet, it was her first contact with the human, unheroic Joyce, the Joyce who now and then liked to have some fun. It made a small dent in her solemnity and it also gave her an intimidating glimpse of the Joyce antlers. For him, it was an irksome reminder that – even with the 'lion-hearted' Miss Weaver – there were strings attached; he had been made to feel answerable, he had been told (more or less) to watch his step, to sober up, to be sensitive to the concerns of others. People had tried telling him this kind of thing before.

Dealings between the two of them, patron and beneficiary, had entered a perilous new phase. When Joyce finally visited London in 1922 (just after the French publication of *Ulysses* and a few months before Miss Weaver's clandestine and much-harassed English edition), he made a point of parading his extravagance: he took taxis when he did not need to, 'tipped the drivers lavishly', and later boasted that he spent about £200 in just over a month; this was not much less than the annual income provided by Miss Weaver. She noted what he was up to, but she had learned her lesson. This time, her response was to increase his income. During his time in London, Joyce's eye trouble had flared up again; his good eye was affected too. Harriet could 'see with her own eyes the wretchedness of his affliction'. She arranged consultations with all the leading London oculists, took lots of conflicting advice and was left in no doubt that the problem was serious and would probably get worse. By the end of his visit, she was fired with a new determination: she would try to save his sight.

It was not possible, Harriet had found, to separate the man – his 'old world manner, a little like her father's', his 'soft voice', his 'charm, wit, great dignity' – from the books she so admired. And she had been wrong to judge him as she would judge herself. And Joyce, since Miss Weaver had shown an interest in his private life, was now ready to let her into as much of it as she could take. He had her measure, he believed: she was susceptible not just to his writings but to his *predicament*. She was not in this for the excitement and the fame, like Sylvia Beach, or for the Bohemian nights out, like McAlmon and the Paris crew, or because she had no choice, like Stani, or because she wanted to star in a literary-historical romance. For ten years she had devoted the best part of her life to his service. She had once stepped out of line, but was seemingly keen to make amends. Her goodwill was like a mother's, limitless.

When Joyce told Miss Weaver that his next great undertaking would be nothing less than a 'history of the world', she was appropriately thrilled – he was taking her seriously, not just as a publisher and patron, but as a literary confidante. Even as she had begun to worry more about his eyesight than about his writings, so he had begun to open up to her about his most private literary schemes – and not just schemes for publication. And he seemed desperate for her approval. In 1924, he began sending her early episodes from his new book, at this stage called simply 'Work in Progress', and fretted when she was slow in her response. To McAlmon he wrote: 'I don't think she likes the tone of my last effusion', to her 'You did not say if you liked the piece' and 'I hope none of the MS was lost'. He prefaced his submissions with explanatory notes – *Anna Livia Plurabelle* (which she *did* like) was 'a chattering dialogue across the river by two washer-women who as night falls become a tree and a stone' and 'Shaun the Post' was 'a description of a postman travelling backwards in the night through the events already narrated'. Also enclosed would be the customary *cris de cœur* about 'work, worry, bad light, general circumstances and the rest'. Harriet was now more deeply stirred by the personal disclosures than by the texts that accompanied them. These she found baffling and self-indulgent. Finding out about new eye-doctors, or worrying about Joyce's increasingly troublesome offspring, or simply sending gifts of cash: these were ways of disguising from him, and from herself, that something had gone wrong. For the first time, she feared that the book he was writing was no good.

The Egoist Press closed down in 1924. Miss Weaver still had stocks of *Ulysses* in her wardrobe, but the book was launched – or as launched as it could be for the moment: it would have to wait until the mid-1930s for the ban on general publication to be lifted. She no longer had a publishing role in Joyce's life, apart from sending him royalty statements and, when necessary, doctoring them in his favour. Why did her opinion matter? The answer to that one, Joyce's friends would say, was pretty obvious. But Harriet, knowing – as only she could – that her beneficence was not at risk, liked to believe that his need for reassurance was more nobly based. Perhaps he himself was less than committed to his peculiar 'world history'? The new book, as revealed to her over the months, was getting ever harder to decipher, let alone enjoy: 'The author's copious notes helped over particulars but not in general. It seemed a defect that his text, unlike the great books that spoke to her directly, had to be teased out round a set of clues before the message was – in some degree – disclosed. And she saw it going on for ever.'

As 'Work in Progress' progressed, others besides Harriet were beginning to voice doubts. Stanislaus told his brother that 'having done the longest day in literature' he was now 'conjuring up the darkest night', and by 1926 both Pound and Wyndham Lewis had demurred. 'It is possible Pound is right,' Joyce said, 'but I cannot go back.' Harriet, who had begun to hint that she was troubled, decided that it was time to take the plunge:

> Some of your work I like enormously – as I am sure you know – especially the more straightforward and character-analytical parts and the (to me) beautifully expressed ghost-parts . . . but I am made in such a way that I do not care much for the output from your Wholesale Safety Pun Factory nor for the darkness and the unintelligibilities of your deliberately-entangled language system. It seems to me you are wasting your genius.

And then, as a nervous afterword: 'I daresay I am wrong and in any case you will go on with what you are doing, so why thus stupidly say anything to discourage you? I hope I shall not do so again.'

After reading this, Joyce took to his bed and stayed there for several days. 'Miss Weaver says she finds me a madman,' he told Robert McAlmon and was not wholly comforted when McAlmon assured him that he was not mad, merely a bit 'touched' – as great artists were supposed to be. Maybe Stanislaus had put his finger on the problem – the new book was obscure because the events in it took place at night: 'It's natural they should not be so clear at night, isn't it now?' Joyce continued to brood, though, and even suggested – earnestly, it seemed – that someone else should be employed to finish the book for him. 'But who is the person? There is no such absurd person as could replace me except the incorrigible god of sleep . . .'

Harriet was appalled by his feverish response. As with the drink, so with the experimental writing. She should have held her peace. From now on, she vowed, she would 'try to say all I can in praise of the pieces and nothing against them'. This was not easy because, as Joyce wrote on, he continued to solicit her opinion:

I find it difficult as I have the feeling all the time that his genius and his immense labours are being to some extent wasted in producing what appears to me to be – to put it baldly – a curiosity of literature. I daresay I am wrong . . . but I cannot help it – and I have neither the art nor the ability to lie adroitly in order to please him. But it distresses me to hurt him and I wish he would not always so insistently ask me how I like the pieces. I *do* like immensely the ending of *Anna Livia* and have told him so.

Harriet wrote this to Sylvia Beach, whose attitude was very different. Miss Beach liked 'Work in Progress' but no longer liked Joyce constantly rifling her till. Harriet rather envied her, as she also perhaps envied Nora. Nora could simply tell her 'genius – so-called': 'Why don't you write sensible books that people can understand?'

Perhaps, Miss Weaver came to think, the fault was not in Joyce but in her own deficiency as a reader. She owed it to him to work harder. In 1928, she went to Paris and Joyce took her through the book, section by section, and she began to believe that she could see its point, that she *would* come to like it after all. In any case, she assured Joyce that, whatever he chose to write, he could depend on her support, 'to his death'. According to a friend: 'Miss Weaver's visit seems to have dispelled a cloud and made JJ more at rest as to the cares of living.' Throughout her short stay in Paris, Harriet was determined not to shrink from Joyce's social life, whatever it might be. A touching glimpse of the pair of them has been preserved. It was the usual Paris set at play: George Antheil, Adrienne Monnier, McAlmon, *et al.*, with Joyce at one point warbling his Irish ballads in tones of 'tenderness, melancholy, bitterness'. And then, with Miss Weaver watching from her sofa, there was 'champagne and dancing': 'everything was gay, stiffness melted. Only Miss Weaver kept her calm and stillness . . . Joyce's silence comes, I think, from a profound weariness of spirit, but Miss Weaver's is like the stillness of a stone, a quality.'

In Paris, a compromise of sorts had been achieved. Joyce continued to send sections of his book, along with glossaries and explanations ('a few shafts of moonlight on the dustier bits') and Miss Weaver took note like a good student and every so often ventured an interpretation of her own. She had now given her 'official' assent to the project, and Joyce could address her as a colleague, a co-worker, but they each knew that the old spontaneity had gone. Harriet feared that she had let him down, that there was a disappointment, a coolness in the tone of his still frequent letters. But then, as her biographers have pointed out:

their friendship had always been at risk. Her role as judge was difficult enough, and so was her role as financier. She had also felt a personal responsibility for looking after his health, and had acted on it. This is the natural concern of a mother. He had fled from his mother, from Mother Ireland and from Mother Church; but the inescapable mother appeared again in the person of his benefactress. Her 'alms' supported him; her frown disturbed or irritated him.

During the 1930s, Joyce surrounded himself with a new group of admirers: 'Bohemian artist types' gave way to an altogether smoother type of personnel: art critics, historians, lawyers, and even a few early 'Joyceans' – including Herbert Gorman, whom he would soon authorise as his biographer. He was turning fifty, about to be a grandfather (his son Giorgio married in 1930), and he now liked to associate with orderly, successful professionals, men of the world. Paul Leon, a Russian-born lawyer and former 'professor of philosophy and sociology', appointed himself as Joyce's secretary and general manager, 'there to handle every situation, to smooth over all sorts of misunderstandings, to protect Joyce from intruders and gatecrashers'. Leon, his wife has testified, 'was more interested in Joyce as a person' than as a writer. When he was asked why he gave up so much of his time to Joyce, he would reply: 'I am most interested in watching [his] processes of creation. He has me look up words in various languages, and his mental process and the metamorphoses of language he indulges in are most fascinating to witness.' The Safety Pun Factory which had so repelled Miss Weaver was for Leon a splendidly equipped laboratory, or workshop: '[Joyce] is writing in a way that nobody understands or can understand. I've found it wonderfully amusing to translate simple ideas into incomprehensible formulas and to feel it may be a masterpiece.'

From Harriet Weaver's point of view, Leon was cut out to be the worst kind of influence on 'Work in Progress'. On the other hand, the appearance in Joyce's life of such a cerebral and omnicompetent factotum was not to be deplored. Harriet could now be certain that, from day to day, someone else was there to 'look after Mr Joyce'. There was a sadness in finding herself excluded from the magic circle but it was a sadness she could live with. Joyce still wrote her regular, amusing letters and from time to time needed practical advice (usually to do with one or other of the lawsuits he liked to have in progress) and she was glad of the free time in which to pursue her own pet literary project (which she had taken over from her other protégé, Dora Marsden): two vast symposia on *Time* and *Space* that would collect and classify the views of 'outstanding philosophers since the time of the Greeks onwards'.

In the mid-1930s, though, Joyce turned to her again – not as a moneybags, specifically, nor as a literary sounding-board, but as 'family': he wanted a nursemaid for his daughter Lucia, whose bouts of mental illness were becoming more frequent, and harder to control. And harder also to be seen as evidence of an unusual creativity: 'Whatever spark of gift I possess has been transmitted to Lucia,' Joyce would say, '[and] has kindled fire in her brain.' As her affliction became more wearing and spectacular, he was obliged to concede that maybe she *was* ill. He agreed to let her be seen by doctors and to attempt the various treatments that were on offer at the time. But he could never accept that one day she would have to be certified and 'put away'. Ill or not, she was a talented artist: a dancer, a writer, a designer of 'lettrines', elaborately wrought initial letters such as he used to decorate his *Pomes Penyeach*: 'a wonder wild/in gentle eyes thou veilest/My blueveined child.'

When Lucia, in a manic phase, expressed the wish to effect a reconciliation between her father and Miss Weaver, Joyce did nothing to prevent her. Maybe he believed that Harriet could pull off one final miracle on his behalf. And perhaps Harriet hoped that by helping Lucia she could reclaim some of her old function as Joyce's principal helpmate. In 1935, she invited Lucia to stay with her in London. The visit was a disaster, ending – after many frantic weeks – with Lucia in a straitjacket and Harriet thoroughly persuaded that the girl was indeed clinically mad. And this was to be the breaking of her long friendship with James Joyce.

Any just reading of Miss Weaver's handling of Lucia would have to give her high marks for fortitude and sensitivity. As Joyce saw it, though, she had finally lined up with the opposition. When he next addressed himself to her, in a letter of June 1936, it was as a father wishing to advance his daughter's artistic career. Lucia's designs for an ABC poem by Chaucer would, he said, be published in July, to mark her birthday. He was soliciting subscriptions:

I believe I can cover most of the expenses of publication of my daughter's alphabet. My idea is not to persuade her that she is a Cezanne but that on her 29th birthday . . . she may see something to persuade her that her whole past has not been a failure. The reason I keep on trying by every means to find a solution for her case (which may come at any time as it did with my eyes) is that she may not think that she is left with a blank future as well. I am aware that I am blamed by everybody for sacrificing that precious metal money to such an extent for such a purpose when it could be done so cheaply and quietly by locking her up in an economical mental prison for the rest of her life.

I will not do so as long as I see a single chance of hope for her recovery, nor blame her or punish her for the great crime she has committed in being a victim to one of the most elusive diseases known to men and unknown to medicine. And I imagine that if you were where she is and felt as she must you would perhaps feel some hope if you felt that you were neither abandoned nor forgotten.

If you have ruined yourself for me as seems highly probable, why will you blame me if I ruin myself for my daughter!

Miss Weaver's response was to offer to share the cost of publishing Lucia's alphabet, and when the book came out she helped with the distribution. In gratitude, Joyce gave her the original designs, just as long ago he had given her the manuscript of his first novel.

It was really a parting of the ways. Since 1931, Harriet had been an industrious worker for the Marylebone branch of the Labour Party, addressing envelopes, raising funds, canvassing around the houses. In 1936, she was secretly recruited by the local Communists. By the time Lucia's little book appeared, politics had taken over the centre of her life. Joyce was no longer dominant. Harriet was still much moved by what she heard of him from Paul Leon and in the winter of 1936, when Leon told her that Joyce was broke and in a deep depression, she sped to Paris and assured him yet again of her support. But this was the last time they were to meet. Back in London, Harriet threw herself into the political struggle with something of the fervour that had once belonged exclusively to Joyce: selling the *Daily Worker* on the Edgware Road, attending anti-fascist rallies, bailing out co-marchers who had ended up in jail. At the Munich crisis, she broke with the Labour Party and declared her Communist allegiance. When, in December 1938, Leon reported that Joyce, after sixteen years, had finally finished his great work, the sixty-two-year-old Miss Weaver was collecting party dues in Baker Street. Leon wrote to her that he could 'easily understand' that current world problems might make Joyce's book seem colossally trivial; its 'accumulation of words' was, he supposed, meaningless 'to the ordinary intelligent reader of today

287

. . . I cannot see anywhere the slightest attempt in it to face or still less to solve these pressing problems':

> But it is impossible to deny that he has acted according to his conscience and that he has actually consumed almost all his substance, physical and spiritual, moral and material, in the writing of a book likely to be received with derision by his illwishers and with pained displeasure by his friends. And in this attitude he has remained true to himself.

Leon had struck exactly the right note, and Harriet was grateful. When *Finnegans Wake* appeared in May 1939, the world's attention was elsewhere, but Miss Weaver made it her business, as usual, to cut out the English reviews and mail them off to Paris. She knew that Joyce liked to see them all, even or perhaps especially the abusive ones, of which – in this case – there were several.

When Joyce died in Zurich in January 1941, Miss Weaver heard the news on her radio: 'Did he say Mr Joyce was dead? . . . But there was no hint of illness.' His death had indeed been sudden: he had been struck down by a duodenal ulcer and died two days after a seemingly successful operation. Harriet had heard little from him since the publication of *Finnegans Wake*, and had not known in advance of his flight from Paris to Zurich in December 1940. Their last significant exchange of letters had been acrimonious: Giorgio's wife Helen had had a nervous breakdown and when Harriet 'expressed sympathy', Joyce had 'construed her remarks as evidence of improper curiosity'. These letters were later destroyed by Miss Weaver, but it seems that this last accusation of Joyce's was 'too much. She had held her tongue for too long':

> He had accused her, at the height of his distress over Lucia, of having long been poisoned against him. The converse was true: it was he who was poisoned in his attitude towards her. She wrote, scathingly, to tell him so.

And then of course she regretted it. In October 1940, after the fall of France, she arranged for £30 a month to be channelled to Joyce through the Irish Minister at Vichy. The last message she received from him was in cable form four weeks before he died. He needed an immediate £300 for 'maintenance family arrears' and to pay for Lucia to be moved from the hospital in France where he had had to leave her.

In a will drawn up in 1931, Joyce had appointed his literary executor: 'I leave all my manuscripts to Harriet Shaw Weaver and direct that she shall have sole decision in all literary matters relating to my writings published or unpublished.' When Harriet accepted the appointment, she did not expect to be called upon to serve: after all, she was six years older than Joyce – indeed in her own will she bequeathed her collection of manuscripts to *him*.

In 1941, Harriet moved to Oxford – her residence in Gloucester Place had been damaged by fire – and there settled into a three-pronged routine: working for the Communist Party (behind the counter at its bookshop and delivering party newspapers), adding to her *Space* and *Time* symposia, and administering the affairs of the James Joyce estate. For a few years after Joyce's death, there was chaos: his family stranded penniless in Zurich, many of his papers lodged inaccessibly in Paris. Miss Weaver was expected to come up with cash, and so she did – although now and then with some reluctance since it was known that the Joyce son was alcoholic. She began to get begging letters from Giorgio that reminded her of his father's wheedling overtures of some twenty years before. Wartime currency restrictions made the business of supporting the Joyces at long distance a bureaucratic nightmare; it was risky too – but the old lion-heartedness prevailed.

By the late 1940s, Joyce's books began to sell, granting Nora (who died in 1951) a brief taste of well-off widowhood: Jim, she conceded, had perhaps been on to something after all. And as the Joyce reputation rocketed, Harriet found herself in charge of a small business that was rather more prosperous and respectable than those she was accustomed to running. She could finally relax. The royalties started to roll in, and she could see for herself that she had served 'her author' well; her guardianship of the Joyce flame had been accomplished when it was most needed, in his lifetime. All that was required now was good management, the sort of low-key administrative chores she quite enjoyed: overseeing copyrights and permissions, vetting permissions and translations, annotating manuscripts, negotiating with libraries and scholars. In her last years, she was approached with awe by a new generation of academic Joyceans, revered by them as the heroine who had picked up the tab.

Needless to say, this was not how Miss Weaver liked her contribution to be viewed. She would get embarrassed when people marvelled at how much she had done for Joyce – 'I did nothing, nothing.' For her part, she was glad of these last years because they offered an opportunity for her to make peace with him, to complete the cycle of their extraordinary friendship. She had started out as a protector of his books and she was grateful that in the end this was again her role. But she was sometimes contrite. As she read the biographies, the memoirs, the selected *Letters*, she could see that she had often failed to make allowances for Joyce's 'utterly overwrought condition'; and as the explicators decoded his 'impenetrable' later writings, she lashed herself for having so troubled him with her 'lack of sympathetic, imaginative understanding'.

To complete the picture, she came to believe that she had been at fault in her handling of the Lucia situation, and here too she tried to make amends. In 1951, after Nora's death, she became Lucia's 'receiver' or legal guardian, and arranged for her to be transferred to a British hospital. Over the years, Harriet visited as often as she could. Indeed, one of her last journeys was to Lucia in Northampton: in autumn 1961, she went there bearing a gift, a water-colour paint-box, tied with pink ribbon. Before handing it over, Miss Weaver 'gazed long and sadly at the packet, as though it epitomised for her the unfulfilled promise of Mr Joyce's daughter'.

# CHAPTER SIXTEEN

# SYLVIA PLATH AND PHILIP LARKIN

For literary keepers of the flame, the Copyright Act of 1911 represented a significant upgrading, an access of power. Under the new law, an author's legatee had fifty years' control of published work, together with perpetual ownership of any writings which remained unpublished at the author's death. Keepers could look forward to a lifetime's reign, a lifetime's proceeds. With fifty years in view, their sense of having a double duty – to respect the dead and to maximise the takings – was bound to seem both more delicate and weightier than under the old rules. Obedience to what the lost loved one 'would have wished' might not always turn out to be good for business.

But then, as we have seen, that obedience had always been elastic. Most readily lauded among keepers of the flame is Max Brod, who defied Franz Kafka's instruction that 'Everything I leave behind me . . . is to be burned unread even to the last page.' Most often vilified is Spencer Curtis Brown, who scorned Somerset Maugham's not dissimilar decree: 'I direct that there shall be no biography or publication of my letters and that my literary executor and trustees are to refuse permission for such publication and any assistance to any person who wishes or attempts such publication.' Max Brod, of course, saved Kafka's now-celebrated novels from the fire; Curtis Brown merely sanctioned a biography: 'Many people may think I have acted wrongly,' he said. 'Only one man could have given me a clear decision, and he was the man who had sufficient confidence in me to place his reputation in my hands.'

Brod's defence, which no one pressed him for, was that when Kafka made his 'will' – actually a note addressed to Brod – he was in one of his depressions (his 'self-critical tendencies had reached their peak') and in any case he had been warned that his instructions would be disobeyed: 'Franz knew that my refusal was in earnest, and at the end, if he had still intended these wishes to be carried out, he would have appointed another executor.' Curtis Brown's defence, which few seem to have quite swallowed, was that 'when Maugham made this stipulation and when I accepted it, neither of us could foresee how many books would be written about him. Some were written with great responsibility, some with apparent lack of it. But even the most conscientious have been unable, for lack of access to the material, to give a true picture of his final tragic years.' Curtis Brown's own 'true picture' of those final years was that the author of *Cakes and Ale* had turned into a fairly poisonous old toad. The sanctioned biography, by Ted Morgan, was strongly supportive of this view.

George Orwell was another who said he wanted no biography, and there are now two 'authorised' versions of his Life, the second of these none too admiring of the dead widow who had authorised and then disowned the first. W. H. Auden asked his executor Edward Mendelson to assist in 'making a biography impossible'. 'Biographies are always superfluous and usually in bad taste,' he used to say, and when he died the estate published his request that friends should destroy any letters they had had from him: how many of them did we'll never know, but in any case by that date – 1973 – most of Auden's correspondence had found its way into the libraries. Auden did not, however, formally veto a biography. After some head-scratching, Mendelson decided that his instructions were 'flexible enough to be bent backwards'. As with Maugham, the executor contended that his hand was forced by a flood of unofficial memoirs. And Auden, the compulsive aphorist, came to his aid: 'What every author hopes to receive from posterity – a hope usually disappointed – is justice.'

T. S. Eliot added a memorandum to his will: 'I do not wish my executors to facilitate or countenance the writing of a biography of me.' His widow Valerie has done what she was told, or asked: she has not sanctioned a biography and her gradual and meticulous unveiling of the poet's letters has made it difficult for unauthorised enquirers to make headway. And yet it is not at all certain that her husband would have approved her publication of his *Waste Land* drafts. And what about the song 'Memory' in *Cats*? 'Memory', says the sleevenote of the *Cats* LP, 'includes lines from and suggested by "Rhapsody on a Windy Night"' together with 'additional material by Trevor Nunn'. Eliot loved the music-hall, we know, and he hungered for theatrical success, but a taste for Marie Lloyd does not necessarily betoken a taste for Andrew Lloyd Webber. Scholars who have had trouble with the Eliot estate on the matter of permissions might well go a bit sulky when they hear Grizabella mew about those 'burnt out ends of smoky days, the stale cold smell of morning/A street lamp dies, another night is over, another day is dawning.'

The Eliot estate is still a so-called 'live' estate, and will remain so until 2015. Until that date, if Mrs Eliot holds to the no-biography ruling, critics will have trouble reading the Eliot life into the Eliot work, and vice versa. When Peter Ackroyd wrote his unsanctioned biography of Eliot in 1984, he was refused permission to quote from the poet's published work, 'except for purposes of fair comment in a critical context' – which is what the law allows. If he had wished to trace in detail the imprint on Eliot's verse of, say, his terrible first marriage, he would have been obliged to tread with feline stealth: a line here, a couple of lines there, with lashings of critical fair comment. As it was, he made no effort to get round the ruling; he merely put up a few signposts, as in: 'The image of a man who believes himself to have committed a crime, and the notion of a secret which leads to guilt and feelings of worthlessness, are significant aspects of [Eliot's] later drama.' Of course, with Eliot, the biographer was fairly certain that his signposts could be followed, that readers knew the work or had it readily to hand. Ackroyd in truth was not much inhibited by the quotation ban: he claimed that it helped him to tell his tale more crisply. It might have been different if the subject had been a fiction writer of large output and small fame.

It might have been different too if Eliot had been like Sylvia Plath and had 'deliberately used the details of [his] everyday life as raw material for art'. Of Plath's case, A. Alvarez has observed:

A casual visitor or unexpected telephone call, a cut, a bruise, a kitchen bowl, a candlestick, everything became usable, charged with meaning, transformed. Her poems are full of references and images which seem impenetrable at this distance but which could mostly be explained by a scholar with full access to the details of her life.

Arguments about what is or should be meant by 'full access' to the details of Sylvia Plath's life have been on the go for the past twenty-five years, and are raging even now. When she committed suicide in 1963, not much was known about her life *or* work. She had published one book of poems, *The Colossus*, a pseudonymous novel, *The Bell Jar*, and she was married to Ted Hughes, a well-known poet from whom she seemed to have learned plenty. The poems that would shortly make her name were written during the last two years of her life; some of them, the most spectacular, during the last weeks. On the Sunday after Plath's death, Alvarez printed an obituary notice in *The Observer*, together with four poems. The impact was immediate, and eerie. In one poem, 'Edge', a woman imagines her own suicide: 'The woman is perfected/Her dead/Body wears the smile of accomplishment.' In another, 'The Fearful':

> This woman on the telephone
> Says she is a man, not a woman.
>
> The mask increases, eats the worm,
> Stripes for mouth and eyes and nose,
>
> The voice of the woman hollows—
> More and more like a dead one,
>
> Worms in the glottal stops.

Read alongside a terse announcement of Plath's death, at the age of thirty-one, the lines seemed to insist on an inquisitive response: 'How?', 'Why?' and 'Who?'

It was not until the late 1960s that these questions were brought up in public. The appearance of *Ariel* in 1965 made it possible, indeed necessary, to make mention of the suicide. Most critics settled for respectful talk about the price Sylvia Plath had had to pay, the 'sacrifice' she had made in order to achieve this last 'blood jet' of brilliantly angry and despairing verse. There was also much emphasis on the so-called 'public' dimension of the poems. Plath's rather modishly dragged-in references to Nazi concentration camps were grasped at as evidence of imaginative courage: 'Sylvia Plath *became* a woman being transported to Auschwitz on the death-trains,' wrote George Steiner. When 'Daddy' was discussed, there was no problem about explaining why Plath imagined her dead father as a Nazi, but there were other bits of the poem which at this stage had to be ignored:

> I made a model of you,
> A man in black with a Meinkampf look

And a love of the rack and the screw,
And I said I do, I do.

Sylvia Plath died intestate, and Ted Hughes inherited her copy-rights. The couple had separated a few months before she died, and not amicably, but they had not divorced. There were two young children of the marriage. Hughes's inheritance was scarcely to be envied. There was a great mass of unpublished writing, principally journals and poems, and not all of it, in his view, deserved to be kept. One of the journals, covering the last weeks of her life, he at once elected to destroy: 'because I did not want the children to see it.' And he may well have felt tempted to deal similarly with certain of the poems. During her last months, much of his wife's creative fury had been aimed at *him*. As executor, he was now required to publicise insults and accusations to which he could make no dignified riposte: how do you *reply* to a good poem – by pointing out that it exaggerates, tells lies?

When Hughes came to assemble the manuscript of *Ariel*, he decided to present the late work 'cautiously'; he 'omitted some of the more personally aggressive poems from 1962, and might have omitted one or two more if she had not already published them in magazines'. (The omitted poems appeared in 1971, in *Winter Trees*.) His policy, it seemed, would be one of gradual disclosure. At the time no one complained. In 1969, he appointed a biographer, Lois Ames, and 'undertook to help her exclusively in the usual way (to give her his own records and recollections, make available Sylvia's diaries, notebooks, correspondence, manuscripts, etc. and to request family and friends to give their full cooperation)'. Contracts were drawn up with publishers in the UK and US, stipulating delivery by 1975. Ames's agreement with Hughes granted her 'exclusive help until December 1977'.

How Lois Ames might have performed we can but guess, for she did not deliver. Over the years her research 'slowed to a standstill'. In the meantime, though, the exclusivity clause could be used to deter other would-be investigators. By the end of the 1960s, there was a burgeoning Plath cult and Hughes began to look to his defences, to exhibit a certain touchiness on the matter of how to 'interpret' his wife's death. He did not seem to mind the event being glorified by the likes of Anne Sexton: 'We talked death with burned-up intensity, both of us drawn to it like moths to an electric light bulb. Sucking on it!' But when the Leavisite critic David Holbrook contended, in 1968, that some of the *Ariel* poems might set a bad example to the young, the estate refused him permission to make quotations from her work. The objection was to Holbrook's use of the terms 'schizoid' and 'insane'. Olwyn Hughes, Ted's sister and by now acting as literary agent to the Plath estate, explained that Holbrook's theories 'seriously misrepresented' the dead poet 'as an individual and as an artist'. Holbrook manfully struck back:

> It may be that in public debate my readers will decide that I am as poor a literary critic as Miss Hughes says I am. But she is still trying to suppress the debate altogether, which is my point. Her implication that an author's agent has the right to decide whether or not a work is good enough as *criticism* to allow copyright permission for it to be published is, I suggest, quite unacceptable to the world of scholarship and letters.

Because Holbrook was constantly writing letters to the newspapers about this or that sickness in the culture, nobody rallied to his aid. But even his worst enemies could see that he did have a point.

Three years later, the estate was at it again, and this time the offender was none other than Alvarez, Plath's first, most influential champion. Of Holbrook, Olwyn Hughes complained that he 'never knew Sylvia Plath in her lifetime'. Alvarez's offence, it soon transpired, was that he did. In 1971, he published a study of suicide, *The Savage God*, in which he gave an account of his relationship with Plath. During her last months, she had from time to time visited him at his London flat, often bearing new poems, which she read aloud to him. A critic's nightmare, one might think, but in this case Alvarez was bewitched. Plath's poems seemed to him an extraordinary vindication of his own critical position. He had lately ridiculed the 'gentility principle' that vitiated most current English verse and had called for a new poetry of psychic risk: the risk was that by voyaging in search of their 'unquiet buried selves' artists might indeed go mad, or die, or both. As he saw it, Plath's was an accidental death; she gambled, and she lost. 'She had always been a bit of a gambler, used to taking risks. The authority of her poetry was in part due to her brave persistence in following the thread of her inspiration right down to the Minotaur's lair.'

In terms of biography, of circumstantial reportage, the memoir was highly reticent: Hughes was a friend. Alvarez knew that the marriage had ended because of Hughes's involvement with another woman, but he said nothing of this; there had, he implied, been merely a collision of two giant talents. It was a surprise, therefore, when – on the appearance in *The Observer* of an extract from *The Savage God* (the first of two, it was announced) – there was an outcry from the Plath estate. Ted Hughes wanted the serialisation stopped, he said, because the memoir had been 'written and published without my having been consulted in any way'. He objected to Alvarez's 'misremembering' of private conversations they had had:

> Mr Alvarez's main *trouvé* is that Sylvia Plath 'gambled' with her death and he uses this to drag her in as an example in close-up, an unusual type of suicide who happened to be his friend (and only incidentally as the now very public poet) to fill the longest and most sensational chapter in his general history of suicide. This particular fantasy of her gamble was, in fact, a notion of mine, which haunted me at the time, and which I aired to him, even though it went against the findings of the coroner, and against other details which I imparted to no one.
>
> His facts are material for fiction, second-hand scraps, glimpses and half-experiences, resurfacing after seven years, imaginatively reshaped and acceptably explained to the author. They have nothing to do with the truth of an event far more important to Sylvia Plath's family than to Mr Alvarez or any of his readers.

It was in order to protect Plath's family, the adult members now and 'her children throughout their future' that he wanted the memoir withdrawn 'from any wider circulation'. *The Observer* cancelled the second extract. Replying to Hughes, Alvarez sounded genuinely hurt and baffled. He could understand Hughes's instinct to defend 'his privacy and that of his children', and he was also aware that the 'authorised version of Sylvia's last months will appear in the official biography' but 'I see no reason why this should stand in the way of an account by another person who was also involved – though, God knows, not very willingly – in the affair.' And as to not having checked it out with Hughes: 'I was not writing a memoir of him: I was writing about Sylvia Plath.'

Alvarez had reason to be puzzled: what *was* it that had got up Hughes's nose? The 'risk' theory might be wrong, but it was just a theory. Robert Lowell, six years before, had written: 'These poems are playing Russian roulette with six cartridges in the cylinder, a game of "Chicken", the wheels of both cars locked and unable to swerve.' This was the preface to the American edition of *Ariel*, which Hughes himself had ushered into print. But Lowell was Lowell, and he had been careful to say 'these poems' and not 'she'. And his only personal recollection of Plath was of her attending one of his Boston University poetry classes in the 1950s, when – he had to admit – she had made more impression than the poems, which somehow never 'sank very deep into my awareness'. He also said nothing about Hughes. Alvarez, on the other hand, had in his memoir attempted to distinguish the Hughes style of self-exploration from that of his wife. The rustic Hughes, it was suggested, lived more familiarly with his dark gods than she could. 'Her intensity was of the nerves, something urban.' Hughes, although as worldly as the next man when he wished to be, was genuinely *primitivo*; he 'had never properly been civilised or had, at least, never properly believed in his civilisation'. But could the author of the blood-drenched *Crow* (1970) seriously object to being thought of as possessing 'a quality of threat beneath his shrewd, laconic manner', 'some dark side of the self which had nothing to do with the young literary man'?

Alvarez's memoir was probably Hughes's first experience of what was to become for him a lifetime's horror. From now on, he was able to perceive, the Plath biography would need to appropriate at least one chapter from the biography of Hughes. Anybody who took an interest in her life could claim the right to poke about in his. Hughes, by all accounts, was a taciturn personality, pre-Plath. There is no evidence that he had any taste for the confessional. His poetry, for all its love of violence, tended to be void of personality. Oddly enough, the best way of getting any near-intimate sense of what he might be like was to consult the verses and stories that he wrote for children.

It was not until the early 1970s that Sylvia Plath became a celebrity in the commercial book world. A rough check of her bibliography shows that about four-fifths of all recorded writings on her – aside from book reviews – was done in that decade. In 1970, *The Bell Jar* was published in the United States and it launched her into stardom. Plath herself once described her first novel as a 'potboiler' and it was turned down in the 1960s by Harper and Row, its 1970 publisher. But with *Ariel* and the suicide behind it, so to speak, this thin study of late-adolescent breakdown was an immediate bestseller, a campus cult, a movie, and so on. And as the women's movement got into its stride, Plath was assimilated to the ideology. Articles with titles like 'Reading Women's Poetry: the Meaning and our Lives' or 'Male Authority and

Female Identity in Sylvia Plath' began appearing in the journals. Post-graduate theses were embarked on: 'The Woman as Hero', 'The Quest for Self', 'Power and Vulnerability in the Poetry of Sylvia Plath'. The girl who won the *Mademoiselle* fiction prize in 1951 was in 1972 up for 'reconsideration' in the inaugural issue of *Ms.* magazine. And as Plath was reconsidered, so was Hughes. Under feminist scrutiny, he was found to epitomise 'the enemy, the monster who had all but murdered her'.

Post-1970, then, Hughes's relationship with the 'audience' was forced to undergo a change. Because of his wife's death, the manner of it, and because of her posthumous literary fame, he now had to justify his privateness. For the poet Hughes there could be not much subtlety of interaction between artist and inquisitor. If he were to burn his own diaries in a fit of privacy, he would surely be accused of interfering with Plath Studies. And the situation was for him further complicated by his knowledge that Plath was an eloquent distortionist; she was very good at making her enemies look bad. Her friends too: she used to describe Ted Hughes adoringly as a 'colossus', 'a large hulking healthy Adam . . . with a voice like the thunder of God', 'a huge Goliath' – praise for which he would later have to pay. She made things up, played roles and put on masks:

> Some were camouflage cliché façades, defensive mechanisms, involuntary. And some were deliberate poses, attempts to find the key to one style or another. They were the visible faces of her lesser selves, her false or provisional selves, the minor roles of her inner drama. Though I spent every day with her for six years, and was rarely separated from her for more than two or three hours at a time, I never saw her show her real self to anybody – except, perhaps, in the last three months of her life.

Hughes believed that he knew Plath, or knew the several Paths – lesser, provisional and real – better than anyone else could. Her death, and the anger that went into it, the death-poems, ought to be understood as a drama of 'rebirth', a destroying of fabricated selves and a breaking through into the 'real'.

Hughes would no doubt have preferred to keep Plath Studies at this level of abstraction. The hate-objects in *Ariel* and *Winter Trees* were often male, admittedly, but they were male-*figures*, archetypes, not individual chaps. For Plath to become 'real' in those last months, she had to conquer and destroy the psychic tyranny of those male-gods who had controlled her lesser lives. Did it matter who, in actuality, they were? A father, a lover, a merging or confusing of the two: this was the radical configuration. When it came to studying the verse, the important evidence was already on display, and if the evidence was justly scrutinised, Plath's fear and hatred of other women could scarcely be ignored. This is perhaps to travesty Hughes's thinking, but he did seem to believe something of the sort. For instance, Judith Kroll's *Chapters in a Mythology* is one of the few books about Plath that Hughes is known to have admired; Kroll's approach is anti-biographical, heavy with archetypes, and expounds a 'false-selves' thesis that roughly corresponds with his.

Perhaps the early Seventies would have been the right time for Hughes to have applied the brakes. He could have brought out a *Collected Poems* and embargoed all other material for fifty years. With only the poems to go on, his accusers would have been thrown back on speculation and hearsay. But then speculation and hearsay could hurt too, as Hughes was soon to learn. In 1976 a deeply unauthorised biography by Edward Butscher appeared in the United States. Butscher in 1972 had solicited the estate's cooperation and had been rebuffed: the Ames arrangement was invoked. He had persisted, though, and his book leaned heavily on the 'living witness' method of research. The witnesses prepared to speak were, of course, no friends of Hughes. During her last chaotic months, Plath had done a lot of talking: more than one neighbour or acquaintance could boast of having been her special confidante. In an attempt to block the book, the estate refused Butscher permission to quote from Plath's writings, but he and his US publisher ignored the ban, reckoning – correctly – that Hughes would not pursue a transatlantic lawsuit. (Many years later, Hughes had cause to regret not suing Butscher. When a film was made of *The Bell Jar*, a Dr Jane Anderson complained that a lesbian character in it had been based on her: she used Butscher's text as evidence. Hughes was arraigned for having 'failed to control what Mr Butscher wrote about the plaintiff' and the whole affair, he said, 'consumed five years and cost several people – but not Butscher – many hundreds of thousands of dollars'.)

As Sylvia Plath's executor, Hughes had a duty, he believed, 'to permit publication of whatever contributes to a fuller appreciation of the author'. Despite all the peculiar circumstances, the overlaps, the general prejudice, his own loathing of biography ought not to be imposed on her. *Ariel*, he had to acknowledge:

supplies little of the incidental circumstances or the crucial inner drama that produced it. Maybe it is this very bareness of circumstantial detail that has excited the wilder fantasies projected by others in Sylvia Plath's name. We respond to the speech, that fascinating substance, which is everywhere fully itself, nowhere diluted and ordinary – but we can only discuss it, or communicate our feelings about it, in terms of those externals, the drama of her psychological makeup, the accidents of her life.

There was a money angle too. By the mid-1970s Hughes did not need his sister to tell him that the Plath industry, now at its peak and not guaranteed to last, could provide security for the two children.

Whatever the reasoning, the estate in the end opted for a policy of staged and monitored publication, releasing a bit here, a bit there. First, in 1976, came *Letters Home*, a collection of Sylvia's letters to Aurelia, her mother. Hughes had given Aurelia the copyright of these on condition that he could retain some measure of control. Thus, when reviewers discovered that there were a number of excisions, they rumbled sternly about censorship. It turned out that, although Hughes *had* asked for certain cuts, not all of these were self-defensive. He removed 'some wicked comments about people she knew' and a few of the more 'syrupy' descriptions of himself. The book's editor, Frances McCollough, was 'amazed to see how much he allowed through'. She herself had had the task of cutting the original manuscript by half. The real problem with *Letters Home* was that the letters themselves were almost unreadably affected. They displayed one of the least endearing of Plath's provisional or unreal selves: the chirpy, high-achieving self she kept on tap for mother. Faced with accusations of a Hughes paint-job, McCollough was obliged to spell out what ought to have been obvious: 'Anyone who remembers his own letters home will recognise at once that if there is a censor's hand at work here, it is the daughter's, not the mother's.'

The estate itself was less level-toned in its response to the reviews of *Letters Home*, possibly because the book's publication coincided with the 'illegal' Butscher Life: the two volumes were being noticed side by side. When Karl Miller, in the *New York Review of Books*, expressed what might to most readers have seemed a decent sympathy for Hughes's plight, Olwyn Hughes accused him of writing 'in guise of indignation on my brother's behalf'. Miller's crime was that he had given more space to Butscher's 'patently rubbishy hotch-potch' than to the near-official *Letters Home*. A belligerence was in the air and

Olwyn was beginning to make a name for herself. As Hughes retreated into a volcanic silence, his sister could be found out-front, mixing it with the 'libbers' and the ghouls, 'who treat Sylvia Plath's family as though they are characters in some work of fiction, or a hundred years dead, and proper subjects for speculation and academic dissection'.

Since the mid-1970s, there have been further, but not dissimilar outbreaks of controversy. The estate has been criticised for censoring Plath's *Journals*, for delaying the *Collected Poems*, for harassing the feminist biographer Linda Wagner-Martin and for leaning on their own appointee, Anne Stevenson, whose 1989 Life of Plath confessed to being 'almost a work of dual authorship' – the co-author being, of course, Olwyn.

The Stevenson biography was a curious affair. As the estate's answer to two decades of misrepresentation, it was always likely to sound somewhat irritably partisan, pro-Hughes, and perhaps if Hughes himself had chosen this opportunity to have his say, the book might have had a more cordial reception. As it was, he distanced himself from the whole enterprise ('Hughes asked me to address all questions relating to his personal life to Olwyn,' Stevenson recalls), and his sister seized the reins. So eager was Olwyn to ensure that Ted should at last be treated fairly that she strong-armed a large part of the biography into an appearance of ill-natured bias, and in the process made Stevenson seem got at and confused – one minute thanking Olwyn for her help, the next complaining that her own input had been 'olwynized', and all in all coming to regret the whole assignment: 'It was clear to me at a very early stage that Olwyn Hughes badly needed to tell her side of Sylvia's story. It was a side no one as yet had heard, chiefly because no one would listen.'

The message of Anne Stevenson's *Bitter Fame* could not in truth have been delivered in person by Ted Hughes: the narrative suggests that only a man of the most saintly temperament could have lived with the devil-woman Plath for twenty-four hours, let alone six years. In the end, after many a wearying explosion, even the ever-patient Hughes had had to get some air. To force such a reading into shape, Plath of course had to be represented at her worst: jealous, success-hungry, manipulative, and – since the childhood loss of her over-adored father – suicidally inclined. She was a victim, to be sure, but not of Hughes, nor of any other dominating male. Her own dis-ordered psyche was to blame. And yet, apart from the poems, there was nothing very heroic about the ways in which she tried to cope with her affliction. Most of the time, she had come over as petty, mean-minded, self-absorbed, a rather shrill and nasty bore. The book reeked of exasperation, and thus rather played into the hands of hostile Plathologists, those commentators who had now and then felt the rough edge of Olwyn's tongue and had retaliated by building small careers out of policing the estate.

In the year of Stevenson's biography, Ted Hughes was obliged to emerge from his burrow to answer charges that really could not be ignored: (a) that his first wife's grave lay derelict and unmarked in a remote Yorkshire churchyard and (b) that on the night of her funeral he had attended a 'highspirited and boisterous party with bongo drums'. In the latter case, Hughes had recourse to the law, and was thus branded as a bully-litigant: the bongo-party anecdote had been dredged from the faulty memory of a near-penniless 82-year-old. On the matter of the grave, he wrote letters to the press, explaining that the headstone, having been regularly vandalised by feminists who objected to the inscription 'Sylvia Plath Hughes', was in the repair shop of a local mason: 'I asked him to give it another go. If he has not yet done so, I'm sure I agree with him that there is no hurry.'

Hughes's account of his trial-by-gravestone was restrained enough, and rather touching. He had originally wanted to put the legal name Sylvia Hughes on the memorial but had then added the Plath because 'I knew well enough in 1963 what she had brought off in that name, and I wished to honour it. That was the beginning and end of my thoughts about the name.' Then came the desecrations: riveted lead letters were levered off the stone, restored, and then removed again – three times. Even the shells and beach pebbles he had placed about the plot were carried off. Small wonder that he now 'simply wished to preserve for a while longer something of the private remnant valued by her living family'. To judge from these letters, Hughes was tired of the whole carry-on, but there was also an anger to be felt, an anger that had been building up over the twenty-five years in which he served as keeper of the Plath inheritance; an inheritance which had come to him but was not really his:

In the years soon after her death, when scholars approached me, I tried to take their apparently serious concern for the truth about Sylvia Plath seriously. But I learned my lesson early. The honourable few who have justified my trust have been few indeed. With others, if I tried too hard to

303

tell them exactly how something happened, in the hope of correcting some fantasy, I was quite likely to be accused of trying to suppress Free Speech. In general, my refusal to have anything to do with the Plath Fantasia has been regarded as an attempt to suppress Free Speech. Where my correction was accepted, it rarely displaced a fantasy. More often, it was added to the repertoire, as a variant hypothesis. It would then become itself a source of new speculations which sooner or later, somewhere or other, would be preferred to it. The truth simply tends to produce more lies . . .

A rational observer might conclude (correctly in my opinion) that the Fantasia about Sylvia Plath is more needed than the facts. Where that leaves respect for the truth of her life (and mine) or for her memory, or for literary tradition, I do not know.

A year before he died, Philip Larkin reviewed Peter Ackroyd's Life of Eliot for *Encounter*, and found himself in two minds. As an ordinary reader, and as a professional librarian, he had to admire Ackroyd's tenacity: the unauthorised biographer had tracked down a great mass of accessible archive material and had managed to come up with a detailed, plausible and widow-proof account of Eliot's life. As a poet who would sooner or later be the subject of similar researches, Larkin was rather less enthralled. Acknowledging the general helplessness of the biographee ('Truly it is not much use trying to put people off'), he was also 'relieved', he said, to find that Ackroyd, for all his diligence, had in the end failed to explain the 'contradictions and paradoxes of Eliot's life and temperament':

> Is it ungrateful to feel relieved? If Eliot wished to live quietly, succeeding in avoiding notice, living and partly living, without making his life a continual allegory, then he had a right to. There was pain, there was dignity, finally there was happiness. Let it go at that.

Larkin was here toying with a fancy: he knew very well that, in the case of Eliot – and in the case of Larkin – biography would never 'let it go at that'. There was an attraction for him, though, in the idea of the Life as mythic silhouette. He liked to project himself as a semi-recluse, 'living and partly living' – a sort of North British Prufrock for whom the question 'Do I dare?' had long ago been answered: 'I do not.' He was not exactly secretive – from poems, interviews and even TV appearances, his readers could piece together a sizeable dossier of facts about where and how he spent his days – but he was thought of as difficult to get to know. And yet, if the work can be believed, he badly wanted to be known: some of his most moving poems contrive a subtle, unsettlable quarrel between revelation and concealment.

On the matter of his posterity, therefore, we would expect Larkin to be torn. On the one hand, he would not have wished to incinerate, or *un*document, the self he usually kept hidden: the romantic, yearning self whose presence in the verse is so poignantly stage-managed – disguised, thwarted, made mock of, now and then permitted to show through. On the other hand, he would not have relished the prospect of his own mysterious 'contradictions and paradoxes' being offered up for explanation in terms of the day-to-day events of his real life. He once commented on how awful it would be if it turned out that, say, Thomas Hardy's view of the human predicament depended on something that had *happened* to him.

As a public figure, Larkin often caricatured his own caricature, but at the same time he wished to keep us guessing: can he really be like that? The grumpiness, the deflating narrowness of vision that typifies the 'Larkin manner' was never so unsociable as to prevent him being rather liked by most of those who read him. He was not quite lovable, as many have said they find John Betjeman, but he could and wished to be located in that same sector of audience-appeal. He was more than usually aware that 'a writer's reputation is twofold: what we think of his work, and what we think of him. What's more, we expect the two halves to relate: if they don't, one or other of our opinions alters until they do.' It sounds obvious but one doubts that Ted Hughes, say, would state the proposition so urbanely.

In a poem called 'Posterity', Larkin once jokily imagined his own biographer as Jake Balokowsky, an American academic hack. Balokowsky would rather be working on Protest Theater, or, better still, teaching school in Tel Aviv, but marriage and kids have kept him in the university rat-race and now, in search of tenure, he finds himself stuck with writing about Philip Larkin. What is Larkin like? someone enquires, and he replies: 'Oh, you know the thing . . . one of those old-type *natural* fouled up guys.' The poem is meant to sound modest and rueful – only a Balokowsky would fix on *me* as a viable topic of research – but is actually alive with self-esteem. The reader is invited to despise the inadequate biographer but is also required to join with him in pondering the strange case of Philip Larkin. ('Posterity' was written in 1968, not a good year in the United States for British right-wing ironists, but then Larkin's American reputation was never quite sky-high and there was maybe always a touch of resentment in his jeering attitude to Yank literary studies – indeed to Yank literature in general. When Robert Lowell sent him his bulky *History* and *Notebook*, he responded with a copy of the forty-page *High Windows*, inscribed: 'From a drought to a deluge'. Lowell laughed but he was not amused.)

As the Hull University librarian, Larkin specialised in collecting modern literary manuscripts and he meticulously hoarded his own memorabilia. From an early age, it seems, he knew himself to be marked for literary greatness, and his own Philip Larkin archive dates back to his mid-adolescence. At sixteen, he began keeping the diary which, by the time he died, ran to twenty-five stout foolscap volumes. He preserved his juvenilia in dated files and arranged his incoming letters in shoe-boxes, A to Z. Very little seems to have been thrown away. These are the expected rituals of the bachelor librarian: the 'life in perfect order' that Larkin himself mocks in *The Less Deceived*. They might seem to sit more oddly, though, with the self-neglecting, can't-be-bothered persona of the later poems: the Mr Bleaney side of him. But Mr Bleaney can perhaps safely be taken as a horror-fantasy; what you end up as if you don't keep your documents in decent trim:

> . . . how we live measures our own nature,
> And at his age having no more to show
> Than one hired box should make him pretty sure
> He warranted no better . . .

When Larkin came to make arrangements for his literary after-life, he set about it with an air of competence. He appointed Anthony Thwaite and Andrew Motion as his literary executors, along with his main beneficiary, Monica Beal Jones. Writing to Motion and Thwaite on the matter of how the executors might divide their duties, he stressed the need for total clarity in the actual wording of his will: 'the one thing the will mustn't be is ambiguous,' he wrote, and again: 'The chief thing about it is that it should be unambiguous'; 'the great thing about a clause such as this is that it should say exactly what I mean.' When the will was signed in July 1985, Larkin was seriously ill in hospital: the document was witnessed by the surgeon who operated on him for throat cancer. He died in December of that year, leaving behind him instructions which are now notorious for their refusal to make sense.

In one clause of the will, Larkin directed that 'all unpublished writings and diaries and texts and manuscripts in any form whether or not published at the date of my death and in my possession at the date of my death shall be destroyed unread'. And, as if this was not sufficiently obscure, a second clause required that his literary executors be consulted 'in all matters concerned with the publication of my unpublished manuscripts and the exploitation of my work both published and unpublished'. What *did* he mean? Was the first clause perhaps meant to refer to biographical material, the second to 'creative' works? Just before he died, Larkin told Monica Jones to 'make sure those diaries are destroyed' and she had hastened to obey: the twenty-five volumes were shredded within hours of his death. Maybe the 'destroy' clause had been drawn up with these and other similarly private documents in mind – hence the insistence that they be unread. The will, though, made no distinction between kinds of writing. The executors were faced with just the sort of dilemma that Larkin had seemed anxious to avoid.

Legal advice was sought and in the view of learned counsel the will was indeed most seriously flawed. Even if Larkin had meant to consign his unpublished writings to the flames, he would have had no legal right to do so: it was 'not possible for a testator to impose on his personal representatives a duty to destroy items unexamined'. The case was cited of *Brown* v. *Burdett* (1882), where a 'direction to block up all the rooms in a house for twenty years was held void'. On this reading, the instruction to destroy was 'repugnant to the benefits sought to be conferred' by other clauses in the will. 'Capricious' was another legal term employed to describe the contradictory decrees: as if the one had been meant whimsically to undermine the other.

The lawyers did not believe that Larkin had been playing games: as they saw it, the will was badly written and needed to be straightened out. The rogue clause, in their view, should be disregarded. And so it was. When Larkin's *Collected Poems*, edited by Thwaite, appeared in 1988, it carried about eighty poems which had not before seen print: a hefty addition, since Larkin's three 'mature' books, *The Less Deceived*, *The Whitsun Weddings* and *High Windows*, totalled a mere eighty-five. Larkin the thrifty was now to be seen as passably prolific. It was as though this most fastidiously bachelor of poets had suddenly acquired a rather messy family life.

And this was the principal objection of those who challenged the executors' 'flouting' of the will. In 1990, a solicitor-bookman called

John Whitehead (who a dozen years earlier had challenged the Auden estate on *its* presentation of the texts) wrote to the papers accusing Thwaite and Motion of having destroyed 'the purity of the Larkin canon for ever and a day, and I can't believe his ghost will ever forgive them'. 'It is a moral point,' he said; Larkin had 'kept the rubbish out. They have put in everything but the kitchen sink.' But what if the eighty 'new' poems had turned out to be late gems, not infant trifles? Would the executors then have been chastised for disobedience? On the question of Larkin's 'purity', there may well have been a case for issuing the unpublished pieces (mostly juvenilia and fragments) as a separate publication, although such a book would have been very hard to sell. But this is to speak not of morality but of editorial tactics. Thwaite's intention was to 'show the growth of a major poet, testing, filtering, rejecting, modulating, achieving'.

Larkin's shade might have found this fairly easy to forgive. There was no disobeying. There was not even much of a dilemma. Larkin chose as his representatives two poets whose attachment to him was as much literary as personal. They were friends but they were literary friends; he would have known that neither Thwaite nor Motion was likely to destroy anything that issued from his pen. For example, they would surely have attempted to preserve the diaries. From what Motion, the biographer-elect, has been able to find out about their contents, these showed Larkin at his most intimate, and at his worst. Even so, says Motion, 'if it had fallen to me to destroy them, I would not have done it'. At the last moment, Larkin made sure that the decision did not fall to him.

Both Thwaite and Motion believe that the ambiguity of Larkin's will was more than just a legal blunder. Thwaite reckons that the wording might have been clarified if Larkin had lived longer. When the inconsistencies were pointed out to him 'he was very ill and very depressed' and possibly past caring. At the same time, he was also 'very likely in two minds':

> Part of him wanted total destruction as the end to a talent that he now saw as dead. Part of him allowed his executors discretion, because he had a scrupulous writer's sense of responsibility. What we as his executors have had to think about, and still think about, is our responsibility to Larkin's work and to posterity.

Motion likewise takes the view that we should look beyond the legalities:

> It seems to me that the contradictions are part of a much larger pattern of ambiguous feelings that he had about everything in his life – from women through work; just everything – and it is therefore not in the least surprising that he left such a will behind him . . . He wanted to set up a circumstance in which he got let off having to take the decision of doing the keeping or destroying, and to devolve it on to others.

These are literary interpretations but Larkin was a literary man. On the unpublished poems, he probably was undecided but perhaps not seriously troubled one way or the other: he had never made any secret of his early debts to Yeats and Auden, and several of the unpublished later pieces had been shown to friends. On the diaries, we can take it that he lost his nerve. Without knowing what was in them, it is probably unwise to guess.

It is too early to attempt to characterise the Larkin keepers of the flame: as this book goes to press, the Letters and the Life are still to come. The odd wording of the will, however, does take us back to the question of executive obedience, of 'what the dead author would have wished'. In Larkin's case – as with Eliot, Auden and indeed Sylvia Plath – it seems that we will never know. But then, 'posterity', as Larkin's bequest seems to acknowledge, will usually turn out to be a muddle. Although invoked as an abstract authority ('Let posterity be my judge') it is in reality a turbulence of weaknesses, an unending jostle of vanities, appetites and fears. And if it is believed that justice triumphs in the end, this is probably because the original arguments, both prosecution and defence, have been forgotten; the witnesses are dust; the laws have been revised. Posterity, like history, should be thought of in the plural. 'Let posterities be my judge' sounds less reassuring but it makes more sense. And it is certainly more Larkinesque.

What then would Larkin himself have said if he had been called on to judge some other writer's posthumous arrangements? Would he have burned the diaries, suppressed the early work? To judge from his own book reviews – on Hardy, say, or Wilfred Owen – he would have wished for everything to be preserved, however embarrassing or nasty. On the other hand, if Hardy's diaries had turned up and were found to be full of 'things you would tell no person', Larkin might have voted for a fifty-year embargo. It takes that length of time, he once opined, for the 'total picture' to emerge, the total picture which, in his case, we will never be vouchsafed:

> That is not to say that we have no picture in the meantime: nearly always we have, but it is put out by precisely the people (widow, family, etc.) who are standing in the way of complete documentation. There may be good human reasons for this, and in any case the interim picture will be far from false, but it will almost certainly require ultimate modification, which (again almost certainly) will come as something of a shock.

# NOTES

## 1. John Donne the Younger

1 Humphry Dunt incident: R. C. Bald, *John Donne: A Life*, Oxford University Press, 1970, p 548.

2 *Whosoever in writing a modern history*: Walter Ralegh, *The History of the World* (1614).

2 *fines impossible to be paid*: Izaak D'Israeli, *Amenities of Literature*, Vol 3, London, 1841, pp 412–13.

3 *ambling unpretence*, re Walton: Austin Dobson, quoted in Edmund Gosse: *The Life and Letters of John Donne*. Vol 1, Heinemann, 1899, p.xiii.

6 *great visiter of ladies*: Sir Richard Baker, *Chronicles of the Kings of England*, quoted in Bald, *John Donne*, p 72.

6 *Prynne* etc: F. A. Mumby, *Publisher and Bookselling*, London 1964, pp 102–3.

7 *England's Helicon*: D'Israeli, *Amenities*, p 278.

7 James I publication: *ibid*, p 289.

9 *verge of extinction*: Gosse, *Life and Letters*, Vol 2, p 298.

10 *incomparable*: see A. J. Smith, 'Donne's Reputation', in *John Donne: Essays in Celebration*, ed. A. J. Smith, Methuen, 1972, p 3.

10 J.D. Jr's Petition to Archbishop of Canterbury: see *The Poems of John Donne*, ed. Herbert J. C. Grierson, Oxford University Press, 1912, lxvi–lxviii.

10 *How these manuscripts*: R. Krueger: 'The Publication of Donne's Sermons', *Review of English Studies*, Vol XV, 1964, pp 159–60.

11 *rent the books in pieces*: Dean of Chichester (1646) quoted in Ronald Berman, *Henry King and the Seventeenth Century*, Chatto, 1964, pp 16–17.

11 *my study was often searched*: 'A Seventeenth Century Jester' in *Gossip of the Seventeenth and Eighteenth Centuries*, ed. John Beresford, 1923, pp 68–9.

11 *no such important work*: Gosse, *Life and Letters*, Vol 2, p 324.

11 *disregarding father's wishes*: Augustus Jessop, *DNB* on Donne the Ygr.

11  *I could find no certain way; the banks of the church*: Beresford, *Gossip*, pp 68–9.

12  *atheistical buffoon*: Thomas Wood, quoted in Bald, *John Donne*, pp 551–2.

## 2. Surviving Shakespeare

16  *Certain Verses*: see Margaret A. Beese, 'John Donne the Younger: Addenda and Corrections to his Biography', *Modern Language Review*, Vol xxxiii, 1938, pp 356–9.

17  *I will gravely tell thee*: W. Davenant, *Gondibert*, Postscript to the Reader, quoted in Mary Edmond, *Rare Sir William Davenant*, Manchester University Press, 1987, p 117.

17  *the courtiers with the Prince of Wales*: Aubrey, *Brief Lives*, ed. Andrew Clark, 1898, Vol 1, p 207.

17  *there was a feature in his face*: *Calamities and Quarrels of Authors* 1881, p 410.

17  Suckling on Davenant: D'Israeli, ibid. see Suckling 'The Sessions of the Poets', (1637).

17  *a Notch in's name*: Edmond, *Davenant*, p 110; see also *Certain Verses*, London, 1653.

18  *transported with Indignation*: Earl of Clarendon, quoted in *DNB*.

18  *a very beautiful woman*: Anthony Wood, quoted in D'Israeli, *Calamities*, p 411.

18  *Pope would tell a story*: *ibid*, pp 411–12.

19  Frank Kermode, 'Shakespeare's Learning', in *Shakespeare, Spenser, Donne*, Routledge, 1971, p 182.

19  *told them plainly*: Suckling, 'Sessions of the Poets', lines 19–20.

21  *He had waited eighteen years*: F. E. Halliday, *The Cult of Shakespeare*, Duckworth, 1957, p 12.

22  *each generation, like each individual*: T. S. Eliot, *The Use of Poetry and the Use of Criticism*, Faber, 1933, p 109.

23  *Nay, even Shakespeare*: Richard Flecknoe, 'Sir William Davenant's Voyage to the Other World: with his Adventures in the Poet's Elizium', 1668; quoted in J. F. Bradley and J. Q. Adams, *The Jonson Allusion Book*, Yale University Press, New Haven, 1922, p 339.

23  *Their quick inventions*: Anon, *ibid*, p 340.

24  *it is no extravagance to suggest*: Sidney Lee, *Pepys and Shakespeare*, Samuel Pepys Club, 1904, p 30.

26  *Behold this fair goblet*: Halliday, *The Cult of Shakespeare*, p 70.

27 *The Gothic glories*: *Gentleman's Magazine*, July 1769, quoted in *ibid*, pp 67–8.

## 3. Be Kind to My Remains: Marvell, Milton, Dryden

30 *It is probable that:* F. S. Tupper, *Proceedings of the Modern Language Association of America*, June 1938, Vol 63, pp 367–88.

34 *For Spenser and Fairfax*: Preface to the Fables, *Dryden: Poetry, Prose and Plays*, ed. Douglas Grant, Hart-Davis, 1952, p 474.

36 *In some very elegant*: *Dryden's Works*, ed. Congreve, Tonson, 1735; see *William Congreve, Letters and Documents*, ed. John C. Hodge, Macmillan, 1964, p 126.

37 *The great lady*: Lord Macaulay, *Literary Essays*, Amalgamated Press, 1905, p 472.

37 *as to nod mechanically*: Edmund Gosse, *The Life of Congreve*, Heinemann, 1924, p 172.

40 *Onely the actions of the just*: *Oxford Book of Seventeenth Century Verse*, ed. H. J. C. Grierson and G. Bullough, Oxford University Press, 1934, p 413.

43 *John Ogilby's The Carolies*: Harvey M. Geduld, *Prince of Publishers. A Study of the Work and Career of Jacob Tonson*, Indiana University Press, 1969, p 204.

44 *The faint cultural overtones*: John Feather, *A History of British Publishing*, Croom Helm, 1988, p 74.

45 *Whereas Printers, Booksellers*: John Feather, 'The Book Trade in Politics. The Making of the Copyright Act of 1710', *Publishing History*, no 8, 1980, pp 19–44.

## 4. Pope's Bullies

46 *The old Tory*: H. B. Wheatley, 'Dryden's Publishers', *Transactions of the Bibliographical Society*, Vol XI, 1912, pp 17–38.

47 *the wish to live his life*: Geduld, *Tonson*, pp 23–4.

47 *Sir: I have lately seen a Pastoral*: quoted in George Sherburn, *The Early Career of Alexander Pope*, Clarendon Press, 1934, p 51.

47 *You will make Jacob's ladder*: Pope, *Works*, ed. Elwin and Coulthorpe, Vol 9, p 545.

49 *Shut, shut the door*: Alexander Pope, 'Epistle to Dr Arbuthnot', *Poetical Works*, ed. Herbert Davis, Oxford University Press, 1966, p 117.

50 *It occurred to him that*: Walter Raleigh, *Six Essays on Johnson*, Clarendon Press, 1910, p 117.

52 *A Crowd of Authours*: description by Richard Savage, quoted in Maynard Mack, *Alexander Pope: A Life*, Yale University Press, 1985, p 457.

52 *A Bookseller advertises his intention*: *ibid*, p 654.

54 *Employ not*: Atterbury to Pope, quoted in *ibid*, p 512.

55 *atheism, spinozaism*: A. W. Evans, *Warburton and the Warburtonians: A Study in some Eighteenth Century Controversies*, Oxford University Press, 1932, p 72.

56 *You have made my system*: Pope, *Works*, Vol 9, p 203.

56 *go down together to posterity*: *ibid*, p 218.

56 *rapturous commendation*: Evans, *Warburton*, pp 84–5.

56 *The style of the great dogmatist*: D'Israeli, *Calamities*, p 323.

57 *they should never go into any hands*: Evans, *Warburton*, p 166.

58 *Are the laws of friendship*: *ibid*, p 169.

58 *I venture to foretell*: D'Israeli, *Calamities*, pp 327–8.

59 *a soured and disappointed . . . secretly hostile*: Evans, *Warburton*, p 177.

59 *wild and pernicious ravings*: Boswell, *Life of Johnson*, Oxford University Press World's Classics, ed. R. W. Chapman, 1980, p 189.

## 5. Boswell's Colossal Hoard

63 *As they returned*: Sherburn, *The Early Career*, p 2.

64 *I'm in love with Mr Pope*: Joseph Spence, *Observations, Anecdotes and Characters of Books and Men*, ed. James M. Osborn, Clarendon Press, 1966, p xxiv.

64 *Colossus bully*: Sherburn, *The Early Career*, p 11.

66 *Sometimes writers of romances*: Donald A. Stauffer, *The Art of Biography in Eighteenth Century England*, Princeton University Press, 1941, pp 66–7.

67 *It is commonly supposed*: *The Idler*, 29 March 1760.

68 *several resolutions*: Boswell, *Life of Johnson*, ed. George Birkbeck Hill, Clarendon Press, 1934; rev. L. F. Powell, p 355.

68 *He did not, in fact*: Boswell's *Life* p 248.

68 *a faithful and affectionate henchman*: Edmund Gosse, *Gray*, Macmillan, 1902, pp 86–7.

69 *brushing his clothes*: *ibid*, p 215.

69 *wearying of the script*: *Correspondence of Thomas Gray*, ed. Paget

Toynbee and Leonard Whibley, Oxford University Press, 1935, pp xxi–xxii.

71 *The fear that his wavering flame*: Frederick A. Pottle, *Pride and Negligence*, McGraw-Hill, 1982, p 6.

71 *it is Boswell who must*: Donald A. Greene, 'Johnson without Boswell', *TLS*, 22 November 1974, pp 1315–16.

72 *the band of modern scholars*: ibid.

73 *a man of the feeblest intellect*: Lord Macaulay, *Literary Essays*, pp 94–5.

74 *though one of the most entertaining*: Walter Scott to John Wilson Croker, 16 January 1830, quoted in Pottle, *Pride and Negligence*, p 41.

76 *the original journals*: ibid, p 42.

77 *once tried to penetrate*: George Birkbeck Hill, 'Boswell's Proof-sheets', *Atlantic Monthly*, November 1894, pp 657–68.

78 *But Macaulay*: John Murray to Lord Talbot of Malahide, 2 July 1911, quoted in Pottle, *Pride and Negligence*, pp 67–8.

79 *I was led into an adjoining room*: C. B. Tinker to Alan G. Thomas, 17 August 1946 [(?)] quoted in David Buchanan, *The Treasure of Auchinleck*, Heinemann, 1975, p 53.

79 *feeling . . . that his life's work lay in ruins*: Pottle, *Pride and Negligence*, p 81.

80 *Everything here*: Buchanan, *Treasure*, p 53.

80 *I'll bet a hat*: ibid, p 54.

81 *tremendous with lumber*: Claude Colleer Abbott: *A Catalogue of Papers Relating to Boswell, Johnson and Sir William Forbes, Found at Fettercairn House*, Clarendon Press, 1936, p xvii.

82 *Nothing had been touched*: ibid, p xxiii.

83 *he brought them together*: Pottle, *Pride and Negligence*, p 187.

## 6. The Frailties of Robert Burns

85 *Sitting one evening*: W. G. Hiscock, 'John Evelyn's Library at Christ Church', *TLS*, 6 April 1951, p 220.

86 *Human nature, like a vast machine*: Isaak D'Israeli, *Literary Miscellanies*, 1801, Vol 3, pp 120–21.

89 *Unacquainted with the necessary requisites*: Robert Burns, *Preface to Poems, Chiefly in the Scottish Dialect*, Kilmarnock, 1786.

89 *purity of expression*: Prof. Dugald Stewart, in James Currie, *The Works of Robert Burns With an Account of his Life and a Criticism of his Writings*, 1820, pp 222–3.

89 *It was, I know, a part of the machinery*: Robert Burns: The Critical Heritage, ed. Donald A. Low, Routledge, 1974, pp 8–9.

89 *the embarrassment of my singular situation*: Letter to Hugh Blair, quoted in David Daiches, *Robert Burns*, Deutsch, 1966, p 226.

90 *I know what I may expect*: ibid, p 225.

90 *I have long studied myself*: ibid, p 213.

90 *Should my farm*: Letters, 1, p 234, quoted in Ronald Thornton, *James Currie, The Entire Stranger, and Robert Burns*, Oliver and Boyd, 1963, p 309.

91 *Burns . . . would not dine but*: ibid, p 310.

91 *I believe it is all over with him*: ibid, p 312.

92 *it gives me great pain*: ibid, p 331.

92 *drinking excessively*: ibid, p 315.

92 *Is thy Burns dead?*: The Poems of Samuel Taylor Coleridge, ed. Ernest Hartley Coleridge, Oxford University Press, 1960, p 159.

93 *The truth is, my dear Syme*: Thornton, *James Currie*, p 321.

93 *those friends in Ayr*: ibid, p 324.

93 *Avaunt the sacrilege*: ibid, p 328.

93 *preserved most of Burns's love letters*: J. DeLancey Ferguson, 'Some Aspects of the Burns Legend', *Philological Quarterly*, no 11, 1932, p 268.

94 *My dear Syme*: Thornton, *James Currie*, p 358.

95 *The very circumstance*: ibid, p 342.

96 *At last, crippled, emaciated*: Heron Memoir quoted in M. Lindsay, The Burns Encyclopedia, Hutchinson, 1959, p 125.

97 *It is the more necessary*: Currie, *The Works*, p 250.

97 *To apply these observations*: ibid, p 251.

98 *His temper now became*: ibid, p 219.

101 *brucellosis, etc*: Richard Hindle Fowler, *Robert Burns*, Routledge, 1988, pp 235–6.

103 *The case of Mr Wordsworth*: Francis Jeffrey, review of 'The Excursion' in *Edinburgh Review*, November 1814.

105 *Wordsworth: A Letter to a Friend of Robert Burns*: Robert Burns, ed. Low, pp 278–91.

108 *Burns initiated a recorded five*: Fowler, *Robert Burns*, p 182.

## 7. Byron and the Best of Friends

109 *What an antithetical mind*: Byron Journal, 13 December 1813; *Robert Burns*, ed. Low, pp 257–8.

110 *All the fairies*: Thomas Babington Macaulay, Review of Moore's *Letters and Journals of Lord Byron: with Notice of his Life*, in *Byron: The Critical Heritage*, ed. Andrew Rutherford, Routledge, 1970, p 296.

110 *things of dark imaginings*: ibid, p 316.

111 *It is unhappily your disposition*: Leslie A. Marchand, *Byron: A Biography*, Vol 2, Knopf, 1957, p 574.

112 *squeeze tears to his memory*: Charles Lamb, quoted in Samuel C. Chew, *Byron in England: His Fame and After-Fame*, Murray, 1924, p 136.

112 *Even detraction*: Hazlitt, 'The Posthumous Poems of Shelley', *Edinburgh Review*, no 40, July 1824, p 494.

112 *Poor Byron! Alas poor Byron!*: Thomas Carlyle, letter to Jane Welsh Carlyle, 19 May 1824, quoted in Rutherford, *Byron: The Critical Heritage*, p 286.

112 *There were individuals*: *The Times*, 15 May 1824.

113 *Alter Ego*: *Lord Byron, Selected Letters and Journals*, ed. Leslie A. Marchand, John Murray, 1982, p 258.

114 *Byron's power of attaching*: Lord Broughton, *Recollections of a Long Life*, John Murray, 1910, Vol 3, p 41.

114 *His principal failing*: Lord Broughton, *Recollections*, Vol 3, p 329.

114 *The Life is Memoranda not Confessions*: Marchand, *Byron*, Vol 2, p 822.

115 *You will perhaps say why*: Ralph Milbanke, Earl of Lovelace, *Astarte*, New Edition, Christophers, 1921, p 102.

115 *With regard to 'the Memoirs'*: Letter from Lord Byron to Cam Hobhouse, 23 November 1821, quoted in Doris Langley Moore, *The Late Lord Byron*, John Murray, 1961, pp 38–9.

115 *after the first access of grief*: Lord Broughton, *Recollections*, Vol 3, p 38.

118 *I do not care whose*: Moore, *The Late Lord Byron*, p 33.

118 *If only Hobhouse*: ibid, p 38.

119 *Poor Byron*: ibid, p 57.

119 *A great poet belongs to no country*: *Medwin's Conversations of Lord Byron*, ed. Ernest J. Lovell Jr, Princeton University Press, 1966, p xv.

120 *Mr Murray is tender of my fame!*: *Medwin*, ed. Lovell, pp 166–8.

120 On Dallas biography: Moore, *The Late Lord Byron*, pp 57–91.

124 *was guilty of incest*: Harriet Beecher Stowe, *Lady Byron Vindicated*, Sampson, Low, Son and Marston, 1870, p 160.

126 *Not the least*: *The Listener*, 9 September 1948; 7 October 1948, pp 382 and 530–31.

## 8. At the Shelley Shrine

128 *In an 1830 debate*: Chew, *Byron in England*, p 260.

128 *Shelley, the writer of some infidel verses*: *Courier*, 5 August 1822, quoted in Richard Holmes, *Shelley: The Pursuit*, Penguin, 1987, p 730.

128 *There is thus another man gone*: Byron to Moore, 8 August 1822, *Lord Byron: Letters and Journals*, ed. Marchand, Vol 9, p 190.

129 *in times past*: Moore, *The Late Lord Byron*, p 96.

129 *I abstain from*: Shelley, *The Poetical Works*, ed. Mary Shelley, Vol 1, Moxon, 1853, p vii.

130 *I have found in the Record Office*: Sylva Norman, *Flight of the Skylark*, Max Reinhardt, 1954, pp 168–9.

131 *She must have seen*: ibid, p 179.

131 *It sounds exquisite*: idem.

131 *Mary accompanied*: Muriel Spark, *Mary Shelley*, Cardinal, 1987, p 143.

131 *built expressly*: Lady Shelley to Trelawney, quoted in A. Glynn Grylls, *Mary Shelley*, Oxford University Press, 1938, pp 286–7.

132 *All Shelley's journals*: Robert Metcalf Smith, *The Shelley Legend*, Scribner's, 1945, p 173.

132 *He was a climber*: T. J. Hogg, *Shelley*, Vol 2, Moxon, 1858, p 46.

132 *He was altogether*: ibid, p 68.

132 *It was with the most powerful feelings of dismay*: *Shelley Memorials from Authentic Sources*, ed. Lady Shelley, Smith, Elder, 1859, p iv.

133 *Our feelings of duty*: ibid.

133 *to give a truthful statement*: ibid, p v.

133 *in a sad and evil hour*: ibid, p 22.

134 *The occurrences*: ibid, p 65.

134 *Of those*: ibid.

134 *most decidedly contradicts*: Richard Garnett, *Macmillan's Magazine*, Vol 11, May–October, 1860, quoted in Smith, *The Shelley Legend*, pp 186–7.

134 *A few facts*: Thomas Love Peacock, *Fraser's*, March, 1862, *ibid*.

134 *guided by the best of feelings*: Edward Dowden to Richard Garnett, 17 May 1885, quoted in *Letters About Shelley*, Hodges, 1917, p 116.

135 *One mistake*: *Shelley Memorials*, ed. Lady Shelley, pp 65–6.

135 *To the family of Godwin*: ibid, p 67.

135 *Godwin's daughter Mary*: ibid, pp 67–8.

136 *I can't be two things at once*: W. M. Rossetti to Richard Garnett, 17 May 1885, in *Letters About Shelley*, pp 21–2.

137 *It is no part of this biography*: Edward Dowden, *The Life of Percy Bysshe Shelley*, Vol 1, Kegan Paul, Trench & Co., 1886, p 428.

137 *An almost literal transcript*: ibid, p 436.

139 *the perhaps dismalest thing*: J. G. Lockhart to Robert Cadell, 20 June 1836; see Davidson Cook: 'Lockhart's Treatment of Scott's Letters', *The Nineteenth Century*, cii, 1927, pp 382–98.

139 *'Lockhart,' he said*: J. G. Lockhart, *The Life of Sir Walter Scott, Bart.*, Adam & Charles Black, 1893, p 753.

140 *'Never shall I forget'*: *Charles Kingsley, His Letters and Memories of His Life*, edited by his wife, Kegan Paul, Trench & Co., 1885, p 349.

141 *One thing we hear greatly blamed*: T. Carlyle, *Westminster Review*, 1838, xxviii, pp 299ff.

141 *The writers of Lives*: Moore, *The Late Lord Byron*, p 383.


## 9. John Forster, of Dickens Fame

144 *By the year 1840*: Harold Nicolson, *The Development of English Biography*, Hogarth Press, 1927, p 125.

145 *At Thackeray's funeral*: John Carey, *Original Copy*, Faber, 1987, p 125.

145 *'toes' to 'fingers'*: *The George Eliot Letters*, ed. Gordon S. Haight, Oxford University Press, 1954, Vol 1, p xiii.

145 *I wish you would burn my letters*: quoted in Richard D. Altick, *Life and Letters*, Knopf, 1965, p 173.

146 *It is with great regret*: *Quarterly Review*, April 1814, p 73.

146 *We scarcely remember to have seen*: *Edinburgh Review*, September 1814, p 398.

147 *in common with*: *Edinburgh Review*, July 1885, p 36.

147 *What would Rousseau have said*: John Keats to Fanny Brawne, 27 February 1820, in *Letters of John Keats, A Selection*, ed. Robert Gittings, Oxford University Press, 1970, p 362.

147 *We shudder at the thought*: 'Modern Biography – Beattie's Life of Campbell', *Blackwood's Magazine*, February 1849, pp 219–24.

149 *I hardly know*: John Forster, *The Life of Charles Dickens*, Chapman & Hall, one-vol edn, 1892, p 261.

150 *ceased to believe*: ibid, p 7.

151 *quite realised the expectations*: John Forster, 'Charles Lamb', *New Monthly Magazine*, Vol XLIII, 1835, pp 198–202.

152 *I was awakened*: *Thackeray: The Letters and Private Papers of W. M. Thackeray*, ed. Gordon N. Ray, Oxford University Press, 1945–6, Vol 1, pp 351–2.

152 *one of those people*: James A. Davies, *John Forster: A Literary Life*, Leicester University Press, 1983, p 186.

152 *a most noisy man*: ibid, p 188.

153 *As I look back*: Percy Fitzgerald, quoted in Arthur Waugh, *A Hundred Years of Publishing*, Chapman & Hall, 1930, p 35.

153 *To you only I say this*: Davies, *John Forster*, p 123.

154 *How often have I*: ibid, p 157.

155 *The course taken*: Forster, *Dickens*, p 328.

156 Forster's will: Davies, *John Forster*, pp 259–62.

## 10. Froude's Carlyle, Carlyle's Froude

158 *It has been the fortune*: Waldo Hilary Dunn, *James Anthony Froude: A Biography*, Oxford University Press, 1961, pp 8–9.

158 *What on earth is the use*: Thomas Carlyle to John Forster, Spring 1848, quoted in Fred Kaplan, *Thomas Carlyle: A Biography*, Cambridge University Press, 1983, p 438.

159 *Mr Carlyle has a good deal to answer for*: Goldwin Smith, *The Edinburgh Review*, July 1858, quoted in Dunn, *Froude*, Vol 1, p 268.

159 *There is such a generous*: ibid, Vol 1, p 209.

160 *Late one afternoon*: J. A. Froude, *Thomas Carlyle: A History of his Life in London, 1834–1881*, Longmans, Green, 1884, Vol 2, pp 254–5.

161 *Somewhere about the middle*: ibid, pp 322–3.

162 *I still mainly mean to burn this book*: quoted by Mary Carlyle in a letter to *The Times*, 4 May 1881; see Waldo Dunn, *Froude and Carlyle: A Study of the Froude–Carlyle Controversy*, Longmans, 1930, p 34.

162 *Ah! and where is it now?* Froude, *Carlyle*, Vol 2, p 359.

164 *Ah me! Ah me!* etc.: quoted from *Letters and Memorials of Jane Welsh Carlyle, Prepared for Publication by Thomas Carlyle*, edited by James Anthony Froude, Vol 3, Longmans, 1883, *passim*.

164 *One day – the middle or end of June*: Froude, *Carlyle*, Vol 2, pp 408–9.

165 *For the first time*: J. A. Froude, *My Relations with Carlyle*, Longmans, 1903, p 13.

165 *I should then have done*: Froude, *Thomas Carlyle*, Vol 2, p 411.

166 *Lady Ashburton was a great lady*: Froude, *My Relations*, p 16.

167 *provided that I was left free*: ibid, p 17.

167 *When she heard*: ibid, pp 20–1.

168 *When any subject was disagreeable*: ibid, p 18.

172 *the more intimately I knew Carlyle*: Dunn, *Froude: A Biography*, p 497.

173 *suffered from constitutional inaccuracy*: Leslie Stephen, quoted by Crichton-Browne in 'Carlyle and Froude' *Contemporary Review*, June 1903, p 35.

174 *If he trusted me at all*: J. A. Froude, journal entry for 8 March 1887, quoted in Dunn, *Froude: A Biography*, p 551.

175 Crichton-Browne attack on Froude: see *Contemporary Review*, June, July, August, September 1903; *British Medical Journal*, 13 June, 1903.

176 *Of him I will make only*: Sir James Stephen to J. A. Froude, 9 December 1886, quoted in Froude, *My Relations*, p 62.

## 11. Keeping House: Tennyson and Swinburne

177 *In the absence of other evidence*: Robert Bernard Martin, *Tennyson, the Unquiet Heart*, Faber, 1983, pp 503–4.

178 *I had to answer many letters*: *Lady Tennyson's Journal*, ed. James O. Hoge, Virginia University Press, 1981, pp 370–1.

178 *She has overwrought herself*: Martin, *Tennyson*, p 504.

179 *jolly Woman*: Edward Fitzgerald, quoted in *ibid*, p 455.

180 *I today/Lord of myself*: quoted in Christopher Ricks, *Tennyson*, Macmillan Press, 1972, pp 148–9.

181 *he himself should be ripped open*: ibid.

181 *The worth of a biography*: Hallam, Lord Tennyson, *Tennyson: A Memoir*, Macmillan, 1897, Vol 2, p 165.

182 *I heard of an old lady the other day*: Martin, *Tennyson*, p 552.

183 *In the story of English Poetry*: Theodore Watts-Dunton, *Old Familiar Faces*, Books for Libraries Press, Freeport, 1970 (orig. 1916), p 135.

184 *a mysterious house in St John's Wood*: Edmund Gosse, 'Confidential Papers' or 'An Essay on Swinburne', Cecil Y. Lang, *The Swinburne Letters*, Vol VI, Yale University Press, New Haven, 1962, p 245.

184 *that these scourgings*: ibid.

185 *He carried his large head*: Edmund Gosse, *The Life of Algernon Charles Swinburne*, Macmillan, 1917, p 284.

186 *Watts-Dunton Cure*: Coulson Kernahan, *Swinburne As I Knew Him*, London, 1919; see Philip Henderson *Swinburne: Portrait of a Poet*, Macmillan, 1974, pp 230–2.

188 *A fitting and beautiful end*: The Times, 16 April 1909.

188 *A magnetic arrow*: Clara Watts-Dunton, 'Walter Theodore Watts-Dunton and I' in Thomas Hake and Arthur Compton-Rickett, *Life and Letters of T. Watts-Dunton*, London, 1916, p 167.

189 *bright-eyed vampire-like*: Helen Rossetti Angeli, daughter of W. M. Rossetti, quoted in Henderson, p 279.

189 *[Swinburne] began to imagine*: Hake/Compton-Rickett, *Life and letters*, p 136.

189 *All around Swinburne's sitting-room*: Posthumous Poems, ed. Edmund Gosse and Thomas James Wise, Heinemann, 1917, pp xxii–xxiii.

190 *sign a form*: Arthur Bell Nicholls to Clement Shorter, 10 July 1895 (Brotherton Collection).

191 *he wants to know*: Thomas J. Wise to Edmund Gosse, 10 May 1909 (Brotherton Collection).

191 *terribly slow to deal with*: ibid.

192 *I lose all power of speech*: E.G. to T.W., 6 October 1909, ibid.

193 *if only the old chap*: T.W. to E.G., 29 April 1912, ibid.

193 *he said: 'Cannot you induce Gosse'*: T.W. to E.G., 27 May 1913, ibid.

194 *I do hope Gosse*: T.W. to E.G., 29 April 1914, ibid.

194 *massively flagellated*: Frank Wilson, letter to *TLS*, 30 January 1969.

## 12. Legends and Mysteries: Robert Louis Stevenson and Henry James

198 *It is a most unhealthful place*: Fanny Stevenson to her mother-in-law, quoted in Margaret Mackay, *The Violent Friend*, Dent, 1968, p 92.

199 *I am not likely to change*: ibid, p 175.

200 *I beg Henley*: Michael Balfour, 'How the Biography of R.L.S. Came to be Written', part 1, *TLS*, 15 January 1960.

201 *They tell, with the zest*: *Vailima Letters, Being Correspondence Addressed by Robert Louis Stevenson to Sidney Colvin*, November 1890–October 1894, Methuen, 1895, p xvii.

202 *I want something definite*: Mrs R. L. Stevenson to Sidney Colvin, 26 June 1898 (Brotherton Collection).

202 *the sense of pressure*: S.C. to Mrs R.L.S., 28 June 1898, *ibid*.

202 *how could I forego*: S.C. to Mrs R.L.S., 31 March 1899, *ibid*.

202 *let me say in all frankness*: Lloyd Osbourne to S.C., 14 April 1899, *ibid*.

203 *I am afraid it is not possible*: Balfour, *TLS*, 15 January 1960.

205 *Tis as that of an angel*: John Connell, *W. E. Henley*, Constable, 1949, pp 365–8.

205 *Henley wanted to savage Fanny*: *ibid*, p 365.

206 *The relations between*: Alan Osbourne, letter to the Editor, *TLS*, 25 March 1960.

207 *the greatest of literary quarrels*: *Henry James: Selected Literary Criticism*, ed. Morris Shapira, Heinemann, 1963, p 158.

207 *Nothing comes up oftener*: Henry James's review of R.L.S. Letters (ed. Colvin, 1899) in *Henry James and Robert Louis Stevenson*, ed. Janet Adam Smith, Hart-Davis, 1948, pp 253–4.

208 *positively make for revelations*: *ibid*, p 254.

208 *It has been his fortune*: *ibid*, p 277.

209 *There are other thoughts*: Balfour, *TLS*, 15 January 1960; see also *Henry James' Letters*, Vol IV, ed. Leon Edel, Harvard University Press, 1984, pp 212–14.

212 *indeed brings up with singular intensity*: *James: Selected Literary Criticism*, ed. Shapira, p 139.

212 *a promise first to look at*: Letter to William Dean Howells, 25 January 1902, in *Henry James' Letters*, ed. Edel, Vol IV, pp 221–5.

213 *when I laid hands on the letters*: *ibid*, p 802.

213 *What would have been thought*: *James: Selected Literary Criticism*, ed. Shapira, p 114.

214 *The reporter and the reported*: *ibid*, p 160.

215 *it has been, it is*: Henry James to Edmund Gosse, 8 April 1895, in *Selected Letters of Henry James and Edmund Gosse*, ed. Rayburn S. Moore, Louisiana State University Press, 1988, p 126.

216 *All the forces of civilisation*: H.J. to William James, quoted in Leon

Edel, *Henry James: The Treacherous Years, 1895–1901*, Hart-Davis, 1969, pp 72–3.

216 *I have fallen upon evil days*: H.J. to W.D. Howells, *ibid*, p 87.

218 *So long as the events are veiled*: Leon Edel, *Henry James: The Master*, Hart-Davis, 1972, p 439.

219 *An aunt of my wife's*: Janet Adam Smith, *John Buchan*, Hart-Davis, 1965, p 472.

219 *at this very time*: *ibid*.

220 *I am greatly touched*: *Henry James' Letters*, ed. Edel, Vol IV, p 806.

221 *Hemingway and others*: see Ernest Hemingway, *Fiesta* or *The Sun Also Rises*, Bantam, 1955, p 90.

221 *a close reader*: *Henry James's Letters*, ed. Percy Lubbock, Macmillan, 1920, Vol 1, p xv.

## 13. Remembering Rupert Brooke

222 *the circumstances have caused me*: Henry James to Edward Marsh, 28 March 1915, quoted in Christopher Hassall, *Edward Marsh, Patron of the Arts,* Longman, 1959, p. 314.

222 *fresh, boyish stunt*: Paul Delany, *The Neo-Pagans: Love and Friendship in the Rupert Brooke Circle*, Macmillan, 1987, p 64.

222 *Insidious*: H.J. to Charles Sayle, 16 June 1909, *Henry James' Letters*, ed. Edel, Vol III, p 524.

222 *What it first and foremost*: Henry James, Preface to Rupert Brooke: *Letters from America*, Sidgwick and Jackson, 1916.

222 *the destruction, on such a scale*: Edel, *Henry James: The Master*, p 524.

223 *they have weakened*: Henry James, interview with *New York Times*, 21 March 1915, quoted in Edel, *Henry James: The Master*, pp 521–2.

223 *The thoughts to which*: Christopher Hassall, *Rupert Brooke*, Faber, 1964, p 515.

224 *slain by bright Phoebus' shaft*: D. H. Lawrence to Ottoline Morrell, 30 April 1915, quoted in Hassall, *Brooke*, p 516.

225 *your nakedness and beauty*: Rupert Brooke to Katherine Cox, 30 March 1912, quoted in Delany, *The Neo-Pagans*, p 170.

225 *radiant youthful figure in gold*: Edward Marsh, *Memoir*, in *Collected Poems of Rupert Brooke*, Sidgwick and Jackson, 1918, p xxiv.

225 *'Rupert Trunk'*: Hassall, *Edward Marsh,* 1959, p xiii.

226 *As I looked back*: Marsh, *Memoir*, p xii.

226 *One's soreness of soul*: Hassall, *Edward Marsh*, p 352.

227 *I don't care what goes*: Rupert Brooke to Dudley Ward, 17 March

1915, in *The Letters of Rupert Brooke*, ed. Sir Geoffrey Keynes, Faber, 1968, p 671.

227 *You are to be my literary executor*: Rupert Brooke to Edward Marsh, 9 March 1915, in *Letters*, ed. Keynes, p 669.

227 *If I can set them free*: Hassall, *Rupert Brooke*, p 517.

227 *I'm telling the Ranee*: Rupert Brooke to Katherine Cox, 10 March 1915, in *Letters*, ed. Keynes, p 669.

227 *as one of his legal heirs*: Hassall, *Edward Marsh*, p 327.

229 *But we must remember*: ibid, p 355.

230 *I found the Memoir*: ibid, p 360.

232 *Brooke's unmanly physical beauty*: Geoffrey Keynes, *The Gates of Memory*, Oxford University Press, 1982, p 165.

233 *inevitably incomplete*: *TLS*, 8 August 1918.

233 *one of the most repulsive*: Virginia Woolf to Ka Cox, quoted in John Lehmann, *Rupert Brooke: His Life and Legend*, Weidenfeld, 1980, p 158.

234 *I think we should do it by August*: Rupert Brooke to Rev. Alan Brooke, 1 January 1915, in *Letters*, ed. Keynes, pp 650–1.

234 *discredit the Rupert Brooke legend*: Keynes, *The Gates of Memory*, p 170.

235 *Intentions became plain*: Delany, *The Neo-Pagans*, pp 78–80.

235 *and he was amazed*: Jon Stallworthy, in conversation with the author, 21 February 1991.

236 *You told me – in the first flush*: Delany, *The Neo-Pagans*, p 154.

237 *those two fat volumes*: Lytton Strachey, *Eminent Victorians*, Penguin, 1986, p 10.

238 *as the war got under way*: Michael Holroyd, *Lytton Strachey: A Biography*, Penguin, 1971, p 509.

239 *Let the biographers labour and toil*: Peter Gay, *Freud, a Life for our Times*, Macmillan, 1989, p xiii.

239 *stripping the mystery*: E. F. Benson, 'On Undesirable Information', *Contemporary Review*, Vol LXVIII, 1895, pp 123–33.

239 *no one is safe*: Frederick Graves, 'The Rakers', *Westminster Review*, Vol CLXXV, 1911, pp 683–6.

## 14. Authorised Lives: Hardy and Kipling

241 *I have not been doing much*: Thomas Hardy to Sir George Douglas, 7 May 1919, *Thomas Hardy: The Personal Notebooks*, ed. Richard H. Taylor, Macmillan, 1978, p xiii.

241 *I have been occupied*, 11 September 1919, *ibid*.

242 *I seemed suddenly to leap*: Florence Hardy to Sidney Cockerell, 26 November 1922, quoted in Robert Gittings and Jo Manton, *The Second Mrs Hardy*, Heinemann, 1979, p 67.

242 *He wanted a housekeeper*: F.H. to Alda, Lady Hoare, 22 July 1914, quoted in Gittings and Manton, *Second Mrs Hardy*, p 71.

242 *I am never so happy*: F.H. to Rebekah Owen, 17 December 1915, quoted in *ibid*, p 72.

243 *Mr Hardy looks very well*: F.H. to Edward Clodd, 16 January 1913 (Brotherton Collection).

244 *I read it with horrible fascination . . . It seems that I am an utter failure*: quoted in Gittings and Manton, *Second Mrs Hardy*, p 79.

244 *very well and amazingly cheerful*: F.H. to Rebekah Owen, 3 December 1916, quoted in *ibid*, p 83.

244 *All I trust*: F.H. to Edward Clodd, 7 March 1913 (Brotherton Collection).

245 *The barest of known facts*: F.H. to Vere H. Collins, 2 July 1922 (Brotherton Collection).

245 *prying, vivisection* etc: *ibid*, 24 June 1922 (Brotherton Collection).

245 *he underwent the strange experience*: Florence Emily Hardy, *The Life of Thomas Hardy, 1840–1928*, Macmillan paperback, 1962, p 270.

246 *Given the circumstances*: *The Life and Work of Thomas Hardy*, ed. Michael Millgate, Macmillan, 1984, p xii.

247 *I do not in truth*: Thomas Hardy to Sidney Cockerell, 28 August 1914 (Colby College, Maine).

247 *I will act loyally*: S.C. to T.H., 30 August 1914 (Brotherton Collection).

247 *Regard me as a parishioner*: T.H. to Vicar of Stinsford, 16 December 1924 (Dorset County Museum).

248 *If Somerset Maugham*: J. B. Priestley, *Saturday Review of Literature*, 1 November 1930.

249 *It is the stab in the back*: Rupert Hart-Davis, *Hugh Walpole*, Hamish Hamilton, 1985, p 316.

249 *There are moments*: F.H. to Siegfried Sassoon, 5 November 1930, quoted in Gittings and Manton, *Second Mrs Hardy*, p 3.

249 *In a recent novel*: F.H. to Rev H. G. B. Cowley, 30 October 1930, quoted in *ibid*, p 2.

249 *as she read through*: *ibid*, p 108.

250 *Richard Purdy revealed*: 'New Editions and Otherwise', *New York Times, Book Review*, 12 May 1940.

251  *transatlantic pirates*: John Sutherland, *Mrs Humphry Ward*, Clarendon Press, 1990, p 129.

251  *to grin and bear it*: ibid, pp 129–30.

252  *As I look back*: Edmund Gosse, *Portraits and Sketches*, Heinemann, 1912, p 215.

253  *Extraordinarily importunate person*: Arthur Waugh, *One Man's Road*, Chapman & Hall, 1931, p 186.

253  *No other man*: Charles Carrington, *Rudyard Kipling, His Life and Work*, Penguin, 1986, p 225.

254  *poor little concentrated*: Henry James to Edmund Gosse, 10 December 1891, quoted in *Henry James' Letters*, ed. Edel, Vol III, Macmillan, 1981, p 364.

254  *'The Long Trail'*: see Martin Seymour-Smith, *Rudyard Kipling*, Macdonald/Queen Anne Press, 1989, p 196 and *passim*.

255  *My mother introduced*: 'Memoir' by Mrs George Bambridge; epilogue to Carrington, *Kipling*, pp 587–97.

257  *the Higher Cannibalism*: Rudyard Kipling, *Something of Myself*, Penguin, 1987, p 146.

257  *If Rud had been*: Mrs A. M. Fleming to Lord Birkenhead, quoted in Lord Birkenhead, *Rudyard Kipling*, Star Books, 1980, p 253.

258  *Birkenhead's contract*: ibid, pp 1–2.

259  *the light of her life*: Mrs J. M. Huntington-Whitely to Charles Carrington, 4 June 1976 (University of Sussex Library).

259  *It is very unpleasant*: Birkenhead, *Kipling*, pp 3–4.

260  *what is important*: T. S. Eliot to W. P. Watt, 11 September 1948 (University of Sussex Library).

260  *Squire thought the biography*: Sir John Squire report, 14 August 1948 (University of Sussex Library).

260  *the only alternative*: W. P. Watt to Mrs George Bambridge, 2 September 1948 (University of Sussex Library).

261  *We had been brought up*: Charles Carrington, 'The Kipling "Mystery" ', *New Statesman*, 2 March 1979.

261  *R. K. had the complete Fascist–Nazi mentality*: Draft Essay on Kipling by A. L. Lyall, 1936 (University of Sussex Library).

261  *We argued powerfully*: Carrington, *New Statesman*.

262  *30 Jan 1896*: Kipling Papers (University of Sussex Library).

262  *9th [May 1896]. Sat.*: Kipling Papers (University of Sussex Library).

263  *WHAT DID*: *Sunday Times*, 13 June 1976.

263  *KIPLING SECRETS*: *Sunday Telegraph*, 6 June 1976.

263  *REVEALED*: *Daily Mail*, 5 October 1978.

263  *Robert Blake was*: 'The Hidden Life of Rudyard Kipling', *Sunday Times*, 8 October 1978.

264  *July 18. Down and down*: Birkenhead, *Kipling*, pp 235–6.

265  *– no description*: Kipling Papers (University of Sussex Library).

266  *downright wicked*: Carrington, *Kipling*, p 553.

## 15. James Joyce's Patron Saint

267  *Few people will love him*: *The Dublin Diary of Stanislaus Joyce*, ed. George Harris Healey, Faber, 1962, p 15.

267  *[James] has extraordinary moral courage*: *ibid*, pp 14–15.

269  *The mystery of esthetic*: James Joyce, *A Portrait of the Artist as a Young Man*, Penguin, 1964, pp 214–15.

270  *His letters home*: Richard Ellmann, *James Joyce*, Oxford University Press paperback, 1966, p 207.

271  *he saw his private quarrels*: *ibid*, p 349.

272  *There has never been any valid*: Herbert Gorman, *James Joyce: A Definitive Biography*, Bodley Head, 1941, p 216.

272  *Who was it said*: Ellmann, *Joyce*, p 348.

273  *Dear Sir: Mr Yeats has been speaking*: *Pound/Joyce: The Letters of Ezra Pound to James Joyce*, ed. Forrest Read, Faber, 1968, pp 17–18.

273  *Let us presume*: *ibid*, p 33.

275  *must have been edited on a mountain top*: Jane Lidderdale and Mary Nicholson, *Dear Miss Weaver*, Faber, 1970, pp 53–4.

276  *we have in working practice*: *ibid*, p 164.

276  *I did my best*: *The Diary of Virginia Woolf*, ed. Anne Olivier Bell, Vol 1, 1915–1919, Penguin, 1979, p 140.

277  *Harriet felt strongly*: Lidderdale and Nicholson, *Dear Miss Weaver*, p 174.

278  *He gave the impression*: Noel Riley Fitch, *Sylvia Beach and the Lost Generation*, Souvenir Press, 1984, pp 62–4.

279  *It was a heavy blow*: *ibid*, p 77.

279  *Mother dear*: *ibid*, p 78.

279  *what she thought about drink*: Lidderdale and Nicholson, *Dear Miss Weaver*, pp 184–5.

280  *The truth probably; I now end*: J.J. to H.S.W., 24 June 1921, quoted in *Selected Letters of James Joyce*, ed. Richard Ellmann, Faber, 1976, pp 281–4.

283  *The author's copious notes*: Lidderdale and Nicholson, *Dear Miss Weaver*, p 259.

283  *Some of your work*: ibid, p 269.

284  *I find it difficult*: ibid, pp 275–6.

284  *Miss Weaver's visit*: Ellmann, *Joyce*, p 612.

284  *everything was gay*: ibid.

285  *there to handle any situation*: Lucie Noel, *James Joyce and Paul L. Leon: The Story of a Friendship*, Gotham Book Mart, New York, 1950, p 8.

285  *Joyce is writing in a way nobody understands*: Ellmann, *Joyce*, p 643.

286  *I believe I can*: J.J. to H.S.W., 9 June 1936, quoted in *Selected Letters*, ed. Ellmann, pp 380–1.

288  *But it is impossible to deny*: Lidderdale and Nicholson, *Dear Miss Weaver*, pp 372–3.

288  *He had accused her*: ibid, pp 377–8.

290  *gazed long and sadly*: ibid, p 454.

## 16. Provisional Posterities: Sylvia Plath and Philip Larkin

291  *Many people may think I acted wrongly*: Spencer Curtis Brown, 'Personal Note' in Ted Morgan, *Somerset Maugham*, Cape, 1980, pp vii–viii.

292  *when Maugham*: ibid.

292  *flexible enough to be bent backwards*: Edward Mendelson, 'Authorised Biography and its Discontents', *Harvard English Studies*, 1978, p 10.

293  *The image of a man*: Peter Ackroyd, *T. S. Eliot*, Cardinal, 1988, p 208.

293  *A casual visitor*: A. Alvarez, 'A Poet and Her Myths', *New York Review of Books*, 28 September 1989, pp 34–6.

295  *omitted some of the most personally aggressive poems*: Sylvia Plath, *The Collected Poems*, Faber, 1981; Introduction by Ted Hughes, p 15.

296  David Holbrook: Letters to *TLS*, 24 October and 7 November 1968.

296  Olwyn Hughes: Letters to *TLS*, 31 October and 14 November 1968.

296  *She had always been*: A. Alvarez, *The Savage God*, Weidenfeld and Nicolson, 1971, p 32.

297  *Mr Alvarez's main trouvé*: Ted Hughes, letter to *TLS*, 19 November 1971.

297  *I see no reason*: A. Alvarez, letter to *TLS*, 26 November 1971.

299  *the enemy, the monster*: Sherry Lutz Zivley, 'Ted Hughes's

*Apologia Pro Matrimonio Suo*', *New England Quarterly*, no 55, June 1982, pp 187–200.

299 *Some were camouflage*: Ted Hughes, Foreword to *The Journals of Sylvia Plath*, Dial Press, New York, 1982, p xii.

300 *consumed five years*: Ted Hughes, letter to the *Independent*, 20 April 1989.

301 *supplies little of the incidental*: Hughes, *Journals*, pp xii–xiii.

301 *Anyone who remembers*: Frances McCullough, letter to *Atlantic Monthly*, August 1976.

301 *in guise of indignation*: Olwyn Hughes, letter to *New York Review of Books*, 30 December 1976.

302 *who treat Sylvia Plath's family*: ibid.

302 *Hughes asked me*: Anne Stevenson, 'The Making of *Bitter Fame*', unpublished lecture, October 1990.

302 *It was clear to me*: ibid.

303 *that his first wife's grave*: Julia Parnaby and Rachel Wingfield, letter to the *Guardian*, 7 April, 1989.

303 *a highspirited and boisterous*: Trevor Thomas, *Sylvia Plath: Last Encounters*, privately published, 1989.

303 *I asked him to give it another go*: Ted Hughes, letter to the *Guardian*, 20 April 1989.

303 *In the years soon after*: ibid.

304 *Is it ungrateful*: Philip Larkin, 'An Unofficial Life', *Encounter*, December 1984, pp 45–6.

305 *a writer's reputation is twofold*: Philip Larkin, *Required Writing*, Faber, 1983, p 228.

306 *the one thing the will mustn't be*: Philip Larkin to Andrew Motion, 3 April 1985.

306 *the chief thing about it*: Philip Larkin to Anthony Thwaite, 14 April 1985.

308 *the purity of the canon*: John Whitehead, quoted in the *Independent on Sunday*, 4 November 1990.

308 *It is a moral point*: John Whitehead, quoted in the *Daily Telegraph*, 27 October 1990.

308 *show the growth*: Anthony Thwaite, Introduction to *Philip Larkin: Collected Poems*, Faber, 1988, p xxxiii.

308 *if it had fallen to me*: Andrew Motion in conversation with the author, January 1991.

308 *Part of him*: Anthony Thwaite, in conversation with the author, January, 1991.

309 *It seems to me*: Andrew Motion, in conversation, January 1991.

309 *things you would tell no person*: Description of diaries by Hull University secretary, who shredded them, quoted in *The Observer Colour Magazine*, 3 March 1991.

310 *That is not to say*: Larkin, *Required Writing*, p 228.

# Index

Abbot, Claude Colleer, 81–2
Abercrombie, Lascelles, 225, 226, 227
Ackroyd, Peter: biography of T. S. Eliot,
  293, 304
Addison, Joseph, 47
Aldington, Richard, 238
Allingham, William, 181
Alvarez, A., 294, 296–8
  *The Savage God*, 296–7, 298
Ames, Lois, 295, 300
Anderson, Dr Jane, 300
Anderson, Robert, 89
Antheil, George, 284
Arbuthnot, Dr John, 50
Arnold, Matthew, 138
Arnold, Thomas, 140, 238
Ashburton, Lady: affair with Carlyle, 160,
  166, 167–8, 174
*Athenaeum, The*, 183
Aubrey, John, 17, 23, 43, 75
  *Brief Lives*, 12, 25
Auden, W. H., 292, 309
Austen, Jane, 181

Baldwin, Earl, 259
Balestier, Beatty, 256, 262
Balestier, Wolcott, 252–4, 256, 263
  collaborates with Kipling on *The
  Naulahka*, 253
  organises simultaneous US publication for
  British authors, 252–3
Balfour, Graham, 203, 209
  *Life of Robert Louis Stevenson* (1901), 204–
  5, 206, 208–9
Balfour, Michael, 206
Balzac, Honoré de, 213
Bambridge, Elsie (*neé* Kipling), 255, 263,
  264, 266

  appoints Birkenhead as Kipling's
    biographer, 258–9
  hires Charles Carrington to replace
    Birkenhead, 260–1
  *Memoir*, 264
  notes on banned Birkenhead manuscript,
    264–5
  orders destruction of mother's diaries,
    262–3
  rejects Birkenhead's version, 259–60
Bambridge, Captain George, 258, 259
Baxter, Charles, 201
Baxter, James, 197
Beach, Sylvia, 278–9, 281, 284
Beattie, James, 81
Beattie, William: *Life of Thomas Campbell*,
  148
Beerbohm, Sir Max, 196
Benson, A. C., 195, 231
Benson, E. F., 239
Betjeman, Sir John, 263, 305
Betterton, Thomas
  devotee of Shakespeare, 23–4
  performance of Hamlet, 23–4
  researcher for Rowe's Life of Shakespeare,
    25–6
Birkenhead, Lord (2nd Earl), 258
  appointed biographer of Kipling, 258
  draft banned by Kipling's daughter, 259–
    60, 262, 263, 264–6
  eventual publication of revised biography,
    263–4
Birrell, Augustine, 175
*Blackwood's Magazine*, 102, 124, 147–9
Blake, Robert, 263–4
Blake, William, 136
Blunt, Wifred Scawen, 127
Bohun, Edmund, 44
Bolingbroke, Henry St John (1st Viscount),
  53–4, 55, 56, 61, 138

attacked by Warburton, 58–9
influenced Pope's *An Essay on Man*, 54, 61
mud-slinging after demise of Pope, 58
receives Pope's unpublished manuscripts, 57
*The Idea of a Patriot King*, 57, 58
*Works*, 59
Bolitho, Hector, 257, 259
Boswell, Alexander, 74–5, 79
Boswell, James, 29, 68, 77, 153, 158
   Abbott's haul of Boswell correspondence at Fettercairn, 81–3
   caricatured by Macaulay, 73, 75, 76
   collection sold to Yale University by Isham, 83
   hoard of private papers, 72–3
   Isham edition of *The Private Papers*, 80–1, 82
   Journal, 73–4, 77–8, 80–1
   *Life of Johnson*, 59, 63, 70–4, 75, 76, 81, 82, 86, 87
   literary executors of, 73–4
   method of biography, 70
   missing papers, 74–81
   purchase of correspondence by Isham, 80–1, 82–3
Boswell, James, jr, 74, 75, 77
   literary heir to Malone, 75
Boswell, Sir James, 74, 76, 77
Brawne, Fanny, 146–7
Brod, Max, 291–2
Broderick, Sir Allen, 15
Brontë, Charlotte, 143, 190
Brooke, Alfred, 226, 229
Brooke, Mary (the Ranee), 226, 227, 228, 237
   disagreement with Marsh over his *Memoir* on Rupert, 228–33, 237
   granted lifelong possession of her son's papers, 227
   Marsh dismissed in her will, 234
Brooke, Rupert, 222–37
   attempt by Keynes to discredit the legend, 234
   Churchill's eulogy, 223
   'Clouds', 224
   *Collected Letters*, 234, 235
   *Collected Poems*, 228, 232
   'Grantchester', 224
   Katherine Cox affair, 226, 227, 236–7
   *Letters from America*, 228
   *Memoir* by Marsh, 228, 229–34, 237

   myth of, 224, 228, 234
   nervous breakdown and flight to South Seas, 224, 225, 226, 228, 232–3, 236
   *1914 and Other poems*, 228
   'Peace', 236
   *Poems* (1911), 222
   *Poems 1914*, 228
   praise from Henry James, 222–3
   sexual proclivities, 224, 225, 233, 234–5
   'The Soldier', 223, 236
   'Tiare Tahiti', 224
   war sonnets, 224, 225, 228, 234, 236
Brooke, William Parker, 226
Brotherton Library, Leeds, 190–1
Browning, Robert, 138, 151, 153, 158
   *Collected Poems*, 152
Buchan, John (later Lord Tweedsmuir), 218, 219
Budgen, Frank, 280
Bulwer, Edward, 179
Bulwer-Lytton, Edward (later 1st Baron Lytton), 151, 152
Burns, Gilbert, 92, 101, 103
Burns, Jean, 90, 91, 92, 93, 105, 107, 108
Burns, Robert, 75, 87–108, 109, 110, 175
   'A Cotter's Saturday Night', 89
   'Ae Fond Kiss', 93
   alcoholism, 96–8, 99, 101
   *Collected Letters*, 100
   cleaning up the image, 100
   committee of executors, 91, 92, 93, 94
   Currie's Life of, 94–9, 101, 103, 105, 106
   Edinburgh edition, 89
   Edinburgh period, 89–90
   frailties, 90–3
   illness theories, 91, 97–101
   improper verses, 88
   Kilmarnock edition, 88–9
   'Merry Muses of Caledonia', 89
   'O, my luve's like a red, red, rose', 100
   position with HM Excise, 90
   posthumous notoriety, 91–4, 99
   subscription appeal, 91–3, 94
   'Tam o' Shanter', 91, 106
   ways with women, 108
   Wordsworth's defence of, 103, 104–7
   Works, posthumous edition of, 93
Burns Club, 100, 101
Burton, Sir Richard Francis, 144
Burton, Lady, 144
Butscher, Edward: unauthorised biography of Sylvia Plath, 300, 301

Byron, Ada, 125
Byron, Lord George Gordon (6th Baron),
    109–27, 128, 129, 142, 150, 223–4
  allegations of incest, 124–6
  *Cain*, 125
  *Childe Harold*, 109, 113, 125
  *Don Juan*, 112, 120
  *English Bards and Scotch Reviewers*, 109
  'Fare Thee Well', 111
  Greek adventure, 111, 112, 113, 123
  *Hours of Idleness*, 120
  *Manfred*, 125
  marriage separation controversy, 110–11,
    124, 125, 133, 218, 219
  Memoirs, 114–18, 119; destroyed by
    Hobhouse, 113, 116–18
  Moore's *Life*, 116, 123–4, 142
  pre-marital letters to Lady Melbourne,
    218–19
Byron, Lady, 110–12, 114–15, 116, 117,
    118–19, 124, 125, 126–7, 219

Campbell, Thomas, 109, 148
Carey, John, 145
Carlyle, Jane Welsh, 152, 160–1, 162–3,
    167–8, 172–3, 174, 175
  edition of her letters, 163–6
  husband's memoir of her, 161–2, 166, 169,
    170, 171
  mental health, 174, 175
  tensions of marriage, 160, 163–5, 167–8,
    174, 175, 178
Carlyle, John, 167, 169
Carlyle, Mary, 163, 168–9, 170–1, 172, 173,
    174, 175
Carlyle, Alexander, 169, 170, 172, 175
  *New Letters and Memorials of Jane Welsh
    Carlyle*, 175
Carlyle, Thomas, 112, 140–1, 142, 152, 155,
    178–9, 182, 239
  affair with Lady Ashburton, 160, 166
  biography of Frederick the Great, 160,
    161, 162
  edition of wife's letters, 163–6
  *French Revolution*, 159, 162
  Froude's biography, 158, 168, 171, 172–4,
    175–6
  impotency charge, 167, 174, 175
  *Letters and Memorials*, 168, 171
  memoir of his wife, 161–2, 166, 169, 170,
    171

relationship with Froude, 158, 160–1,
    164–70
  *Reminiscences*, 169, 170–1, 173
  remorse on death of wife, 161–3, 164–5,
    170, 172, 175, 243
Carrington, Charles, 262, 263, 265
  hired as official biographer of Kipling,
    260–1
  *Life* of Kipling, 261, 263, 264
  *The British Overseas*, 261
censorship by printers, 276
Chapman, R. W., 82
Chapman and Hall, publishers, 153, 158
Charles I, 2, 17
Charles II, 14, 20, 21, 22, 44
Chatterton, Thomas, 87, 103
  forgeries exposed, 75
Chaucer, Geoffrey, 34
Chaworth, Mary, 218
Churchill, Sir Winston, 223, 225
  eulogy on Rupert Brooke, 223
Cibber, Colley, 22
Civil War, English, 17–18, 25
Clairmont, Claire, 128, 137
Clarendon, Edward Hyde, earl of, 17–18
Clarendon Press, 82
Clinton, Lord, 82
Clodd, Edward, 243, 245, 250
Cobham, Lord Richard, 38
Cockerell, Sydney, 246–8, 249
  executor of Hardy, 246–8
  ingratiation with Hardy, 246
  quarrel with Florence Hardy, 247–8
Coleridge, Samuel Taylor, 86
  lines of Burns, 92
  *The Lyrical Ballads*, 86
Collier, Jeremy: attacks Congreve in *View of
    the Immorality and Profaneness of the
    English Stage*, 36
Colum, Padraic, 272
Colvin, Sir Sidney, 197, 199, 200, 201–3,
    204–5, 206, 207
  delay in producing biography of Robert
    Louis Stevenson, 202–3
  edition of Stevenson's *Letters* (1899), 208,
    209
  *Memoir* of RLS (1921), 203
  relinquishes writing of the biography, 203
Condell, Henry, 19, 20
Congreve, William, 47
  attacked by Jeremy Collier, 36
  early retirement from the drama, 36–7

introduces Dryden's *Works*, 36
last poem, 38
literary heir to Dryden, 38
refusal of Dryden's bequest, 37–8
*The Double Dealer* preface by Dryden, 35–6
*The Way of the World*, 36, 37
Coningham-Sterling, Anthony, 193
Cooke, Thomas, 30–1
copyright law and practice
    Act for the Encouragement of Learning, 1710 (first Copyright Act), 44–5, 47
    Act of 1842 improves author's control, 144
authors' rights not defined in seventeeth century, 41–2
Berne Union (1885) for international copyright protection, 251
    Copyright Act (1911), 291
    injunction against publication of Byron correspondence, 122
    sixteenth-seventeenth century, 6
    transatlantic piracy, 251–2
    US Chace Act (1891), 251, 252, 253
Cornford, Frances, 224, 229, 235
Cowley, Abraham, 40–1
Cox, Katherine, 227
    affair with Rupert Brooke, 226, 236–7
    liaison with Henry Lamb, 236–7
Crichton-Browne, Sir James, 99–100, 175
Croker, John Wilson, 75–6, 83, 179, 180
    edition of *Life of Johnson*, 75, 76, 102
    review of Keats, 102
Cromek, R. H.: *Reliques of Robert Burns*, 102
Cromwell, Oliver, 20, 22, 32
Cromwell, Richard, 51
Cross, John Walter, 144, 145
Cross, Mary Ann (George Eliot), 144, 145, 239, 275
    *Adam Bede*, 275
Crousaz, Jean Pierre de, 54–5, 61
Cunningham, Alexander, 91, 92–3, 94
Curll, Edmund, 50–3, 64
    battle with Alexander Pope, 50, 51–3, 55
    fake memoirs of celebrities, 50, 66
    *Popiad*, 51
Currie, Dr James, 94–9, 175
    diagnosis of the illness and death of Burns, 97–8, 99, 100, 102
    Life of Burns, 95–9, 101, 103, 105, 106, 108
Curtis Brown, Spencer, 291, 292

Dallas, Rev. Alexander, 121, 122
Dallas, R. C., 120–2
    *Private Correspondence of Lord Byron* etc., 121–2; injunction by Hobhouse against its publication, 122
Davenant, Sir William, 16–23, 24, 25, 34
    consigned to the Tower, 18
    *Epithalamion*, 20
    *Gondibert*, 16–18
    guardian of Shakespeare, 18–23
    performance in the Civil War, 17–18
    personal appearance, 17
    ridiculed by satirists, 17–18
    stages Shakespeare productions, 21–3
    *The Siege of Rhodes*, 20
    *The Witts*, 16
De La Mare, Sir Walter, 226, 227, 234
Dekker, Thomas, 42
Delany, Paul, 236
    *The Neo-Pagans, Friendship and Love in the Rupert Brooke Circle*, 234
Dent, E. J., 228, 229
*Des Imagistes*, 273
Dickens, Catherine, 149, 154–5
Dickens, Charles, 149–50, 151, 152, 158
    *David Copperfield*, 149
    Forster's biography, 154–6
    friendship with Forster, 149, 153
    *Household Words*, 149
    *Our Mutual Friend*, 149
*Dictionary of National Biography*, 1, 12, 17, 99, 193, 239
Digby, Kenelm, 40
D'Israeli, Izaak, 8, 56–7
    *Curiosities of Literature*, 86
Dobson, Austin, 252
Donne, Dr John (the Elder), 1–15, 37
    *Anniversaries*, 7
    *Biathanatos*, 11
    *Death's Duell* (final sermon), 3–4, 5
    death-bed extravaganza, 3–4
    disgrace and imprisonment due to marriage, 5
    *Essays in Divinity*, 12
    executors, 4, 5
    first subject of a literary biography, 1
    'Heap of Riddles', 9
    Izaak Walton's Life of, 2–3, 4, 5, 8, 37, 40
    *Juvenilia*, 6
    *Letters to Severall Persons of Honour* (1651 edition), 11

monument in St Paul's, construction of, 4
*Poems*, 6
publication of poems, 8–10
prose safeguarded and published by son, 10–11
*XXVI Sermons*, 11, 12
Donne, John (the Younger), 1–15, 18, 20
acquitted of unlawful killing, 1
character-sketches of, 12–13
*Donnes Satyr*, 13–15
Entry in *Dictionary of National Biography*, 1
intervention as custodian of father's estate, 5–7, 9–10
Last Will and Testament, 14–15
other writings, 16, 17
safeguarding of father's prose, 10–11
Dorling, Taprell, 257–8, 259
Dowden, Edward: biography of Shelley, 137–8
Doyle, Colonel, 117
Drummond, William, 41
Dryden, John, 34–9, 42, 53, 55
champion and refiner of Shakespeare, 21–3, 34
chooses Congreve as his literary heir, 35–8
defends native literary tradition, 34–5
Last Will and Testament, 39
liaison with publisher Jacob Tonson, 46–7
*Life of Plutarch*, 46
*Love's Triumphant*, 39
Malone's edition, 75
*Miscellanies*, 46
poems, 22, 35
'To My Dear Friend Mr Congreve', 35–6
translation of *Iliad*, 46
*Works* (1718) introduced by Congreve, 36
Dunlop, Mrs, 93, 95
benefactress of Burns, 89–90
Dunt, Humphry, 1, 5, 12

Edel, Leon, 219–21, 269
Edgcumbe, R.: *Byron, the last phase*, 218, 219
*Edinburgh Review*, 102, 105, 146–7
attack on the Lake Poets, 102
Wordsworth's riposte, 103–4
*Egoist, The*, 272
publishes extracts of *Ulysees*, 276
serialises *A Portrait of the Artist as a Young Man*, 273–4, 275
Egoist Press, 276, 282
Eldon, Lord, 122

Eliot, George, *see* Cross, Mary Ann
Eliot, Thomas Stearns, 9, 29, 259–60, 292–3, 309
Ackroyd's biography, 293, 304
*Waste Land*, 292
Eliot, Valerie, 292, 293
Elizabeth I, 34
Ellmann, Richard, 278
*Joyce*, 270
Elwin, Warwick, 157
Elwin, Whitwell, 157
Empson, William, 31–2
*Encounter*, 304
Evelyn, John, 20, 85
*Diaries*, 86
letters from Wotton House, 85
Evelyn, Lady, 85, 86

Fairfax, Edward, 34
Feather, John, 44
Fielding, Henry, 66
Fitzgerald, Edward, 179
Fitzgerald, Percy, 153
Fitzwilliam Museum, Cambridge, 246
Flaubert, Gustave, 211–12
*Letters*, 212
Flecknoe, Richard, 23
Fleming, Mrs A. M., 257, 259
Forbes, Sir William: Boswell's chief literary executor, 73, 81, 83–4
Forman, Mr, 147
Forster, John, 149–57, 158, 166
biography of Landor, 154
friendship with Dickens, 149, 153
*Life of Dickens*, 154–6
*Life of Goldsmith*, 149, 153
reconstruction of Leigh Hunt, 150–1
Fowler, Richard Hindle, 100–1
*Fraser's Magazine*, 160, 193
Freud, Sigmund, 238–9
Froude, James Anthony, 158–61, 164–76, 181–2
accused of malpractice, 172–3
biography of Carlyle, 158, 168, 171, 172–4, 175–6, 239
edition of Carlyle's *Reminiscences*, 170–1, 173
editor of *Fraser's Magazine*, 160
*History of England*, 158, 159
*My Relations with Carlyle*, 174, 175
*Nemisis of Fate*, 158–9

publishes *Letters and Memorials* by Carlyle, 171
relationship with Carlyle, 158, 160–1, 164–70
Frye, Northrop, 86
Fuller, Thomas: *Worthies*, 24

Garnett, Richard, 133, 134, 136, 137
Garrard, Flo, 256
Garrick, David, 26, 28, 29
Gaskell, Elizabeth, 143
*Gentleman's Magazine*, 26–7, 120
George I, 53
George V, 257, 265, 271
Gibson, Wilfred, 227
Gifford, William, 116, 118
Gladstone, William Ewart, 144, 182
Goldsmith, Oliver, 71, 153
Forster's *Life*, 149, 153
Goncourts' *Journals*, 213
Gorman, Herbert, 285
Gosse, Sir Edmund, 9, 12, 69–70, 190, 191–5, 197, 209, 215, 231, 248, 252, 253
biography of Swinburne, 185, 194–5, 237
*Confidential Paper*, 195
Grant Richards, publishers, 271, 273, 275
Graves, Robert, 187
Gray, James, 103
Gray, Thomas: doctoring of his letters by William Mason, 68–70
Greene, Donald, 72–3
Greene, Robert, 23
Greville, Fulke, 2
Grierson, Herbert, 9
Guiciolli, Countess, 124

hagiography, rebirth of, 144
Halifax, Lord, 258
Hamilton, Emma, Lady, 146
Hardy, Emma, 242–6, 249–51
illness and death, 245
husband's remorse, 243–4, 246
venomous diaries, 243, 244, 246
Hardy, Florence, 241–51
adjustments to the *Life*, 249–50
assists with husband's biographical deception, 241, 244, 246–7
claims authorship of *Life*, 247
disagreement with Cockerell, 247–8
marital unhappiness, 242, 244

Hardy, Thomas, 241–51, 252, 305, 309
critics of his work, 245
destroys papers, 241, 247
*Jude the Obscure*, 243, 245
*Life of Thomas Hardy*: self-biography deception (ghost-*Life*), 241, 244, 246–7, 248, 249–50, 256
remorse at death of Emma, 243–4
reticence, 245
*Satires of Circumstance*, 244
unhappy marriages, 242–4
Harper and Row, publishers, 298
*Harper's Monthly*, 252, 253
Harvard University, 221
Hazlitt, William, 112
Heinemann, William, publishers, 253
Heming, John, 19, 20
Hemingway, Ernest, 221
Henley, W. E., 197, 198, 199–200, 203, 204, 205, 208, 253, 254
debunks biography of Robert Louis Stevenson by Graham Balfour, 205
quarrel with RLS, 199–200, 205
Henrietta Maria, Queen, 17
Henry VIII, 159
Herbert, George: Izaak Walton's Life of, 40
Heron, Robert: *Memoir* on Burns, 96
Hill, Edmonia, 256
letters from Kipling, 257
Hill, George Birbeck, 77
Hobhouse, John Cam (later Lord Broughton), 118–19, 120, 121–4, 141–2
Byron's literary executor and alter ego, 113–15
destruction of Byron's memoirs, 113, 116–18
injunction against publication by Dallas of Byron's correspondence, 122
Hogarth, Georgina, 154
Hogarth, Mary, 153
Hogarth Press, 276
Hogg, Thomas Jefferson: attempted Life of Shelley, 132–3
Holbrook, David, 296
Holroyd, Michael, 238
Hood, Thomas, 145
*Memorials* by his children, 144
Horton, Wilmot, 117
Houghton, Lord, 184
Housman, A. E., 195–6
Howells, William Dean, 216
Huebsch, Ben, publisher, 275

Hughes, Olwyn, 296, 301–2, 303
Hughes, Ted, 294, 305
  Crow (1970), 298
  loathing of biography, 300
  poetry, 298
  problems of guarding the Plath estate,
    295–304
  trial-by-gravestone, 303
Hume, Patrick, 47
Hunt, Leigh, 112, 123, 128
  reconstructed by Forster, 150–1
  The story of Rimini, 150
Hyatt, A. H., 242
  The Pocket Thomas Hardy, 242

Inge, Dean, 223, 224
Ingelow, Jean, 252
Irving, Edward, 162, 169, 174
Isham, Lieutenant-Colonel Ralph Hayward,
    80–3, 84
  edition of The Private Papers of Boswell,
    80–1, 82
  collection sold to Yale University, 83
  purchase of Boswell correspondence, 80–
    1, 82–3
  wins claim to Boswell papers discovered
    at Fettercairn, 83

James, Harry, 220–1
James, Henry, viii, 198, 200, 205, 206–21,
    224, 226, 228, 241, 252, 254
  advice to Edward Marsh on Memoir of
    Rupert Brooke, 230–1
  destroys own archive, 219–20
  dislike of Wilde, 215
  essay in praise of Rupert Brooke, 222–3
  failure of Guy Domville, 209, 214, 215,
    216, 217
  final years and rebirth in Rye, 216–21
  Life of W. W. Story, 212
  Notes of a Son and a Brother, 212–13, 218
  perusal of Byron papers, 219
  selection of Letters by Lubbock, 221
  spellbound by myth of Robert Louis
    Stevenson, 207
  The Aspern Papers, 139, 207, 210
  'The Beast in the Jungle', 214
  'The Birthplace, 1903', 27–8
  'The Middle Years', 217
  'The Real Right Thing', 210–11
  The Sacred Fount, 215
  The Turn of the Screw, 218
  theories of biographical disclosure, 209–
    14, 218

  unsuccessful New York edition of
    writings, 217, 218
James, William, 212–13, 218
James I: publishing of his own works, 7–8
Jeffrey, Francis, 162, 169
  article on Burns, 102, 104
  criticism of Wordsworth in the Edinburgh
    Review, 102–3
  Wordsworth's riposte, 103–4, 107
Jessop, Canon Augustus: hostility towards
    Donne the Younger, 12–13
Jewsbury, Geraldine, 160, 161, 167, 174, 175
Johnson, Dr Samuel, 21, 26, 36, 37–8, 41,
    49, 75, 81, 86, 158
  biography by John Wain, 72
  Boswell's Life, 59, 63, 70–4, 75, 76, 81,
    82, 86, 87
  Dictionary, 68
  homage in preface to Shakespeare, 28–9
  Idler article (1760), 67–8
  Life of Pope, 52–3, 56, 65
  Life of Savage, 65–6, 67, 72
  Lives of the Poets, 35, 65
Jones, Monica Beal, 306, 307
Jonson, Benjamin, 7, 8, 16, 19, 21, 23, 25,
    40
Joyce, Giorgio, 285, 288, 289
Joyce, Helen, 288
Joyce, James, 267–90
  Anna Livia Plurabelle, 282, 284
  cause adopted by Ezra Pound, 272–5
  death in Zürich, 288
  Dubliners, 270, 271, 273, 275
  exile from Dublin, 269, 270; revisiting,
    271
  expensive tastes, 278, 281
  Finnegans Wake, 287–8
  Harriet Weaver becomes his patron, 274–
    86; breaking of the friendship, 286–7;
    criticism from, 283; financial help, 277,
    278, 281, 288; manages the estate, 289–
    90
  manuscripts left to Harriet Weaver, 288–9
  move to Paris, 278–9
  perceived persecutions and betrayals,
    269–70, 271
  Pomes Penyeach, 286
  Portrait of the Artist as a Young Man, A,
    268–9, 270; published in the United
    States, 275–6; serialised in The Egoist,
    273–4, 275
  'Shaun the Post', 282

*Ulysees*, 270, 274, 276, 280; attempts to
  publish by Harriet Weaver, 276–9;
  banned, 279, 282; English edition, 281;
  extracts published in *The Egoist*, 276;
  French publication, 281; serialised in US
  *Little Review*, 278
'Work in Progress', 270, 282, 283, 284,
  285
Joyce, Lucia, 270, 286–7, 288, 290
Joyce, Nora, 269, 270, 271, 277, 278, 284,
  289, 290
Joyce, Stanislaus, 267, 271, 281, 283
  Dublin Diary, 267–8
Jung, Carl, 278

Kafka, Franz, 291–2
Keats, John, 129, 150, 180, 239
  letters to Fanny Brawne, 146–7
Kermode, Frank, 19
Keynes, Sir Geoffrey, 231, 232, 234, 235
  discredits the Rupert Brooke legend, 234
  selection of Brooke's *Letters*, 234, 235
Killigrew, Thomas, 15, 20, 21
King, Bishop Dr Henry, 7, 10–11, 15, 40
  executor of Donne, 4, 5
Kingsley, Charles, 140, 144, 172
Kingsley, Mrs, 144, 172
Kipling, Carrie, 254–8
  daughter orders destruction of her diaries,
    262–3
  destroys Kipling's letters to Edmonia Hill,
    257
  diaries, 262–3, 264
  domination of Kipling, 254–6
  Kipling's executor, 257–8
Kipling, John, 255, 256
Kipling, Josephine, 255, 262
Kipling, Rudyard, 252, 253–66
  Birkenhead's banned biography, 258–60,
    262, 263, 264–6
  Carrington's *Life*, 261, 263, 264
  co-author of *The Naulahka*, 253
  dominated by wife, 254–6, 262
  letters to Edmonia Hill, 257
  marriage, 254, 256, 263
  posthumous requirements, 256
  simultaneous publication of novels in the
    US, 253
  *Something of Myself*, 256–7
  *The Light that Failed*, 253
  'The Long Trail', 254
  unrequited loves, 256, 257

Knowles, John, 181, 182
Kroll, Judith: *Chapters in a Mythology*, 300

Lake Poets, 102, 104
Lamb, Caroline, 113
Lamb, Charles, 151, 158
Lamb, Henry, 236–7
Landon, Letitia, 153
Landor, Robert Eyres, 151, 152, 154, 158
Larkin, Philip, 304–10
  ambiguity of will, 306–9
  *Collected Poems*, 307
  diaries, 306, 308; destruction of, 307
  *High Windows*, 306, 307
  'Posterity', 305
  *The Less Deceived*, 306, 307
  *The Whitsun Weddings*, 307
Laud, Archbishop William, 10
  war against books, 6
Lawrence, D. H., 224
  prosecution of *The Rainbow*, 276
Lawrence, T. E., 261
Leigh, Augusta, 110, 116, 117, 121, 124,
  125, 126
Leith, Colonel, 194
Leith, Mary Disney, 190, 193, 194–5
  *Undercliff*, 194–5
Leon, Paul, 285, 287–8
L'Estrange, Roger, 46
letters, use of in constructing biography,
  69–70
Lewis, Wyndham, 279, 280, 283
*Listener* extract, 126–7
literary celebrity, first, 49
Lockhart, John Gibson, 75, 102, 104, 142
  *Life of Scott*, 102, 139–41, 168
  reviews in *Blackwood's*, 102
London Library, founding of, 158
Lovelace, Lady Anne, 126, 127, 218–19
Lovelace, Lord Ralph: *Astarte*, 125–6, 218–19
Lovell, John W., publishers, 252, 253
Lowell, Robert, 297–8, 306
  *History* and *Notebook*, 306
Lubbock, Percy: selection of Henry James
    *Letters*, 221
Lucan, Marcus, 24
Luttrell, Henry, 117
Lyall, Archie, 261

McAlmon, Robert, 280, 281, 282, 283, 284
Macaulay, Thomas Babington, 36, 37–8, 74,
  83, 109

caricatures Boswell, 73, 75, 76, 78, 102
McCollough, Frances, 301
McCormick, Mrs Harold, 278
McClure, S. S., publishers, 253
Machiavelli, Niccolò, 14
Mack, Maynard, 62
McLehose, Mrs James, 93–4
Macmillan, publishers, 247
Mallet, David, 58, 59
Malone, Edmund, 73, 75, 76, 83
  Dryden edition, 75
  Shakespeare edition, 75
Marchmount, Lord, 60
Marlborough, Sarah, Duchess of, 37, 38, 58
Marriot, Thomas, 8
  publication of Donne's poems, 8–10
Marsden, Dora, 274, 275, 286
Marsh, Sir Edward, 223, 235, 237, 273
  attachment to Rupert Brooke, 225, 226
  Brooke's literary executor, 227–8
  dismissed by Mary Brooke, 234
  Georgian Poetry, 224, 225
  Memoir on Brooke, 228, 229–34, 237
  objections from Mary Brooke, 229–33
  publishing Brooke's work, 228–9
Martin, Robert Bernard, 177, 178
Marvell, Andrew: Miscellaneous Poems, 1681,
  allegedly published by landlady, 30–3
Mason, Philip, 263
Mason, William: doctored 'biography' of
  Thomas Gray, 68–70
Maugham, Somerset, 262, 291, 292
  biography by Ted Morgan, 292
  Cakes and Ale, 248–9, 292
Maunsell and Co., publishers, 271
Maurois, André, 238
Maxwell, Dr William, 98, 99
Medwin, Thomas
  conversations of Lord Byron, 119–20
  Life of Shelley, 130
Melbourne, Lady: letters from Byron, 218
Mendelson, Edward, 292
Menken, Adah, 184, 193, 195, 196
Miller, Karl, 301
Millgate, Michael, 246
Milton, John, 18, 32–4, 90
  Areopagicita, 43
  'Lycidas', 33
  royalties negotiated for Paradise Lost, 43
  Tonson's edition of Paradise Lost, 47
  verse in praise of Shakespeare, 39
  view of posterity, 39

Milton, Mrs, 43
Mitford, John, 69–70
Monnier, Adrienne, 284
Moore, Doris Langley, 118, 126
Moore, Thomas, 109, 115, 116, 117, 118,
  119, 128
  Life of Byron, 116, 123–4, 142
Morgan, Ted: biography of Maugham, 292
Morley, John: English Men of Letters series,
  239
Motion, Andrew, 306, 308, 309
Mountford, John: executor of Donne, 5
Muller, Max, 140
Murray, John, 77–8, 114, 115, 119, 120, 123
  acquiesces in destruction of Byron's
    memoirs, 116, 117, 118
  founds Quarterly Review, 102
  rejects Boswell Journals, 78

Nelson, Admiral Lord: letters to Lady
    Hamilton, 146, 147
Nesbitt, Cathleen, 228, 229, 233
New Monthly Magazine, 179
New Statesman, 243
Newcastle, Duke of, 65
Newman, John Henry, 158
Newton, A. Edward, 80
Nicholls, Arthur Bell, 190
Nicol, William, 92
Nicolson, Sir Harold: Development of English
    Biography, 144
Nightingale, Florence, 237, 238
Norman, Sylva, 131
Norton, Charles Eliot, 153, 172–3, 174
novel-biographies of the eighteenth century,
    66–7

Ogilby, John: The Carolies, 43
Orwell, George, 292
Osbourne, Alan, 206
Osbourne, Belle, 201
Osbourne, Lloyd, 200, 202–3, 206, 207, 208
Osbourne, Mrs, 205
Owen, Wilfred, 234, 309

Pall Mall Magazine, 205
Palmer, Mary: allegedly assumes
    widowhood of Marvell and publishes
    his Miscellaneous Poems, 30–3
Paris, 278–9, 284, 288, 289
patronage system in the seventeenth century,
    42

Peacock, Thomas Love, 134, 142
Pepys, Samuel, 22–4
Peterkin, Alexander: defence of Burns in
  *Review of the Life of Robert Burns*, etc.,
  101, 102, 103
Plath, Aurelia, 301
Plath, Otto, 302
Plath, Sylvia, 293–304, 309
  Alvarez memoir, 294, 296–8
  *Ariel*, 294, 295, 296, 298, 299, 300–1
  biographies: *Bitter Fame* (Anne Stevenson),
    302–3; unauthorised version (Edward
    Butscher), 300, 301
  *Collected Poems*, 302
  cult figure, 295, 298–9
  'Edge', 294
  husband's difficulties in protecting her
    estate, 295–304
  *Journals*, 302
  *Letters Home*, 301
  poems, 294–5, 296, 297, 298, 299, 300,
    302
  suicide, 293, 294, 295, 296–7, 298, 299
  *The Bell Jar*, 294, 298, 300
  *The Colossus*, 294
  'The Fearful', 294
  *Winter Trees*, 295, 299
Plutarch: *Lives*, 2
Poe, Edgar Allan, 239
Pope, Alexander, 18–19, 37, 38–9, 48–62,
    63, 64
  *An Essay on Man*, 54, 55, 61
  annotations by Warburton, 59–60
  appetite for self-promotion, 49–50
  case of the 'Atossa' verses, 57–8
  copyrights left to Warburton, 57
  first literary celebrity, 49
  *Iliad*, 53
  Johnson's *Life of Pope*, 52–3, 65
  launched by Tonson, 47
  natural disadvantages, 49
  outsmarting Edmund Curll, 50, 51–3, 55
  *Shakespeare*, 39, 55
  support from Warburton, 55–6
  *The Dunciad*, 39, 51–2, 61, 63, 104
  'The Temple of Fame', 48–9
  unpublished manuscripts left to
    Bolingbroke, 57
  *Works*, Warburton's 1751 edition, 60–2
Pottle, Frederick A., 82, 83
Pound, Ezra, 195, 278, 283
  espouses the Joyce cause, 272–5

*Letters of Ezra Pound to James Joyce*, 273
Priestley, J. B., 248–9
private letters, first case against the use of,
  41
Procter, Mrs B. W., 182
Proust, Marcel, 278
Prynne, William, 6
Purdy, Richard, 250

*Quarterly Review*, 102, 116, 146, 179, 193
Quinn, John, 273, 275

Ralegh, Sir Walter (1552–1618), 2
Raleigh, Sir Walter (1861–1922), 196
reductivism, style of, 104–5
Reich, Clara, 188–9
Restoration and the reopening of London
  theatres, 20, 22
Reynolds, Sir Joshua, 74
Riddell, John, 88
Riddell, Maria, 88, 93, 94, 95
Rogers, Rev. Charles, 77
Rogers, Samuel, 109
Romantic writers, 86, 143, 150
Roscoe, William, 96
Rosenberg, Isaac, 234
Rossetti, Christina, 136
Rossetti, Dante Gabriel, 136
Rossetti, William Michael, 138
  edits Shelley's poems with Memoir, 136
  executor for his brother and sister, 136–7
Rousseau, 71, 118, 147, 196, 267
Rowe, Nicholas
  first critical editor of Shakespeare, 24
  'Some Account of the Life', 24–6, 47
Royal Literary Fund, 150, 273
royalties negotiated by Milton for *Paradise
  Lost*, 43
Ruffhead, Owen: biography of Alexander
  Pope, 64–5
Ruskin, John, 172, 173
Russell, G. W. (A.E.), 270
Russell-Smith, Denham, 235
Rymer, Thomas, 22

Sand, George, 213
Sassoon, Siegfried, 234, 248
Savage, Richard, 53
  Johnson's *Life*, 65–6, 67, 72
Scott, Geoffrey, 80
Scott, Sir Walter, 74, 75–6, 109, 139–40
  Lockhart's *Life of Scott*, 102, 139–41, 168

Scribner's publishers, 218
serialisation deals with US magazines, 252
Sextion, Anne, 295–6
Shadwell, Thomas, 22
Shakespeare, William, 18–29, 47, 181, 220, 239
  bardolatry, 26–8
  championed by Davenant and Dryden, 18–23, 34
  First Folio (1623), publication of, 19
  Hamlet, 23–4
  homage in Dr Johnson's preface, 28–9
  Milton's praise in verse, 39
  Restoration and seventeenth-century attitudes towards, 22–5
  Rowe's Life of, 24–6
Shakespeare and Co., 279
Sharpe, Thomas, 26
Shelley, Harriet, 129, 130, 132, 133–4, 135, 136, 137
Shelley, Lady Jane, 131, 138, 143
  guardian of the Shelley papers, 131–2
  issues Shelley Memorials, 133–6, 138
  marriage to Shelley's son, 131
Shelley, Mary, 128, 129–31, 132, 133, 134, 135, 137
  edited Works of husband, 129
  Lodore, 137
Shelley, Sir Percy, 129, 131, 136, 143
Shelley, Percy Bysshe, 128–38, 142–3, 150, 239
  adoration of Byron, 128
  Dowden's biography, 137–8
  Hogg's attempted Life, 132–3
  poems edited by William Rossetti, 136
  scandals, 129
  The Necessity of Atheism, 128
Shelley, Sir Timothy, 129, 130
Shenstone, William, 128
Sheppard, Jack, 234
Sherburn, George, 59
Shirley, James, 40
Shorter, Clement, 190
Sydney, Sir Philip, 7
  family prevents piracies of Astrophel and Stella, 1
  Life written by Fulke Greville, 2
Simmons, Samuel, 43
simultaneous publication in US of works by British authors, 252–3
Sitwell, Fanny, 199, 203, 204, 206
Sligo, Marquess of, 123

Smith, F. E. (later 1st Earl Birkenhead), 258
Southey, Robert, 109, 112, 162, 169
Spence, Rev. Joseph, 63–4, 65
  abandons plans for biography of Alexander Pope, 64
  Anecdotes, 65, 75
Spenser, Edmund, 34
  Faerie Queene dedications, 42
Sprat, Dr Thomas, 40
  Life of Cowley 41, 69
Squire, Sir John, 260
Stallworthy, Jon, 235
Stanley, Dean: Life of Thomas Arnold, 140
Stationers' Company, 44
  copyright practice, 6
  Register, 44, 45
Stauffer, Donald A.: The Art of Biography in Eighteenth Century England, 66–7
Steiner, George, 294
Stephen, Sir James, 174, 176
Stephen, Leslie, 174
  Dictionary of National Biography (1882), 239
Stevenson, Anne, 302
  Bitter Fame, 302–3
Stevenson, Fanny, 197, 198–202, 204, 205–7, 208, 254, 255
  influence on Robert Louis Stevenson, 197, 198–200
  post-Stevenson career and death, 205–6
Stevenson, Robert Louis, 197–209, 214, 215, 216, 253, 255
  Balfour's Life, 204–5, 208–9
  Collected Works, 201
  Colvin's edition of Letters (1899), 208, 209
  Edinburgh years, 197, 203, 204
  influence of wife, 197, 198–200
  myth of, 207
  quarrel with Henley, 199–200, 205
  relations with Mrs Sitwell, 203–4
  South Seas idyll legend, 201, 204
  strain of marriage, 201
  Vailima Letters, 201
  Weir of Hermiston, 202
Stone, Major, 76
Story, William Wetmore, 212
  Life by Henry James, 212
Stowe, Harriet Beecher, 124–5
Strachey, James, 224, 233, 235, 236, 238
Strachey, Lytton, 159, 236–40, 243
  Eminent Victorians, 237–8, 241, 266
Stratford-on-Avon, 24, 25–8, 75
  bardolatry, 26–8

subscription selling of works in the
seventeenth century, 42
Suckling, Sir John, 17
Sullivan, John, 270
Sutherland, John, 251
Swift, Dean Jonathan, 53, 138
'On the Death of Dr Swift', 50–1
Swinburne, Algernon Charles, 138, 184–96,
197–8
Gosse biography, 194–5, 237
Letters (1918), 190
personal appearance, 185
Poems and Ballads – Second Series, 185
Posthumous Poems (1917), 190
row over his biography, 190–5
saved from the bottle by Watts–Dunton,
184, 185–6, 189
succumbs to the custodial regime of
Watts–Dunton, 185–7
taste for flagellation, 185
Works (1925–7), 190
Swinburne, Isabel, 189, 193, 194
Swinburne, Lady, 185
Syme, John, 91, 92, 93, 94, 95
friendship with Burns, 91
Symonds, John Addington, 138

Talbot de Malahide, Lord, 77, 78, 79
Talbot de Malahide, Lady Emily, 77
Talbot de Malahide, James (later Lord), 77,
79
Talbot de Malahide, Lady Joyce, 79, 80–1
sells Boswell correspondence, 80
Talbot, Colonel Milo, 77
Taylor, John, 23, 24
Temple, William, 73, 76
letters from Boswell, 76
Tennyson, Alfred Lord, 153, 177–83, 186,
241
In Memoriam, 177
Poems (1832), 179
sensitivity to criticism, 178, 179–81, 182
son's biography, 182–3
'To—, after Reading a Life of Letters',
180–1, 220
Tennyson, Emily, 177
helps son with biography and Tennyson,
182–3
Journal, 178, 181, 182
physical breakdown, 178, 181
protective towards husband, 177–8, 179
Tennyson, Hallam, 181

Alfred, Lord Tennyson: A Memoir, 182–3,
237
Ternan, Ellen, 149, 155
Thackeray, William Makepeace, 144–5, 150
Pendennis, 152
Theobald, Lewis, 39, 55
Thompson, Edward, 31
Thrale, Mrs, 71
Thwaite, Anthony, 306, 307, 308
Times, The, 170, 171, 188, 263
Byron obituary, 112–13
Times Literary Supplement, The (TLS), 206,
233
Tinker, Professor Chauncy B., 78–80, 83
edition of Boswell letters, 78–9
Tonson, Jacob, 46–8, 50
edition of Paradise Lost, 47
first publisher to influence literary taste, 47
launches Alexander Pope, 47
liaison as publisher with Dryden, 46–7
publication of Rowe's Shakespeare, 47
Trelawney, Edward John, 128, 131, 142
Trieste, 270, 271, 272–4
Tupper, Fred S., 30, 31
Twain, Mark, 137

Upcott, William: acquisition of Evelyn
letters, 85–6

Vallon, Annette, 108
Voltaire, 36, 71

Wagner, Richard, 239
Wagner-Martin, Linda, 302
Wain, John: biography of Dr Johnson, 72
Waller, Edmund, 34
Walpole, Hugh, 216, 249
Walton, Izaak, 10, 15, 64
Life of Donne, 2–3, 4, 5, 8, 10, 37, 40
Life of George Herbet, 40
Warburton, Dr William (later Bishop), 63
annotations, 59–60
attacks Bolingbroke, 58–9
commissions biography of Alexander
Pope, 64–5
defends Pope, 55–6, 61–2
edition of Pope's Works (1751), 60–2
receives Pope's copyright, 57
Ward, Dudley, 226, 231, 234
Ward, Mrs Humphry, 252
Robert Elsmere, 251

Warton, Joseph: *Essay on the Genius and Writings of Pope*, 64
Watt, A. P., 259, 261
Watt, William, 260
Watts-Dunton, Theodore, 183–94, 197
  *Aylwin*, 188–9
  executor and beneficiary of Swinburne's will, 188
  saves Swinburne from drink, 184, 185–6, 189
  marriage, 188
  takes custody of Swinburne, 185–7
Waugh, Arthur, 253
Weaver, Harriet Shaw, 274–90
  attempts to publish *Ulysees*, 276–9
  breaking of friendship with Joyce, 286–7
  criticises Joyce, 283
  English edition of *Ulysees*, 281
  finances Joyce, 277, 278, 281, 288
  guardian of Joyce's daughter, 290
  inherits Joyce manuscripts, 288–9
  managing Joyce's literary estate, 289–90
  patron saint of Joyce, 274–86
  *Space* and *Time* symposia, 286, 289
  takes up left-wing politics, 287, 289
  visit to Joyce in Paris, 284
Web, Mary, 15
Wentworth, Lady Judy, 126
Westbrook, Eliza, 133
Wharton, Edith, 218
Whitehead, John, 308
Whitman, Walt, 136
Wilde, Oscar
  disliked by Henry James, 215

imprisonment, 214, 215
  *The Importance of Being Earnest*, 214
Wilson, Sir Angus, 264, 266
  Kipling biography, 264
Wise, Thomas, 190–4
  prince of literary figures, 190
Wood, Anthony, 18, 25
  character-sketch of Donne the Younger, 12, 14
Woolf, Virginia, 174, 233
  *Diary of Virginia Woolf*, 276–7
Woolson, Constance Fennimore, 214
Wordsworth, William, 86, 87, 103, 109, 162
  attacked by Francis Jeffrey, 102–3
  defence of Burns, 103, 104–7
  Immortality Ode, 103
  'Letter to a Friend of Robert Burns', 105–7
  *Poems in Two Volumes*, 103
  'Resolution and Independence', 103
  riposte to criticism by Jeffrey in *Edinburgh Review*, 103–4, 107
  *The Excursion*, 103
  *The Lyrical Ballads*, 86
  *The Prelude*, 108
  *White Doe at Rylestone*, 103
Wycherley, William, 38–9, 47, 51, 53

Yale University: purchase of Boswell collection, 83
Yeats, W. B., 270–1, 272–3, 309

Zola, Emile, 213
Zürich, 288, 289